THE

# ECCLESIASTICAL HISTORY

OF THE

# SECOND AND THIRD CENTURIES

THE

# ECCLESIASTICAL HISTORY

OF THE

## Second and Third Centuries

ILLUSTRATED FROM THE WRITINGS OF TERTULLIAN

BY

JOHN, BISHOP OF BRISTOL

MASTER OF CHRIST'S COLLEGE

AND

REGIUS PROFESSOR OF DIVINITY IN THE UNIVERSITY OF CAMBRIDGE

Wipf and Stock Publishers
199 W 8th Ave, Suite 3
Eugene, OR 97401

The Ecclesiastical History of the Second and Third Centuries
Illustrated from the Writings of Tertullian
By Kaye, John
ISBN: 1-59752-672-X
Publication date 5/4/2006
Previously published by Griffith Farran & Co., 1893

# PREFACE TO THE SECOND EDITION.

SOON after the first edition of this work issued from the Press, I received a copy of a German work on the writings of Tertullian, published at Berlin in 1825, by Dr. August Neander, under the title of *Antignosticus Geist des Tertullians, etc.* As it is probable that few other copies have yet reached England, a short account of its object and contents may not be unacceptable to the reader.

The learned author states in his preface that he is engaged in writing an Ecclesiastical History of the first three centuries, a portion of which will be occupied by an inquiry into the different forms under which the Christian doctrine developed itself; in other words, into the different doctrinal and practical systems which arose during that period. The authors of those systems he divides into two classes, the Idealists and the Realists; the Idealists he again divides into the Ultra, from whom the Gnostics took their rise, and the Moderate, who formed the Alexandrian school. Of the Realists, he conceives Tertullian to be the proper representative. His object therefore is, by an analysis of Tertullian's writings, to present his readers with an accurate view of the Realist system. He had done the same with reference to the Gnostic system, in a work which I have not seen.

In pursuing this object, he classes the writings of Tertullian under three heads.

I. Those which were occasioned by the relation in which the Christians of Tertullian's day stood to the heathen, which were either composed in defence of Christianity and in confutation of heathenism, or referred to the sufferings and conduct of Christians in time of persecution, and to their intercourse with the heathen.

II. Those which related to the Christian life, and to the discipline of the Church.

III. Tertullian's dogmatical and polemical works.

I. Under the first head he mentions, as composed before Tertullian's secession from the Church—

The tract ad Martyres,
The tract de Spectaculis,[1]
The tract de Idololatriâ,
The two books ad Nationes,

[1] I have classed the tracts *de Spectaculis* and *de Idololatriâ* among the works probably composed by Tertullian after he became a Montanist; nor do Dr. Neander's arguments appear to me of sufficient weight to establish a different conclusion. He supposes these tracts to have been occasioned by the public festivities which took place after the defeat of Niger and Albinus (pp. 14, 32); and contends that Tertullian, if he had been then a Montanist, would, instead of resorting exclusively to arguments drawn from Scripture, have also appealed to the authority of the New Prophecy (p. 26). But the references to passing events are of too general a character to warrant us in deciding positively upon the time when the treatises were written; and Dr. Neander himself admits (p. 112) that in the tract *de Spectaculis* Tertullian uses stronger language respecting the incompatibility of the military life with the profession of Christianity than in the tract *de Coronâ*, which was certainly composed after he became a Montanist. This single fact, in my opinion, outweighs all the arguments on the other side.

The Apology,[1]
The tract de Testimonio Animæ;

as composed after Tertullian became a Montanist—

The tract de Coronâ,[2]
The tract de Fugâ in Persecutione,
Scorpiace,
The tract ad Scapulam.

II. Under the second head, Dr. Neander classes

The tract de Patientiâ,[3]
The tract de Oratione,[4]
The tract de Baptismo,
The tract de Pœnitentiâ,
The two books ad Uxorem,
The two books de Cultu Fœminarum,

among the works composed by Tertullian before he became a Montanist.

The tract de Exhortatione Castitatis,
The tract de Monogamiâ,

[1] Dr. Neander supposes the two books *ad Nationes* to have been anterior to the *Apology*, respecting the date of which he agrees with Mosheim (pp. 58, 76 note). He infers also (p. 79), from the answer to the charge of *unprofitableness* brought against the Christians by their enemies, that Tertullian could not have imbibed the ascetic spirit of Montanism when he wrote the *Apology*. But the validity of this inference may be questioned, as it is certain that Tertullian sometimes varied his language with his object.

[2] The largess alluded to in the tract *de Coronâ* was, according to Dr. Neander, that given to the military on account of the victories of Severus over the Parthians (p. 114). If this supposition is correct, we must assign the year 204 as the probable date of the tract.

[3] Dr. Neander remarks that a comparison of the modes in which Tertullian applies the parables of the Lost Sheep and of the Prodigal Son in the tract *de Patientiâ*, c. 12, and in that *de Pudicitiâ*, c. 9, will prove the former to have been written before his secession from the Church (p. 168).

[4] Dr. Neander considers the additional chapters of the tract *de Oratione* genuine.

The tract de Pudicitiâ,
The tract de Jejuniis,
The tract de Virginibus velandis,[1]
The tract de Pallio,[2]

among those written after he recognised the prophecies of Montanus.

III. Of the works which fall under the third head, Dr. Neander thinks that one only was written before Tertullian became a Montanist—the tract *de Præscriptione Hæreticorum.* The rest were written by him when a Montanist.

The five books against Marcion.
The tract adversus Valentinianos.
The tract de Carne Christi.
The tract de Resurrectione Carnis.
The tract adversus Hermogenem.
The tract de Animâ.
The tract adversus Praxeam.[3]
The tract adversus Judæos.[4]

[1] From the following passage in the second chapter of this tract ("Sed eas ego Ecclesias proposui, quas et ipsi Apostoli vel Apostolici viri condiderunt, et puto *ante quosdam.* Habent igitur et illæ eandem consuetudinis auctoritatem, tempora et antecessores opponunt magis quam posteræ istæ"), and from other incidental expressions, Dr. Neander infers that the custom against which it was directed prevailed in the Church of Rome.

[2] With respect to this tract, Dr. Neander interprets the expression, "Præsentis imperii triplex virtus, Deo tot Augustis in unum favente," of Severus, Caracalla, and Geta, and supposes the tract to have been composed about the year 208. He conjectures also that Tertullian was induced, after the death of his wife, to adopt the ascetic mode of life, and, in consequence, to wear the pallium, the peculiar dress of the ἀσκηταί (p. 310).

[3] Dr. Neander thinks with Blondel (p. 487) that the Bishop of Rome mentioned in the first chapter of the tract *against Praxeas,* was Eleutherus: Allix was disposed rather to fix upon Victor.

[4] On this tract Dr. Neander has written a short dissertation, the object of which is to prove that the ninth and following chapters are spurious. In our remarks

Dr. Neander gives a more or less detailed analysis of each tract, and occasionally introduces (most frequently in considering the works included under the last head) the sentiments of other ecclesiastical writers on the points under discussion—a proceeding foreign from the plan which I had proposed to myself. He is always learned and ingenious, but not altogether free from that love of hypothesis for which the German writers are remarkable.

There is an appendix to the work, containing two dissertations,—one on the last part of the tract *adversus Judæos;* the other on Tertullian's doctrine respecting the Lord's Supper, which Dr. Neander supposes to be something intermediate between that of Justin and Irenæus, whom he asserts to have maintained (he does not allege any passages in proof of the assertion) the doctrine of consubstantiation, and the doctrine of Origen, who did not allow that any divine influence was united to the outward signs *as such*, but thought that the object of sense was the symbol of the object of the understanding, *only* to the worthy receiver; though, in addition to that symbolical relation, he conceived a sanctifying influence to be united with

upon Semler's theory respecting Tertullian's works, we stated that he grounded an argument on the fact that a considerable portion of the third book *against Marcion* is repeated in the tract *against the Jews.* Dr. Neander draws a different inference from this fact. He observes that many of the passages thus repeated, however suitable to the controversy between Tertullian and Marcion, are wholly out of their place in a controversy with a Jew. He concludes, therefore, that Tertullian, having proceeded as far as the quotation from Isaiah in the beginning of the ninth chapter of the tract *against the Jews*, from some unknown cause left the work unfinished; and that the remainder of the tract was afterwards added by some person, who thought that he could not do better than complete it, by annexing what Tertullian had said on the same passage of Isaiah in the third book *against Marcion*, with such slight variations as the difference of circumstances required. The instances alleged by Dr. Neander in proof of this position are undoubtedly very remarkable; but, if the concluding chapters of the tract are spurious, no ground seems to be left for asserting that the genuine portion was posterior to the third book *against Marcion*, and none consequently for ass rting that it was written by a Montanist.

the *whole rite* in the case of those who are capable of receiving that influence. Dr. Neander thinks that *to eat the flesh and drink the blood of Christ* meant, in Tertullian's view of the subject, *to appropriate to ourselves the divine* λόγος *who appeared in the nature of man, and to enter into a living union with Him through faith.* He thinks also that in the words, "Caro corpore et sanguine Christi vescitur, ut et anima de Deo saginetur," Tertullian intended to say that, while the body, in a supernatural manner, comes into contact with the body of Christ, the soul receives into itself the divine life of Christ. Dr. Neander justly remarks that on other occasions Tertullian speaks as if the bread and wine were merely representative signs of the body and blood of Christ. It may be doubted, therefore, whether, in arguing upon the above expressions, he has made sufficient allowance for the peculiarities of Tertullian's style. If, however, he is correct, Tertullian must be classed with those who maintain a real presence of Christ's body in the Eucharist, but in a spiritual, not in a gross corporeal sense. Dr. Neander appears himself to consider the bread and wine as mere symbols.

In the body of Dr. Neander's work are also two disquisitions,—one on a passage in the third chapter of the tract *de Coronâ*, where Tertullian speaks of various customs observed in the Church on the authority of tradition; the other on an obscure passage in the fourteenth chapter of the tract *de Jejuniis*, from which Dr. Neander infers that the practice of fasting on a Saturday already existed in the Western Church.

If the reader will compare Dr. Neander's classification of Tertullian's writings with that which I have ventured to suggest, he will find that the difference between us is not great; and with respect to some of the tracts on which we differ, the learned author expresses himself with great diffidence. He was too well aware of the dubious character of the proofs on which his conclusions necessarily rest, to adopt a more decided language. I was myself restrained by similar considerations from hazarding any positive decision of many of the controverted points connected with Tertullian's life and writings. It would have been no difficult task to bring forward the different passages produced by preceding writers upon those points; to add others of equally, or more, doubtful application to the subject in debate; and after the parade of a formal discussion, to pronounce between the contending parties. Such a proceeding would have been very imposing, and have carried with it an appearance of great learning and profundity; but it would at last have been only solemn trifling. When the facts are not merely scanty, but susceptible of different interpretations,[1] it seems to follow as a necessary consequence, that the mind must remain in a state of suspense; and an author ought at least to escape censure for avowing doubts which he really feels. Diffidence may imply a defect both in the moral and intellectual character; but it is surely less offensive in itself, and less likely to be injurious in its consequences, than that presumptuous rashness which ventures to deliver peremptory decisions where there are scarcely materials even for forming an opinion.

I was naturally anxious to ascertain the opinion of Dr. Neander

[1] For instance, Dr. Neander asserts that Tertullian had once been a heathen, and produces, in support of the assertion, the first sentence in the tract *de Pœnitentiâ* (p. 3). "Pœnitentiam, hoc genus hominum, quod et ipsi retro fuimus," etc. He afterwards (p. 5) alludes to the passages in the tracts *de Exhortatione Castitatis*, c. 7, and *de Monogamiâ*, c. 12 ("Nonne et Laici Sacerdotis sumus?" and "Sed quum extollimur et inflamur adversus Clerum, tunc unum omnes sumus," etc.), which have been alleged, in order to disprove the fact of Tertullian's admission into the priesthood, but thinks that they do not disprove it. In both cases Tertullian speaks in the first person and in the plural number; yet in the former we are to suppose that he spoke in his own, in the latter in an assumed character. Surely there is something very arbitrary in these decisions.

respecting the instances of the exercise of miraculous powers mentioned by Tertullian, and the accounts of visions which occur in his writings. The learned author accounts for the story of the female who came back from the theatre under the influence of a demoniacal possession, by supposing that, being conscience-stricken, she returned the answer recorded by Tertullian, under the persuasion that she was possessed by an evil spirit who made use of her organs of speech.[1] The story of the man who was chastised in a vision because his servants had suspended garlands on his door in his absence, may, Dr. Neander thinks, be accounted for on psychological principles.[2] The view which he takes of the subject of visions is, that the fermentation at first produced by Christianity in the nature of man was accompanied by many extraordinary phenomena not likely to occur in a similar manner at all times. New powers were imparted to human nature, and those which had been before concealed were brought into action. Moreover, the necessities of the infant Church called for many unusual interpositions of Providence. Great caution would of course be requisite in forming a judgment respecting those phenomena, since it would be easy to confound that which was natural with that which was divine; and into this error the turn of Tertullian's mind would render him peculiarly liable to fall, by disposing him to regard all such appearances as divine revelations. In a subsequent part of his work, Dr. Neander mentions the story of a female to whom the soul was exhibited in a corporeal shape

[1] *De Spectaculis*, c. 26 (p. 31, note).

[2] *De Idololatriâ*, c. 15 (p. 54). I do not perfectly comprehend the meaning of this observation. It is very easy to conceive that a man of a superstitious temper might have been so affected on finding that his servants had complied with what he deemed an idolatrous practice, as to dream that he was severely chastised for their misconduct. But Tertullian's words convey the idea that the chastisement was real. "Scio fratrem per visionem eâdem nocte *castigatum graviter* quod januam ejus, subito annuntiatis gaudiis publicis, servi coronâssent." Are we to suppose that the impression made on the mind by the dream affected the body, and produced the same feeling of soreness as if the beating had been real?

—as an instance of Tertullian's readiness to consider visions as communications from heaven.[1] Although Dr. Neander has not expressed himself decidedly, I infer from the general tenor of his observations, that he objects altogether to the notion that the exercise of miraculous powers was intended to be confined to any particular persons or to any particular age. He supposes Tertullian to have asserted that the possession of the extraordinary gifts of the Spirit was the peculiar characteristic of an apostle, and regards this assertion as a proof of Montanism.[2] He speaks also of the impropriety of confining the *charismata* to the apostolic age. To what I have before said on this disputed subject I will now add, that we usually infer what *will be* the future course of the divine government from considering what it *has been;* and thus Christians living towards the end of the second century—who had either themselves conversed, or had heard the accounts of others who had conversed, with men who had witnessed the exercise of miraculous powers—could not be justly charged with credulity for expecting the continuance of the same powers in the Church. Centuries have since elapsed, during which no miraculous narrative deserving of credit can be produced. Our case, therefore, is widely different. They who contend that, because the first teachers of the gospel were endowed with miraculous powers in order to prove their divine commission, it is not unreasonable to suppose that similar powers would be imparted to those who in subsequent ages went forth to convert heathen nations, may fairly be called upon to produce an instance, subsequent to the times of the immediate successors of the apostles, in which such powers have been actually conferred.

[1] *De Animâ,* c. 9 (p. 465).

[2] The passage on which Dr. Neander builds this inference is in the tract *de Exhortatione,* c. 3: "*Proprie* enim Apostoli Spiritum Sanctum habent in operibus prophetiæ, et efficaciâ virtutum, documentisque linguarum; non ex parte, quod cæteri," p. 242.

Dr. Neander's notions respecting the authority ascribed by the early Christians to tradition seem to coincide with my own. He says, "These two fountains of the knowledge of the doctrine of faith—the collection of the apostolic writings and oral tradition—sent forth streams, flowing by the side of each other through all communities which agreed in the essentials of Christianity, and especially through the communities which were of apostolic foundation. But as the stream of tradition necessarily became more turbid in proportion as the distance from the apostolic times increased, the writings of the apostles were designed by Providence to be an unadulterated source of divine doctrine for every age. Though on some occasions the Christians of those days might appeal solely to the authority of tradition, they uniformly maintained that the doctrine of Christianity in all its parts might be deduced from Holy Writ" (p. 312).

The spirit in which Dr. Neander's remarks on Tertullian are conceived is widely different from that in which it has been fashionable of late years to think and speak of the Fathers. M. Barbeyrac, whose views were directed to the systematic development of the principles of ethics, looking only at Tertullian's defects, regarded him as an author who was incapable either of thinking naturally, or preserving a just medium; who delivered himself up to the guidance of his African imagination, which magnified and confounded all the objects presented to it, and did not allow him to consider any one with attention; who, in short, had disfigured the morality of the gospel by his extravagances, and thereby inflicted a serious injury on Christianity itself. Dr. Neander, on the contrary, to whose mind the image of the Christian community, as it existed under the immediate superintendence of the apostles, appears to be continually present, discovers in Tertullian the working of that spirit which animated the early converts; and regarding him as a man whose whole soul was absorbed in his desire to promote the practical influence of the gospel, is little disposed to speak with harshness of errors which arose from the overflowings of Christian zeal.[1] Looking rather to the internal feeling than to the terms in which it is expressed, he discerns matter for commendation in passages in which others have found nothing but extravagance and absurdity. The concluding passage of the tract *de Spectaculis*, which called forth Gibbon's animadversions, appears to Dr. Neander to contain a beautiful specimen of lively faith and Christian confidence; though he wishes that the vehemence of Tertullian's zeal had been tempered by a larger infusion of Christian love.[2] He ventures even to defend the celebrated

[1] I have, in the fourth chapter of the present work, examined certain passages of Tertullian's writings, from which it has been inferred that he did not recognise the distinction between the clergy and laity. Dr. Neander accounts (p. 204) for the apparent inconsistency in his language, by supposing that he stood on what may be termed the boundary mark of two periods,—the period of original simple Christianity, and the period of the establishment of a system of Church-authority. During the former period there was a perfect equality among Christians; no distinction of orders; all were priests. The separation of the clergy from the laity, and the gradation of ranks among the former, were subsequently introduced by injudicious attempts to transfer the institutions of the Mosaic to the Christian dispensation. This view of the subject frequently occurs in Dr. Neander's work; but I must confess my inability to reconcile it either with the statements contained in the Acts of the Apostles and in the Epistles, or with the natural course of things. If the Church of Christ on earth was *in fact* what it is *in theory*, the distinction between the clergy and laity would doubtless be unnecessary. But where are we to look for the period of original simple Christianity of which Dr. Neander speaks? Even the apostles found themselves under the necessity of appointing particular orders of men for the accomplishment of particular objects, and of making new regulations in order to correct the abuses which from time to time sprang up. The distinction, therefore, of the clergy from the laity, and of orders among the clergy, arose out of the necessities of what Dr. Neander elsewhere (p. 341) calls that frail compound of spiritual and sensual—human nature; not out of any designed imitation of the Mosaic institutions. After it had once been established, we might naturally expect to find the language of the Old Testament respecting the Jewish priesthood applied to the Christian: at first only in the way of analogy, but subsequently perhaps to promote the interested views of ambitious men. Dr. Neander has pointed out a remarkable instance of the application of the phraseology of the Old Testament to the celebration of the Eucharist in the tract *de Oratione*, c. 14 (p. 184, note).

[2] P. 34.

declaration, "Certum est, quia impossibile,"[1] which has contributed more than any other circumstance to bring Tertullian's writings into discredit; and says with great truth, that how strangely soever it may sound when separated from the context, yet when taken in connexion with what precedes, it is only an exaggerated mode of stating that a Christian readily admits, on the authority of Revelation, that which men, who rely solely on the conclusions of their own reason, pronounce impossible. There can be no doubt that Dr. Neander has entered more deeply into Tertullian's character, and has, in consequence, been enabled to form a juster estimate of his merits and defects, than the philosophical jurist or the sceptical historian. Yet there are, perhaps, occasions in which Dr. Neander himself has interpreted Tertullian's expressions too strictly; and, though aware of the difficulty of referring the opinions of a man on whom the feeling of the moment had so much influence, to general principles, he has not always been able to resist the temptation to generalize, and has in consequence extracted from Tertullian's words a train of thought of which he himself was probably never conscious.[2]

I will now proceed to mention the principal additions and alterations which have been made in this second edition.

In chapter i. p. 42, n. 1, the reader will find a passage disproving Semler's assertion that Eusebius has never mentioned Miltiades as a writer against the heretics. The passage is in the *Eccl. Hist.* l. v. c. 28.

In chapter iii. p. 88, I had given an erroneous account of the exordium of the tract *de Testimonio Animæ*, having

[1] *De Carne Christi*, c. 4, p. 394.

[2] P. 380.

substituted in the place of the argument there urged by Tertullian, that which he uses in the passage in the *Apology*, to which I had referred in the note. The error is now corrected.

In chapter v. p. 172, n. 2 (note 209, first edition), the reader will find an attempt to reconcile the apparent inconsistencies in Tertullian's language respecting the state of the soul during the interval between its separation from the body and the general resurrection.

In chapter vi. p. 226 (p. 453, first edition), I have inserted a note containing a reference to the custom which existed in Tertullian's time, of reserving a portion of the consecrated bread, and eating it at home before every other food. Dr. Neander thinks that this custom gave rise to the practice of administering the communion only in one kind. He observes also that the practice of daily communion appears from the writings of Tertullian to have then prevailed, at least in the African Church. See *de Idololatriâ*, c. 7.

There are some minor alterations which it is unnecessary to specify; and at the end of the volume will be found a list of addenda, some of which have been suggested to me by the perusal of Dr. Neander's work. Notwithstanding all the care which I have been able to bestow, the learned reader will doubtless discover additional errors and omissions. One mistake has, however, been imputed to me, of which I have not been guilty. I have never mentioned, incidentally or otherwise, that Stephen, Bishop of Rome, was contemporary with Tertullian.

In the introduction to the present work I have stated that *the object which I proposed to myself in my lectures on the writings of Tertullian was, to employ them, as far as they could be employed, in filling up Mosheim's outline* of ecclesiastical history. After this explicit declaration, it may appear almost unnecessary to add that I never intended to compose *an* Ecclesiastical History of the Second and Third Centuries. My labours were directed to an humbler object—to assist in collecting materials for a future historian of the Church. My persuasion has always been, that a good ecclesiastical history of that or any other period will never be composed until the works of each writer who flourished during the period have been examined, and the information which they supply, collected and arranged under different heads. I did not mean to propose Mosheim's arrangement as the best which could be devised; I followed it because his history is that which is in most general use among theological students in this country. I deem it also most essential to the successful execution of such a plan, that the testimony of each author should be kept as distinct as possible. If I may form a judgment from Dr. Neander's preface, his view of the subject nearly coincides with my own. He there states that he has published a volume on the Gnostic system, which must necessarily include an examination of the work of Irenæus; a friend, at his request, is employed on the writings of Cyprian: in the volume of which I have now given a short account, we have the spirit of Tertullian, the representative of the Realists; there remain, therefore, for consideration only the Moderate Idealists of the Alexandrian school, whose opinions will be found in the writings of Clemens and Origen. Having thus prepared the way by analysing the works of the five principal authors of the second and third centuries, the learned author will proceed to the completion of his ecclesiastical history of that period. With the design of facilitating the composition of a similar history, I had, in the fulfilment of the duties of my office, before I lectured on the writings of Tertullian, examined the writings of the Fathers who preceded him; whether I shall at any future period be able to lay before the public the result of the examination must depend upon the time which I can spare from other avocations.

# TABLE OF CONTENTS.

---

## CHAPTER II.

### ON THE EXTERNAL HISTORY OF THE CHURCH.

## CHAPTER III.

### ON THE STATE OF LETTERS AND PHILOSOPHY.



---

## CHAPTER IV.

### ON THE GOVERNMENT OF THE CHURCH.



---

## CHAPTER V.

### ON THE DOCTRINE OF THE CHURCH

---

## CHAPTER VI.

### ON THE CEREMONIES USED IN THE CHURCH.

## CHAPTER VII.

### CONCERNING THE HERESIES AND DIVISIONS WHICH TROUBLED THE CHURCH.

# THE ECCLESIASTICAL HISTORY

OF THE

# SECOND AND THIRD CENTURIES.

## INTRODUCTION.

THE following pages contain the substance of a course of lectures delivered by the author, as Regius Professor of Divinity, in the Lent and Easter terms of 1825. He had previously delivered two courses on the writings of the Fathers; and the plan which he then pursued was, first to give a short account of the author's life; next an analysis of each of his works; and lastly, a selection of passages, made principally with a view to the illustration of the Doctrines and Discipline of the Church of England. The peculiar character of the writings of the earlier Fathers pointed out this as the mode in which the information to be derived from them might be most clearly and usefully exhibited to the theological student. In proceeding, however, to the writings of Tertullian, the next in order of time to those whose works had been previously reviewed, it occurred to the author that a different mode might be adopted with advantage; and that they might be rendered subservient to the illustration of ecclesiastical history in general. They who have read Mosheim's work require only to be reminded that he divides the history of the Church into two branches, external and internal. Under the former he comprehends the prosperous and adverse events which befell it during each century; under the latter, the state of learning and philosophy, the government, doctrine, rites and ceremonies of the Church, and the heresies which divided its members and disturbed its tranquillity, during the same period. This arrangement was not an original idea of Mosheim; the Centuriators of Magdeburgh had before adopted nearly a similar plan. His work is, moreover, of a very compendious character, designed to present his readers with a general and connected view of the history of Christianity from its first promulgation; and to assist their studies, by directing them to the sources from which, if they are so disposed, they may derive more particular and detailed information. The object, therefore, which the author proposed to himself in his Lectures on the Writings of Tertullian, was to employ them, as far as they could be employed, in filling up Mosheim's outline, by arranging the information which they supply under the different heads above enumerated. Still, it was necessary for him so far to adhere to his original plan as to prefix a brief account of Tertullian himself, in order that the student might be enabled accurately to distinguish the portion of ecclesiastical history which his writings serve to illustrate, as well as justly to appreciate the importance to be attached to his testimony and opinions.[1]

——o——

## CHAPTER I.

### ON TERTULLIAN AND HIS WRITINGS.

THE following account of Tertullian[2] is given by Jerome:[3]—

"Tertullian a presbyter, the first Latin writer after Victor and Apollonius, was a native of the province of Africa and city of Carthage, the son of a proconsular centurion:[4] he

[1] The edition of Tertullian's works, to which the references in the following pages are made, is that of Paris, 1675.

[2] He is called in the MSS. of his works Quintus Septimius Florens Tertullianus; and in the concluding sentence of the tract *de Virginibus Velandis* he calls himself Septimius Tertullianus. But whether that sentence is genuine may be reasonably doubted. The same remark applies to the concluding words of the tracts *de Baptismo* and *de Exhortatione Castitatis*. The final mention of Tertullian in the latter is omitted in the *Codex Agobardi*. Jerome calls him Septimius Tertullianus. *Ep. ad Fabiolam sub fine*.

[3] *Catalogus Scriptorum Ecclesiasticorum*.

[4] A proconsular centurion appears to have been a species of officer who was constantly in attendance upon the proconsul to receive his commands. See the note of Valesius in Euseb. *Eccl. Hist.* l. ii. c. 2. This part of Jerome's account has been supposed to be founded on a passage in the *Apology*, c. 9: "Infantes

was a man of a sharp and vehement temper, flourished under Severus and Antoninus Caracalla, and wrote numerous works, which, as they are generally known, I think it unnecessary to particularize. I saw at Concordia in Italy an old man named Paulus. He said that, when young, he had met at Rome with an aged amanuensis of the blessed Cyprian, who told him that Cyprian never passed a day without reading some portion of Tertullian's works; and used frequently to say, 'Give me my master,' meaning Tertullian. After remaining a presbyter of the Church until he had attained the middle age of life, Tertullian was, by the envy and contumelious treatment of the Roman clergy, driven to embrace the opinions of Montanus, which he has mentioned in several of his works under the title of the New Prophecy; but he composed, expressly against the Church, the treatises *de Pudicitiâ*, *de Persecutione*, *de Jejuniis*, *de Monogamiâ*, and six books *de Ecstasi*,[1] to which he added a seventh *against Apollonius*.[2]

penes Africam Saturno immolabantur palam usque ad proconsulatum Tiberii, qui ipsos Sacerdotes in iisdem arboribus templi sui obumbraticibus scelerum votivis crucibus exposuit, teste militiâ patriæ nostræ, quæ id ipsum manus illi proconsuli functa est." Rigault says that one MS. reads "Patris nostri."

1 The six books *de Ecstasi* and the seventh *against Apollonius* are lost. Montanus pretended that he was frequently thrown into a species of rapture or ecstasy; and that, while in that state, he saw visions and received communications from the Spirit, which enabled him to foretell future events. This circumstance was urged by his opponents as an argument against the truth of his pretensions to inspiration; and Miltiades, of whom Tertullian speaks with respect, wrote a treatise to show that a prophet ought not to speak in ecstasy, περὶ τοῦ μὴ δεῖν προφήτην ἐν ἐκστάσει λαλεῖν. Eusebius, *Eccl. Hist.* l. v. c. 17. Tertullian wrote his books *de Ecstasi* in defence of Montanus; and a passage in the fourth book *against Marcion*, c. 22, will put the reader in possession of his notions on the subject of prophetic inspiration. He is speaking of the Transfiguration, when, according to St. Luke, St. Peter knew not what he said; on which Tertullian observes, "Quomodo nesciens? utrumne simplici errore, an ratione quam defendimus in causa Novæ Prophetiæ, gratiæ ecstasin, id est, amentiam convenire? In Spiritu enim homo constitutus, præsertim quum gloriam Dei conspicit vel quum per ipsum Deus loquitur, necesse est excidat sensu, obumbratus scilicet virtute divinâ, de quo inter nos et Psychicos (the name given by Tertullian to the orthodox) quæstio est." Comp. *adv. Marc.* l. i. c. 21, *sub fine;* l. v. c. 8, *sub fine; adv. Praxeam*, c. 15. In like manner Tertullian supposes that in the deep sleep or ecstasy (ἔκστασιν in the Septuagint) into which Adam was thrown, when his rib was taken from him to form Eve, he was enabled to predict the perpetual union of Christ and the Church: "Nam etsi Adam statim prophetavit magnum illud Sacramentum in Christum et Ecclesiam" (the reference is to Ephesians v. 31). "'Hoc nunc os ex ossibus meis et caro ex carne meâ. Propter hoc relinquet homo patrem et matrem, et adglutinabit se uxori suæ et erunt duo in carnem unam,' accidentiam Spiritûs passus est; cecidit enim ecstasis super illum, Sancti Spiritûs vis, operatrix Prophetiæ." *De Animâ*, c. 11. Tertullian is very fond of this notion respecting the deep sleep or trance into which Adam was thrown; we find it again *de Virgin. Vel.* c. 5; *de Animâ*, c. 21, 45; *de Jejuniis*, c. 3.

2 Apollonius is mentioned as an opponent of Montanus by Eusebius, *Eccl. Hist.* l. v. c. 18.

He is reported to have lived to a very advanced age, and to have composed many other works which are not extant."

The correctness of some parts of this account has been questioned. Doubts have been entertained whether Tertullian was a presbyter. It is certain that he was married, for among his works are two treatises addressed to his wife. How then were the Roman Catholics to dispose of a fact which appeared to militate strongly against their favourite doctrine of the celibacy of the clergy? The easiest mode was to deny that he ever became a presbyter; and, in support of this opinion, two passages,[1] in which he appears to speak of himself as a layman, have been quoted from works supposed to have been written when he was far advanced in life. On these passages Allix remarks that the course of Tertullian's argument in some measure compelled him to speak in the first person;[2] and he opposes to them one from the treatise *de Animâ*,[3] in which our author states that he remained in the church, or place of religious assembly, after the people were dismissed, for the purpose of recording and investigating the accounts given by a Christian female, to whom visions were vouchsafed, of what she saw in her spiritual ecstasies; an office which, in the opinion of Allix, would not have been assigned him had he not been a presbyter. It must, however, be confessed that this passage is by no means decisive of the controversy; and we must be content to receive the fact of Tertullian's admission to the priesthood, as the majority of Roman Catholic divines have received it, upon the authority of Jerome. We shall hereafter have occasion to notice the different conjectures proposed by them, in order to deprive their Protestant opponents of the argument which the example of Tertullian supplies in favour of a married priesthood.

Another question has been raised respecting the place where Tertullian officiated as a presbyter; whether at Carthage, or at Rome. That he at one time resided at Carthage may be

[1] "Vani erimus si putaverimus, quod Sacerdotibus non liceat, Laicis licere. Nonne et Laici Sacerdotes sumus? Scriptum est, regnum quoque nos et Sacerdotes Deo et Patri suo fecit." *De Exhort. Castit.* c. 7. Again, "Sed quum extollimur et inflamur adversus Clerum, tunc unum omnes sumus, tunc omnes Sacerdotes, quia Sacerdotes nos Deo et Patri fecit. Quum ad peræquationem disciplinæ Sacerdotalis provocamur, deponimus infulas, et impares sumus." *De Monogamiâ*, c. 12.

[2] *Dissertatio de Tertulliani Vitâ et Scriptis*, c. 2.

[3] C. 9.

inferred from Jerome's account; and is rendered certain by several passages in his own writings.[1] Allix supposes that the notion of his having been a presbyter of the Roman Church owed its rise to Jerome's statement, that the envy and abuse of the Roman clergy impelled him to espouse the party of Montanus. Optatus[2] and the author of the work *de Hæresibus*, which Sirmond edited under the title of *Prædestinatus*, expressly call him a Carthaginian presbyter.[3] Semler, however, in a dissertation inserted in his edition of Tertullian's works (c. 2), contends that he was a presbyter of the Roman Church. We know, he argues, that Tertullian visited Rome; for he speaks of the profusion of pearls and precious stones which he saw there.[4] Eusebius tells us that he was accurately acquainted with the Roman laws,[5] and on other accounts a distinguished person at Rome. He displays, moreover, a knowledge of the proceedings of the Roman Church with respect to Marcion and Valentinus,[6] who were once members of it, which could scarcely have been obtained by one who had not himself been numbered among its presbyters. The question is of little importance, nor do the arguments on either side appear to be of so convincing a nature as to warrant a peremptory decision. Semler admits that, after Tertullian seceded from the Church, he left Rome and returned to Carthage.

Jerome does not inform us whether Tertullian was born of Christian parents, or was converted to Christianity. There are passages in his writings which seem to imply that he had been a Gentile:[7] yet he may perhaps mean to describe, not his own condition, but that of Gentiles in general before their conversion. Allix and the majority of commentators understand them literally, as well as some other passages in which he speaks of his own infirmities and sinfulness.[8]

[1] *De Pallio*, c. 1. *Apology*, c. 9. *Scorpiace*, c. 6. *De Res. Carnis*, c. 42.

[2] *Adv. Parmenianum*, l. i.

[3] C. 26.

[4] *De Cultu Fœminarum*, l. i. c. 7. "Gemmarum quoque nobilitatem vidimus Romæ," etc.

[5] *Eccl. Hist.* l. ii. c. 2. It should, however, be observed that Valesius, following Rufinus, understood the words τῶν μάλιστα ἐπὶ 'Ρώμης λαμπρῶν to mean that Tertullian had obtained distinction among Latin writers.

[6] *De Præscriptione Hæreticorum*, c. 30.

[7] "Pœnitentiam hoc genus hominum, quod et ipsi retro fuimus, cæci, sine Domini lumine, naturâ tenus norunt." *De Pœnitentiâ*, c. 1. "Nobis autem et via nationum patet, in quâ et inventi sumus." *De Fugâ in Persec.* c. 6. "Et nationes, quod sumus nos." *Adv. Marc.* l. iii. c. 21. "Hæc et nos risimus aliquando; de vestris fuimus." *Apology*, c. 18.

[8] *De Cultu Fœm.* l. ii. c. 1. *De Res. Carnis*, c. 59. *De Pœnitentiâ*, c. 4, 12.

His writings show that he flourished at the period specified by Jerome, that is, during the reigns of Severus and Antoninus Caracalla, or between the years 193 and 216; but they supply no precise information respecting the date of his birth, or any of the principal occurrences of his life. Allix places his birth about the year 145 or 150; his conversion to Christianity about 185; his marriage about 186; his admission to the priesthood about 192; his adoption of the opinions of Montanus about 199; and his death about 220: but these dates rest entirely upon conjecture.

As the most remarkable incident in Tertullian's life was his adoption of the errors of Montanus, it will be necessary to give some account of that heresiarch. We find in Eusebius[1] the statement of an anonymous author, supposed by Lardner and others to be Asterius Urbanus, who wrote it about thirteen years after the death of Maximilla, one of the prophetesses who accompanied Montanus. From this statement we learn that he began to prophesy at Ardabau, a village in that part of Mysia which was contiguous to Phrygia, while Gratus was proconsul of Asia; that many persons were induced to believe him divinely inspired, particularly two females, Maximilla and Priscilla or Prisca, who also pretended to possess the same prophetic gifts; that the fallacy of their pretensions was exposed, and their doctrine condemned; and that they were themselves excommunicated by different synods held in Asia. The same anonymous author adds that Montanus and Maximilla hanged themselves; and that Theodotus, one of the earliest supporters of their cause, was taken up into the air and dashed to pieces by the spirit of falsehood, to whom he had consigned himself under the expectation that he should be conveyed into heaven. The author, however, tells us that he does not vouch for the truth of either of these stories.

Considerable difference of opinion prevails respecting the exact period when Montanus began to prophesy. The date of the proconsulship of Gratus has not been ascertained; but in speaking of the persecution in which the martyrs of Lyons and Vienne suffered, Eusebius says,[2] that Montanus and his com-

*De Patientiâ*, c. 1. In the tract *de Idololatriâ*, c. 4, he says of himself, "Et quid ego modicæ memoriæ homo?"

[1] *Eccl. Hist.* l. v. c. 16.

[2] *Eccl. Hist.* l. v. c. 3. The martyrs addressed letters to the brethren in Asia and Phrygia, as well as to Eleutherus, bishop of Rome, respecting the New

panions then began to be spoken of as prophets in Phrygia. The seventeenth year of Marcus Antoninus, or the year 177, is assigned by Eusebius himself as the date of the persecution in Gaul. In speaking also of the works of Apollonius of Hierapolis, who flourished about the year 170, Eusebius says [1] that he wrote against the Cataphrygian heresy, of which Montanus then began to lay the foundations. Epiphanius [2] places the rise of this heresy in the nineteenth year of Antoninus Pius, or the year 157, in which date he is followed by Pearson and Beausobre; Baratier places it as early as 126. Lardner decides in favour of the date assigned by Eusebius, whose authority on chronological questions is more to be relied upon than that of Epiphanius.

It appears from the account given by the anonymous author already quoted, that the followers of Montanus were numerous and powerful.[3] One of them, named Themiso, possessed sufficient influence to prevent Zoticus and Julian, the bishops of Comana and Apamea, from questioning the evil spirit by whom they supposed Maximilla to be inspired. The general opinion of Christians in those days, founded as they conceived on apostolic authority, was that the spirit of prophecy would remain in the Church until the second coming of Christ.[4] They felt, therefore, a predisposition to lend an attentive ear to one who assumed the character of a prophet; and though the trances and ecstatic raptures and fanatical ravings of Montanus might disgust and repel the judicious and sober-minded, they would be regarded by the credulous and wondering multitude as the surest signs of divine inspiration.

From a long extract, given by Eusebius [5] out of the writings of Apollonius against the Montanists, we collect that their leader was charged with recommending married persons to separate;

Prophecy. Irenæus does not expressly mention the Montanists, but is supposed to allude to them twice, l. iii. c. 11, p. 223; l. iv. c. 61. Clemens Alexandrinus twice mentions the Cataphrygians. *Strom.* l. iv. p. 511. *A.* l. vii. p. 765 c.

[1] *Eccl. Hist.* l. iv. c. 27.

[2] *Hær.* 28 or 48.

[3] We know from Tertullian that one of the bishops of Rome (learned men are not agreed respecting the particular bishop) was disposed for a time to recognise the prophetic character of Montanus. *Adv. Praxeam*, c. 1.

[4] The anonymous author urges (c. 17) as an argument against the Montanists, that there had been no succession of prophets among them since the death of Maximilla. She appears from Epiphanius to have herself foreseen this objection, and to have furnished her followers with an answer by declaring that after her no prophetess would appear, but the end of the world would come.

[5] *Eccl. Hist.* l. v. c. 18.

with laying down laws respecting fasts;[1] with calling Pepuza and Tymium, villages of Phrygia, Jerusalem, to which he wished to gather all the nations of the earth. He seems to have established a regular body of preachers, to whom he assigned salaries, which he paid out of contributions raised from his followers, under the name of oblations. Of Maximilla and Priscilla, Apollonius relates that they left their husbands when they joined themselves to Montanus; and he accuses the Montanists in general of converting religion into a source of profit, as well as of being licentious in their conduct. He confirms the statement of the anonymous writer respecting the attempt made by certain bishops to try the spirit in Maximilla whether it was of God; and mentions Themiso as a man of great wealth, who wrote a catholic epistle in defence of Montanism. Of himself he says that he composed his work forty years after Montanus began to prophesy.

The account given by Epiphanius of the Montanists is[2] that they received both the Old and New Testaments, believed in the resurrection of the dead, and maintained the catholic doctrine of the Trinity. Their error consisted in supposing that Montanus, Maximilla, and Priscilla were divinely inspired; and maintaining that the recognition of the Charismata, or spiritual gifts, announced by Montanus, was of absolute necessity. The larger portion of the account of Epiphanius is taken up in refuting the notions of Montanus respecting inspiration; and proving that the prophets both of the Old and New Testaments, at the time when they delivered their predictions, were in a state of complete self-possession, and perfectly understood what they said. He gives some specimens of the prophecies of Montanus and his female associates, which are of the most extravagant character.[3] In one of them Montanus says, "I am the Lord God who dwell in man." In another, "I am no angel or ambassador: I myself, God the Father, am come." Yet Epiphanius seems not to have understood these expressions as designed to convey the idea that Montanus represented himself to be God the Father. Otherwise he would scarcely have said that the Montanists agreed with the Catholic Church respecting the Father, Son, and Holy Ghost. According to the anonymous author quoted by Eusebius, Maximilla predicted that wars and tumults — according to Epiphanius, that the end of the world—would closely follow her

[1] The expression is ὁ νηστείας νομοθετήσας. Montanus did not merely himself observe additional fasts, but enjoined the observance of them by others.

[2] *Hær.* 28 or 48.

[3] Sect. 4, 10, 11, 12, 13.

decease. The former observes, in confutation of her predictions, that in the interval of thirteen years which had elapsed between her death and the time at which he wrote, the world and the Church had enjoyed profound peace; the latter that, although she had been dead 220 years, the world still continued to exist. Epiphanius mentions also the respect entertained by the Montanists in his day for a desolate spot in Phrygia called Pepuza, once the site of a town, which had been levelled with the ground; and adds that they expected the heavenly Jerusalem to descend there. To the general head of Cataphrygians he refers a number of minor sects, called Quintilliani, Pepuziani, Priscilliani, Artoturitæ, and Tascodrugitæ.[1] The first three were so called in consequence of a vision seen by a female, of the name of Quintilla or Priscilla,[2] at Pepuza. The Artoturitæ derived their name from using bread and cheese in the celebration of Eucharist; nad the Tascodrugitæ from their custom of putting the forefinger on the nose in the act of prayer; τασκὸς in the Phrygian language signifying a stake, and δροῦγγος a nose or beak.

The foregoing statements respecting the doctrines and opinions of Montanus are in great measure confirmed by the notices scattered over Tertullian's works. We find him, on the authority of the New Prophecy, enforcing the necessity of frequent fasts; if not actually condemning marriage, yet on all occasions giving a decided preference to a life of celibacy, and positively pronouncing second marriages unlawful; maintaining that favourite notion of enthusiasts in all ages of the Church, that the heavenly Jerusalem would descend on earth, and that the saints would reign there for a thousand years.[3] We find him also uniformly asserting the orthodoxy of the Montanists upon the fundamental doctrines of Christianity; though with respect to the Trinity they appear to have introduced certain novel illustrations of the generation of the

[1] *Hær.* 29 or 49.

[2] Tertullian wrote his treatise *de Baptismo* against a female named Quintilla, who denied the necessity and efficacy of baptism. He describes her as belonging to the sect of Cainites (Caiani), wild and profligate fanatics, who called Cain their father, and regarded with particular veneration Esau, Corah, Judas, and all the characters noted in Scripture for their opposition to the will of God. Perhaps, therefore, Tertullian called Quintilla a Cainite from analogy only, because she set herself against a divine ordinance, not because she was actually a member of the sect.

[3] In confirmation of this notion, Tertullian narrates a prodigy which occurred in Judea, and was witnessed by the army then on its march into the east. For forty successive days, early in the morning, a city was seen suspended from heaven. *Adv. Marcionem*, l. iii. c. 24.

Son from the Father.[1] We learn further from Tertullian that Montanus denied to the Church the power of granting absolution to persons guilty of flagrant offences—particularly to adulterers and fornicators—and maintained that Christians were not at liberty to avoid persecution by flight, or to purchase their safety with money.

Mosheim asserts,[2] on the authority of the work already quoted under the title of *Prædestinatus*, that among his other doctrines Montanus taught the approaching downfall of the Roman Empire, which would be followed by the appearance of Antichrist, and the second coming of our Lord to avenge the persecutions inflicted on His saints. The more judicious and sober-minded Christians would naturally take alarm at the open avowal of tenets, the necessary effect of which must be to render their religion obnoxious to the ruling powers, and to bring upon them fresh hardships and sufferings. We have seen that Maximilla predicted the speedy approach of those wars and tumults which were to precede the end of the world; and there are passages in Tertullian's works[3] which lead to the suspicion that he entertained similar sentiments. He appears, however, to have felt the necessity of concealing them, and is betrayed by the struggle between his conviction and his prudence into occasional inconsistency of language. He sometimes speaks as if Christians ought, at others as if they ought not, to pray for the speedy consummation of all things.[4]

One question still remains to be considered—What was the precise nature of the pretensions of Montanus? The two passages, quoted by Epiphanius from his Prophecies, would at first sight lead us to suppose that he gave himself out to be God the Father. Some writers have thought that he pretended to be the Holy Ghost, who was incarnate in him, as the Word was in Jesus. Mosheim appears at different times

[1] "Protulit enim Deus Sermonem, quemadmodum etiam Paracletus docet, sicut radix fruticem, et fons fluvium, et Sol radium." *Adv. Praxeam*, c. 8.

[2] "De rebus Christianis ante Constantinum." *Sæculum Secundum*, c. 67.

[3] See particularly the concluding chapter of the tract *de Spectaculis*, where Tertullian's exultation at the prospect of the approaching triumph of the Christians, and of the punishment of their adversaries, nearly gets the better of his discretion. "Quale autem spectaculum *in proximo* est adventus Domini jam indubitati, jam superbi, jam triumphantis?" See also *de Oratione*, c. 5.

[4] Compare *Apology*, c. 32, 39; *ad Scapulam*, c. 2, with *de Oratione*, c. 5; *de Res. Carnis*, c. 22, *sub in.*

to have held different opinions on the subject. In his work *de Rebus Christianorum ante Constantinum*,[1] he thus speaks of Montanus: "Homo nullius nominis, minime malus, naturâ tristis, debilisque judicii, morbo quodam animi in tantam incidebat amentiam, ut *Spiritum Sanctum seu Paracletum illum qui animaverat Apostolos Jesu Christi, divinitus sibi obtigisse* contenderet ad res futuras maximi momenti prædicandas, et morum vitæque disciplinam, priori ab Apostolis traditâ sanctiorem et meliorem, tradendam." But in his *Ecclesiastical History*,[2] he gives the following account of the pretensions of Montanus: "Montanus pretended to be the Paraclete or Comforter, whom the Divine Saviour, at His departure from the earth, promised to send to His disciples to lead them into all truth. Neither have they," he adds, "who inform us that Montanus pretended to have received from above the same Spirit or Paraclete, which formerly animated the apostles, interpreted with accuracy the meaning of this heretic. It is therefore necessary to observe here that Montanus made a distinction between the Paraclete promised by Christ to His apostles and the Holy Spirit that was shed upon them on the day of Pentecost; and understood by the former a divine teacher, pointed out by Christ under the name of Paraclete or Comforter, who was to perfect the gospel by the addition of some doctrines omitted by our Saviour, and to cast a full light upon others which were expressed in an obscure and imperfect manner, though for wise reasons which subsisted during the ministry of Christ. This Paraclete, Montanus represented himself to be." It is scarcely necessary to observe that the former statement is directly at variance with the latter, which Mosheim professes to have collected from an attentive perusal of Tertullian's writings. As my own perusal of the same writings has conducted me to the conclusion that the former, not the latter, is the correct representation of the pretensions advanced by Montanus, I shall proceed to state the reasons on which my opinion is founded.

Mosheim refers to no particular passage. Let us first turn to the commencement of the treatise *de Virginibus velandis*, which contains the fullest and most connected account of Tertullian's notions respecting the Paraclete. Having laid down what he calls the immutable rule of faith respecting the Father and the Son, Tertullian goes on to say "that those parts of the

[1] *Sæculum Secundum*, c. 66. [2] *Century* ii. c. 5, p. 237, note.

Christian dispensation which relate to the life and conversation of Christians admit of change and improvement. On this very account our Lord sent the Paraclete; to the end that, as the weakness of man's nature rendered him incapable of bearing the whole truth at once, the Christian rule of life might by degrees be carried to perfection by Him who was substituted in the place of the Lord, *i.e.* the Holy Spirit.[1] Man in his earliest state was directed by the fear of God implanted in his nature; under the law and prophets he was in his infancy; under the gospel, in his youth; but now, through the Paraclete, he has reached the state of perfect manhood." In this passage the Paraclete and the Holy Spirit are clearly identified.

We will now proceed to the tract *de Monogamiâ*, in which Tertullian is endeavouring to establish the superior sanctity of a life of celibacy, and contending that the apostle's words, "It is better to marry than burn," imply only a permission granted in condescension to the infirmities of human nature.[2] "Whether, then," he proceeds, "we look to the grounds on which the permission was granted, or to the preference given to a state of celibacy (in the preceding words of St. Paul, 'It is good for a man not to touch a woman'), the evident tendency of the apostle's reasoning is to do away the permission to marry. This being so, why may not *the same Spirit*, coming after the days of the apostles at the appropriate time (there being, according to the Preacher, a time for all things) for the purpose of leading Christians into all truth,—why may not, I say, *the same Spirit* have imposed a final and complete restraint upon the flesh, and called men away from marriage, not indirectly, but openly?—especially as St. Paul's argument, that 'the time is short,' is much more forcible now that 160 years have elapsed since he wrote his Epistle. Had such been the injunction of the Paraclete, ought you not thus to have reasoned with yourself? This is in truth the ancient discipline exhibited in the flesh and will of the Lord (who was not married), and afterwards in the

[1] "Ab illo vicario Domini, Spiritu Sancto." Tertullian's notion was that when our Lord ascended into heaven, He sent the Holy Spirit to carry on the gospel dispensation. Thus in the tract *de Præscriptione Hæreticorum*, c. 13: "Misisse vicariam vim Spiritûs Sancti, qui credentes agat;" and again, c. 28: "Neglexerit officium Dei villicus, Christi vicarius."

[2] C. 3: "Igitur si omnia ista obliterant licentiam nubendi," etc. It should be observed that Tertullian's professed object, in the second and third chapters of the tract *de Monogamiâ*, is to show that although the injunctions of the Paraclete were new and burdensome to human weakness, Christ had prepared the minds of His followers to expect that such would be their character. Compare c. 14.

recommendations and examples of His apostles. This is the holiness to which we were originally destined. The Paraclete introduces no new doctrine; He now definitely enjoins that of which He before gave warning; He now requires that for which He has hitherto been content to wait. Reflect upon these observations, and you will easily be convinced that it was competent to the Paraclete to limit man to a single marriage; since He might (in perfect consistency with the doctrine of Christ and His apostles) have forbidden marriage altogether: and if you rightly understand the will of Christ, you will admit it to be credible that the Paraclete would curtail a liberty which might with propriety have been wholly taken away. Nay, you will acknowledge that, in this case also, the Paraclete is your advocate, since He has not imposed upon your weakness the obligation of absolute and undeviating continence." Surely the fair inference to be deduced from the comparison of this and the preceding passage is, not that Montanus pretended to be the Paraclete,[1] or made a distinction between the Paraclete promised by Christ to His apostles and the Holy Spirit that was shed upon them on the day of Pentecost; but that Montanus conceived himself to be inspired by the same Spirit as the apostles, though it was his peculiar office to close as it were the Christian revelation, and to place in a clear and refulgent light those sublime truths, those doctrines of perfection, which, during Christ's residence upon earth, His disciples had not been able to bear, but which had been in a progressive state of development since the descent of the Holy Spirit on the day of Pentecost. To say that the Holy Spirit inspired the apostles, and the Paraclete Montanus, is to make a distinction only of words; if, as is evident from the general tenor of Tertullian's writings, he identified the Holy Spirit with the Paraclete.[2] It is true that Tertullian generally speaks of the New Prophecy as proceeding from the Paraclete; but this is not invariably the case. In the treatise *against Praxeas*, he calls it the prophecy of the Holy Spirit.[3] He makes a dis-

[1] So far was Tertullian from supposing that Montanus was the Paraclete, that he did not even conceive the revelations of the Paraclete to have been confined to him. For in the tract *de Res. Carnis*, c. 11, he quotes some words, as spoken by the Paraclete through the prophetess Prisca: "De quibus luculenter et Paracletus per Prophetidem Priscam, 'Carnes sunt et carnem oderunt.'"

[2] He uses the word Paracletus to designate the Third Person in the Holy Trinity. "Ita connexus Patris in Filio, et Filii in Paracleto, tres efficit cohærentes, alterum ex altero." *Adv. Praxeam*, c. 25. And in the tract *de Jejuniis*, c. 13, we find "Spiritus Sanctus—qua Paracletus, id est, advocatus."

[3] "Hic interim acceptum a Patre munus effudit, Spiritum Sanctum, tertium

tinction between the revelations vouchsafed to the apostles and to Montanus with respect to their different degrees of perfection; but none with respect to the source from which they were derived. For in the tract *de Præscriptione Hæreticorum*, he says that "the Paraclete was the Teacher of the apostles when they went forth to preach unto the Gentiles;"[1] and, in the tract *de Resurrectione Carnis*, that "the Holy Spirit, having previously allowed some doctrines to remain involved in a certain degree of obscurity in order to prove the faith of Christians, had now removed all ambiguities by a clear and explicit development of the whole mystery of the gospel, through the New Prophecy which had been poured out abundantly from the Paraclete."[2] My conclusion is, that the pretensions of Montanus were correctly represented by Augustine, when he said of him and his two female associates, "Adventum Spiritûs Sancti a Domino promissum in se *potius* quam in Apostolis fuisse asserunt;"[3] and by Philaster, according to whom the Montanists held that the fulness of the Holy Spirit was not given to the apostles, but to Montanus.[4] This is also the view taken by Lardner;[5] who says that "the followers of Montanus supposed God to have made some additional revelations by him for the perfection of believers." But when Lardner, speaking of the comparative importance attached by the Montanists to the revelations made to their leader and to the apostles, contends that "they could not think this inspiration of Montanus equal to that of the apostles, as it did not relate to the great articles of faith, but chiefly to matters of external order and discipline," he certainly does not give an accurate representation of the opinions of our author; who ought perhaps so to have reasoned, but in fact reasoned otherwise. Tertullian, who believed that Montanus was commissioned to complete the Christian revelation, could not deem him inferior to the apostles, by whom it was only obscurely

nomen divinitatis et tertium gradum majestatis, unius prædicatorem monarchiæ sed et οἰκονομίας interpretatorem, si quis sermones Novæ Prophetiæ *ejus* admiserit," c. 30.

[1] "Quod si nationibus destinati doctores Apostoli, ipsi quoque doctorem consecuti erant Paracletum," c. 8.

[2] "Sed quoniam nec dissimulare Spiritum Sanctum oportebat, quo minus et hujusmodi eloquiis superinundaret, quæ nullis hæreticorum versutiis semina subspargerent, imo et veteres eorum cespites vellerent, idcirco jam omnes retro ambiguitates et quas volunt parabolas apertâ atque perspicuâ totius sacramenti prædicatione discussit per Novam Prophetiam de Paracleto inundantem." *Sub fine.*

[3] *Liber de Hæresibus*, c. 26.

[4] *Hæres. Cataphryges.*

[5] *History of Heretics.* Of the Montanists, c. 19.

and imperfectly developed; nor can Lardner's statement be reconciled with the distinguished appellation of πνευματικοὶ, or spiritual, which Tertullian confers on the Montanists; while he brands with the epithet of ψυχικοὶ, or animal,[1] those who, though they believed all the fundamental articles of the Christian faith, rejected the new revelation from the Paraclete.

Tertullian's works furnish presumptive proof that the effusions of Montanus and his female associates had been committed to writing. A passage has been already cited containing a saying of the prophetess Prisca;[2] and in the treatises *de Fugâ in Persecutione* and *de Pudicitiâ* are citations from the discourses of Montanus.[3] Yet the work, from which Epiphanius made his extracts, could not have been known to our author. Had he been acquainted with it, he could scarcely have failed in his treatise *against Praxeas* to give some explanation of expressions which appear at first sight to identify Montanus with God the Father.

Such were the tenets and pretensions of Montanus, as far as we can collect them from the writings of authors who lived near his time; and particularly of Tertullian, who appears to have adopted all his peculiar opinions. Some of his followers are said to have fallen into great errors both of doctrine and practice, though we may reasonably suspect that they were in many instances charged with crimes which existed only in the invention of their accusers. Montanus was evidently a man of weak intellects, who was induced partly by a superstitious temper, partly by the desire of distinction, himself to pursue, and to recommend to others, an ascetic course of life.[4] The austerity of his doctrine and practice naturally gained him admirers and

[1] "Homines solius animæ et carnis." *De Jejuniis*, c. 17.

[2] Note 38.

[3] "Spiritum vero si consulas, quid magis Sermone illo Spiritus probat? namque omnes pene ad Martyrium exhortatur non ad fugam, ut et illius commemoremur 'Publicaris, inquit: bonum tibi est. Qui enim non publicatur (παραδειγματίζεται) in hominibus, publicatur in Domino. Ne confundaris: justitia te producit in medium. Quid confunderis, laudem ferens? Potestas fit quum conspiceris ab hominibus.' Sic et alibi, 'Nolite in lectulis, nec in aborsibus et febribus mollibus optare exire, sed in Martyriis, ut glorificetur qui est passus pro vobis.'" *De Fugâ in Persec.* c. 9. "Si et Spiritum quis agnoverit, audiet et fugitivos denotantem," c. 11. "Hoc ego magis et agnosco et dispono, qui ipsum Paracletum in Prophetis Novis habeo dicentem, 'Potest Ecclesia donare delictum,' sed non faciam, ne et alia delinquant." *De Pudicitiâ*, c. 21.

[4] The anonymous author in Eusebius imputes the conduct of Montanus to this motive.

followers; and he confirmed his empire over their minds by professing to see visions, and to receive revelations from heaven. Perhaps he had succeeded in persuading himself that he was divinely inspired. Fanaticism is for the most part combined with fraud in the character of the religious impostor; nor is it improbable that, in the state of exhaustion to which the body of Montanus was reduced by the length and frequency and severity of his fasts, his mind might occasionally become disordered, and he might mistake for realities the creations of a distempered fancy.

The notion that the doctrine of the gospel was not publicly delivered by the apostles in its full perfection, but that certain important truths were reserved which the minds of men were not yet able to bear, does not appear to have been peculiar to the school of Montanus. The Valentinians held a similar language, and supposed these mysterious truths to relate to their extravagant and unintelligible fancies respecting the Pleroma and the successive generations of Æons.[1] Even among the orthodox, a notion not altogether dissimilar very generally prevailed. The principal object of the *Stromata* of Clemens Alexandrinus is to point out the distinction between the Christian who is perfected in knowledge (γνωστικὸς), and the great mass of believers; and to lay down rules for the formation of this perfect character. He does not indeed, like Montanus, profess to communicate truths which he had received by immediate revelation from above, and of which the apostles were ignorant. He supposes them to have been revealed by Christ to Peter, James, and John, at the time of the Transfiguration, and to Paul at a subsequent period; and to have been by them orally transmitted to their successors in the superintendence of the Church.[2] When, however, we come to inquire into the nature of this sublime knowledge,[3] we find that it consisted of subtle explanations of the doctrine of the Trinity and of other

[1] *De Præscriptione Hæreticorum*, c. 25.

[2] Eusebius says *after the resurrection*, *Eccl. Hist.* l. ii. c. 1. Compare Clem. Alex. *Strom.* l. i. p. 322, l. 18. p. 323, l. 23. p. 324, l. 26; l. vi. p. 771, l. 14. p. 774, l. 27. p. 802, l. 36. p. 806, l. 25. Ed. Potter. Mr. Rennell, in his *Proofs oj Inspiration*, has inadvertently referred to the first of these passages as bearing testimony to the inspiration of the New Testament, p. 46.

[3] Clemens says that he is not at liberty to disclose fully and openly wherein this γνῶσις consists, as it is of too pure and spiritual a nature to be comprehended by Christians in general, l. i. p. 327, l. 41. The notion, if not originally suggested y certain passages in St. Paul's Epistles, was at least defended by a reference to them. *Strom.* l. v. p. 683, l. 18.

Christian doctrines; of allegorical and mystical interpretations of Scripture; and of moral precepts not widely differing from those, the observance of which was enjoined by Montanus, though carried to a less degree of extravagance. For instance, Clemens[1] does not pronounce second marriages positively unlawful, but says that a man who marries again after the decease of his wife falls short of Christian perfection. The notions of Clemens bear a close affinity to mysticism, and are calculated to form a sort of philosophic Christian, raised far above the sensible world, and absorbed in sublime contemplations; those of Montanus would lead men to place the whole of virtue in bodily austerities and acts of mortification: both may be justly charged with having assisted in paving the way for the introduction of the monastic mode of life.

There is nothing more flattering to the pride of man than the persuasion that he is the favoured depositary of knowledge which is unattainable by the generality of his fellow-creatures; that, while they are destined to pass their lives amidst thick clouds and darkness, he, with a select few, is permitted to bask in the meridian sunshine of divine truth. Both the philosophy and the religion of the Gentile world had their external and internal doctrines; and from them in an evil hour the distinction was introduced into the Church of Christ. Clemens Alexandrinus is the earliest Christian writer in whose works any allusion to it appears; and we say that he introduced the distinction in an evil hour, because on it and on the account which he gives of its origin, are founded the two principal arguments urged by Roman Catholics in defence of their doctrinal and other corruptions. When driven from every other point, they fly, as to a last refuge, to the *disciplina arcani* and to oral tradition; and though the writings of Clemens afford no countenance whatever to the particular errors which the Romish Church is anxious to maintain, yet it derives no small advantage to its cause from the statement of so early a writer—that Christ communicated important truths to the apostles, which were neither intended for the ear, nor adapted to the comprehension of the great body of believers, and which had come down to his own time through the medium of oral tradition.

But to return to Tertullian, his adoption of the opinions of Montanus has, without the slightest semblance of truth, been imputed by Pamelius and others to disappointed ambition. He

[1] *Strom.* l. iii. p. 548, l. 26.

was indignant, they say, because he was defeated in his pretensions to the see, either of Rome or Carthage. The true cause of his defection from the Church is to be sought in the constitution and temper of his mind; to which the austere doctrines and practice of the new prophet were perfectly congenial, and of which the natural warmth and acerbity were, as Jerome informs us, increased by the censures, perhaps by the misrepresentations, of the Roman clergy.[1]

Before we quit this part of the subject, it will be necessary to obviate an objection, which the foregoing statement may possibly suggest. "What reliance, it may be asked, can we place upon the judgment, or even upon the testimony of Tertullian, who could be deluded into a belief of the extravagant pretensions of Montanus? or what advantage can the theological student derive from reading the works of so credulous and superstitious an author?" These are questions easily asked, and answered without hesitation by men who take the royal road to theological knowledge: who either through want of the leisure, or impatience of the labour, requisite for the examination of the writings of the Fathers, find it convenient to conceal their ignorance under an air of contempt. Thus a hasty and unfair sentence of condemnation has been passed upon the Fathers, and their works have fallen into unmerited disrepute. The sentence is hasty, because it bespeaks great ignorance of human nature, which often presents the curious phenomenon of a union of the most opposite qualities in the same mind; of vigour, acuteness, and discrimination on some subjects, with imbecility, dulness, and bigotry on others. The sentence is unfair, because it condemns the Fathers for faults which were those, not of the individuals, but of the age: of the elder Pliny and Marcus Antoninus as well as of Tertullian. It is, moreover, unfair, because the persons who argue thus in the case of the Fathers, argue differently in other cases. Without intending to compare the gentle, the amiable, the accomplished Fénélon, with the harsh, the fiery, the unpolished Tertullian, or to class the spiritual reveries of Madame Guyon with the extravagances of Montanus and his prophetesses, it may be remarked that the predilection of Fénélon for the notions of the mystics betrayed a mental weakness, differing in degree, rather than in kind, from that which led Tertullian to the adoption of Montanism. We do not, however, on account of this weakness in Fénélon, throw aside his works

[1] *Catalogus Scriptorum Ecclesiasticorum.*

as utterly undeserving of notice, or deem it a sufficient ground for questioning the superiority of his genius and talent; we regard with surprise and regret this additional instance of human infirmity, but continue to read Telemachus with instruction and delight. Let us show the same candour and sound judgment in the case of the Fathers; let us separate the wheat from the tares, and not involve them in one indiscriminate conflagration. The assertion may appear paradoxical, but is nevertheless true, that the value of Tertullian's writings to the theological student arises in a great measure from his errors. When he became a Montanist, he set himself to expose what he deemed faulty in the practice and discipline of the Church. Thus we are told indirectly what that practice and that discipline were; and we obtain information which, but for his secession from the Church, his works would scarcely have supplied. In a word, whether we consider the testimony borne to the genuineness and integrity of the books of the New Testament, or the information relating to ceremonies, discipline, and doctrines of the Primitive Church, Tertullian's writings form a most important link in that chain of tradition which connects the apostolic age with our own.

Attempts have been made to arrange Tertullian's works in chronological order;[1] with how little success we may judge from the diversity of opinions which has prevailed among learned men respecting the date of a single tract, that entitled *de Pallio.*

[1] For the better understanding of the remarks upon Tertullian's writings, the dates of the principal events connected with the reign of Severus are inserted as given by the Benedictines in their learned work, *L'Art de Verifier les Dates.*

| | A.D. |
|---|---|
| Commencement of the reign of Severus, | 193 |
| Defeat of Niger, | 195 |
| Taking of Byzantium, | 196 |
| Defeat of Albinus, | 197 |
| Caracalla associated in the empire, | 198 |
| War against the Parthians, | 198 |
| Severus returns from that war, | 203 |
| Celebration of the secular games, | 204 |
| Plautianus put to death, | 204 or 205 |
| War in Britain, | 208 |
| Wall built by Severus, | 210 |
| Death of Severus, | 211 |
| Caracalla born, | 188 |
| —— called Cæsar, | 196 |
| —— ,, Augustus, | 198 |
| Geta born, | 189 |
| —— called Cæsar, | 198 |
| —— ,, Augustus, | 208 |

It appears that Tertullian had exchanged the Roman toga for the pallium, which was worn by the Greeks and by those who affected to be called philosophers. This change of dress excited the ridicule and censure of his fellow-citizens of Carthage; and he composed the treatise *de Pallio* in answer to their attacks. Pamelius, with whom Scaliger agrees, supposes that it is the earliest of Tertullian's works now extant, written immediately after his conversion to Christianity, on which occasion he put on the pallium, the garment then universally worn by Christians. Salmasius contends that the pallium was the dress, not of Christians in general, but of presbyters only; and that the tract was consequently written after the admission of Tertullian into that order. Allix[1] differs both from Pamelius and Salmasius, and affirms that the pallium was worn only by those Christians who adopted an ascetic course of life; he concludes, therefore, that the tract was written shortly after Tertullian openly professed himself a Montanist. Each of the three critics supports his opinions by quotations from the tract itself; and there is one passage which at first sight would lead the reader to hope that the date might be ascertained with a considerable degree of precision. Tertullian[2] says that three persons were then united in the administration of the empire, and that the world enjoyed profound peace. Unfortunately, the commentators cannot agree among themselves whether the three emperors were Severus, Antoninus Caracalla, and Albinus,[3] or Severus, Antoninus Caracalla, and Geta;[4] or whether the profound peace of which Tertullian speaks was that which followed the suppression of Niger's revolt, or that which the empire enjoyed during the latter years of the life of Severus. Semler[5] leans to the former opinion, but admits that the question is involved in great obscurity. In fact, the style of the treatise is so declamatory and rhetorical, that no inference can be safely drawn from particular expressions. To me,[6] however, it appears to have been

1 *Dissertatio de Tertulliani vitâ et scriptis*, c. 6.

2 "Quantum urbium aut produxit, aut auxit, aut reddidit præsentis Imperii *triplex Virtus!* Deo tot Augustis in unum favente, quot census transcripti!" etc., c. 2.

3 A. S. 196.

4 A. S. 208.

5 *Dissertatio in Tertullianum*, c. 1.

6 This inference I draw from the following passages:—"Enimvero quum hanc *primum* sapientiam vestit, quæ vanissimis superstitionibus renuit, tunc certissime pallium super omnes exuvias et peplos augusta vestis, superque omnes apices et titulos sacerdos suggestus; deduc oculos, suadeo, reverere habitum unius interim erroris tui renuntiatorem," c. 4, *sub fine*. And again, "Sed ista pallium loquitur. 'At ego jam illi etiam divinæ Sectæ ac Disciplinæ commercium confero.' Gaude pallium, et exulta; melior jam te Philosophia dignata est, ex quo Christianum vestire cœpisti," c. 6.

written as a defence of the general adoption of the pallium at that period by the Christians of Carthage; or perhaps of its adoption by himself in particular, because he deemed it more suitable to the Christian character.

The only work which supplies positive evidence of its date, is the first book *against Marcion.* In c. 15, Tertullian says that he is writing in the fifteenth year of the reign of the Emperor Severus, or the year 207.[1] There is also positive evidence in this book that the author was, when he wrote it, a believer in the prophecies of Montanus.[2]

In a passage from the tract *de Monogamiâ,*[3] already referred to, Tertullian says, that 160 years had elapsed since St. Paul addressed his First Epistle to the Corinthians. Pamelius in consequence assigns the year 213 as the date of the tract, conceiving that the First Epistle to the Corinthians was written in 53. But in the first place, learned men are not agreed respecting the exact date of the Epistle, some fixing it as late as 59; and in the next, it is highly probable that Tertullian did not speak with precision, but used round numbers. In the first *Address ad Nationes* our author says, in one place that 250 years, in another that 300 years had not yet elapsed since the birth of Christ:[4] it is evident, therefore, that in neither instance did Tertullian mean to express the precise number.

Unable to discover in the works themselves any marks by which their dates may be precisely ascertained, later critics have been content to divide them into two classes; those written before Tertullian adopted the errors of Montanus, and those written afterwards. But even on this point a diversity of opinions subsists, and the commentators are not agreed to which of the two classes each work belongs. Unless indeed the tract contains some allusion to the Paraclete or to the New Prophecy, we are not warranted in positively asserting that it was written by a Montanist; nor does the absence of all such allusion justify a contrary inference. The subject of the tract might afford its author no opportunity of disclosing his belief in the inspiration of Montanus; while, on the other hand, the mere

1 "Ad decimum quintum jam Severi Imperatoris."

2 "Sed etsi nubendi jam modus ponitur, quem quidem apud nos Spiritalis Ratio, Paracleto Auctore, defendit, unum in Fide matrimonium præscribens," c. 29.

3 C. 3. See page 12.

4 The first number occurs in c. 7, the second in c. 9.

fact that one of the tenets maintained by that heresiarch occurs in a particular work, is not of itself sufficient to prove that Tertullian, when it was written, was professedly a Montanist. There were in that age, as in most ages of the Church, two parties, the advocates of a milder and of a severer discipline. In the latter class would be many whose opinions respecting the course of life to be pursued by a Christian would not differ widely from those of Montanus, although they might give no credit to his pretended revelations from heaven. The natural disposition of Tertullian would incline him to the more rigid side; yet it is probable that a gradual change was effected in his sentiments, and that, as he advanced in years, they continually assumed a harsher and more uncompromising character. Such is the usual progress of opinion, and we know that on two points at least this change actually took place in his case,—the readmission of penitents into the Church, and the degree of criminality to be attached to a second marriage. As the inclination to the severe discipline of Montanus always existed in Tertullian's mind, and increased by slow and almost imperceptible degrees, it is scarcely possible, in the absence of all external testimony, to draw a well-defined line of separation between the works which were and those which were not composed before his secession from the Church. Having premised these observations respecting the difficulty of arriving at any certainty on the subject, I will proceed to state the result of my own examination of Tertullian's writings.

The tracts *de Pœnitentiâ*, *de Oratione*, and *de Baptismo* are allowed by the majority of commentators to have been written before Tertullian had become a follower of Montanus.

Erasmus doubted the genuineness of the tract *de Pœnitentiâ*, partly on account of its superiority in point of style to the acknowledged works of Tertullian, and partly because it contains opinions at variance with those which he has expressed in the tract *de Pudicitiâ*. In the former,[1] he expressly says that all crimes without exception committed after baptism may once, but only once, be pardoned by the Church upon repentance; in the latter,[2] he denies that adulterers, as well as idolaters and murderers, can ever be reconciled to the Church. But in the commencement of the tract *de Pudicitiâ*[3] he himself alludes to

[1] See c. 7, 8, 9. [2] See c. 5.
[3] C. 1. "Erit igitur et hic adversus Psychicos titulus, *adversus meæ quoque sententiæ retropenes illos societatem*," etc.

this change in his sentiments, which is also mentioned by Jerome;[1] and the necessary inference from a comparison of the passages is, that the tract *de Pœnitentiâ* is genuine, and that it was composed while Tertullian was yet a member of the Church.

A passage in the fifth chapter of Hilary's *Commentary on St. Matthew*[2] implies that Tertullian composed the treatise *de Oratione* before he quitted the communion of the Church. It is certain that he mentions the *Shepherd of Hermas*[3] without bestowing upon it any of those opprobrious epithets which he employs in the treatise *de Pudicitiâ*,[4] written after he became a Montanist.

Allix thinks that he discovers traces of a leaning to Montanism in the tract *de Baptismo.* He founds his suspicions on an allusion to the name of Pisciculi,[5] which Tertullian applies to the Christians, and on the mention of Charismata.[6] But with respect to the latter term, there appears to be no reason for restricting it to the revelations of Montanus; and with respect to the appellation of Pisciculi, though Allix may be right in supposing it to have been borrowed by Tertullian from the Sibylline verses, the work, according to him, either of Montanus or a Montanist, yet the majority of learned men are of opinion that the forgery of the Sibylline verses was prior to the rise of the heresy of Montanus. There is in my opinion a far more suspicious passage in this book,[7] where Tertullian says that three persons compose a church; a notion which frequently occurs in

[1] Epistle to Damasus on the parable of the Prodigal Son: "Unde vehementer admiror Tertullianum in eo Libro, quem de Pudicitiâ adversum Pœnitentiam scripsit et sententiam veterem novâ opinione dissolvit, hoc voluisse sentire."

[2] "De Orationis autem Sacramento necessitate nos commentandi Cyprianus vir Sanctæ memoriæ liberavit. Quamquam et Tertullianus hinc volumen aptissimum scripserit; sed *consequens* error hominis detraxit scriptis probabilibus auctoritatem.'

[3] C. 12.

[4] C. 10.

[5] "Sed nos Pisciculi secundum ἰχθῦν nostrum Jesum Christum in aquâ nascimur," c. 1. Cicero says (*de Divinatione*, l. ii. c. 54, or 111) that the original Sibylline verses were acrostics; and in the eighth book of the spurious verses are some acrostics commencing with the initial letters of the words Ἰησοῦς Χριστὸς, Θεοῦ Υἱὸς, Σωτὴρ, of which letters the word ἰχθῦς is composed; but, according to Lardner, there is no good ground to think that Tertullian has alluded to these acrostics. *Credibility of the Gospel History*, c. 29.

[6] "Petite de Domino peculia, gratias, distributiones charismatum subjiciente," c. 20, *sub fine.*

[7] "Quum autem sub tribus et testatio fidei et sponsio salutis pignerentur, necessario adjicitur Ecclesiæ mentio; quoniam ubi tres, id est, Pater et Filius et Spiritus Sanctus, ibi Ecclesia quæ trium corpus est," c. 6.

the works confessedly written after he became a believer in the New Prophecy.

Allix, in like manner, discovers a leaning to Montanism in the two treatises *ad Uxorem;* in the former of which Tertullian dissuades his wife, in case she should survive him, from contracting a second marriage; in the latter, fearful that she might be unwilling to impose upon herself so severe a restraint, he cautions her at least not to marry a heathen. This condescension to human weakness is so utterly at variance with the harsh language which he applied to second marriages after he became a Montanist, that I cannot assent to the opinion of Allix.

In the tract *ad Martyres* is an allusion[1] to a practice which then prevailed, of restoring penitents to the communion of the Church, at the request of persons confined in prison on account of their profession of Christianity. If we compare the tone of this allusion with the pointed condemnation of the practice in the tract *de Pudicitiâ*,[2] we must, I think, conclude that Tertullian was not yet a convert to Montanism when he wrote the tract *ad Martyres*. The death of the philosopher Peregrinus, which happened between the years 164 and 170, is mentioned in c. 4; and the concluding sentence has been supposed, with great appearance of probability, to relate to the numerous executions, particularly of persons of the senatorial order, which took place after the defeat and death of Albinus;[3] though it may perhaps relate to the death of Plautianus.

A comparison of the different modes in which Tertullian speaks of flight in time of persecution, in the tracts *de Patientiâ*[4] and *de Fugâ in Persecutione*, will lead to the conclusion that the former was written while he was yet a member of the Church.

The treatise *adversus Judæos* is supposed by Pamelius to have been written in the year 198; by Allix (after Baronius) in 208. Allix grounds his opinion on the expressions respecting the state of the Roman empire which occur in c. 7, and which he con-

[1] C. 1. "Quam pacem quidam, in Ecclesiâ non habentes, a Martyribus in carcere exorare consueverunt. Et ideo eam etiam propterea in vobis habere et fovere et custodire debetis, ut si forte et aliis præstare possitis."

[2] C. 22.

[3] A. S. 197.

[4] C. 13. "Si fuga urgeat, adversus incommoda fugæ caro militat." The fair inference from these words appears to be that flight in time of persecution is allowable.

ceives to be applicable only to the latter years of the reign of Severus; but they are so general that no inference as to the date of the tract can be safely drawn from them.

Allix infers from the mention of Charismata in the tract *de Præscriptione Hæreticorum*,[1] that it was written after Tertullian became a Montanist. But, as was observed with respect to the tract *de Baptismo*, the context suggests no reason why we should restrict the word to the peculiar gifts of the Paraclete of Montanus. Allix also quotes a passage from the first book *against Marcion*, from which he argues that it was prior to the tract *de Præscriptione Hæreticorum*;[2] the context leads me to an opposite conclusion. Besides, had the tract been written by a Montanist, some mention of the Paraclete would probably have been introduced into the short summary of faith given in c. 13; as is the case in the first chapter of the tract *de Virginibus velandis*. The conclusion also warrants the inference that it was written before all the treatises against particular heresies.[3] It was certainly prior to the tract *de Carne Christi*.[4]

It was also prior to the tract *against Hermogenes*,[5] in the first chapter of which there is an allusion to it. Allix thinks that Tertullian was a Montanist when he wrote *against Hermogenes*, because he charges that heretic with marrying repeatedly;[6] but I doubt whether the words are sufficiently precise to warrant the inference.

Great diversity of opinion prevails among the commentators respecting the date of the *Apology*. Allix appears to me to have shown satisfactorily that it was written, not at Rome, but at

[1] C. 29.

[2] "Sed *alius libellus* hunc gradum sustinebit *adversus Hæreticos*, etiam sine retractatu doctrinarum revincendos, quod hoc sint de Præscriptione Novitatis. Nunc quatenus admittenda congressio est, interdum, ne *compendium Præscriptionis ubique advocatum* diffidentiæ deputetur, regulam Adversarii prius prætexam, ne cui lateat in quâ principalis quæstio dimicatura est," c. 1.

[3] C. 45. "Sed nunc quidem generaliter actum est a nobis adversus hæreses omnes, certis et justis et necessariis præscriptionibus repellendas a conlatione Scripturarum. De reliquo, si Dei gratia annuerit, etiam specialiter quibusdam respondebimus."

[4] C. 2. "Sed plenius ejusmodi præscriptionibus adversus omnes hæreses alibi jam usi sumus."

[5] C. 1. "Solemus Hæreticis compendii gratiâ de posteritate præscribere."

[6] C. 1. "Præterea pingit illicite, nubit assidue. Legem Dei in libidinem defendit."

Carthage;[1] and it was addressed, not to the Senate, but to the governors of Proconsular Africa.[2] He has not, however, been equally successful in proving that it was written so late as the year 217. I cannot discover in the passage in which Tertullian speaks of the reformation of the Papian laws any reason for thinking that Severus was then dead;[3] I should rather infer the contrary. The allusion to the conspiracies which were daily detected at the very time when the book was written,[4] as well as the enumeration of the barbarous nations which either then were, or had recently been, at war with Rome,[5] correspond to the events which took place during the reign of Severus; and as the work contains internal testimony that the Christians were then suffering persecution, why may it not have been written soon after the promulgation of the law by which the Christians were forbidden to make proselytes, that is, about the year 204?[6] The date assigned by Mosheim, in a tract written expressly on the subject, is 198. It was not to be expected that any marks of Montanism would appear in the *Apology*.

The two books entitled *ad Nationes* have come down to us in so imperfect a state that it is difficult to ascertain whether they were designed to be a distinct work from the *Apology*, or whether Tertullian at first wrought his materials into this form, which he

[1] Speaking of Rome, Tertullian says, c. 9, "Ecce in illâ religiosissimâ urbe Æneadum;" and in c. 21, *sub fine*, he thus addresses the Romans: "Ut ad vos quoque, dominatores gentium, aspiciam;" and again, in c. 35, "Ipsos Quirites, ipsam vernaculam septem collium plebem, convenio:" modes of expression which he would scarcely have used had the tract been written at Rome.

[2] In designating the persons to whom the *Apology* is addressed, he styles them in general Præsides; thus, "Veritatis extorquendæ Præsides," c. 2. "Ex ipsis etiam vobis justissimis et severissimis in nos Præsidibus," c. 9. "Hoc agite, boni Præsides," c. 50. In c. 2 he uses the expression, "Hoc imperium cujus ministri estis;" and from a passage in c. 45, "Deum non Proconsulem timentes," it may fairly be inferred that he was writing in a province governed by a proconsul.

[3] "Nonne vanissimas Papias Leges, quæ ante liberos suscipi cogunt quam Juliæ matrimonium contrahi, post tantæ auctoritatis senectutem heri Severus constantissimus Principum exclusit?" c. 4.

[4] "Unde Cassii et Nigri et Albini?" and again, "Sed et qui nunc scelestarum partium socii aut plausores quotidie revelantur, post vindemiam parricidarum racematio superstes," etc., c. 35. This passage appears to relate to the triumph of Severus after his return from the Parthian war, and to the conspiracy of Plautianus, which took place about the year 204.

[5] C. 37. "Plures nimirum Mauri et Marcomanni ipsique Parthi."

[6] The part taken by the Syrians of Palestine in favour of Niger greatly irritated Severus, and probably gave occasion to this law. *Ælii Spartiani Severus*, p. 902 C. From the words of the historian it might be inferred that the law applied only to Palestine. "In itinere Palæstinis plurima jura fundavit. Judæos fieri sub gravi pœna vetuit. Idem etiam de Christianis sanxit," p. 904. Speaking shortly afte of the inhabitants of Alexandria, he says, "Multa præterea *his* jura mutavit."

afterwards thought proper to change. The arguments are for the most part the same as those urged in the *Apology*, and are frequently expressed in the same words. Allix fancied that he found an allusion to the assumption of the title of Parthicus by Caracalla,[1] and concluded, therefore, that these books were written after the death of Severus; but I suspect that the allusion existed only in his own fancy.

The tract *de Testimonio Animæ* was subsequent to the *Apology*, to which it contains a reference. "Ut loco suo edocuimus ad fidem earum (Divinarum Scripturarum) demonstrandam," c. 5. The reference is to the nineteenth chapter of the *Apology*, in which Tertullian establishes the superior antiquity of the Hebrew Scriptures to the literature of the Gentiles.

The terms in which Tertullian speaks,[2] in his *Address to Scapula*, of the favour shown by Severus to the Christians, in consequence of the cure wrought upon him by one of their body named Proculus, lead to the conclusion that the work was composed after that Emperor's death. There is in this tract an allusion to the destruction of Byzantium, which took place in the year 196;[3] as well as to a preternatural *extinction* of the sun's light, which occurred at Utica, and which Allix supposes to have been an eclipse of the sun that happened in the year 210. He agrees with Scaliger and Holstenius in thinking that this was one of the latest of Tertullian's works, and written about the year 217. In c. 4, Tertullian mentions Cincius Severus among the governors who treated the Christians with lenity. This governor was put to death by Severus after the defeat and death of Albinus.[4] The tract contains no traces of Montanism, yet was probably written after the author became a Montanist.

The treatises in which we find positive allusions to the

[1] "Ita vero sit, quum ex vobis nationibus quotidie Cæsares, et Parthici, et Medici, et Germanici," l. i. c. 17. Allix drew his inference from a passage in the life of Caracalla which goes under the name of *Ælius Spartianus.* "Datis ad Senatum, quasi post victoriam, literis Parthicus appellatus est; nam Germanici nomen patre vivo fuerat consecutus," p. 930 D. The circumstance here alluded to occurred not long before the death of Caracalla in 217. But the titles of Parthicus and Germanicus had been so frequently conferred upon emperors that it cannot be affirmed with any degree of certainty that a particular allusion to Caracalla was intended.

[2] C. 4. The cure was performed by the use of oil. Severus laboured under an arthritic complaint. *Ælii Spartiani Severus*, p. 903 D.

[3] C. 3. "Extincto pene lumine."

[4] A.D. 198. *Ælii Spartiani Severus*, p. 902 A.

prophecies of Montanus are those—*de Coronâ*,[1] *de Animâ*,[2] *de Virginibus velandis*,[3] *de Resurrectione Carnis*,[4] *against Praxeas*,[5] the first,[6] third,[7] fourth,[8] and fifth[9] books *against Marcion*, and the tracts *de Fugâ in Persecutione*, *de Monogamiâ*, *de Jejuniis*, and *de Pudicitiâ*. The four last-mentioned tracts are stated by Jerome to have been composed by our author in direct opposition to the Church, and their contents fully confirm the statement. With respect to their order, we know only that the tract *de Monogamiâ* was prior to that *de Jejuniis*,[10] which contains a reference to it.

Gibbon affirms it "to be evident that Tertullian composed his treatise *de Coronâ* long before he was engaged in the errors of Montanus."[11] I am afraid that the historian was induced to adopt this opinion because it assisted him in transferring the sentiments expressed by Tertullian from the followers of Montanus to the primitive Christians in general; and thereby to confirm his representation of their rashness and extravagances. But the allusion to the New Prophecy in the first chapter affords a complete refutation of the assertion. Gibbon also supposes the event which gave occasion to the treatise to have happened at Carthage, when a donative was distributed to the soldiers by the Emperors Severus and Caracalla, and consequently before the title of Cæsar was conferred on Geta, that is, before the year 198. But should we allow the correctness of this date to be better ascertained than it really is, the only inference to be drawn from it would be, that even at that early period Tertullian had openly avowed his belief in the prophecies of Montanus. There is, moreover, in this tract an allusion to a tract on *Public Spectacles*,[12] which Tertullian composed in Greek; if it agreed with the Latin tract now extant, he was probably a Montanist when he wrote it. Tertullian appears in the tract *de Coronâ* to announce his intention of writing the *Scorpiace*.[13]

The second book *against Marcion* affords an example of the difficulty of accurately determining from the treatises themselves

[1] C. 1. "Qui prophetias ejusdem Spiritûs Sancti respuerunt."
[2] Cc. 9, 11, 55, 58. There is in this tract, c. 55, an allusion to the martyrdom of Perpetua, which is supposed to have happened about the year 203.
[3] Cc. 1, 17. [4] C. 11. [5] Cc. 1, 2, 8, 13, 30. [6] C. 29. [7] C. 24.
[8] C. 22. [9] C. 16. "Ut docent Veteres et Novæ Prophetiæ."
[10] C. 1. [11] Chapter 15, note 49.
[12] "Sed et huic materiæ propter suaviludios nostros Græco quoque stilo satisfecimus," c. 6, *sub fine*.
[13] C. 1. "Sed de quæstionibus confessionum alib docebimus."

whether the author was a Montanist when he composed them; for it contains no decisive marks of Montanism. The same remark is applicable to the tract *de Carne Christi*, though we find in it an express reference to the fourth book *against Marcion*,[1] and to the *Scorpiace*,[2] in which we also find a reference to the works *against Marcion*. Jerome, in his work *against Vigilantius*, c. 3, says that the latter tract was written against the Cainites, a branch of the Gnostics, who appear to have spoken contemptuously of martyrdom, and to have dissuaded Christians in times of persecution from exposing themselves to danger by an open profession of their faith; contending that he was the true martyr, μαρτὺς, who bore testimony to the gospel by his virtuous life and conversation.[3] Here, then, we might expect to find strong proofs of Tertullian's Montanism; yet they do not occur. There is in the *Scorpiace* an allusion to the establishment of the Pythian games at Carthage, as if it had recently taken place.[4]

If the Proculus, whom Tertullian calls Proculus noster,[5] and mentions with respect in his treatise *against the Valentinians*, was the same, to whose dispute or dialogue with Caius both Eusebius and Jerome refer,[6] we may fairly conclude that Tertullian was a Montanist when he composed the treatise.

Allix infers that the tract *de Spectaculis* was written after Tertullian became a Montanist, because in enumerating the privileges of the Christian, he mentions that of asking revelations from heaven.[7] The introduction of the New Jerusalem in the last chapter,[8] when compared with the final chapter of the fourth book *against Marcion*, supplies in my opinion far more decisive proof of his Montanism. Allix has shown satisfactorily that it was written, not at Rome, but at Carthage.[9] It was prior to the

[1] C. 7. "Audiat igitur et Apelles quid jam responsum sit a nobis Marcioni eo libello, quo ad Evangelium ipsius provocavimus." The reference is to c. 19.

[2] C. 5. "Longum est ut Deum meum bonum ostendam; quod jam a nobis didicerunt Marcionitæ." The reference is to the second book. From c. 1 and c. 4 it appears that the *Scorpiace* was written during a time of persecution.

[3] Compare Irenæus, l. iii. c. 20; l. iv. c. 64; and Clemens Alexandrinus, l. iv. c. 4, p. 571, l. 10.

[4] "Adhuc Carthaginem singulæ civitates gratulando inquietant, donatam Pythico Agone post stadii senectutem," c. 6.

[5] C. 5.

[6] *Hist. Eccl.* l. vi. c. 20. *Catalogus Scriptorum Eccl. sub Caio.*

[7] C. 29. "Quod revelationes petis."

[8] "Qualis Civitas nova Hierusalem?"

[9] "Quanta præterea Sacra, quanta Sacrificia præcedant, intercedant, succedant, quot Collegia, quot sacerdotia, quot officia moveantur, sciunt homines illius urbis

tract *de Idololatriâ*[1] and the first book *de Cultu Fœminarum*,[2] which contain references to it. These two tracts, therefore, were probably written after Tertullian became a Montanist, though they contain no decisive marks of Montanism. In the tract *de Idololatriâ*[3] Allix fancies that he discovers an allusion to the festivities which took place at Carthage, when the birthday of Geta was celebrated in the year 203.

The notion that three persons compose a church has been already mentioned as indicative of Montanism.[4] It occurs in the tract *de Exhortatione Castitatis*:[5] yet I am led to infer, from a comparison of this tract with that *de Monogamiâ*, that Tertullian, when he wrote it, had not embraced the tenets of Montanus in all their rigour.

Perhaps we shall not deviate very widely from the truth, if we adopt the following classification of Tertullian's works, without attempting to arrange them in the order in which they are written.

Works probably written while he was yet a member of the Church:—

De Pœnitentiâ.
De Oratione.
De Baptismo.
The two books ad Uxorem.
Ad Martyres.
De Patientiâ.
Adversus Judæos.
De Præscriptione Hæreticorum.[6]

Works certainly written after he became a Montanist:—

First book against Marcion.
Second book against Marcion.[7]

(Romæ) in quâ Dæmoniorum conventus consedit," c. 7. "Proinde tituli: Olympia Jovi, quæ sunt Romæ Capitolina," c. 11. Observe also the use of the word Præsides in the last chapter.

[1] C. 13. [2] C. 8. [3] C. 15. [4] P. 48.

[5] C. 7. "Sed ubi tres, Ecclesia est, licet Laici." Compare *de Pudicitiâ*, c. 21. Pamelius supposes that the three persons alluded to in the latter passage were Montanus, Maximilla, and Priscilla; but, as it appears to me, without sufficient grounds.

[6] Referred to in the first book *against Marcion*, c. 1; *adv. Praxeam*, c. 2; *de Carne Christi*, c. 2; *adv. Hermogenum*, c. 1.

[7] Referred to in the *Scorpiace*, c. 5. In the treatise *de Animâ*, c. 21, where the allusion is to c. 5. *De Res. Carnis*, cc. 2, 14.

De Animâ.[1]
Third book against Marcion.
Fourth book against Marcion.[2]
De Carne Christi.[3]
De Resurrectione Carnis.[4]
Fifth book against Marcion.
Adversus Praxeam.
Scorpiace.[5]
De Coronâ Militis.
De Virginibus Velandis.
De Exhortatione Castitatis.
De Fugâ in Persecutione.
De Monogamiâ.[6]
De Jejuniis.
De Pudicitiâ.

Works probably written after he became a Montanist:—

Adversus Valentinianos.
Ad Scapulam.
De Spectaculis.[7]
De Idololatriâ.
The two books de Cultu Fœminarum.

Works respecting which nothing certain can be pronounced:—

The Apology.
The two books ad Nationes.
The Tract de Testimonio Animæ.[8]
De Pallio.
Adversus Hermogenem.

[1] Referred to in the tract *de Res. Carnis*, cc. 2, 17, 45. Compare cc. 18 and 21.

[2] Referred to in the tract *de Carne Christi*, c. 7.

[3] Referred to in the tract *de Resurrectione Carnis*, c. 2. See also the concluding words of the tract *de Carne Christi*.

[4] Referred to in the fifth book *against Marcion*, c. 10.

[5] In c. 4, Tertullian speaks as if he had already refuted all the heretics.

[6] Referred to in the tract *de Jejuniis*, c. 1.

[7] Referred to in the tract *de Idololatriâ*, c. 13, and in the first book *de Cultu Fœminarum*, c. 8. In the tract *de Coronâ*, c. 6, is a reference to the Greek tract *de Spectaculis*.

[8] Subsequent to the *Apology*, see c. 5. Prior to the tract *de Carne Christi*, in the twelfth chapter of which it is quoted.

In addition to the works already enumerated, Tertullian composed others not now extant:—

A treatise entitled de Paradiso.[1]
Another, de Spe Fidelium.[2]
Six books de Ecstasi,[3] and a seventh against Apollonius, mentioned by Jerome in his account of our author.
A tract against the Apelliaci, or followers of Apelles.[4]
A tract against Hermogenes,[5] entitled de Censu Animæ.

In the treatise *de Animâ,* Tertullian mentions his intention of discussing the questions of Fate and Free-Will, upon the principles of the gospel.[6]

Jerome mentions other works of Tertullian:—

One de vestibus Aaron.[7]
One ad Amicum Philosophum:[8] Jerome's words are, "Et nunc eadem admoneo, ut, si tibi placet scire quot molestiis virgo libera, quot uxor astricta sit, legas Tertullianum ad Amicum Philosophum, et de Virginitate alios libellos, et beati Cypriani volumen egregium." Among Tertullian's works now extant, there is none entitled *ad Amicum Philosophum;* and I should have supposed that Jerome referred to the tract *de Exhortatione Castitatis,* had he not in his first book *against Jovinian* said that Tertullian wrote upon the subject of celibacy in his youth.

In the index to Tertullian's works given in the *Codex Agobardi* appear the three following titles: De Animæ Summissione, De Superstitione Sæculi, De Carne et Animâ. The tracts themselves are not extant in the MS.; which appears at one time to have contained the tracts *de Paradiso* and *de Spe Fidelium.*

[1] Mentioned in the tract *de Animâ,* c. 55, and in the fifth book *against Marcion,* c. 12.
[2] Mentioned in the third book *against Marcion,* c. 24, and by Jerome in his account of Papias.
[3] There is an illusion to the books *de Ecstasi* in the fourth book *against Marcion,* c. 22.
[4] Mentioned in the treatise *de Carne Christi,* c. 8.
[5] Mentioned in the treatise *de Animâ,* cc. 1, 3, 22, 24.
[6] C. 20.
[7] *Epistola ad Fabiolam de veste Sacerdotali, sub fine.*
[8] Epistola 22, *ad Eustochium de Custodiâ Virginitatis.* I am in doubt whether Jerome here alludes to tracts expressly entitled *de Virginitate,* or means only that Tertullian had in various works written on the advantages of the unmarried state.

Mosheim classes the Montanists amongst the illiterate sects;[1] but this epithet is wholly inapplicable to Tertullian, who appears to have been acquainted with every branch of science and literature that was studied in his day. Eusebius[2] mentions particularly his knowledge of Roman law,[3] which displays itself in his frequent use of legal terms; and his quotations embrace not only the poetry and history, but also the natural philosophy[4] and medical science of antiquity.[5] The Greek language must have been familiar to him, as he composed in it three treatises,[6] not now extant. So great indeed was his reputation for genius and learning that, notwithstanding his secession from the Church, succeeding ecclesiastical writers always speak of him with high respect. Cyprian, as we have seen, called him his master, and never passed a day without reading some portion of his works. We cannot, however, among the merits of Tertullian, reckon that of a natural, flowing, and perspicuous style. He frequently hurries his readers along by his vehemence, and surprises them by the vigour as well as inexhaustible fertility of his imagination; but his copiousness is without selection; and there was in his character a propensity to exaggeration, which affected his language and rendered it inflated and unnatural. He is indeed the harshest and most obscure of writers, and the least capable of being accurately represented in translation. With respect to his Latinity, I know only one critic who has ventured to speak in its commendation—the late Gilbert Wakefield; between whom and Tertullian, widely as they differed upon doctrinal questions, there appear to have been some points of resemblance. Both possessed great stores of acquired knowledge, which they produced in and out of season; both were deficient in taste, discrimination, and judgment. In one of his letters to Mr. Fox, Mr. Wakefield complains that the "words of Tertullian, Arnobius, Apuleius, Aulus Gellius, and Ammianus Marcellinus, are usually marked in dictionaries as inelegant and of suspicious authority, when they are, in reality, the most genuine remains

[1] *Cent.* ii. c. 5, sect. 23.
[2] *Hist. Eccl.* l. ii. c. 2.
[3] See the tract *de Animâ*, c. 6, *sub fine.*
[4] He appears to have been well acquainted with Pliny.
[5] See the tract *de Animâ*, cc. 2, 6.
[6] Those *de Spectaculis* (see *de Coronâ*, c. 6), *de Virginibus velandis*, c. 1, and *de Baptismo*, c. 15. For additional proof of his knowledge of Greek, see *adv. Marcionem*, l. ii. cc. 9, 24. l. iii. cc. 15, 22. l. iv. cc. 8, 11, 14. l. v. c. 17; *de Præscript. Hæret.* c. 6; *adv. Hermogenem*, cc. 19, 40; *adv. Praxeam*, c. 3; *ad Scapulam*, c. 4; *de Idololatriâ*, c. 3. He sometimes speaks as if he was acquainted with Hebrew. See *adv. Marc.* l. iv. c. 39; *adv. Praxeam*, c. 5; *adv. Jud.* c. 9.

of pure Roman composition," or as he previously expressed himself, "of the language of the old comedians and tragedians, of Ennius and Lucilius."[1] I am far from intending to assert that this statement is wholly destitute of foundation. When I have myself been obliged to consult the dictionaries for the meaning of some strange and portentous word which crossed me in my perusal of Tertullian's works, I have occasionally found that it had been used by Plautus; but the general opinion which I have formed respecting Tertullian's Latinity cannot be better expressed than in the words of the learned Ruhnken: "Fuit nescio quis—qui se pulchre de Latinâ Linguâ meriturum speraret, si verba et verborum constructiones ex Tertulliano—in Lexicon referret. A cujus sententiâ dici vix potest quantopere dissentiam. Sit Tertullianus quam velis eruditus, sit omnis peritus antiquitatis; nihil impedio; Latinitatis certè pessimum auctorem esse aio et confirmo. At usus est sermone eo quo tunc omnes Afri Latinè loquentes utebantur.

Δωρίσδεν δ' ἔξεστι, δοκῶ, τοῖς Δωριέεσσιν.

Ne hoc quidem concesserim. Nam si talis Afrorum sermo fuit, cur, non dicam Apuleius et Arnobius scriptores priscæ elegantiæ studiosi, sed Cyprianus, etc., aliter locuti reperiuntur? Quid ergo? Fecit hic, quod ante eum arbitror fecisse neminem. Etenim quum in aliorum vel summâ infantiâ tamen appareat voluntas et conatus bene loquendi, hic, nescio quâ ingenii perversitate, cum melioribus loqui noluit, et sibimet ipse linguam finxit duram, horridam, Latinisque inauditam; ut non mirum sit per eum unum plura monstra in Linguam Latinam, quam per omnes Scriptores semi-barbaros, esse invecta."[2]

In the preceding remarks we have all along taken for granted that the works, the dates of which we have been investigating, were composed by an individual named Tertullian. This fact we conceived to be established by testimony precisely similar to that by which the genuineness of the works of every author is ascertained—by the testimony of writers whose proximity to the times in which he lived, and whose opportunities of information rendered them competent to form a correct opinion on the subject. We are told that Cyprian, who was Bishop of Carthage within forty years after the period at which Tertullian lived there, held his works in the highest estimation; and in confirmation of this statement we find that Cyprian frequently repeats, not only

[1] Letter 54. [2] *Præfatio ad Schelleri Lexicon.*

the sentiments, but even the words contained in the writings now extant under his name. We find Eusebius,[1] a diligent inquirer into all points connected with ecclesiastical history, quoting within a century after Tertullian's death one of his works which had been translated into Greek, and speaking of him as well known in the capital of the world.[2] We find Jerome, who has left us a catalogue of ecclesiastical authors accompanied by succinct accounts of their lives and writings, quoting various works of Tertullian without giving the slightest hint that he entertained a doubt of their genuineness. We find him quoted by Augustine,[3] who had resided at Carthage and made inquiries there respecting the sect which bore his name; and by subsequent writers, who may be deemed too far removed from his time to be received as independent witnesses. Here surely is a chain of testimony sufficient to satisfy even a sceptical mind. It did not, however, satisfy that of Semler, who in a dissertation, inserted in his edition of Tertullian's works,[4] endeavours to fix a mark of spuriousness, not only upon them, but also upon the writings which are extant under the names of Justin Martyr and Irenæus. His theory is, that all those works, though bearing the names of different authors, proceeded from one and the same shop established at Rome; and were the produce of the joint labours of a set of men, who entered into a combination to falsify history and corrupt the Scriptures, principally with the view of throwing discredit upon certain persons, Marcion, Valentinus, etc., whom they thought fit to brand with the title of heretics.[5] This, it must be allowed, is a theory which, for novelty and singularity, will bear a comparison with the boldest speculations of the German critics. Let us therefore inquire upon what foundations it rests; first observing that we neither profess, nor deem it incumbent upon us, to give a full and complete solution of all the doubts and difficulties which an ingenious mind may frame,

[1] L. ii. c. 2. The only work of Tertullian quoted by Eusebius is the *Apology*, which he states to have been translated into Greek, and with which alone he appears to have been acquainted. He was perhaps little versed in the Latin language, and had never met with the tracts composed by Tertullian himself in Greek, which were of less general interest than the *Apology*.

[2] If we adopt the interpretation suggested by Valesius, after Rufinus, of the words τῶν μάλιστα ἐπὶ Ῥώμης λαμπρῶν, "inter Latinos Scriptores celeberrimus," the inference will be strengthened.

[3] *Liber de Hæresibus*, 86. *Tertullianistæ*.

[4] *Halæ Magdeburgicæ*, 1770.

[5] "Ex unâ atque eâdem officinâ quidam libri videntur prodiisse quos studiosissimè solebant variis et diversis Scriptoribus dividere. Antiquissima fuit hæc Societas et impensa sive ab uno sive a duobus diligentia, quæ cum *Romanâ* illâ, tam Græcâ quam Latinâ, Societate novâ videtur sic cohærere ut communi consilio operam dederint." Sect x. See also the concluding section.

in order to disprove the genuineness of works written sixteen centuries ago. Were this requisite, vain would be the attempt to establish the genuineness of any work of great antiquity; for by the mere lapse of time many facts and circumstances are consigned to oblivion, the knowledge of which can alone enable us to dispel all obscurity and to reconcile all seeming contradictions. In these cases we must not expect demonstration, but be content to weigh probabilities and ascertain on which side the evidence preponderates.

To proceed then to Semler's proofs, or rather surmises, for the latter appears the more appropriate term. He first complains that the allusions contained in these books to the life and history of their author are very scanty and obscure, and afford no useful information.[1] He even insinuates that the works themselves, like the writings of the Sophists, were mere exercises of wit, and that the historical facts and marks of time were introduced by the author in order to give his fiction an appearance of reality.[2] But this insinuation is utterly unsupported by proof. The author, whoever he may be, certainly meant his readers to suppose that he lived in the time of Severus; and his statements in many points accord, in none are at variance with the accounts handed down to us by the historians of that Emperor's reign. The manners and customs which he describes, the transactions to which he alludes, correspond with the information which we derive from other sources. Still his works may be wholly of a fictitious character; he may have invented the circumstances which are supposed to have occasioned them—the calumnies against which he defends the Christians—the persecutions which he exhorts them to bear with constancy—the heretical opinions which he undertakes to confute; and he may have occasionally interspersed historical facts in order to give his inventions an air of probability. All this we may allow to be possible. But what are we to think of the Montanism of our author? was that also fictitious? What could induce a member of Semler's new Roman society, who comes forward at one time as the apologist for Christianity and the vehement champion of orthodoxy, to assume at another the character of a separatist from the Church? This fact appears to be wholly irreconcilable with Semler's

[1] "Solent autem mediocria et parum luculenta esse, quæ horum Librorum Auctor *de se et de suis rebus* commemorat." Sect. i.

[2] "Solet enim hic Scriptor *Declamatorum* imitari exemplum qui ipsi *confingunt* argumenti, quod sibi desumpserunt, *tempus*, et omnes illas rerum Appendices quibus tempora solent commodè et studiosè distingui." Sect. i.

theory. It should also be observed that the few notices of Tertullian's personal history which occur in his works are not introduced with any parade, or in order to answer a particular purpose, but in that incidental manner which has usually been deemed most strongly indicative of truth.

Semler next proceeds to consider Jerome's account of Tertullian, on which he remarks that had Jerome been able to discover more particulars of our author's life, he would certainly have inserted them.[1] This is by no means clear; for the extreme conciseness with which he has drawn up his notices of ecclesiastical writers proves that he made no laborious researches into the history of their lives, but contented himself with such information as happened to fall in his way. Semler further conjectures that even the particulars in Jerome's brief account were not derived from independent sources, but collected from Tertullian's works.[2] This may be partly true; he might have inferred from different passages that Tertullian was born in Africa, resided at Carthage, and flourished during the reigns of Severus and Caracalla. But, not to mention the story respecting Cyprian's admiration of Tertullian, for which he gives his authority, whence did he learn that Tertullian remained a presbyter of the Church until he reached the middle age of life, and was extremely old when he died? It may be doubted whether the generality of readers, unless they had previously learned the fact from some other source, would infer, from the perusal of the works now extant, that Tertullian had ever been admitted to the order of priesthood.

Semler finds another difficulty in Jerome's account, which begins thus: "Tertullianus presbyter nunc demum primus post Victorem et Apollonium Latinorum ponitur." The obvious meaning of these words is that Jerome had at length, after enumerating so many Greek authors, arrived at the place which Tertullian's name was to occupy; he being the first Latin ecclesiastical writer after Victor and Apollonius of whom Jerome had before spoken. Semler thinks that the more accurate statement would have been that Tertullian was the first *presbyter* who used the Latin language, and that this was in fact Jerome's

[1] "Hæc Hieronymus; qui profecto, si plura requirere atque discere potuisset ad historiam Tertulliani facientia, haud dubie hic omnino perscripsisset." Sect. 2.

[2] "Nisi quidem putemus talia Hieronymum ipsum conjecturis reperisse ex variis horum scriptorum locis." Sect. ii.

meaning;[1] an assertion in which few of his readers will, I conceive, be disposed to acquiesce. But how, asks Semler, can Tertullian be called the first presbyter who used the Latin language, when he himself says that he composed several treatises in Greek? I must confess myself at a loss to discover the slightest inconsistency between the two statements. If an author composes three treatises in Greek, and two or three and twenty in Latin, may he not with propriety be classed among Latin writers? It is probable that Jerome had never met with Tertullian's Greek compositions; it is nearly certain that Eusebius had not.

"But," continues Semler, "in the beginning of the treatise *de Testimonio Animæ*, the author alludes to certain Christian writers who had employed profane literature, and appealed to the works of the Gentile poets and philosophers in defence of Christianity. This, he contends, is a mere fiction of the author's brain.[2] In vain, he says, shall we seek in the history of the Church for a confirmation of this statement; in vain try to discover any traces of those learned works by which the early apologists for Christianity asserted its cause. Had such writings ever existed, they could not have been unknown to Eusebius and Jerome, who are, however, entirely silent on the subject." These are bold affirmations. Let us inquire how far they are supported by proof. The ecclesiastical writers whom Tertullian mentions by name are Justin Martyr, Tatian, Miltiades, and Irenæus.[3] All of these wrote treatises in defence of Christianity against paganism. The works of Justin and Tatian are still extant, and prove their authors to have been, as Lardner expresses himself respecting the latter, "men of reading and well acquainted with the Greek learning."[4] We are also in possession of the *Apology*

1 "Optare licet, ut Hieronymus scripsisset et narrâsset accuratius, Tertullianus *Latinorum* presbyter *primus* est; nempe id vult Hieronymus eorum hominum, qui Romæ *Latinâ linguâ* uti solebant, Tertullianus fuit *primus presbyter*. At hic idem Tertullianus *Græcarum multarum Scriptionum* se auctorem dixit; quomodo igitur *Latinorum* dicitur primus esse Romanus presbyter?" Sect. x.

2 "*Confictum* est hoc argumentum universum declamatorum more; nisi putamus hujus generis scriptores, tam antiquos, tam frugiferos, adeo oblivioni statim addictos fuisse, neglectosque et deperditos omnino; ut ne Eusebius quidem vestigium vel notam talium scriptorum reperire potuerit, qui in isto *opere de Preparatione Evangelicâ* id omnino egit, quod hic Tertullianus dicit *suo jam tempore* quosdam instituisse. Eusebius vero nihil quicquam ejus rei didicit, nec Hieronymus aliquid reperire potuit. Audemus, igitur, statuere scriptorem *talia ultro confinxisse*, ex suo ingenio rem illam arbitratum." Sect. x.

3 *Adversus Valentinianos*, c. 5. He also mentions Clemens Romanus and Hermas, but they do not appear to have written in defence of Christianity.

4 *Credibility of the Gospel History*, c. 13.

of Athenagoras, and the work of Theophilus *against Autolycus*; both of which were prior in time to the *Apology* of Tertullian, and contain, especially the former, frequent references to profane literature as well as arguments drawn from the heathen philosophy in defence of Christianity. But the most extraordinary part of Semler's statement is that which respects Jerome; among whose works is an epistle, entitled *ad Magnum Oratorem*,[1] and written expressly to defend his own practice of mixing together profane and sacred literature in his writings. In this epistle he appeals to the authority of preceding ecclesiastical writers who had pursued the same plan, mentioning by name Quadratus and Aristides, who presented their *Apologies* to the Emperor Adrian, and describing the work of the latter as almost entirely composed of opinions taken from the philosophers.[2] He adds that Apollinarius, Dionysius of Corinth, Tatian, Bardesanes, and Irenæus had carefully pointed out the different philosophical sects to which the origin of each heretical opinion then prevalent might be traced. He states that Cyprian had even been censured, because in his work *against Demetrianus* he had confined himself entirely to scriptural testimonies, the authority of which Demetrianus did not acknowledge, and had not appealed to the poets and philosophers, whose authority a heathen could not have disputed. The apologists for Christianity were well aware that no writings which did not bespeak an acquaintance with the learning and philosophy of the age, would gain a moment's attention from a heathen philosopher; and they accordingly adapted their mode of reasoning to the temper and prejudices of the persons with whom they had to deal. The remarks with which Tertullian prefaces his tract *de Testimonio Animæ* are meant as an apology for deviating from the established course, and appealing, not to the speculations of the philosophers, but to the testimony borne by the soul of man in favour of the doctrines of Christianity.

"But even," continues Semler, "if such works as those to which Tertullian is supposed to allude had really existed, since they were written in Greek, and at places remote from Rome and Carthage, he could not possibly have procured them."[3] Why not? Was the communication between the different parts of

[1] Ep. 84. [2] *Contextum Philosophorum sententiis.*

[3] "Pamelii sententiam vel illud evertit; Tertullianus Romæ, Carthagine, tot scriptorum libellos, qui inter Græcos satis remoti ab istis urbibus vivebant, nancisci non potuit." Sect. x.

the Roman Empire so difficult that years must elapse before a work published in Greece could be known at Rome or Carthage? Let us hear the opinion of Gibbon. Speaking of the public roads as they existed in the time of the Antonines, he says that "they united the subjects of the most distant provinces by an easy and familiar intercourse."[1] With respect to the Christians in particular, he states that, by the institution of provincial synods, which took place towards the end of the second century, a regular correspondence was in the space of a few years established between the most remote Churches.[2] We find accordingly the Churches of Vienne and Lyons well acquainted with the state of the Asiatic Churches; and Irenæus, the Bishop of Lyons, acting the part of a mediator between the latter and the Roman pontiff, in the dispute which arose respecting the celebration of Easter.

The mention of Irenæus leads me to consider another of Semler's objections. "Who," he asks, "can read the works of Irenæus which are now extant without being convinced that the author was alike deficient in talent and information?[3] Yet Tertullian has designated him as a minute inquirer into all kinds of learning (or doctrine). Does not this grossly inapplicable eulogium clearly bespeak the sophist and declaimer?" To this objection we reply, that we are scarcely competent to form an opinion respecting the talent of Irenæus from a work which, with the exception of part of the first book and some scattered fragments, is extant, not in the original, but in a barbarous Latin translation. From the portions of the original which still remain we should infer that he possessed one of the most useful qualifications of an author — that of being able to write perspicuously upon a very obscure and unpromising subject. What ground, moreover, is there for supposing that Tertullian, in pronouncing this eulogium upon Irenæus, referred only to the single work, now extant, against the Gnostics? Eusebius gives a list of other works written by him, and uniformly speaks of him as a person to

[1] Chap. i. p. 51. Ed. 4to. [2] Chap. xv. p. 491.

[3] "Quis autem sine tædio et stomacho legat istam declamationem, 'Irenæus, *omnium doctrinarum curiosissimus explorator?*' Nos certè statuimus, hoc encomium monstro non carere. Ea, quæ nobis supersunt, Irenæi profecto hominis ingenium humile et parum excultum præ se ferunt; ista vero Tertulliani nostri scripta sic turgent rerum fere omnium copiâ et varietate, ut in ipsum hoc maximè conveniat hunc scriptorem id diligenter egisse, ut *omnium doctrinarum curiosissimus explorator* videretur." Sect. x.

whose authority great weight was attached in all ecclesiastical concerns.[1]

But Tertullian, it seems, was not content with praising; he also borrowed from Irenæus, and that too without acknowledgment.[2] His treatise *against the Valentinians* is not merely an imitation; it is in many places a translation of the first book of that author's work; yet he gives not the slightest intimation of the source from which he has drawn so largely. How are we to account for this extraordinary fact? Only, as Semler would persuade us, by adopting his theory, that there existed a club of authors who "sent forth their own productions into the world under borrowed names, and appeared at one time as the Greek Irenæus, at another as the Latin Tertullian." But if this were so, whence arises the great inequality which Semler himself has discovered between them? How comes it that, while the works of Tertullian exhibit such an extent and variety of knowledge, those of Irenæus, according to Semler, betray a miserable poverty of intellect and learning?[3]

The close resemblance between Tertullian and Irenæus in the case alluded to may, in our opinion, be satisfactorily accounted for. The design of the first book of Irenæus and of Tertullian's treatise is precisely the same—to explain the doctrine of the Valentinians respecting the generation of Æons; and thus the common subject of the two writers would naturally lead them to pursue the same order, and almost to use the same language. Most strange, indeed, is Semler's assertion that Tertullian has not even named Irenæus; whom he has named, even in the very passage which Semler quotes, in conjunction with Justin, Miltiades, and Proculus.[4] He there states that all these writers

[1] *Hist. Eccl.* l. v. c. 26.

[2] "Jam novæ rei alius superest observatio, quæ non parum facit ad illustrandam hujus suspicionis rationem. Ista enim Irenæi, quæ sunt nostris in manibus, scripta, si comparantur cum his Tertulliani nostri, mirifice conveniunt. Scimus autem Tertullianum istum esse illorum primum qui Irenæi nomen recitant inter scriptores; nempe *omnium doctrinarum curiosissimum exploratorem* dicebat Irenæum noster Tertullianus. Si vero ille Irenæus Lugduni scripsit istos libros adversus hæreses, quomodo Tertullianus isto jam tempore hoc (l. hos) libros oculis et manibus usurpavit suis? Quo autem jure sic fecit Tertullianus, ut ex Græco illo textu Irenæi sublegeret sua et *Latinè repeteret*, quæ ille creditur scripsisse Græcè? Atque sic quidem, ut ne nominaverit quidem Irenæum, quem tamen Latinè exscribebat? Viderint Lectores quid statuendum putent de istâ causâ: nobis certè non videtur monstro carere." Sect. xii.

[3] See the quotation from section x. in note 166.

[4] "Nec undique dicemur ipsi nobis finxisse materias quas tot jam viri sancti-

had refuted the Valentinians; and declares that it is his earnest wish to imitate them, not only in this work of faith (the refutation of heresy), but in all others. He has therefore told his reader, as plainly as he could, that in this treatise he is only an imitator; and his occasional deviations from the statement of Irenæus convince me that he did not borrow from him alone, but also from the other writers whom he has mentioned.

Semler, however, has other objections in reserve, founded on this very passage from the tract *against the Valentinians*.[1] "How happens it that Tertullian alludes to and speaks respectfully of Miltiades, who, as we learn from Eusebius, composed a work expressly against the prophecy of Montanus?" This question will perhaps be best answered by another. Would not a forger of writings in Tertullian's name carefully have avoided such an appearance of inconsistency? The fact appears to be perfectly reconcilable with the history and character of Tertullian, as far as they can be collected from his writings; since, at the very time when he was defending Montanus against the Church, he constantly professed his agreement with the Church in all fundamental articles of faith.[2] It is wholly irreconcilable with Semler's theory.

"But what are we to think of the extraordinary reason

tate et præstantiâ insignes, nec solum nostri Antecessores sed ipsorum Hæresiarcharum contemporales, instructissimis voluminibus et prodiderunt et retuderunt: ut Justinus Philosophus et Martyr, ut Miltiades Ecclesiarum Sophista, ut Irenæus omnium doctrinarum curiosissimus explorator, ut Proculus noster virginis senectæ et Christianæ eloquentiæ dignitas: quos in omni opere fidei, quemadmodum in isto, optaverim assequi. Aut si in totum hæreses non sunt, ut qui eas pellunt finxisse credantur, mentietur apostolus prædicator illarum. Porro si sunt, non aliæ erunt quam quæ retractantur. Nemo tam otiosus fertur stylo, ut materias habens fingat." *Adv. Valentin.* c. 5.

[1] Section iv. note 27. "Miltiades vero? Ecquid tandem illud est, Ecclesiarum Sophista? quid tandem est? Putamusne Tertullianum legisse aliquid hujus Miltiadis? Miltiadis aliquas scriptiones Eusebius" (*Hist. Eccles.* l. v. c. 17) "ex Rhodone nominat contra *Montanum, Priscillam et Maximillam*: contra gentes et Judæos; sed contra Gnosticos aut Hæreticos nihil. Cur ergo hic excitatur, quasi scripserit adversus Valentinianos?" Though Eusebius may not have mentioned or seen any work of Miltiades against the Gnostics, such a work may have been known to Tertullian. So this note stood in the first edition. I have since met with a passage in which Eusebius, on the authority of an anonymous author, speaks of Miltiades as having written against the heretics. καὶ ἀδελφῶν δέ τινων ἐστὶ γράμματα πρεσβύτερα τῶν Βίκτορος χρόνων, ἃ ἐκεῖνοι πρὸς τὰ ἔθνη ὑπὲρ τῆς ἀληθείας καὶ πρὸς τὰς τότε αἱρέσεις ἔγραψαν· λέγω δὲ Ἰουστίνου, καὶ Μιλτιάδου, καὶ Τατιανοῦ καὶ Κλήμεντος, καὶ ἑτέρων πλειόνων ἐν οἷς ἅπασι θεολογεῖται ὁ Χριστός. *Eccl. Hist.* l. v. c. 28.

[2] *De Jejuniis*, c. 1.

assigned by Tertullian for introducing the names of Miltiades and the rest?[1] He supposes that he may be charged with inventing the strange opinions which he imputes to the Valentinians, and thinks it necessary to guard himself against the charge by appealing to the authority of Justin Martyr, etc. Have we not here a strong indication of the mere sophist and declaimer, aware that he is about to advance statements for which there is no foundation in fact, and anxious to anticipate the feeling of incredulity which their improbability would naturally excite?" That this construction should be put upon the passage by Semler is not surprising. His theory required that he should so interpret it. But in me it excites no surprise that an author, who was about to detail opinions so extravagant as those entertained by the Valentinians, should apprehend that his readers might suspect him of attempting to impose upon them the fictions of his own brain as the religious tenets of others. In the tract *de Baptismo*, we find Tertullian offering a similar apology for the extravagance of an opinion which he undertakes to refute, and affirming with great solemnity that he had himself heard it advanced.[2]

Semler grounds another argument in support of his theory on the fact that a considerable portion of the third book *against Marcion* is repeated almost word for word in the treatise *against the Jews*.[3] But the difficulties arising out of this fact are not greater on the supposition that Tertullian was the real author of both the works, than on the supposition that they were composed by others in his name. I know no reason why an author should be precluded from repeating the same arguments in the same words, when an occasion presents itself on which they are equally applicable. Such was the case which we are now con-

[1] Section iv. note 27. Semler introduces the passage quoted in note 170 by the following words:—"Ipse hic scriptor videtur (sicut dici solet) se prodere sicut sorex: nam hoc ipso libro adversus Valentinianos, c. 5, *sic scribit*." He then gives the passage at length, and subjoins, "Totus hic locus videtur aliquid monstri prodere. Si omnino Romæ alibique vivebant homines hæretici, eos igitur non solus Tertullianus noverat: Christiani alii similiter hanc Hæreticorum causam sciebant. Itaque non intelligimus quâ ratione amoliatur hic scriptor eam suspicionem, quâ dici ipse possit sibi finxisse materias."

[2] The opinion was proposed in the form of a dilemma. The apostles did not receive Christian baptism, inasmuch as they were baptised with the baptism of John. Either, therefore, the apostles have not obtained salvation, or Christian baptism is not of absolute necessity to salvation. After stating the opinion, Tertullian adds, "Audivi, Domino teste, ejusmodi, ne quis me tam perditum existimet, ut ultrò exagitem, libidine styli, quæ aliis scrupulum incutiant," c. 12.

[3] Sect. ix.

sidering. Both Marcion and the Jews denied, though on different principles, that Jesus was the Messiah predicted in the Old Testament. Both, therefore, were to be refuted by showing that the prophecies respecting the Messiah were actually accomplished in him; and this is the object of the two passages in which we find so close a resemblance. When Tertullian had the argument ready stated and arranged to his hand, it would surely have been an egregious waste of time to amuse himself in varying the language, especially as the passages in question consist entirely of expositions of prophecies. He does, however, make such alterations as the difference of the circumstances under which he is writing appears to require. It should be observed that the treatise *adversus Judæos* is expressly quoted by Jerome as the work of Tertullian.[1]

It would be foreign from the immediate object of this volume to discuss the reasons assigned by Semler for asserting that the works now extant under the names of Justin and Irenæus contain manifest plagiarisms from Clemens Alexandrinus, and that they are consequently spurious.[2] He admits that they are quoted as genuine by Eusebius;[3] and this circumstance alone will probably, in the opinion of sober critics, outweigh a thousand conjectures unsupported by positive evidence.

I have devoted so much time to the examination of Semler's *Dissertation*, not on account of its intrinsic value, which I am far from estimating highly, but out of regard to the distinguished place which has been assigned him among Biblical critics.[4] His object evidently is to destroy the authority of Justin, Irenæus, and Tertullian; but he does not fairly and openly avow it; he envelops himself in a cloud, and uses a dark mysterious language, designed to insinuate more than it expresses. The reader finds his former opinions unsettled, yet is not told what he is to substitute in their place; and is thus left in a disagreeable state of doubt and perplexity.

Had Semler contented himself with saying that Tertullian, in his tract *against the Valentinians*, had done nothing more than copy the statements of preceding writers, and consequently

[1] In his comment on the ninth chapter of Daniel.

[2] Sect. xiv., xv., xvi.

[3] *Hist. Eccl.* l. v. c. 8, l. iv. c. 18.

[4] The most valuable part of Semler's *Dissertation* is, in my opinion, that which relates to Tertullian's quotations from Scripture, and to the Latin version from which he derived them; to this I shall perhaps recur hereafter.

could not be deemed an independent witness to the tenets of those heretics—had he said, with respect to our author's writings in general, that the natural vehemence of his temper betrayed him into exaggeration, and caused him to indulge in a declamatory tone, which renders it often difficult to determine to what extent his expressions are to be literally understood, and his statements received as matters of fact—had Semler even gone further, and contended that there was reasonable ground for suspecting that Irenæus[1] and Tertullian had, either through ignorance or design, occasionally misrepresented the opinions of the Gnostics, and imputed to them absurdities and extravagances of which they were never guilty,—had he confined his assertions within these limits, they would probably have met with the concurrence of all who are conversant with the subject. But when he proceeds, upon surmises such as we have been now considering, and in opposition to the unanimous voice of ecclesiastical antiquity, to denounce the writings of Irenæus and Tertullian as the offspring of fraud and imposture—as the productions of men who had combined together for the purpose of palming forgeries on the world—he overleaps the bounds of sober and rational criticism, and opens a door to universal incredulity.

—o—

## CHAPTER II.

### ON THE EXTERNAL HISTORY OF THE CHURCH.

Having in the preceding chapter laid before the reader an account of the life and writings of Tertullian, we shall now proceed, in conformity with the arrangement adopted by Mosheim, to collect from his works such passages as serve to illustrate the external history of the Church during the period in which he flourished. In the first place, then, he bears explicit testimony to the wide diffusion of Christianity in his day.[2] To refute the charges of disloyalty and disaffection to the emperors

[1] We should always bear in mind that far the greater portion of the work of Irenæus is extant only in a barbarous Latin translation, which lies under heavy suspicions of interpolation.

[2] "Obsessam vociferantur civitatem: in agris, in castellis, in insulis Christianos: omnem sexum, ætatem, conditionem, etiam dignitatem transgredi ad hoc nomen quasi detrimento mœrent." *Apology*, c. 1.

which had been brought against the Christians, he thus appeals to the patience with which they bore the injuries and cruelties inflicted on them. "Not," he says, "that we are destitute of the means of resistance, if our Christian principles allowed us to resort to them.[1] Though we date our existence only from yesterday, we have filled every part of your empire; we are to be found in your cities, your islands, your camps, your palaces, your forum. . . . So great are our numbers that we might successfully contend with you in open warfare; but were we only to withdraw ourselves from you, and to remove by common consent to some remote corner of the globe, our mere secession would be sufficient to accomplish *your* destruction, and to avenge *our* cause. You would be left without subjects to govern, and would tremble at the solitude and silence around you—at the awful stillness of a dead world." In another place Tertullian tells Scapula, the proconsul of Africa, that if the persecution against the Christians were persisted in, the effect would be to decimate the inhabitants of Carthage.[2] He elsewhere speaks also of the immense revenue which might be collected, if each Christian was allowed to purchase the free exercise of his religion for a sum of money.[3]

After we have made all reasonable allowance for any exaggeration into which Tertullian may have been betrayed, either by the natural vehemence of his temper, or by his anxiety to enhance in the eyes of the Roman governors the importance of the cause which he is pleading, the above-cited passages will justify the belief that the Christians in his day composed a numerous and respectable portion of the subjects of Rome. Nor were the triumphs of the gospel confined within the limits of the Roman Empire. "Christ is preached among the barbarians"[4] is the incidental, and therefore less suspicious expression of Tertullian. "We witness," he says, while arguing against the Jews, "the accomplishment of the words of the Psalmist (as applied by St. Paul), 'their sound is gone out

[1] "Quid tamen de tam conspiratis unquam denotâstis," etc. ? *Apology*, c. 37.

[2] *Ad Scapulam*, c. 5. In c. 2, speaking of the Christians, he says, "Quum tanta hominum multitudo, pars pene major civitatis cujusque, in silentio et modestiâ agimus."

[3] "Tanta quotidie ærario augendo prospiciuntur remedia censuum, vectigalium, collationum, stipendiorum: nec unquam usque adhuc ex Christianis tale aliquid prospectum est, sub aliquam redemptionem capitis et sectæ redigendis, quum tantæ multitudinis nemini ignotæ fructus ingens meti possit." *De Fugâ in Persecutione*, c. 12.

[4] "Et apud barbaros enim Christus." *De Coronâ*, c. 12.

into all the earth, and their words unto the ends of the world.' For not only the various countries from which worshippers were collected at Jerusalem on the day of Pentecost, but the most distant regions have received the faith of Christ. He reigns among people whom the Roman arms have never yet subdued: among the different tribes of Getulia and Mauritania,—in the furthest extremities of Spain, and Gaul, and Britain,—among the Sarmatians, Dacians, Germans, and Scythians,—in countries and islands scarcely known to us by name."[1] The language is declamatory; yet such a representation would not have been hazarded, unless it had been realized to a considerable extent, in the actual state of Christianity.

In speaking of the numerous converts continually added to the Church, and of the extension of its limits, Tertullian contents himself for the most part with simply stating the fact. Convinced of the divine origin of the gospel, he ascribed the triumphs of the cross to the power of God bringing to pass in the fulness of time the events which had been foretold by the prophets, without deeming it necessary to go in quest of secondary causes of the rapid progress of Christianity. But though he has not expressly directed his attention to the development of the means which the Almighty was pleased to employ in the establishment of the empire of the gospel, we may collect from his writings much interesting information on the subject.

The success which attended the preaching of the apostles, and their immediate successors, is doubtless to be principally ascribed to the supernatural powers, by the exercise of which they proved their divine commission. But the writings of Tertullian furnish little reason for supposing that the preachers of the gospel in his day were indebted for their success to the display of similar powers. He asserts indeed that Christians possessed the power of expelling demons,[2] of curing diseases, of healing the wounds occasioned by the bites of

[1] *Adversus Judæos*, c. 7. "Quem exaudierunt omnes gentes, id est, cui omnes gentes crediderunt, cujus et prædicatores Apostoli in Psalmis David ostenduntur," etc.

[2] "Edatur hic aliquis sub tribunalibus vestris, quem dæmone agi constat. Jussus a *quolibet* Christiano loqui, Spiritus ille tam se dæmonem confitebitur de vero, quam alibi Deum de falso." *Apology*, c. 23. See also cc. 37, 43. "Quod calcas Deos nationum, quod dæmonia expellis, quod medicinas facis." *De Spectaculis*, c. 29; *de Testimonio Animæ*, c. 3.; *ad Scapulam*, c. 2; *de Coronâ*, c. 11; *de Idololatriâ*, c. 11.

serpents;[1] but he casts a doubt upon the accuracy of his own statement, by ascribing to Christians in general those extraordinary gifts which, even in the days of the apostles, appear to have been confined to them, and to the disciples upon whom they laid their hands.[2]

The miraculous powers conferred upon the apostles were the credentials by which they were to prove that they were the bearers of a new revelation from God to man, and thus to mark the commencement of a new era in the order of the divine dispensations. We might, therefore, infer from the purpose for which they were conferred that they would in process of time be withdrawn.[3] That they have been withdrawn is a fact which few Protestants will controvert, though great difference of opinion prevails respecting the precise period to which we must refer this important alteration in the circumstances of the Church. Gibbon has endeavoured to convert what he terms the insensibility of the Christians to the cessation of miraculous gifts into an argument against their existence at any period. "So extraordinary an event must," he argues, "have excited universal attention, and caused the time at which it happened to be precisely ascertained and noted. But in vain do we consult ecclesiastical history in the hope of assigning a limit to the period during which supernatural powers subsisted in the Church: we find pretensions to them advanced in every age, and supported by testimony no less weighty and

1 "Nobis fides præsidium, si non et ipsa percutitur diffidentiâ signandi statim et adjurandi et unguendi bestiæ calcem. Hoc denique modo etiam Ethnicis sæpe subvenimus, donati a Deo eâ potestate quam Apostolus dedicavit, quum morsum viperæ sprevit." *Scorpiace*, c. 1.

2 It is not intended by this remark to convey the idea that all upon whom the Apostles laid their hands were endowed with miraculous powers; but that the imposition of hands was the mode in which the apostles communicated those gifts to others. See Acts vi. 6 (compared with vi. 8 and viii. 6), viii. 17, 18, xix. 6.

3 A view somewhat similar seems to have been taken by Pascal in the following extract from his *Pensées*, which has been pointed out to me by a learned friend. "Jésus Christ a fait des miracles, et les Apôtres en-suite, et les premiers Saints en ont fait aussi beaucoup: parce que les Propheties n'etant pas encore accomplies et s'accomplissant par eux, rien ne rendoit témoignage que les Miracles. Il etoit prédit que le Messie convertiroit les nations. Comment cette prophetie se fut-elle accomplie sans la conversion des nations? et comment les nations se fussent-elles converties au Messie, ne voyant pas ce dernier effet des Propheties qui le prouvent? Avant donc qu'il fût mort, qu'il fût resuscité, et que les nations fussent converties, tout n'etoit pas accompli. Et ainsi il a fallu des miracles pendant tout ce tems-là. Maintenant il n'en faut plus pour prouver la vérité de la Religion Chrétienne: car les Propheties accomplies sont un miracle subsistan ." *Diverses preuves de Jésus Christ*, c. 16.

respectable than that of the age which preceded it."[1] The inference which he manifestly intends his readers to draw, is that, as pretensions to miraculous gifts had been asserted in all ages, and continued to be asserted even at the time when he wrote, and every reasonable man was convinced of their cessation, those pretensions were in all ages equally unfounded.

The argument is plausible, and is urged with the author's wonted ingenuity and address. Yet the supposition that miraculous powers were *gradually* withdrawn from the Church appears in a great measure to account for the uncertainty which has prevailed respecting the period of their cessation. To adopt the language of undoubting confidence on such a subject would be a mark no less of folly than presumption; but I may be allowed to state the conclusion to which I have myself been led, by a comparison of the statements in the book of Acts with the writings of the Fathers of the second century. My conclusion then is, that the power of working miracles was not extended beyond the disciples upon whom the apostles conferred it by the imposition of their hands. As the number of those disciples gradually diminished, the instances of the exercise of miraculous powers became continually less frequent, and ceased entirely at the death of the last individual on whom the hands of the apostles had been laid. That event would, in the natural course of things, take place before the middle of the second century: at a time when, Christianity having obtained a footing in all the provinces of the Roman Empire, the miraculous gifts conferred upon its first teachers had performed their appropriate office—that of proving to the world that a new revelation had been given from heaven. What, then, would be the effect produced upon the minds of the great body of Christians by their gradual cessation? Many would not observe, none would be willing to observe it; for all must naturally feel a reluctance to believe that powers, which had contributed so essentially to the rapid diffusion of Christianity, were withdrawn. They who remarked the cessation of miracles would probably succeed in persuading themselves that it was only temporary, and designed by an all-wise Providence to be the prelude to a more abundant effusion of supernatural gifts upon the Church. Or if doubts and misgivings crossed their minds, they would still be un-

[1] Chap. xv. p. 477, ed. 4to. We have given only the purport of Gibbon's observations.

willing openly to state a fact, which might shake the steadfastness of the friends, and would certainly be urged by the enemies of the gospel as an argument against its divine origin. They would pursue the plan which has been pursued by Justin Martyr, Theophilus, Irenæus, etc.; they would have recourse to general assertions of the existence of supernatural powers, without attempting to produce a specific instance of their exercise. The silence of ecclesiastical history respecting the cessation of miraculous gifts in the Church is to be ascribed, not to the insensibility of Christians to that important event, but to the combined operation of prejudice and policy—of prejudice which made them reluctant to believe, of policy which made them anxious to conceal the truth.

Let me repeat that I offer these observations with that diffidence in my own conclusions which ought to be the predominant feeling in the mind of every inquirer into the ways of Providence. I collect from passages already cited from the book of Acts, that the power of working miracles was conferred by the hands of the apostles only; and consequently ceased with the last disciple on whom their hands were laid. I perceive in the language of the Fathers,[1] who lived in the middle and end of the second century, when speaking on this subject, something which betrays, if not a conviction, at least a suspicion, that the power of working miracles was withdrawn, combined with an anxiety to keep up a belief of its continuance in the Church. They affirm in general terms that miracles were performed, but rarely venture to produce an

[1] In confirmation of this remark, I refer the reader to the following passages of Tertullian's works. In the tract *de Pudicitiâ* he is contending that the Church possesses not the power of pardoning certain offences; but foreseeing that the example of the apostles, who had pardoned those offences, might be objected to him, he thus anticipates the objection: "Itaque si et ipsos beatos Apostolos tale aliquid indulsisse constaret, cujus venia a Deo, non ab homine, competeret, non ex disciplinâ, sed ex potestate fecisse." The meaning is, that the apostles pardoned those offences, not in the ordinary course of church discipline, but by a peculiar power vested in themselves. "Nam et mortuos suscitaverunt, quod Deus solus: et debiles redintegraverunt, quod nemo nisi Christus: immo et plagas inflixerunt, quod noluit Christus; non enim decebat eum sævire qui pati venerat. Percussus est Ananias et Elymas, Ananias morte, Elymas cæcitate, ut hoc ipso probaretur Christum et hæc facere potuisse. Sic et prophetæ cædem et cum eâ mœchiam pœnitentibus ignoverant, quia et severitatis documenta fecerunt. Exhibe igitur et nunc mihi, apostolice, prophetica (f. legendum *Apostolica et Prophetica*) exempla, et (f. ut) agnoscam divinitatem, et vindica tibi delictorum ejusmodi remittendorum potestatem. Quod si disciplinæ solius officia sortitus es, nec imperio præsidere, sed ministerio, quis aut quantus es indulgere? qui neque Prophetam, nec Apostolum exhibens, cares eâ virtute cujus est indulgere," c. 21. It is evident that the whole argument proceeds on the supposition that the miraculous powers which had been exerted by the prophets and apostles no longer

instance of a particular miracle. Those who followed them were less scrupulous, and proceeded to invent miracles; very different indeed in circumstances and character from the miracles of the gospel, yet readily believed by men who were not disposed nicely to examine into the evidence of facts which they wished to be true. The success of the first attempts naturally encouraged others to practise similar impositions upon the credulity of mankind. In every succeeding age miracles multiplied in number, and increased in extravagance, till at length, by their frequency, they lost all title to the name, since they could no longer be considered as deviations from the ordinary course of nature.[1]

But to return to Tertullian. The only specific instances which he mentions of the exercise of supernatural powers relate to the exorcism of demons. He is contending in the *Apology*[2] that the gods of the heathen are no other than demons; of which assertion he offers the following proof: "Bring," he says, "before your tribunals a man possessed with a demon: the evil spirit, if commanded by a Christian, will speak and confess himself a demon. In like manner, produce a person supposed to be inspired by one of your deities: he, too, will not dare to give a false reply to a Christian, but will confess that his inspiration proceeds from a demon." In the tract *de Spectaculis*[3] we find a story of a female who went to the theatre, and returned possessed by a demon. The unclean spirit, when asked by the exorcist how he dared to assault a Christian, replied, "I was justified in so doing, for I found her on my own ground."[4]

subsisted; since, if they did subsist, the individual possessing them might exercise the apostolic or prophetic privilege of pardoning the offences in question. Again, in c. 22: "Sic enim Dominus potestatem suam ostendit: 'quid cogitatis nequam in cordibus vestris? Quid enim facilius est dicere Paralytico, Dimittuntur tibi peccata, aut surge et ambula? Igitur ut sciatis filium hominis habere dimittendorum peccatorum in terrâ potestatem, tibi dico, Paralytice, surge et ambula'" (Matt. ix.). "Si Dominus tantum de potestatis suæ probatione curavit, ut traduceret cogitatus et ita imperaret sanitatem, ne non crederetur posse delicta dimittere; non licet mihi eandem potestatem in aliquo sine iisdem probationibus credere." In the tract *de Præscriptione Hæreticorum*, where Tertullian calls upon the heretics to declare what miracles had been wrought by the founders of their several sects, it is worthy of remark that he does not appeal to any instance of the exercise of miraculous powers in his own day, c. 30. See also c. 44.

[1] Gibbon, c. xxviii. p. 99, ed. 4to.

[2] C. 23, quoted in note 7.

[3] "Nam et exemplum accidit, Domino teste, ejus mulieris quæ theatrum adiit et inde cum dæmonio rediit. Itaque in exorcismo quum oneraretur immundus Spiritus quod ausus esset fidelem adgredi. 'Constanter et justissimè quidem, inquit, feci: in meo eam inveni,'" c. 26.

[4] See also the tract *ad Scapulam*, c. 4. "Nam et cujusdam notarius, quum a dæmone præcipitaretur, liberatus est; et quorundam propinquus et puerulus. Et quanti honesti viri, de vulgaribus enim non dicimus, aut a dæmoniis aut valetu-

Surely if miraculous powers still subsisted in the Church, the writings of Tertullian would have supplied some less equivocal instances of their exercise.

Gibbon has animadverted on the evasions of Middleton respecting the clear traces of visions to be found in the apostolic Fathers.[1] Yet it appears to me that Middleton might have admitted their existence without any detriment to the main position of his essay. His object was to prove that, after the apostolic age, no standing power of working miracles existed in the Church—that there was no regular succession of favoured individuals upon whom God conferred supernatural powers, which they could exercise for the benefit of the Church of Christ whenever their judgment, guided by the influence of the Holy Spirit, told them that it was expedient so to do. This position is perfectly compatible with the belief that God still revealed Himself in dreams to pious members of the Church, for their especial comfort and instruction. The distinction between the two cases has been expressly pointed out by Middleton himself. When, however, we examine the visions recorded in Tertullian's writings, we shall feel great difficulty in believing that they were revelations from heaven. He mentions a Christian female to whom visions were frequently vouchsafed in the time of divine service.[2] They related for the most part to points which had formed the subject of previous discussion. On one occasion, a question having arisen respecting the soul, it was exhibited to her in a corporeal state. He tells another story of a female, who saw in a dream a linen cloth, on which was inscribed, with accompanying expressions of reprobation, the name of an actor whom she had heard that very day at the theatre.[3] Tertullian adds that she did not survive the dream five days. An unfortunate man, whose servants, on the occasion of some public rejoicing, had, without his knowledge, suspended garlands over his doors, was for this involuntary offence severely chastised in a vision;[4] and a female, who had somewhat too liberally displayed her person, was thus addressed by an angel in a dream, "Cervices, quasi applauderet, verberans: 'Elegantes, inquit, cervices, et merito nudæ.'"[5] It should be observed that all these visions are

dinibus remediati sunt!" In the tract *de Exhortatione Castitatis*, c. 12, *sub fine*, is a story of a man who married a second wife under the idea that she was barren; but she proved pregnant; preternaturally, as our author would insinuate. See also two stories in the tract *de Animâ*, c. 51.

[1] Chap. xv., note 71.
[2] *De Animâ*, c. 9.
[3] *De Spectaculis*, c. 26.
[4] *De Idololatriâ*, c. 15.
[5] *De Virginibus velandis*, c. 17.

introduced in confirmation of some opinion for which Tertullian is at the time contending. His enthusiastic temper readily discovered in them indications of a divine origin ; the unprejudiced reader will probably come to a different conclusion.

But though miraculous gifts might have ceased in the Church, the Almighty might still interpose for its protection, and for the advancement of its interests, by especial and visible manifestations of His power. An instance of such interposition is recorded in the writings of Tertullian, which is generally known by the name of the Miracle of the Thundering Legion. He asserts in the *Apology*,[1] as well as in the *Address to Scapula*,[2] that Marcus Antoninus became a protector of the Christians, because during his expedition into Germany he, together with his army, was preserved from perishing with thirst by a seasonable shower of rain, procured by the prayers of his Christian soldiers. In support of his assertion, he appeals to a letter of the Emperor, in which the deliverance of the army was ascribed to this cause ; he does not, however, affirm that he had himself seen the letter. The story has been repeated by subsequent writers, and has received, as might be expected, considerable additions in the transmission. Not only were the Roman soldiers preserved by the seasonable shower, but the army of the enemy was destroyed by a storm of thunder and lightning which accompanied it.[3]

That during the German war the Roman army suffered severely from want of water, and was relieved from a situation of great peril by a seasonable shower of rain, is a fact which does not rest on the single authority of Tertullian. It is recorded by several profane writers, and confirmed by the indisputable testimony of the Antonine column. Nor was Tertullian singular in regarding the event as preternatural: the heathen historians did the same. But while Tertullian ascribes the deliverance of the Emperor to the prayers of his Christian soldiers, Dion Cassius gives the credit of it to certain magical rites performed by an Egyptian named Arnuphis ;[4] and on the Antonine column it is attributed to the

1 "At nos e contrario edimus protectorem, si literæ M. Aurelii gravissimi imperatoris requirantur, quibus illam Germanicam sitim Christianorum forte militum precationibus impetrato imbri discussam contestatur," c. 5.

2 "Marcus quoque Aurelius in Germanicâ expeditione, Christianorum militum orationibus ad Deum factis, imbres in siti illâ impetravit," c. 4.

3 *Hist. Eccl. Eusebii*, l. v. c. 5. Apollinarius, who was prior to Tertullian, appears to have mentioned the storm of thunder and lightning.

4 See the *Epitome of Dion* by Xiphilinus. Marcus Antoninus, p. 246 C, ed. H. Steph. 1568.

immediate interposition of Jupiter Pluvius. This latter circumstance completely disproves Tertullian's statement respecting the existence of a letter in which the Emperor ascribed his deliverance to the prayers of his Christian soldiers—a statement, indeed, neither reconcilable with his general character, nor with the harsh treatment experienced by the Christians during his reign.

Referring the reader to Lardner[1] for a full account of all that has been said by learned men on the subject of this story, I shall content myself with remarking that, as told by Tertullian, it contains nothing miraculous. The Roman army was reduced to great extremity—the Christian soldiers who were present put up prayers to God for deliverance—and a seasonable shower of rain relieved the army from its perilous situation. Tertullian indeed wishes his reader to infer that the shower was the consequence of the prayers of the Christian soldiers; that, unless they had prayed, the shower would not have fallen. But this is to assume an acquaintance with the designs of Providence, which man can obtain only by immediate revelation. The pious mind, persuaded that the course of this world is ordered by the divine governance, naturally has recourse to prayer in the hour of danger; and after the danger is passed, it pours forth its gratitude to God for having so ordered events as to admit of a compliance with its petitions. But it presumes not to ascribe such efficacy to its prayers as would imply that God had been induced by them to alter the course of His government. To represent events, which are in themselves of a character strictly natural, a storm for instance, or an earthquake, as produced by an especial interposition of divine power, exerted in compliance with the prayers of men, is to speak the language, not of genuine piety, but of superstition. Yet such was the language of Tertullian's day. We find in his writings numerous instances of the same disposition to ascribe events to the immediate interference of the Almighty. The Christians in Africa had been deprived of their burial grounds;[2] Tertullian represents a total failure of the harvest, which occurred shortly after, as a punishment inflicted upon the pagan inhabitants for this act of injustice. He accounts

[1] *Heathen Testimonies*, Marcus Antoninus, sect. iii.

[2] "Sicut et sub Hilariano præside, quum de areis sepulturarum nostrarum adclamâssent, '*Areæ non sint*,' Areæ ipsorum non fuerunt; messes enim suas non egerunt," c. 3. Our author plays upon the double meaning of the word area, which signifies a threshing-floor as well as an enclosure. *Ad Scapulam*, c. 3.

in a similar manner for an extraordinary quantity of rain which had fallen in the year preceding that in which his *Address to Scapula* was written.[1] He speaks of flames which appeared to hang by night over the walls of Carthage, and of an almost total *extinction* of the sun's light at Utica, and discovers in them infallible presages of the impending wrath of Heaven. To the same wrath he imputes the calamities which had befallen those Roman governors who had been particularly active in their persecution of the Christians.

I shall take this opportunity of offering a few remarks upon another fact, not of a miraculous nature, related by Tertullian. He says, in the *Apology*,[2] that the Emperor Tiberius, having received from Palestine an account of those supernatural events which proved the Divinity of Christ, proposed to the Senate that He should be received among the deities of Rome—that the Senate rejected the proposal—that Tiberius retained his opinion, and menaced all who brought accusations against the Christians. In a subsequent passage Tertullian states that the account was sent to Tiberius by Pilate, who was in his conscience a Christian;[3] and adds an expression which implies that worldly considerations alone prevented Tiberius from believing in Christ. The story is repeated by Eusebius,[4] who appeals to Tertullian as his authority for it. Lardner, after a detailed examination of the objections which have been made to its truth, pronounces it deserving of regard.[5] Mosheim also seems to be of opinion that it ought not to be entirely rejected.[6] Gibbon treats it as a mere fable, but some of his arguments appear to me far from convincing. One

[1] *Ad Scapulam*, c. 3.

[2] "Tiberius ergo, cujus tempore nomen Christianum in seculum introivit, annuntiata sibi ex Syriâ Palestinâ, quæ illic veritatem illius divinitatis revelaverant, detulit ad Senatum cum prærogativâ suffragii sui. Senatus, quia non ipse probaverat, respuit. Cæsar in sententiâ mansit, comminatus periculum accusatoribus Christianorum," c. 5. In this passage Pearson would read "quia non *in se* probaverat," for "quia non *ipse* probaverat," and interpret the sentence thus: *The Senate rejected the proposal because Tiberius had not approved a similar proposal in his own case—had himself refused to be deified.* Lardner contends that this must be the meaning, even if *ipse* is retained. But a sentence which precedes, "Vetus erat decretum, ne qui Deus ab Imperatore consecraretur, *nisi a Senatu probatus*," shows that *ipse* refers to *Senatus: the Senate refused because it had not itself approved the proposal;* and so the passage was translated in the Greek version used by Eusebius.

[3] "Ea omnia super Christo Pilatus, et ipse jam pro suâ conscientiâ Christianus, Cæsari tunc Tiberio nuntiavit. Sed et Cæsares credidissent super Christo, si aut Cæsares non essent seculo necessarii, aut si et Christiani potuissent esse Cæsares," c. 21.

[4] *Hist. Eccl.* l. ii. c. 2.

[5] *Heathen Testimonies*, c. 2.

[6] *Ecclesiastical History*, *Cent.* i. c. 4.

is founded on a misrepresentation of Tertullian's statement: "We are required," says Gibbon,[1] "to believe that Tiberius protected the Christians from the severity of the laws many years before such laws were enacted, or before the Church had assumed any distinct name or existence." Now Tertullian says not a word about any protection from the severity of the laws, afforded by Tiberius to the Christians; he merely says that Tiberius threatened all who accused them. This threat appears to me to have referred to the inveterate hostility manifested by the Jews against Christ and His disciples, which had come to the Emperor's knowledge through the account transmitted by Pilate. Tertullian could not intend to say that any laws against the Christians were in force during the reign of Tiberius, since he has declared more than once that Nero was the first Emperor who enacted any such laws.[2] I must, however, confess my own opinion to be that the story is liable to just suspicion. It rests entirely on the authority of Tertullian. How happened it that so remarkable a fact, as a public proposal from the Emperor to the Senate to receive Christ among the gods of Rome, escaped the notice of every other writer? Justin Martyr, who on two different occasions appeals to what he calls the Acts of Pilate,[3] in confirmation of the gospel narrative of our Saviour's sufferings and miracles, is silent respecting the proposal of Tiberius to the Senate.

But to proceed with the information supplied by Tertullian's works respecting the causes which contributed to the rapid growth of Christianity during the latter part of the second century. We have seen that they furnish no ground for ascribing the success of its teachers at that period to the exercise of miraculous powers. They enable us, however, to ascertain that, by the pious zeal and diligence of its professors, powerful engines had been set at work to promote the diffusion of the gospel. Of these, Mosheim has noticed two:[4] the translation of the New Testament into different languages, and the composition of numerous Apologies for the Christian faith. The writings of Tertullian, which contain quotations from nearly all the books of the New Testament, render it highly probable that a Latin

[1] Chap. xvi. p. 556, ed. 4to.

[2] *Apology*, cc. 5, 21; *ad Nat.* l. i. c. 7; *Scorpiace*, c. 15.

[3] *Apol.* i. pp. 76 C, 84 C. The Acts of Pilate here referred to were the daily transactions of his government, registered in a book, a copy of which was probably sent to Rome.

[4] *Century* ii. part i. c. i.

translation existed in his day.[1] By such a translation the history and doctrines of the gospel would be rendered accessible to a large portion of the subjects of the Roman Empire, who had previously derived their notions of the new religion only from report, and that perhaps the report of enemies anxious to misrepresent it. They were now enabled to judge for themselves, and to perceive how admirably all its precepts are adapted to promote the well-being of society, and to diffuse universal happiness. The favourable impression produced upon the minds of men by the perusal of the sacred books was doubtless confirmed and increased by the numerous Apologies for Christianity to which Mosheim alludes. Among these the *Apology* of Tertullian has always held a distinguished place, and there is perhaps no better mode of conveying to the mind of the reader an accurate notion of the general condition of the Christians in the second century—of the difficulties with which they had to contend, and of the principles on which they acted—than by laying before him a brief summary of its contents. It will be necessary, however, to offer by way of preface a few remarks respecting what may be called the legal position of the Christians at that period, or the point of view in which they were regarded by the Roman laws.

Mosheim [2] says that "in the beginning of the second century there were no laws in force against the Christians; for the Senate had annulled the cruel edicts of Nero, and Nerva had abrogated the sanguinary laws of his predecessor Domitian." Gibbon [3] also infers from Pliny's celebrated letter to Trajan that, when the former accepted the government of Bithynia, "there were no general laws or decrees of the Senate in force against the Christians; and that neither Trajan nor any of his virtuous predecessors, whose edicts were received into the civil and criminal jurisprudence, had publicly declared their intentions concerning the new sect." If, however, we attach any weight to the statements of Tertullian, the conclusions both of Gibbon and

[1] Semler indeed insinuates that the works, extant under Tertullian's name, contain the first specimens of a Latin translation. "Itaque videmur hic ipsa *primordia Latinæ Translationis* occupare et deprehendere." And again, "Aut illud scivit (Tertullianus) *tam pauca esse adhuc Evangelii Latini exemplaria* (nulla forte alia, quam hoc primum, suum ipsius)," etc., sect. iv. Yet he asserts that Tertullian, or whoever the author might be, never used a Greek MS.: "De eo enim satis jam certi sumus, etsi solent viri docti aliter statuere, hunc scriptorem oculis suis manibusque nunquam usurpâsse Græcum ullum codicem *Evangeliorum* aut *Epistolarum*," etc., *ibid.*

[2] *Century* ii. part i. c. 2.

[3] Chap. xvi. p. 540, ed. 4to.

Mosheim are erroneous. In the first book *ad Nationes*,[1] Tertullian expressly says that, while all the other edicts of Nero had been repealed, that against the Christians alone remained in force. In the *Apology*,[2] after having stated that Nero and Domitian were the only Emperors who had persecuted the Christians, he says, as we have already seen, that Marcus Antoninus became their protector in consequence of the miraculous deliverance of his army in the German expedition.[3] "Not," he adds, "that the Emperor abrogated the punishment enacted against them, but he indirectly did away its effect, by denouncing a heavier punishment against their accusers.[4] What, then," our author proceeds, "are we to think of laws which none but the impious, the unjust, the vile, the cruel, the trifling, the insane enforce? of which Trajan partly frustrated the effect by forbidding all inquiries to be made after Christians? which neither Adrian, though a searcher out of all new and curious doctrines, nor Vespasian, though the conqueror of the Jews, nor Pius, nor Verus, called into operation?" The whole tenor of this passage manifestly assumes the existence of laws which, though generally allowed to slumber by the justice and humanity of the Emperors, might yet at any moment be converted into instruments wherewith to injure and oppress the Christians. It is evident also from Pliny's letter[5] and Trajan's answer, that the only offence laid to their charge by the informers was their religion; and that, in the estimation both of the Emperor and the proconsul, the mere profession of Christianity constituted a crime deserving of punishment.

[1] "Et tamen permansit, omnibus erasis, hoc solum institutum Neronianum," etc., c. 7. Compare the *Apology*, c. 4. "Sed quoniam, quum ad omnia occurrit veritas nostra, postremo legum obstruitur auctoritas adversus eam," etc.

[2] C. 5. Tertullian says that Domitian's persecution was of short duration, and that the Emperor himself put a stop to it.

[3] P. 106.

[4] "Sicut non palam ab ejusmodi hominibus pœnam dimovit, ita alio modo palam dispersit, adjectâ etiam accusatoribus damnatione, et quidem tetriore. Quales ergo *leges istæ*, quas adversus nos soli exequuntur impii, injusti, turpes, truces, vani, dementes? quas Trajanus ex parte frustratus est, vetando inquiri Christianos; quas nullus Hadrianus, quanquam curiositatum omnium explorator; nullus Vespasianus, quanquam Judæorum debellator; nullus Pius, nullus Verus impressit." *Apol.* c. 5. "Quoties enim in Christianos desævitis, partim animis propriis, partim *legibus* obsequentes?" c. 37. "Quis denique de nobis alio nomine queritur? quod aliud negotium patitur Christianus, nisi suæ sectæ?" *Ad Scapulam*, c. 4.

[5] Pliny's words are, "Interrogavi ipsos an essent Christiani; confitentes iterum ac tertio interrogavi, supplicium minatus: perseverantes duci jussi. Neque enim dubitabam, qualecunque esset quod faterentur, pervicaciam certè et inflexibilem obstinationem debere puniri." L. x. ep. 97. Trajan answers, "Conquirendi non sunt; si deferantur et arguantur, puniendi sunt."

But whether there were, or were not, any laws in force expressly directed against the Christians, it is certain that their situation was most precarious. It appears indeed to have depended in a great measure on the temper and disposition of the governor of the province in which they lived. If he happened to be rapacious, or bigoted, or cruel, it was easy for him to gratify his favourite passion, by enforcing against the Christians the penalties of laws, originally enacted without any reference to them; such, for instance, as Trajan's[1] edict against companies and associations, and the law[2] which forbade the introduction of any new deity whose worship had not been approved by the Senate. If, on the contrary, he was just and humane, he discountenanced all informations against them, suggested to them the answers which they ought to return when brought before the tribunals, and availed himself of every pretext for setting them at liberty.[3] Thus, while in one part of the empire they were suffering the most dreadful persecution, in another they were at the very same moment enjoying a certain degree of ease and security. For even the power of the governors was not always sufficient to ensure their safety, or to prevent them from falling victims to the angry passions of the populace; at all times difficult to be repressed, but rising to an ungovernable pitch of fury at the celebration of the public games and festivals.[4] On these occasions the intimidated magistrates too often deemed it expedient to yield to the clamorous demands of the multitude, and to gratify their sanguinary impatience by suspending the tardy forms of law, and delivering the Christians to instant death.

The *Apology* of Tertullian is, as has been already observed,[5]

[1] See Pliny's letter above cited, and the *Apology*, cc. 38, 39, 40, where our author complains of the injustice of classing the Christians among the illegal associations, "illicitæ factiones." See also the tract *de Jejuniis*, c. 13. "Nisi forte in Senatus-consulta et in Principum mandata, coitionibus opposita, delinquimus."

[2] See the *Apology*, c. 5, quoted in note 2, p. 55 of this chapter.

[3] In the *Address to Scapula*, c. 4, are recorded the names of several governors who displayed great lenity in their treatment of the Christians; but the latter appear to have regarded the evasions, suggested by the kindness of their judges, with distrust, as the devices of Satan to shake their stedfastness, and to betray them into a criminal compromise of their faith. See the *Apology*, c. 27; *Scorpiace*, c. 11.

[4] "Quoties etiam, præteritis vobis, suo jure nos inimicum vulgus invadit lapidibus et incendiis?" *Apology*, c. 37. "Neque enim statim et a populo eris tutus, si officia militaria redemeris." *De Fugâ in Persec.* c. 14. "Odisse debemus istos conventus et cœtus Ethnicorum, vel quod illic nomen Dei blasphematur, illic in nos quotidiani leones expostulantur, inde persecutiones decernuntur, inde tentationes emittuntur." *De Spectaculis*, c. 27.

[5] Chap. i. p. 52.

addressed to the governors of Proconsular Africa, and we learn from the commencement that their attention and jealousy had been excited by the increasing number of the Christians;[1] but that, instead of being induced to inquire into the real nature of a religion which attracted so many proselytes, they suffered themselves to be hurried away by their prejudices, and condemned it unheard. So great indeed was their ignorance, that they mistook even the name of the new sect; calling those who belonged to it, not Christiani, but Chrestiani.[2] Tertullian[3] exposes, with great power of argument and eloquence, the injustice of punishing Christians merely because they were Christians, without inquiring whether their doctrines were in themselves deserving of hatred and punishment. He complains that in their case alone all the established forms of law were set aside, and all the rules usually observed in the administration of justice violated.[4] Other criminals were heard in their own defence, and allowed the assistance of counsel; nor was their own confession deemed sufficient to their condemnation. The Christian, on the contrary, was simply asked whether he was a Christian; and either his sentence was pronounced as soon as he had admitted the fact, or such was the strange infatuation of the judges, the torture was inflicted in order to compel him to retract his confession and deny the truth; whereas in all other cases torture was applied in order to extract the truth, and to compel the suspected party to confess his guilt. Tertullian dwells for some time upon the gross injustice of these proceedings, as well as upon the inconsistency exhibited by Trajan in his letter to Pliny, in which, at the very moment that he forbade all search to be made after the Christians, he ordered them to be punished as malefactors when brought before the tribunals.

The *Apology* furnishes many striking proofs of the unreasonableness and blindness of the hatred which the enemies of the gospel had conceived against its professors. The Christians were accused of the most heinous crimes,—of atheism, infanticide, of holding nocturnal meetings, in which they abandoned themselves to the most shameful excesses.[5] In vain did they challenge their opponents to make good these horrible charges. In vain did

[1] C. I. [2] C. 3. [3] C. I.
[4] C. 2. Compare *ad Scapulam*, c. 4.
[5] Cc. i. 7, 8. One of the opprobrious appellations applied to the Christian was "Tertium Genus," the precise meaning of which Tertullian does not appear himself to have understood. *Ad Nationes*, l. i. cc. 7, 8, 19. See also *Scorpiace*, c. 10; *de Virgin. vel.* c. 7.

they urge the utter improbability that any body of men should be guilty of such atrocious, such unnatural acts, especially of men, the fundamental article of whose belief was that they should hereafter be summoned before the judgment-seat of God, there to give an account of the deeds done in the flesh.[1] "You are determined," says Tertullian, "to close your eyes against the truth, and to persist in hating us without a cause. You are compelled to witness the salutary influence of Christianity in the reformed lives and morals of those who embrace it; but you quarrel with the effect, however beneficial, in consequence of your hatred of the cause from which it proceeds. Even virtue ceases in your estimation to be virtue when found in a Christian; and you are content that your wives shall be unchaste, your children disobedient, and your slaves dishonest, if they are but careful to abstain from all communication with this detested sect."

Tertullian alludes to an ancient law, which prohibited even the Emperor from introducing the worship of any new deity, unless it had been previously approved by the Senate.[2] As the worship of Christ had not received this preliminary sanction, the Christians, by the profession of their religion, manifestly offended against the law; and Tertullian speaks as if this was the principal ground of the accusations against them. It was not, however, their sole offence: they were charged, not only with introducing a new deity, but with abandoning the gods of their ancestors. Tertullian replies, that the accusation came with an ill grace from men who were themselves in the daily habit of disregarding and violating the institutions of antiquity; but he does not attempt to deny its truth. On the contrary, he boldly maintains that the Christians had done right in renouncing the worship of gods, who were in reality no gods, but mortals to whom divine honours had been ascribed after death, and whose images and statues were the abode of evil spirits, lurking there in ambush to destroy the souls of men.[3]

The absurdity and extravagance of the heathen mythology open to Tertullian a wide field for the exercise of his eloquence and wit;[4] and while at one time he ironically apologises for the readiness with which the magistrates and people gave credit to the horrible reports circulated against the Christians, on the

[1] C. 3.
[2] Cc. 5, 6. See p. 59.
[3] Cc. 10, 11, 22, 23, 27.
[4] Cc. 12, 13, 14, 15.

ground that they believed stories equally horrible respecting their own deities, at another he warmly inveighs against the gross inconsistency of imputing to a Christian as a crime that which was not deemed derogatory to the character of a god.

But the prejudice and bigotry of the enemies of the gospel induced them, not only to believe the most atrocious calumnies against its professors, but also to entertain the most erroneous and ridiculous notions respecting the objects of Christian worship.[1] Not content with falling into the double error, first, of confounding the Christians with the Jews, and next of receiving as true the idle tales related by Tacitus respecting the origin and fortunes of the Jewish people,[2] they persisted in accusing the Christians of worshipping the head of an ass; although, as our author justly observes, the Roman historian [3] had himself furnished the means of disproving his own statement, by relating that, when Pompey visited the temple of Jerusalem, and entered the Holy of Holies, he found there no visible representation of the Deity. Since they could give credit to so palpable a falsehood, we cannot be surprised at their believing that the sun and the cross were objects of worship in the new religion,—a belief to which the forms of Christian devotion might appear to an adversary to lend some countenance. In replying to these calumnies, Tertullian takes the opportunity of stating in spirited and eloquent language the Christian notions of the deity, and of insisting upon the genuineness and antiquity of the Jewish Scriptures, by which the knowledge of the one supreme God, of the creation of the world, and of the origin of mankind, had been preserved and transmitted from age to age.[4] The superior antiquity of Moses and the prophets to the poets and legislators of Greece is repeatedly urged by our author as an irrefragable proof (weak as the argument may appear to us) of the superior claim of the Mosaic institutions to be received as a revelation from heaven.[5]

It has been remarked that the treatment of the primitive Christians formed a solitary exception to that system of universal toleration which regulated the conduct of the Roman government towards the professors of other religions. Gibbon appears to have assigned the true reason of this deviation from its usual policy, when he observes that, while all other people professed a national religion, the Christians formed a

[1] C. 16. [2] *Hist.* l. v. c. 4. [3] *Hist.* l. v. c. 9.
[4] Cc. 17, 18, 19, 20, 21. [5] C. 47.

*sect.*[1] The Egyptian, though he deemed it his duty to worship the same birds and reptiles to which his ancestors had paid their adorations, made no attempt to induce the inhabitants of other countries to adopt his deities. In his estimation, the different superstitions of the heathen world were not so much at variance that they could not exist together. He respected the faith of others, while he preferred his own. But Christianity was from its very nature a proselyting religion. The convert not only abandoned the faith of his ancestors, and thereby committed an unpardonable offence in the eyes of a Gentile, but also claimed to himself the exclusive possession of the truth, and denounced as criminal every other mode of worship. When we consider this striking distinction between the character of Christianity, and of every other form of religion then existing, we shall feel less surprise that it was regarded by the ruling powers with peculiar feelings of jealousy and dislike, or that it was excepted from the general system of toleration. In vain did Tertullian insist upon the right of private judgment in matters of faith; in vain expose the strange inconsistency of tolerating the absurd superstitions of Egypt, and at the same time persecuting the professors of a religion which inculcated the worship of one pure, spiritual, omniscient, omnipotent God, —a God in every respect worthy to receive the adorations of intelligent beings.[2] By thus asserting that the God of the Christians was the only true God, he unavoidably destroyed the effect of his appeal to the understanding, the justice, and the humanity of the Roman governors.

Sometimes the Christians fell into an error not uncommon with very zealous advocates; they urged arguments which were easily retorted upon themselves, and were even converted into pretences for persecuting their religion. We have seen that they were in the habit of accounting for events by the immediate interposition of Providence; of ascribing favourable events to their own prayers, and calamities to the divine displeasure, excited by the cruelties inflicted upon them.[3] The pagans, in answer, appealed to the continually increasing power and glory of Rome during the seven centuries which preceded the birth of Christ, and contended that this long series of prosperity was to be attributed solely to that piety towards the gods which had always formed a striking feature in the national

[1] Chap. xvi. p. 523, ed. 4to.

[2] Cc. 24, 28, *ad Scap.* c. 2.

[3] P. 54.

character.[1] "But how," they asked, "are we to account for the calamities by which the empire has been visited, since the odious sect of Christians appeared? How, but by their impiety and crimes, which have drawn down upon us the wrath of Heaven? By tolerating their existence we have in fact become partakers of their guilt. Let us then hasten to repair our error, and to appease the anger of the gods by utterly rooting out their enemies from the earth."[2] The stated returns of the public games and festivals were, as has been already observed,[3] the occasions on which the blind and inhuman zeal of the deluded populace displayed itself in all its ferocity. Every feeling of compassion was then extinguished, and the cry of "Christianos ad Leonem" resounded from every part of the crowded amphitheatre.

Another ground of accusation against the Christians was, that they refused to sacrifice to the gods for the safety of the Emperor.[4] Tertullian admits the fact, but answers that their refusal arose, not from any feeling of disrespect or disaffection, but from the well-grounded conviction that the gods of the heathen were mere stocks and stones, and consequently incapable of affording the Emperor protection. "Far from being indifferent to his welfare, we put up daily petitions in his behalf to the true, the living, the eternal God, in whom kings reign, and through whose power they are powerful. To that God we pray, in full confidence that He will hear our prayers, and grant the Emperor a long life, a peaceful reign, and every public and private blessing." "Do not," Tertullian adds, "trust merely to my assertions: consult our sacred books: you will there find that we are expressly enjoined to pray for kings and those in authority."

As the Christians cautiously abstained from every act which in the least approximated to idolatry, the seasons of public festivity were to them seasons of the most imminent danger.[5] Their abhorrence of every species of excess, their refusal to join in obstreperous or indecent expressions of joy, to illuminate their houses in the day-time, or to hang garlands over their doors, were construed by their adversaries into certain marks of disloyalty. Tertullian answers this charge by appealing to the uniform tenor of their conduct; "a less equivocal proof," he adds, "of our affection towards our sovereign than those

[1] Cc. 25, 26. [2] C. 40. [3] P. 59.
[4] Cc. 29, 30, 31, 32, 33, 34. [5] Cc. 35, 36, 38, 39.

outward demonstrations of joy which have been displayed in our own time by men who at the very moment were plotting his destruction.[1] As our religion teaches us to disregard and despise the honours and riches of this world, we are not liable to be led astray by those feelings of avarice and ambition which impel others to disturb the public tranquillity; and if you would take the trouble of informing yourselves of what passes in our assemblies, and at our love-feasts, far from finding reason to view them with jealousy as dangerous to the State, you would acknowledge that their necessary tendency is to increase our love towards God and towards our neighbour—to make us better men and better subjects."

But though the enemies of the gospel might be compelled to allow that a Christian was a peaceable, they still accused him of being an unprofitable citizen.[2] The charge, however, if we may judge from Tertullian's answer, resolved itself principally into this, that the Christians brought no offerings to the temples, and contributed nothing towards defraying the expenses of the public games, or to the support of those trades which were more immediately connected with the pomps and ceremonies of idolatry. In his remarks upon this charge, Tertullian expressly affirms that the Christians in his day did not affect a life of solitude and abstraction, but dwelt in the world, and laboured in their several callings and occupations, like other men. In like manner they disclaimed all singularity of dress or diet, freely using the gifts of Providence, but careful not to abuse them. "They indeed," says Tertullian, "who minister to the vicious and criminal passions of mankind—pimps, assassins, and fortune-tellers—may complain with truth that the Christians are unprofitable to them. But all who think that the best man is the most useful citizen, must admit the claim of the Christian to that character, whose religion teaches him that not only his actions, but his very thoughts must be pure, and who regulates his conduct by a reference, not to the imperfect laws of man, the penalties of which he might hope to evade, but to the perfect law of that God, from whom nothing can be hid, and whose vengeance it is impossible to escape."

Unable either to fix any stain upon the morals of the Christians, or to substantiate the charges of irreligion and disloyalty against them, their enemies proceeded in the last place to

[1] *Ad Scapulam*, c. 2.

[2] Cc. 42, 43, 44, 45.

undervalue Christianity itself, and to represent it as a mere species of philosophy.[1] "The philosophers," they said, "inculcate innocence, justice, patience, sobriety, charity; and what do the Christians more?" "Be it so," is Tertullian's reply: "why then do you deny to us alone the indulgence which you extend to every other sect? But look at the effects of Christianity, and you will be forced to confess that it is something more than a species of philosophy; how otherwise can you account for the altered lives and morals of its professors—a change which philosophy has never yet produced in its votaries?"

The conclusion of the *Apology* points out to us one cause of the rapid growth of Christianity, which has been overlooked by Mosheim—the admirable courage and constancy with which the Christians bore the torments inflicted upon them by their persecutors.[2] "Proceed," says Tertullian to the provincial governors, "proceed in your career of cruelty, but do not suppose that you will thus accomplish your purpose of extinguishing the hated sect. We are like the grass, which grows the more luxuriantly the oftener it is mown. The blood of Christians is the seed of Christianity. Your philosophers taught men to despise pain and death by words; but how few their converts compared with those of the Christians, who teach by example! The very obstinacy with which you upbraid us is the great propagator of our doctrines. For who can behold it, and not inquire into the nature of that faith which inspires such supernatural courage?[3] Who can inquire into that faith, and not embrace it? who can embrace it, and not desire himself to undergo the same sufferings in order that he may thus secure a participation in the fulness of the divine favour?"

I cannot quit this part of my subject without briefly noticing Gibbon's remarks on the Apologies published by the early Christians, in behalf of themselves and their religion.[4] He admits that they expose with ability the absurdities of polytheism, and describe with eloquence and force the innocence and sufferings

[1] C. 46.

[2] C. 50. In the *Scorpiace*, our author argues as if sufferings voluntarily endured in the defence of a religion prove not merely the sincerity of the sufferer's persuasion but also the truth of the religion. "Cæterum pati oportebat omnem Dei prædicatorem et cultorem qui ad Idololatriam provocatus negâsset obsequium, secundum illius quoque rationis statum, quâ et præsentibus tunc et posteris deinceps commendari veritatem oportebat, pro quâ fidem diceret passio ipsorum Defensorum ejus, quia nemo voluisset occidi, nisi compos veritatis," c. 8.

[3] Compare *ad Scapulam*, c. 5.

[4] Chap. xv. near the end.

of their brethren. But when they attempt to demonstrate the divine origin of Christianity, then in his opinion they entirely fail; and the only feeling which they excite in the mind of the reader is regret that the cause was not defended by abler advocates. He particularly blames them for insisting more strongly upon the predictions which announced, than upon the miracles which accompanied the appearance of the Messiah.[1] But in these remarks the historian seems to me to proceed upon the erroneous supposition that the *Apology* of Tertullian, and other works of a similar nature, were designed to be regular expositions of the evidences of Christianity. Such an idea never entered into the writer's mind. His immediate business was to defend Christianity against the attacks of its enemies—to correct their misrepresentations, and to refute their calumnies—to persuade them that it was not that combination of folly and crime which they supposed it to be—that, in a word, they were bound to examine before they condemned it. The object, therefore, at which he principally aimed was not to marshal its evidences, but to give a full and perspicuous account of its doctrines and moral precepts. Yet when he explains the notion of the Supreme Being, entertained by the Christians, he adverts, though concisely, to the grounds on which their belief was founded. He shows that the testimony, borne to the existence of an Almighty Creator of the universe by His visible works without, and by the voice of conscience within us, is confirmed by the Jewish Scriptures; the claims of which to be received as a divine revelation he rests upon their superior antiquity, not only to the literature, but even to the gods of Greece, and upon the actual accomplishment of many of the prophecies contained in them.[2] When again he proceeds to explain those doctrines which are more peculiarly Christian, he says that Christ was proved to be the Word of God, as well by the miserable state to which, agreeably to the prophecies of the Old Testament, the Jewish nation was reduced in consequence of its rejection of Him, as by the miracles which He wrought during His residence upon earth.[3] I know not what further evidence of the divine origin of Chris-

[1] In the third book *against Marcion*, Tertullian assigns the reason why he considers the evidence of miracles as not alone sufficient to establish the truth of Christianity. Christ Himself, he says, warned His disciples that many would come in His name, showing signs and wonders. (Matt. xxiv. 24.) It was therefore necessary to the complete establishment of His pretensions that He should not only work miracles, but should in all respects fulfil the predictions of the prophets respecting His character and office, c. 3.

[2] *Apology*, cc. 17, 18, 19, 20.

[3] C. 21.

tianity Tertullian could be expected to produce in a work designed to explain what it was, not to prove whence it was derived. But had the latter been his professed object, are we competent to decide upon the train of reasoning which he ought to have pursued in order most readily to accomplish it? Arguments, which appear to us the most forcible, might have been thrown away upon the persons whom he was addressing; and we may surely give him credit for knowing by what means he was most likely to produce conviction in their minds. He has frequent recourse to the argument *ad hominem;* which, however lightly it may weigh in the estimation of the dispassionate and reflecting reader of the present day, was not without its effect in silencing the clamours of malice and of ignorance. They who think with Daillé[1] that the exquisite wisdom and transcendent beauty of the rule of life prescribed in the gospel constitute the strongest and surest proof of its divine origin, will also think that Tertullian, by simply stating the doctrines of Christianity, and appealing to the Scriptures in confirmation of his statement, adopted the most efficacious mode of extending its influence.

We have seen that the persecutions inflicted on the Christians, far from retarding, contributed, in the opinion of Tertullian, to accelerate the progress of the gospel. The Church was not insensible to the advantages which its cause derived from the intrepid constancy of its members; but it was too well aware of the infirmity of human nature not to know that even the sincerest conviction of the truth of Christianity might not always be sufficient to support the convert in the hour of danger. In order, therefore, to excite his courage, the sufferings of martyrdom were invested with peculiar privileges and honours. It can scarcely be necessary to remark that the original signification of the word Martyr is "a witness;" and though in later times the appellation has been generally confined to those who proved the sincerity of their faith by the sacrifice of their lives, in the time of Tertullian[2] it was used with greater latitude, and comprehended all whom the profession of Christianity had exposed to any severe hardship, such as imprisonment or loss of property—those who are now usually distinguished by the name of Con-

1 "La Sagesse exquise et l'inestimable beauté de la discipline même de Jésus Christ est, je l'avoue, le plus fort et le plus sûr argument de sa Vérité." Quoted by Dr. Hey in his *Lectures*, Book I. end of c. 13.

2 Thus in the tract *de Præscriptione Hæreticorum*, c. 3. "Si etiam Martyr apsus de regulâ fuerit."

fessors.[1] To this lax use of the term *martyr* must be chiefly ascribed the erroneous persuasion which has been so carefully cherished by the Church of Rome respecting the number of martyrs, strictly so called; for though it may have been greater than Dodwell was willing to allow, it is certain that his opinion approaches much nearer to the truth than that of his opponents.[2]

We shall, however, form a very inadequate idea of the sufferings endured by the primitive Christians, if we restrict them to the punishments inflicted by the magistrates, or to the outrages committed by a blind and infuriate populace. Many who escaped the sword and the wild beasts were destined to encounter trials of the severest kind, though their sufferings attracted not the public attention. When we consider the species of authority exercised by heads of families in those days, and the hatred by which many were actuated against Christianity, we may frame to ourselves some notion of the condition of a wife, a child, or a slave, who ventured to profess a belief in its doctrines.[3] This alone was deemed a sufficient cause for repudiating a wife, or disinheriting a son; and Tertullian mentions by name a governor of Cappadocia, who avenged the conversion of his wife by persecuting all the Christians of the province.[4] So heinous indeed was the offence that it cancelled all obligations.[5] He who committed it became at once an outcast from society, and was considered to have forfeited his claim to the good offices of his nearest kinsman; nor were instances wanting, if

[1] Tertullian sometimes applies the term Confessor to one who was imprisoned on account of his religion. "Et quum in carcere fratrem vult visitari, Confessoris imperat curam." *Scorpiace*, c. 11.

[2] Tertullian, we believe, mentions only five martyrs by name: St. Peter, who was crucified, and St. Paul, who was beheaded at Rome during Nero's persecu tion; *de Præscriptione Hæreticorum*, c. 36; *adv. Marcionem*, l. iv. c. 5; *Scorpiace*, c. *ult.* Perpetua, of whose martyrdom an account is still extant under the title of *Passio Perpetuæ ac Felicitatis; de Animâ*, c. 55. Rutilius, who having for some time avoided persecution by flight, and even, as he conceived, secured his safety by the payment of a sum of money, was suddenly seized, and, after undergoing severe torments, cast into the flames; *de Fugâ in Persecutione*, c. 5, and Justin, *adv. Valentinianos*, c. 5. Tertullian relates also that St. John the Evangelist was cast into a cauldron of boiling oil, and came out unhurt. *De Præscript. Hæret.* c. 36.

[3] "Uxorem jam pudicam maritus, jam non zelotypus, ejecit: filium jam subjectum pater, retro patiens, abdicavit: servum jam fidelem dominus, olim mitis, ab oculis relegavit: ut quisque hoc nomine emendatur, offendit." *Apology*, c. 3.

[4] *Ad Scapulam*, c. 3.

[5] In the first tract *ad Nationes*, Tertullian says that informations were frequently laid against the Christians by their slaves, c. 7. "Quid? quum domestici eos vobis prodant? omnes a nullis magis prodimur: quanto magis, si atrocitas tanta sit quæ justitiâ indignationis omnem familiaritatis fidem rumpit."

Tertullian's expressions are to be literally understood, in which a brother informed against a brother, and even a parent against a child.[1]

Yet, amidst the trials and afflictions to which he was subjected, the convert was not entirely destitute even of earthly consolation. The affection and esteem of the *brethren* in some degree compensated the loss of his former friends, the alienation of his kindred, and the contempt and insults of the world. We in the present day can form only a faint conception of the intimacy of that union which subsisted between the primitive Christians, and was cemented by a community of danger as well as of faith and hope. The love which they bore to each other excited the astonishment, though it could not subdue the hostility, of their heathen persecutors.[2] But they naturally regarded, with feelings of peculiar affection and respect, those members of the Church who were called to suffer in its cause. The Christian, when imprisoned on account of his religion, was supported by the reflection, that his brethren anxiously watched over his fate, and that no exertion would be wanting on their part to mitigate its severity—that he should be maintained during his confinement by their voluntary contributions[3]—that devout females would flock to his prison to kiss his chains,[4] and penitents to obtain through his intercession a speedier restoration to the communion of the Church.[5] If he escaped with life, he knew that he should become the object of the most reverential regard—that he should be held up by the Church as

[1] I speak doubtfully, because there is something in our author's mode of expressing himself which leads me to suspect that no such instances had actually fallen within his own knowledge; but that he inferred that they had occurred, because our Lord had declared that they would occur. "Quum autem subjicit, *Tradet autem frater fratrem, et pater filium in mortem, et insurgent filii in parentes et mortificabunt eos;* manifestè iniquitatem istam in cæteros pronuntiavit, quam in Apostolis non invenimus. Nemo enim eorum aut fratrem aut patrem passus est traditorem, quod plerique jam nostri. Dehinc ad Apostolos revocat: *Et eritis odio omnibus propter nomen meum:* Quanto magis nos, quos a parentibus quoque tradi oportet!" *Scorpiace*, c. 9. "Sed et fratres nostros et patres et filios et socrus et nurus et domesticos nostros ibidem exhibere debebis, per quos traditio disposita est," c. 10.

[2] *Vide* "inquiunt, ut invicem se diligunt." *Apology*, c. 39.

[3] *Apology*, c. 39; *ad Martyres*, cc. 1, 2; *de Jejuniis*, c. 12.

[4] "Quis in carcerem ad osculanda vincula Martyris reptare patietur?" *Ad Uxorem*, l. ii. c. 4.

[5] "Quam pacem quidam in Ecclesiâ non habentes a Martyribus in carcere exorare consueverunt." *Ad Martyres*, l. i. After Tertullian had seceded from the Church, he denied that it possessed the power of pardoning crimes of a heinous nature, and ridiculed the notion that attention ought to be paid to the intercession of a martyr. *De Pudicitiâ*, c. 22.

an example to all its members, and possess a prior claim to its dignities and honours.[1] If he was destined to lose his life, he had been taught that martyrdom was a second and more efficacious baptism[2]—that it washed away every stain[3]—and that, while the souls of ordinary Christians passed the interval between their separation from the body and the general resurrection in a state of incomplete enjoyment, that of the martyr was secure of immediate admission to the perfect happiness of heaven.[4]

When such were the privileges conferred, both in this and in the next world, by suffering for the faith of Christ, it is not surprising that men of an ardent and enthusiastic temper should aspire to the crown of martyrdom, and eagerly encounter persecution. Nor can it be dissembled that some of the early Fathers, in their anxiety to confirm the faith of the convert, and to prevent him from apostatizing in the hour of trial, occasionally spoke a language calculated to encourage men to make that gratuitous sacrifice of life, to which the sober decision of reason must annex the name and the guilt of suicide.[5] It may be asked, perhaps, "what surer mark there can be of that love of God, in which consists the perfection of the Christian character, than an earnest desire to be removed from this world of vanity and sin, and to be admitted to the immediate perception of the Divine Presence? When Tertullian says,[6] that the Christian's only concern respecting this life is that he may as speedily as possible exchange it for another, in what does his language differ from that of St. Paul, who tells the Philippians that he has "a desire to depart, and to be with Christ"?[7] But this desire was tempered

1 "Sed alium *ex martyrii prærogativâ* loci potitum indignatus." *Adv. Valentinianos*, c. 4. See *de Fugâ in Persecutione*, c. 11.

2 *De Patientiâ*, c. 13; *Scorpiace*, c. 6, *sub fine; de Pudicitiâ*, c. 9, *sub fine*, c. 22; *de Baptismo*, c. 16.

3 *Apology, sub fine.* "Omnia enim huic operi delicta donantur."

4 "Nemo enim, peregrinatus a corpore, statim immoratur penes Dominum, nisi *ex martyrii prærogativâ*, Paradiso scilicet, non inferis, deversurus." *De Resur. Carnis*, c. 43; *Scorpiace*, c. 12. "Ad ipsum divinæ sedis ascensum." *De Patientiâ*, c. 13.

5 "Denique cum omni sævitiâ vestrâ concertamus, etiam ultrò erumpentes, magisque damnati quam absoluti gaudemus." *Ad Scapulam*, c. 1. "Absit enim ut indigne feramus ea nos pati quæ optamus," c. 2. See also c. 5.

6 "In primis, quia nihil nostra refert in hoc ævo, nisi de eo quam celeriter excedere." *Apology*, c. 41.

7 C. 1, v. 23. Tertullian refers more than once to this very passage. "Cupidi et ipsi iniquissimo isto sæculo eximi, et recipi ad Dominum, quod etiam Apostolo votum fuit." *Ad Uxorem*, l. i, c. 5. "Ipso Apostolo festinante ad Dominum." *De Exhort. Castitatis*, c. 12. See also *de Spectaculis*, c. 28.

and controlled in the mind of the apostle by a feeling of implicit resignation to the will of God. He must abide in the flesh so long as his ministry could be useful to the Philippians; and it was not for him to determine for how long a period his usefulness would continue. Though he was prepared—though he longed for the summons to depart — he did not venture to anticipate it; and, far from courting martyrdom, he employed all warrantable methods of preserving his life. Tertullian himself, in the *Apology*,[1] discriminates accurately between the case of a Christian who voluntarily denounces himself, and that of one who, when brought before the magistrate, professes his gladness that he is called to suffer on account of his faith. He supposes a heathen to ask, "Why do you complain of being persecuted when it is your own wish to suffer?" His answer is, "No doubt, we wish to suffer; but in the same manner that a soldier wishes for the battle. He wishes to obtain the spoil and glory consequent upon victory, but would gladly avoid the danger to which he will be exposed, though he does not shrink from it. So we, though we endure your persecutions in the hope of finally obtaining the reward of our fidelity, would gladly avoid them, could we do so consistently with our allegiance to Christ."

While, however, we condemn that immoderate anxiety to obtain the honours of martyrdom which appears to have been too prevalent among the primitive Christians, let us not involve, in one indiscriminate censure, all who either became their own accusers before the magistrates, or refused to save themselves by flight, or by any other innocent means, from the certain death which awaited them. The moral character of the act must depend upon the motive by which it was dictated. The name of suicide is justly applied to that voluntary sacrifice of life which originates in distrust of the goodness or impatience of the visitations of God—in disgust at the world—or in a presumptuous desire to seize, before the appointed time, the rewards reserved in heaven for the faithful followers of Christ. But who can fail to discern the clear distinction between these cases and the noble refusal of Socrates to save his life by escaping from prison? —a refusal dictated by a feeling of reverence for the laws of his country, and a conviction that he was bound to obey them even

[1] "Ergo, inquitis, cur querimini quod vos insequamur, si pati vultis, quum diligere debeatis per quos patimini quod vultis? Plane volumus pati; verum eo more, quo et bellum nemo quidem libens patitur, quum et trepidare et periclitari sit necesse; tamen et præliatur omnibus viribus, et vincens in prælio gaudet qui de prælio querebatur, quia et gloriam consequitur et prædam," c. 50.

unto death. In like manner it may be presumed that, when the primitive Christians voluntarily presented themselves before the tribunal of the magistrate, they were frequently actuated by a more justifiable motive than the desire of securing the honours of martyrdom. They might hope to arrest the violence of an angry governor by convincing him of the inutility of persecuting men who, far from dreading or avoiding any punishments which he could inflict, came forward to meet them. They might hope to excite a feeling, if not of compassion, at least of horror, in his mind, by showing him that he must wade through a sea of blood in order to accomplish his purpose. Such is the construction put by Lardner upon the conduct of the Asiatic Christians,[1] who during a persecution presented themselves in a body before the tribunal of Arrius Antoninus, the proconsul.[2] He regards as an act of well-timed as well as generous self-devotion, that which Gibbon produces as an instance of the indiscreet ardour of the primitive Christians.[3] His view is, in my opinion, confirmed by the context; for Tertullian introduces the story by observing that the Christians voluntarily presented themselves in order to convince the governors that they were not afraid of death;[4] and afterwards calls upon Scapula, the proconsul of Africa, whom he is addressing, to reflect how many thousands he would destroy, and what utter ruin he would bring upon Carthage, if he persisted in his cruel intentions. Whatever might be the motive which dictated the act, its effect certainly was to put an end to the persecution. Antoninus, after he had ordered a few to be led away to punishment, either influenced by compassion, or observing that the resolution of the survivors was unshaken, dismissed them with the exclamation, "Miserable men! if you wish to die, have you not precipices or halters?"

We find, as we might expect from the change which took place in Tertullian's opinions, some inconsistency in his language respecting the conduct to be pursued by Christians in times of persecution. As he advanced in life, his notions became continually more severe. We have already observed that, in the

[1] *Heathen Testimonies*. Observations on Pliny's letter, sect. vii.

[2] Learned men are not agreed respecting the individual of whom this story is told. Lardner supposes him to have been the maternal grandfather of Antoninus Pius, who was proconsul of Asia during the reign of Nerva or Trajan. Gibbon supposes him to have been Antoninus Pius himself, who was also proconsul of Asia. Casaubon fixes upon an Arrius Antoninus who was murdered during the reign of Commodus. *Ælii Lampridii Commodus*, p. 870.

[3] Chap. xvi. p. 552, ed. 4to.

[4] *Ad Scapulam*, c. 5.

tract *de Patientiâ*,[1] he speaks as if it were allowable for a Christian to consult his safety by flight. But in the tract *de Fugâ in Persecutione*—which was written after his secession from the Church, and is described, perhaps too harshly, by Gibbon, as a compound of the wildest fanaticism and most incoherent declamation—he denounces flight in time of persecution as an impious attempt to resist the divine will. "Persecutions," he argues, "proceed from God, for the purpose of proving the faith of Christians;[2] the attempt, therefore, to avoid them is both foolish and wicked:[3] foolish, because we cannot escape the destiny assigned us by God; wicked, because by fleeing from persecution we appear to set ourselves in opposition to His will, and to accuse Him of cruelty. Our Saviour, it is true, said to His disciples, 'When they persecute you in one city, flee to another.'[4] But this injunction applied only to their particular circumstances: had they been cut off in the very outset of their ministry, the gospel could not have been diffused throughout the world. The same reason will account for the conduct of Christ in withdrawing Himself from the fury of the Jews.[5] His bitter agony in the garden, which is urged in defence of flight in time of persecution, was designed to refute by anticipation the heretical notion that He had neither a human body nor soul; and His prayer to God—'Let this cup pass from me'—will not justify us in endeavouring to flee from danger, since He immediately subjoined, 'Not my will, but Thine be done.'"

Allusion has already been made to a passage in the tract which we are now considering,[6] where Tertullian speaks of the immense revenue which might be collected if each Christian was allowed to purchase the free exercise of his religion for a sum of money.[7] This measure indeed had not been resorted to as a source of revenue to the State, but it had suggested itself to the avarice of the provincial governors as an excellent expedient for replenishing their private coffers; and we find that not only individuals, but whole Churches, were in the habit of purchasing exemption from persecution. Tertullian, as might be expected, condemns this practice in the strongest terms.[8] "Christians," he says, "who have been redeemed with the precious blood of

[1] See the passage quoted in chap. ii. note 4, p. 24. Compare *ad Uxorem*, l. i. c. 3. "Etiam in persecutionibus melius est ex permissu fugere de oppido in oppidum, quam comprehensum et distortum negare. Atqui isti beatiores, qui valent beati testimonii confessione non excidere."

[2] Cc. 1–5.

[3] C. 4.

[4] C. 6. Matt. x. 23.

[5] C. 8.

[6] Note 3, p. 46.

[7] C. 13.

[8] C. 11, *ad fin.*

Christ may not redeem their lives with money. If such a practice was to become universal, no instance of martyrdom could occur. God would no longer be glorified by the sufferings of His faithful servants, and thus one end of the Christian dispensation would be defeated."

Two of Tertullian's treatises relate expressly to the subject of martyrdom. One of them, entitled *ad Martyres*, is a brief address to certain Christians who had been cast into prison on account of their religion, pointing out to them various topics of consolation, and exhorting them to courage and constancy under their sufferings. It might be supposed that the duty of preparation for the cruel fate which awaited them would have left them neither time nor inclination to engage in disputes with each other.[1] They appear, however, to have disagreed in prison, and part of Tertullian's address is taken up in warning them not to allow the enemy of their salvation to gain a triumph by their dissensions. Their disputes appear from our author's expressions to have been of a personal character. *Our* Reformers in Queen Mary's days, when confined in prison and expecting to be brought to the stake, wrote and dispersed tracts against each other on the doctrine of Predestination.

With respect to the other tract, entitled *Scorpiace*, we have already observed that it was directed against the Gnostics and Valentinians, who denied that a Christian was under any obligation to encounter martyrdom.[2] "God," they said, "cannot desire the death of the innocent; nor can Christ, who died for man, wish man to die in turn for Him." The aim, therefore, of our author is to show that it is the bounden duty of Christians to endure the severest sufferings rather than do any act which can be construed into a participation in idolatry. The heinousness of that sin in the sight of God is proved by the numerous denunciations in the Old Testament against it;[3] and by the severe punishments inflicted on the Israelites, for adopting the rites of their idolatrous neighbours. But when God forbids us to commit idolatry, He evidently forbids us to shrink from any danger to which we may be exposed by our refusal to commit it;[4] to shrink, for instance, from martyrdom, if we should be called to so severe a trial of our faith. This conclusion our

[1] C. 1. [2] C. 1. See chap. ii. p. 29. [3] Cc. 2, 3.
[4] C. 4. This notion is carried to the utmost pitch of extravagance in the tract *de Idololatriâ*, c. 22.

author supports by references to the example of Daniel, and the three Jews who were thrown into the fiery furnace by Nebuchadnezzar, for refusing to bow down to the golden image.[1] He appears, however, to have been aware that these references would have little weight with the Gnostics and Marcionites, who denied that the God of the Old Testament was the supreme God.[2] He contends, therefore, that when God calls men to suffer for the gospel, far from deserving, as the Valentinians insinuated, on that account to be censured as cruel, He affords a striking proof of His goodness, by enabling us to vanquish in turn the enemy of our salvation by whom Adam was vanquished.[3]

From the Old Testament Tertullian proceeds to the New, and argues that one principal object of our Saviour's discourses to His disciples was to confirm their faith, and prepare them cheerfully to encounter the persecutions which awaited them.[4] The interpretation which the apostles put upon the words of Christ is, he adds, manifest both from their writings and their conduct. The former are full of allusions to the dangers and difficulties to which the professors of the gospel would be exposed, and of exhortations to support them with constancy;[5] and with respect to the latter, the violent deaths of many of the first disciples sufficiently proved that they did not think themselves at liberty to shrink from martyrdom.[6]

Some of the evasions suggested by the Valentinians for the purpose of enabling the convert at once to save his life and satisfy his conscience, afford amusing instances of the deception which men continually practise on themselves.[7] "Our Saviour's words," they argued, "are, He who denies *me* before men, him will I deny before my Father. Christ does not say, He who denies that he is a Christian; this, therefore, may be denied without incurring the penalty of exclusion from heaven." The heathen magistrates appear to have been aware of this equivocation; for after the party accused had denied that he was a Christian, they compelled him also to deny and blaspheme Christ. The Valentinians also contended that, as St. Paul enjoins Christians to be subject to the higher powers, without limiting the injunction, he meant that they were to obey the magistrate, even when commanded to abjure Christianity.[8]

1 C. 8. 2 C. 5. 3 C. 6. 4 Cc. 9–12.
5 Cc. 12, 13, 14. 6 C. 15. 7 C. 9. Matt. x. 33.
8 C. 14. Rom. xiii. 1.

Another of their fancies was that, when Christ directed His followers to confess Him before men, He alluded to a confession to be made, not before the race of men existing upon earth—the vile work of the Demiurge—but before those to whom the name of men really belongs, the Valentinian Powers and Æons.[1] It must, however, be admitted that Tertullian occasionally displays no less dexterity than his opponents in misinterpreting Scripture and wresting it to his own purpose. Thus he says that the fear which, according to St. John, is cast out by perfect love, is the fear of persecution.[2]

Though we attempt not to justify the language used by many of the Fathers on the subject of martyrdom, we cannot forbear observing that a reference to the circumstances of the times will probably induce us to moderate our censure of them for using it. They lived when the profession of Christianity was attended with the greatest danger—when the Christian was liable at any moment to be dragged by the malice or avarice of his neighbours before the tribunal of the magistrates, and to be offered the dreadful alternative of renouncing his faith, or dying a cruel and ignominious death. They knew how greatly the cause of the gospel was either promoted or injured by the behaviour of its professors under this severe trial. They resorted, therefore, to every argument which was in their opinion calculated to prepare the mind of the convert for the arduous conflict, and to enable him to subdue the natural apprehension of pain and death. But, unhappily, instead of adhering closely to the example of the apostles,[3] and instructing their brethren to encounter persecution, not merely with firmness, as the lot to which they were especially called by their profession, but with cheerfulness and joy, since they thereby became partakers in their blessed Master's sufferings—instead of confining themselves to these sound and reasonable topics of exhortation, they represented martyrdom as an object to be ambitiously sought; forgetting that, although resignation to the will of God, and a patient enduring of the afflictions with which He is pleased to visit us, are the surest signs of a genuine piety, to go as it were in quest of suffering, and to court persecution, is in reality to tempt Him, and bespeaks an impatient and presumptuous temper, most foreign from the Christian character.

[1] C. 10.

[2] C. 12. 1 John iv. 18. The same interpretation is repeated in the tract *de Fugâ in Persecutione*, c. 9.

[3] 1 Pet. iv. 12.

We have seen that Tertullian complains of the total disregard of the established forms of law manifested by the heathen magistrates in their proceedings against the Christians.[1] They appear also, in the punishments which they inflicted, to have been more intent upon gratifying their own ferocity, or that of an exasperated populace, than upon complying with the edicts of the Emperor. From a passage in the *Address to Scapula*, we may conclude that death by the sword was the punishment appointed in the case of the Christians;[2] but Tertullian says that in many instances they had been burned—"a severity of punishment," he adds, "to which even criminals convicted of sacrilege or treason are not doomed." Nor were the governors content with inflicting bodily sufferings on their unhappy victims. Those more refined and ingenious torments, which Gibbon supposes to have existed only in the inventions of the monks of succeeding ages, were, if we may believe Tertullian, actually resorted to in his day.[3] The primitive Christians scrupulously complied with the decree pronounced by the apostles at Jerusalem, in abstaining from things strangled and from blood; when, therefore, they were exhausted by long fasting, food containing blood was offered to them, in the hope that they might be seduced into an act of disobedience.[4] Tertullian states also that attempts were frequently made to overcome the chastity of the female martyrs; and that, instead of being exposed to the wild beasts, they were consigned to the keepers of the public stews, to become the victims either of seduction or of brutal violence.[5]

I shall proceed to notice some other facts mentioned by Tertullian, which, though they do not relate immediately to the history of his own times, are yet worthy of observation. In the tract *against the Jews*, he says that Christ suffered in the reign of Tiberius Cæsar, in the consulship of Rubellius Geminus and

[1] P. 120.

[2] "Pro tantâ innocentiâ, pro tantâ probitate, pro justitiâ, pro pudicitiâ, pro fide, pro veritate, pro Deo vivo (f. vivi) cremamur, quod nec sacrilegi, nec hostes publici, verum nec tot majestatis rei pati solent. Nam et nunc a Præside Legionis et a Præside Mauritaniæ vexatur hoc nomen, sed gladio tenus, sicut et a primordio mandatum est animadverti in hujusmodi," c. 4. Compare *ad Nationes*, l. i. c. 18. "Incendiali tunicâ." And *ad Martyres*, c. 5. "In tunicâ ardente."

[3] Chap. xvi. p. 544, ed. 4to.

[4] *Apology*, c. 9; *de Monogamiâ*, c. 5. "Et libertas ciborum et sanguinis solius abstinentia, sicut ab initio fuit."

[5] "Nam et proxime ad *Leonem* damnando Christianam, potius quam ad *Leonem*, confessi estis labem pudicitiæ apud nos atrociorem omni pœnâ et omni morte reputari." *Apology, sub fine*. See also *de Pudicitiâ*, c. 1.

Fusius Geminus, in the month of March, at the time of the Passover, on the eighth of the calends of April, on the first day of unleavened bread.[1] He had previously said that Augustus survived the birth of Christ fifteen years; and that Christ suffered in the fifteenth year of Tiberius Cæsar, being then about thirty years of age.[2] It is allowed that the consulship of the Gemini corresponded to the fifteenth year of the reign of Tiberius; and as we know from St. Luke's Gospel that our Saviour began to preach in that year, those writers who contend that His ministry lasted only for a single year refer to Tertullian as maintaining that opinion. To these passages, however, has been opposed another from the first book *against Marcion*,[3] in which it is said that Christ was revealed in the twelfth year of Tiberius. The correct inference, therefore, appears to be that Tertullian believed our Saviour's ministry to have continued for three years, but mistook the year in which He was revealed for the year in which He suffered. As it forms no part of my plan to discuss the difficulties attending the chronology of our Saviour's life, I shall content myself with referring the reader to Mr. Benson's work on that subject.[4]

Tertullian[5] more than once speaks of a census taken during the reign of Augustus, the documents relating to which were preserved in the Roman archives, and, according to him, afforded

[1] C. 8, *sub fine.* Compare c. 10, *sub fine.*

[2] "Post enim Augustum, qui supervixit post nativitatem Christi, anni 15 efficiuntur: cui successit Tiberius Cæsar, et imperium habuit annis 22, mensibus 7, diebus 20. Hujus quintodecimo anno imperii passus est Christus, annos habens quasi 30 quum pateretur," c. 8. Tertullian affirms also that Christ was born in the forty-first year of the reign of Augustus, of which he dates the commencement from the death of Cleopatra.

[3] C. 15. "At nunc quale est ut Dominus a 12 Tiberii Cæsaris revelatus sit?" In a subsequent chapter Tertullian speaks as if the ministry of Christ had commenced in the fifteenth year of Tiberius Cæsar; but he then appears to be stating the opinion of Marcion. "Anno 15 Tiberii, Christus Iesus de cœlo manare dignatus est, Spiritus Salutaris," c. 19. So in l. iv. c. 7. "Anno quintodecimo principatûs Tiberiani, proponit (Marcion) eum descendisse in civitatem Galilææ Capharnaum, utique de cœlo creatoris, in quod de suo ante descenderat."

[4] C. vii. sect. i. p. 274.

[5] "Cujus nemo adhuc certus de tribu, de populo, de domo? de censu denique Augusti, quem testem fidelissimum Dominicæ nativitatis Romana Archiva custodiunt?" *Ad Marcionem*, l. iv. c. 7. We must bear in mind that Tertullian is arguing with a heretic, who affirmed that Christ was not born at all, but descended upon earth a perfect man. Again, c. 19, "Sed et census constat actos sub Augusto nunc (f. tunc) in Judæâ per Sentium Saturninum." And c. 36, "Vel de recentibus Augustianis censibus adhuc tunc fortasse pendentibus." See also *de Carne Christi*, c. 2. "Molestos semper Cæsaris census." In the treatise *de Pallio*, c. 1, Sentius Saturninus is mentioned as having presided at the ceremonies which attended the admission of Carthage among the colonies of Rome.

incontestable evidence of our Lord's nativity. He states, however, that this census was taken by Sentius Saturninus, and consequently appears to contradict the account given by St. Luke, who ascribes it to Cyrenius. In this, as in the former case, I shall not attempt to examine the solutions of the difficulty which have been proposed by different learned men, but shall refer the reader to Lardner.[1] One circumstance, however, seems worthy of observation. Tertullian[2] uniformly appeals to the census as establishing the descent of Christ from David through Mary, whose genealogy he also supposes to be given in St. Matthew's Gospel.[3] In the *Apology*,[4] Tertullian states that the miraculous darkness at our Lord's crucifixion was denied by those who did not know that it had been predicted, and therefore could not account for it; "yet," he adds, "it is mentioned in your, *i.e.* the Roman archives." Gibbon[5] thinks that, instead of *archivis vestris*, we should adopt the reading of the *Codex Fuldensis*, *arcanis vestris*, and understand the reference to be to the Sibylline verses, which relate the prodigy exactly in the words of the gospel. It is certain that Tertullian[6] speaks of the sibyl as a true prophetess, but we have just seen that he occasionally appeals to documents in the Roman archives in confirmation of his statements, and I observe that Semler retains the reading *archivis*.[7]

I will conclude my remarks on the external history of the Church, as illustrated by the writings of Tertullian, with briefly adverting to the few notices which can be collected from them respecting the condition of the Jews in his time. He describes[8]

[1] *Credibility of the Gospel History.* Objections against Luke ii. 1, 2, considered.

[2] "Ex stirpe autem Jesse deputatum, per Mariam scilicet inde censendum. Fuit enim de patriâ Bethlehem, et de domo David, sicut apud Romanos in censu descripta est Maria, ex quâ nascitur Christus." *Adv. Judæos*, c. 9. Compare *adv. Marc.* l. iii. cc. 17, 20. l. iv. cc. 1, 36. "Qui vult videre Iesum, David filium credat per virginis censum." See also l. v. c. 1, and c. 8, where there is a very fanciful application of Isaiah xi. 1. Compare *de Carne Christi*, c. 21.

[3] *De Carne Christi*, c. 22.

[4] "Eodem momento dies, medium orbem signante sole, subducta est. Deliquium utique putaverunt, qui id quoque super Christo prædictum non scierunt; ratione non deprehensâ, negaverunt. Et tamen eum mundi casum relatum in archivis vestris," c. 21.

[5] Chap. xv. note 194.

[6] *Ad Nationes*, l. ii. c. 12, *sub fine.* The verses there quoted may be found in the *Apology* of Athenagoras, c. 26, *De Pallio*, c. 2. See *Salmasius in loco.*

[7] See note 5, p. 79.

[8] "Dispersi, palabundi, et cœli et soli sui extorres vagantur per orbem, sine homine, sine Deo rege, quibus nec advenarum jure terram patriam saltem vestigio

them as dispersed throughout the world, having neither God nor a fellow-mortal for their king; not allowed to set foot upon their native land; reduced, in a word, to a state of the lowest degradation.

## Appendix to Chapter II.

By the kindness of the Rev. Samuel Hey, Rector of Steeple Ashton, and of Dr. Richard Hey, of Hertingfordbury, I have been put in possession of twelve lectures on ecclesiastical history, read by their brother—the Rev. Dr. John Hey, late Norrisian Professor of Divinity in the University of Cambridge—in the chapel of Sidney College, in the years 1768 and 1769. Two of them relate to the miracles of the primitive Church; and I willingly take this opportunity of confirming my own opinion on this interesting subject, by that of one of the most acute, most impartial, and most judicious divines of modern times. The reader, in perusing the following extracts, should bear in mind that at the time when Dr. Hey wrote, the controversy excited by Dr. Middleton's Essay was still fresh in the recollections of men.

After some preliminary remarks, Dr. Hey observes:—"The authors on both sides of this question, concerning the reality of the miraculous powers in the primitive Church, seemed to have looked too far *before* them; and to have argued the point with too much regard to the *consequences* which were likely to follow from its being determined in this manner or in that. Those who defend the pretensions of the Fathers do it through fear, lest, if they should appear indefensible, the cause of Christianity should suffer by the condemnation of its early propagators. Those who accuse the Fathers of superstition, weakness, or falsehood, consider what indelible disgrace they shall bring upon popery by showing the impurity of the sources from which all its distinguishing doctrines have taken their rise. But why, in searching after the *truth*, should we give the least attention to any consequences *whatsoever?* We know with certainty beforehand that error of

salutare conceditur." *Apology*, c. 21. Compare *adv. Judæos*, c. 3. "Unde Israel in novissimo tempore dignosci haberat, quando secundum sua merita in sanctam civitatem ingredi prohiberetur." See also c. 13, and *de Pudicitiâ*, c. 8. Ecclesiastical writers sometimes speak as if Adrian's prohibition applied only to the precincts of Jerusalem or Ælia; at others, as if it extended to the whole territory of Judæa. See Gibbon, c. xv. note 19, and the note of Valesius *ad Eusebii Eccl. Hist.* l. iv. c. 6; Justin Martyr, *Apology*, i. p. 84 B.

every kind, if it is not an evil in itself, is always productive of evil in some degree or other; and that to distinguish truth from falsehood is the likeliest method we can take to make our conduct acceptable to God and beneficial to man. Nothing can be more groundless than the fears which some men indulge lest the credit of Christianity should suffer along with the reputation of several of its professors, or more weak than considering *that* a sufficient reason for defending the veracity of the Fathers at all events. There are some miracles recorded in ecclesiastical history which are too childish and ridiculous for *any one* to believe; and there are *some indisputable* records of the vices of the Christians, and more particularly of the clergy: so that, if Christianity can suffer by *such* objections (for which there is no kind of foundation in reason), it has *already* suffered, even in the estimation of those who think the objections of weight. All agree (at least all Protestants) that there have been pious frauds and forged miracles, as well as that the sacred order have been in some ages extremely vicious. The only difference then is in the *degree* of this charge, or rather about the century with regard to which it ought to take place; but what difference can such a circumstance as that make in respect of the divine origin of Christianity? We may therefore, without fear or scruple, enter upon the discussion which I have been proposing, and probe every apparent wound with resolution and accuracy.

"But as all reasoning on subjects of this nature must have its foundation in *facts* (for we can no more argue upon points of history without ascertaining *facts*, than upon points of philosophy without experiments), the first part of our business is to collect from ecclesiastical writers *narratives* of *those* miracles wrought, or pretended to be wrought, in the Christian Church which seem to be most worthy of our attention, and most likely to afford our judgment ground for a determination.

"Previous, however, to such enumeration, it will be proper to mention a circumstance of importance, viz. that for fifty years after the ascension of Christ none of the Fathers made any pretensions to the possession of miraculous powers. We have already spoken in a former lecture of those Fathers who are called the Apostolic, of Ignatius, Polycarp, Barnabas, Hermas;[1] now it is an historical truth not to be omitted that not one of those pious men, though they were the principal governors of the

[1] Hermas had visions. *Note of Dr. Hey.*

Church, and the immediate successors of the apostles in that government (as well as their companions and friends), ever speaks of himself as capable of counteracting the ordinary powers of nature: they all endeavour to inculcate the morality and religion of the gospel, but that merely as *men*, possessed indeed of the sense and meaning of the sacred writers, but entirely void of their extraordinary power. This fact, though not wholly uncontroverted, is very nearly so; some ambiguous expressions concerning the graces and gifts of the Holy Spirit have been, not without great violence, extended to signify an extraordinary communication with the Deity—but no one has so much as *pretended* that such communication was ever meant to answer any further end than that of strengthening the weakness of human nature against the terrors of persecution. I only affirm, however, that none of the apostolic Fathers speaks of *himself* as endued with a power of working miracles. We must not absolutely say that no miracles have ever been said to be wrought about the time they lived, because there is a very celebrated letter extant from the Church of Smyrna, giving an account of the martyrdom of Polycarp, which is said to have been attended with circumstances sufficiently miraculous. This account I shall beg leave to repeat from an eminent writer."

Having given an extract from this letter, as well as from the account of the martyrdom of Ignatius, Dr. Hey proceeds:—"These miracles are mentioned because they are said to have been performed concerning those two apostolic Fathers, who never ventured to assume the power of performing any themselves." After briefly noticing the miracle of the thundering legion, of which he observes that "there seems sufficient reason for being cautious about ranking it amongst the genuine miracles performed in favour of the Christian religion," he adds the following remarks:—"Though the apostolic Fathers stand clear of all imputations of vanity or falsehood on the score of claiming miraculous powers, yet those whom we mentioned next in order, when we considered the subject of studying the writings of the Fathers, declare openly that such were in their time indisputably exercised in the Church. I mean Justin Martyr, Irenæus, Theophilus Bishop of Antioch, and Tertullian. We might add Origen, and indeed every other writer after them till the Reformation; and there is no effort of the divine power so great which they do not boast of having exerted. Of all sorts of miracles ever performed, one would expect men to be the most cautious of assuming *the power of raising the dead;* and yet Irenæus says that this was frequently done on necessary occasions, and that men so raised had lived amongst them many years. Irenæus only affirms this *in general*, without mentioning any *particular instance*, and it is somewhat strange that no instance was ever produced in the three first centuries, insomuch that the heathens gave no credit to the affirmations of the Fathers upon this head. 'Tantum enim,'[1] says Irenæus, 'absunt ab eo ut mortuum ipsi excitent, ut ne quidem credant hoc in totum posse fieri.' There is not, however, the same want of instances with regard to the other branches of miracles said to have been performed in the Church, namely, seeing visions, prophesying, healing diseases, curing demoniacs, and some others."

Dr. Hey passes in the second of the two lectures to what he terms the later miracles of the Church; those which are said to have been wrought in the interval between the establishment of Christianity by the civil power, and the time at which he wrote; and having remarked that many of them were proved to be impostures, he supposes with respect to others the question to be asked—"whether those should not be credited which have been strongly attested, and their falsity never proved?"

"In answer to this," he proceeds, "we may observe, in the first place, that to any one who has been conversant in history, and has seen the credulity of some, and the pious frauds of others, the want of regard to conscience in promoting the views of a party, whether civil or religious, with the many actual violations of truth which have been fully exposed, it is absolutely *impossible* to believe the common run of miraculous stories; no evidence can equal the prior probability which we have of their falsehood. Then there are many relations of preternatural events which no one believes (or perhaps a very trifling party), though they have been attested with all possible formality and exactness. The Abbé Paris is mentioned by every one on this subject: he only died in 1735. The variety of miracles which

[1] The whole passage is as follows:—"Tantum autem absunt ab eo ut mortuum excitent, quemadmodum Dominus excitavit, et Apostoli per orationem, et in fraternitate sæpissime propter aliquid necessarium, eâ quæ est in quoque loco Ecclesiâ universâ postulante per jejunium et supplicationem multam, reversus est Spiritus mortui et donatus est homo orationibus sanctorum, ut ne quidem credant hoc in totum posse fieri," l. ii. c. 56. Again, c. 57: "Jam etiam, quemadmodum diximus, et mortui resurrexerunt, et perseveraverunt nobiscum annis multis." Instead of the *heathens*, Dr. Hey should have said the *heretics*, for of them Irenæus is speaking.

were said to have been performed at his tomb is truly surprising in an improved age; but not less so the strength, the precision, the regularity of the attestations of them, taken before magistrates of the greatest gravity and authority. Mons. de Montgeron, a person of eminent rank in Paris, published a select number of them in a pompous volume in quarto, which he dedicated to the king, and presented to him in person, being induced to the publication of them, as he declares, by the incontestable evidence of the facts, by which he himself, from a libertine and professed deist, became a sincere convert to the Christian faith. And yet no one *now believes* these facts; the Jesuit party *never* owned their belief of them, for the Abbé was a Jansenist, and the miracles were to support the interests of the Jansenists; though the Jesuits profess to believe the miracles of the Fathers which we have been relating, and which are not near so well attested as those of the Abbé Paris.

"If, then, some of the ecclesiastical miracles are to be *disbelieved*, and the later, which we are to disbelieve, are better attested than the early, in what century shall we draw the line between the credible and the incredible? It is a difficult matter, and the difficulty cannot but affect the general credit of Church miracles, if joined to other collateral proofs of the fallibility of their evidence.

"There is another remarkable instance, in which the greatest number of witnesses, and the firmest *temporary* opinion concerning the truth of the facts, have not been able to perpetuate an error—and that is the affair of *witchcraft*. No miraculous fact in the Church has ever been better proved, if so well, as the supernatural operations of witches. All the nations of Christendom have so far taken their powers for granted as to provide legal remedies against them,—nay, even capital punishments for their supposed crimes. At this time there subsist in this university one, if not several foundations for annual sermons, to be preached against them. It is shocking to think of the number of poor wretches who have suffered cruel deaths on account of this superstition; and yet there does not now seem to remain the least trace of it amongst liberal people, or indeed in any rank whatsoever.[1] If we consider how an incredulous person, during its existence, would be blamed for opposing the united sense of

[1] We are afraid that Dr. Hey here overrates the intelligence of the people of this country.

all Christian nations—the testimony of numbers of impartial people—the purport of the wisest laws, we shall at least contract a candid indulgence towards those who are unable to believe the relations of St. Jerome. In short, as Dr. Middleton says, 'the incredibility of the thing prevailed, and was found at last too strong for human testimony.'[1]

"Far different from those we have been speaking of, are the miracles of the gospel—rational, benevolent, seasonable, of *extensive* use, disinterested, free from superstition and moroseness, promoting good morals, called out by the greatness of the occasion in a series, coincident with the purposes of God manifested in prior revelations of His will. Nor would even these have justly gained the assent of mankind had the *internal* evidence of the gospel plainly contradicted the *external*,—had the precepts which it promulgated been evidently unworthy of the Deity, and productive of the misery of human nature, instead of meriting the angelic eulogium which they received when the heavenly choir sang, 'Glory to God, peace on earth, and good-will towards men.'"[2]

—o—

## CHAPTER III.

### ON THE STATE OF LETTERS AND PHILOSOPHY.

MOSHEIM commences his internal history of the Church in each century with an account of the state of letters and philosophy. In the second century his observations principally relate to the new system of philosophy, or, to speak more accurately, to that mixture of Platonism and Christianity which was introduced by Ammonius Saccas at Alexandria. On this subject the writings of Tertullian afford no information. Not

[1] Dr. Middleton does not seem to fall far short of Mr. Hume *On Miracles*. *Note of Dr. Hey*.

[2] A miracle to *me* can only be what *I judge is done* with, and *could not be done* without, divine power: I am liable to be deceived both as to what *is* done, and what *can be* done: every miracle therefore must be scrutinized by every man, and the nature and tendency of it called in to assist the judgment as to the *fact*, and the *powers of man*, etc., under the *laws of nature*. *Note by Dr. Hey*, written in 1783.

that he was unacquainted with the tenets of the different sects—his works, on the contrary, show that he had studied them with diligence and success; or that he entertained that mortal enmity to philosophy and letters which Mosheim imputes to the Montanists in general, for he appears even to have thought that the philosophers, who opposed the polytheism of their countrymen, were in some measure inspired by the spirit of truth;[1] but he clearly saw, and has, in his controversial writings against the heretics, pointed out the pernicious consequences to the interests of Christianity, which had resulted from the attempt to explain its doctrines by a reference to the tenets of the philosophers.[2] "They indeed by a lucky chance might sometimes stumble upon the truth, as men groping in the dark may accidentally hit upon the right path; but the Christian, who enjoys the benefit of a revelation from heaven, is inexcusable if he commits himself to such blind and treacherous guidance."[3]

Although, however, the writings of Tertullian afford us no assistance in filling up the outline sketched by Mosheim of the state of learning and philosophy in the second century, an examination of his own philosophical or metaphysical notions will, we trust, supply some curious and not uninteresting information. We will begin, therefore, with the treatise *de Testimonio Animæ*, the object of which is to prove that the soul of man bears a natural testimony to the truth of the representation, given in Scripture, of the divine nature and attributes. In a short exordium,[4] Tertullian points out the inconsistency and perverseness of the heathen, who usually paid a blind deference to the decisions of the philosophers, but renounced their authority at the very time when they approached most nearly to the truth—when their doctrines most closely resembled those of Christianity.

1 "Idem (Socrates) et quum aliquid de Veritate sapiebat, Deos negans," etc. *Apology*, c. 46. "Taceo de Philosophis, quos, superbiâ severitatis et duritiâ disciplinæ ab omni timore securos, nonnullus etiam afflatus Veritatis adversus Deos erigit." *Ad Nationes*, l. i. c. 10.

2 "Quid ergo Athenis et Hierosolymis? quid Academiæ et Ecclesiæ? quid Hæreticis et Christianis? Nostra institutio de porticu Solomonis est, qui et ipse tradiderat Dominum in simplicitate cordis esse quærendum. Viderint qui Stoicum, et Platonicum, et Dialecticum Christianismum protulerunt. Nobis curiositate opus non est post Christum Iesum, nec inquisitione post Evangelium." *De Præscriptione Hæretic.* c. 7. He traces the origin of all the heresies by which the peace of the Church was disturbed to the heathen philosophy: "Ipsæ denique hæreses a Philosophiâ subornantur." *Ibid.* "Cum Philosophis—Patriarchis, ut ita dixerim, Hæreticorum." *De Anima*, c. 3. See also c. 18, and the *Apology*, c. 47.

3 *De Anima*, c. 2. "Nonnunquam et in tenebris aditus quidam et exitus deprehenduntur cæcâ felicitate."

4 Compare the *Apology*, c. 46.

He then proceeds to address the soul, enumerating at the same time the opinions entertained by the philosophers respecting its origin. "Stand forth," he says, "O soul, whether, as the majority of philosophers affirm, thou art divine and immortal, and therefore incapable of falsehood; or whether, according to the solitary opinion of Epicurus, thou art not divine, because mortal, and therefore under a stricter obligation to speak the truth; whether thou art brought down from heaven, or taken up from the earth; whether thou art formed from numbers or from atoms; whether thine existence commenced with that of the body, or thou wast subsequently introduced into the body: whatever thine origin, and in whatever manner thou makest man a rational animal, capable of sense and knowledge—stand forth."[1] "I do not, however," he adds, "address myself to the soul in an artificial state, such as it becomes after it has been tutored in the schools of philosophy, but to the soul in its natural state, possessing only that knowledge which it has either within itself or learns immediately from its Creator."

The testimony which, according to Tertullian, the soul bears to the unity of God, consists in exclamations like the following, which burst forth involuntarily from the mouths even of pagans, in common conversation:—"God grant that it may be so"—"If God will."[2] "How happens it," asks our author, still addressing the soul, "that instead of naming any one of the numerous deities who are the objects of heathen worship, you use the word *Deus*, and thus unconsciously bear testimony to the existence of one supreme God?" In like manner the soul evinces its knowledge of the attributes of God, of His power and goodness, by exclaiming, "God bless you; God is good; I commend you to God; God sees all things; God will repay:" as it evinces its knowledge of the author of evil, by the execrations which it pronounces against demons.[3] By the fear also of death, by its innate desire of fame, and by involuntary expressions of feeling respecting the dead, it declares its consciousness that

[1] "Consiste in medio, Anima, seu divina et æterna res es, secundum plures philosophos, eo magis non mentiens; seu minimè divina, quoniam quidem mortalis, ut Epicuro soli videtur, eo magis mentiri non debens; seu de cœlo exciperis seu de terrâ conciperis; seu numeris, seu atomis concinnaris; seu cum corpore incipis, seu post corpus induceris; unde unde et quoquo modo hominem facis animal rationale, sensûs et scientiæ capacissimum," c. 1. In c. 4 are briefly enumerated the opinions of the different philosophers respecting the state of the soul after death.

[2] C. 2.

[3] C. 3.

it shall exist in another state, and its anticipation of a future judgment.[1]

"Such is the testimony which the soul bears to the unity and attributes of God, and to the reality of a future state of retribution. Such the language which it speaks, not in Greece only, or at Rome, but in every age and in every clime. Common to all nations, this language must have been derived from a common source, must have been dictated by nature, or rather by the God of nature, by Him who created the soul. But you will say, perhaps, that these exclamations, which burst as it were involuntarily from the lips, are not the result of a consciousness in the soul of its Divine Author, impressed upon it by Himself, but are merely habitual modes of speech used in common conversation, almost without meaning, and transmitted either by written or oral tradition. Be it so. Whence then were they derived by the man who first used them? The notion must have been conceived in the soul before it was delivered to the tongue, or committed to writing. To account for the general use of these expressions by saying that they have been handed down by written tradition, is in fact to trace them to God Himself; for the earliest writings in the world are the Jewish Scriptures, of which the authors were *divinely* inspired. It matters little whether we say that this consciousness was impressed immediately by God upon the soul, or that the soul acquired it through the medium of His revealed Word." [2]

The confirmation which the natural testimony of the soul affords to the truth of Christianity was evidently a favourite topic with Tertullian.[3] He urges the same argument in the *Apology*,[4]

[1] C. 4.

[2] Cc. 5, 6.

[3] Compare *de Animâ*, c. 41; *de Carne Christi*, c. 12; *de Resurrectione Carnis*, c. 3; *adv. Marcionem*, l. i. c. 10.

[4] C. 17. I insert the whole chapter as highly deserving the reader's attention. "Quod colimus Deus unus est, qui totam molem istam cum omni instrumento elementorum, corporum, spirituum, verbo quo jussit, ratione quâ disposuit, virtute quâ potuit, de nihilo expressit in ornamentum majestatis suæ, unde et Græci nomen mundo κόσμον accommodaverunt. Invisibilis est, etsi videatur; incomprehensibilis, etsi per gratiam repræsentetur; inæstimabilis, etsi humanis sensibus æstimetur; ideo verus et tantus est. Cæterum quod videri communiter, quod comprehendi, quod æstimari potest, minus est et oculis quibus occupatur, et manibus quibus contaminatur, et sensibus quibus invenitur. Quod vero immensum est, soli sibi notum est; hoc est quod Deum æstimari facit, dum æstimari non capit. Ita eum vis magnitudinis et notum hominibus objicit et ignotum. Et hæc est summa delicti nolentium recognoscere quem ignorare non possunt. Vultis ex operibus ipsius tot ac talibus quibus continemur, quibus sustinemur, quibus oblectamur, etiam quibus exterremur—vultis ex animæ ipsius testimonio com-

and Milner in his *History of the Church*, though little disposed to think highly of our author, admits that he "scarce remembers a finer observation made by any author in favour both of the natural voice of conscience, and of the patriarchal tradition of true religion; for both may fairly be supposed concerned."

In the short preface to the tract of which we have been speaking, Tertullian assigns the cause of his frequent recurrence to this mode of reasoning. To press the enemies of the gospel with arguments drawn from profane literature was, he says, useless; though they allowed the premises, they were always ready with some pretext for evading the legitimate conclusion. To bring forward arguments founded on Scripture was still more unavailing; they did not admit its authority. How then were they to be convinced, or at least silenced? By an appeal to the testimony borne to the existence of one supreme God, by the natural voice of conscience, and by the works of creation.[1] To this testimony, therefore, Tertullian appeals; and in thus appealing, far from thinking that he could be accused of pursuing a course derogatory to the honour or injurious to the interests of the gospel, he conceived that he was offering the strongest evidence in confirmation of its truth, by showing that the revelation which God has been pleased to make of Himself, in His

probemus? quæ licet carcere corporis pressa, licet institutionibus pravis circumscripta, licet libidinibus et concupiscentiis evigorata, licet falsis Diis exancillata, quum tamen resipiscit, ut ex crapulâ, ut ex somno, ut ex aliquâ valetudine, et sanitatem suam potitur, Deum nominat, hoc solo nomine quia proprio Dei veri. *Deus magnus, Deus bonus*, et *quod Deus dederit*, omnium vox est. Judicem quoque contestatur illum. *Deus videt*, et *Deo commendo*, et *Deus mihi reddet.* O testimonium animæ naturaliter Christianæ! Denique pronuntians hæc, non ad Capitolium, sed ad cœlum respicit. Novit enim sedem Dei vivi; ab illo et inde descendit."

[1] The following are selected from numerous passages in which Tertullian appeals to this testimony:—"Tractandum et hic de revelationis qualitate, an dignè cognitus sit (Deus), ut constet an verè; et ita credatur esse, quem dignè constiterit revelatum. Digna enim Deo probabunt Deum. Nos definimus Deum primo naturâ cognoscendum, dehinc doctrinâ recognoscendum. Naturâ, ex operibus; doctrinâ, ex prædicationibus." *Adv. Marc.* l. i. c. 18. Compare l. ii. c. 3; *adv. Valentinianos*, c. 20. "Denique ante legem Moysi scriptam in lapideis tabulis, legem fuisse contendo non scriptam, quæ naturaliter intelligebatur et a Patribus custodiebatur. Nam unde Noe justus inventus, si non illum naturalis legis justitia præcedebat?" *Adv. Judæos*, c. 2; *de Virginibus vel.* cc. 1, 16. "Nos unum Deum colimus, quem omnes naturaliter nostris; ad cujus fulgura et tonitrua contremiscitis: ad cujus beneficia gaudetis." *Ad Scapulam*, c. 2. "Si enim anima, aut divina aut a Deo data est, sine dubio datorem suum novit." *De Testim. Animæ*, c. 2. "Quum etiam ignorantes Dominum nulla exceptio tueatur a pœnâ, quia Deum in aperto constitutum, et vel ex ipsis cœlestibus bonis comprehensibilem ignorari non licet, quanto cognitum despici periculosum est!" *De Pœnitentiâ*, c. 5; *de Spectaculis*, c. 2; *de Coronâ Militis*, c. 6; *ad Nationes*, l. ii. c. 5.

visible works and in the soul of man, is in perfect harmony with that contained in His written Word.

But though approved, as we have seen, by Milner, Tertullian's reasoning will be far, we suspect, from commanding universal assent in the present day. Since the publication of Dr. Ellis's work, entitled *The Knowledge of Divine Things from Revelation*, it has become the fashion with many to treat, not merely as vain and idle, but even as presumptuous and almost impious, every attempt to prove the existence and attributes of God from the visible works of creation, or from the internal constitution of man. "Unless," we are told, "the idea of a God had in the first instance been communicated to the mind; unless God had Himself taught it to our first parents, and it had thus been transmitted through succeeding generations; no contemplation of the works of creation—no induction from the phenomena of the natural and moral world, could ever have enabled mankind to discover even His existence. But as soon as we are taught that there is a Creator necessarily existent and of infinite perfections, our understandings readily admit the idea of such a Being; and we find in the natural world innumerable testimonies to the truth of the doctrine."

Now we are ready to grant that man never *did* by reasoning *à posteriori* discover the existence of God; or in Warburton's words, that "all religious knowledge of the Deity and of man's relation to Him was revealed, and had descended traditionally down (though broken and disjointed in so long a passage) from the first man."[1] Still this concession does not, in our estimation, affect the only important part of the question; which is not, whether man ever did, *without previous intimation of a Supreme Being*, reason from the works of creation to the existence of a Creator; but whether, if he had so reasoned, he would have reasoned correctly.

When, however, it is affirmed that man not only never *did*, but never *could* so have reasoned, we must be permitted to examine the arguments by which the assertion is supported. Why then could not man discover the existence of God from the contemplation of the works of creation, etc.? "Because, it is said, between matter and spirit, things visible and invisible, time

[1] *Doctrine of Grace*, Book III. c. 2. Warburton is speaking in the person of an opponent of Natural Religion.

and eternity, beings finite and beings infinite, objects of sense and objects of faith, the connexion is not perceptible to human observation." And we are therefore to conclude that, unless we had been taught that there *is* a spiritual, invisible, eternal, infinite Being, we never could have arrived at the knowledge of that Being. Yet the same writers contend that the fact is no sooner proposed than it commands the assent of the understanding. What then are the grounds on which that assent is given? The mere statement cannot alone be sufficient to produce conviction. The truth is that the understanding assents, because the fact proposed agrees with our previous observations—with the previous deductions of reason. Reason tells us that there are in the nature of man faculties for the existence of which we cannot account by any modification of matter known to us—thought, memory, invention, judgment. Reason tells us that no bounds can be set to time or space; hence we are led to admit the existence of a spiritual, eternal, infinite Being. The reasoning is equally valid, whether we apply it in confirmation of a fact which has been revealed to us, or without any previous revelation infer that fact from it. The latter is doubtless by far the more difficult operation; but we are now speaking only of its possibility or impossibility. The same series of proofs by which we establish a known truth might surely have conducted us to the knowledge of that truth.[1]

Let us suppose a sceptic to ask why we believe the existence of God: what must be our reply? According to the writers whose opinions we are now considering, "this truth was originally made known by revelation." But if the sceptic proceeded to deny, as he probably would, the authority of the revelation, by what arguments must we endeavour to convince him? The answer is, "We must necessarily refer him to those testimonies, which the natural and moral phenomena of the world abundantly supply, of a Creator all-wise, powerful, good." It is admitted, then, by the very answer that those testimonies are sufficient to prove to the sceptic the existence of God; and is not this, in fact, to give up the point in dispute?

Perhaps, however, there may be some who will foresee this

[1] To borrow an illustration from science. For how long a period were the ablest mathematicians employed in endeavouring to effect the passage from finite to infinite, or from discrete to continuous, in geometry? The discovery was at length made, and therefore was at all times possible.

inevitable consequence of referring the sceptic to testimonies drawn from the natural and moral world, and will answer, "We can prove the authority of the revelation by historical investigation. We possess certain records, the genuineness of which we have ascertained. These declare that at a certain time a revelation was made from Heaven, and that the person who was sent to make it, attested the truth of His mission by miracles." Perhaps the sceptic will reply that no human testimony can establish the credit of a miracle. How is this objection to be answered but by a reference to the natural world? by showing that what we call the course of nature, from which a miracle is said to be a deviation, is in fact only a system appointed by the God of nature, and consequently liable to be suspended or altered according to His pleasure? Or perhaps the sceptic may say that pretensions to miraculous powers have abounded in all ages; and that, as such pretensions have in the majority of instances been shown to be false, we may reasonably conclude that they were so in all. To meet this objection, we must refer to the criteria of miracles, which are all deductions of human reason, and show that the purposes for which the miraculous powers are said to have been exerted were consonant to just conceptions of the divine nature and attributes; and those conceptions derived from sources extraneous and independent of the revelation itself. For we must not, in the first instance, say that we obtain the knowledge of the nature and attributes of God from a revelation, and then prove the truth of that revelation by a reference to the knowledge so obtained.

But is not this, it will be asked, to constitute human reason the judge of the divine dispensations? Is it not to say that man, blind and ignorant man, can certainly determine what ought and what ought not to proceed from God? By no means. It is only to compare one set of facts with another; to compare the conceptions of the divine nature, which we derive from the perusal of the Bible, with those which we derive from the contemplation of the phenomena of the natural and moral world. If the written word and the visible world both proceed from the same author, they cannot but agree in the testimony which they bear to His character and attributes.

Men, it is true, have not unfrequently been induced by the love of paradox, by the desire of obtaining a reputation for superior talent and acuteness, or by other motives of a similar description, to assert the all-sufficiency of human reason, and to deny the necessity of a revelation. Hence many good and pious Christians have run into the opposite extreme, and been disposed to regard all who have recourse to reason and the light of nature in the investigation of religious truth as little better than infidels, puffed up with a presumptuous conceit of their own knowledge, and sitting in judgment on the fitness of the divine procedure. Yet what just ground is there for these heavy accusations? Is not reason the gift of God? Does not the light of nature emanate from the author of nature? from Him who is the fountain of light? In what then consists the presumption of endeavouring to trace the divine character and operations by means of that light which God has Himself supplied? The knowledge of divine things which we acquire by the proper exercise of our various faculties on the phenomena of the visible world, is as strictly the gift of God as that which we derive from the perusal of His revealed Word.

Warburton, in the second and third chapters of the third book of the *Doctrine of Grace*, has pointed out with his usual acuteness the causes in which the existing disposition to undervalue and condemn the argument *à posteriori* originated. In their endeavours to defend our holy religion, divines, instead of taking their stand upon the firm basis of truth, have been too apt to shift their ground, and think opinions right in proportion as they were further removed from those of the adversary with whom they were immediately contending. Hence they have continually run into extremes; sometimes exalting human reason above all due bounds, at other times as unjustly depreciating it. In the seventeenth century fanaticism was the error against which the clergy had principally to contend; and in order to place themselves at the greatest possible distance from it, they took every opportunity of launching forth into the praises of human reason, and asserting its sufficiency to the discovery of divine truth, till the gospel at length came to be spoken of as a mere republication of the religion of nature. The infidel was not slow in availing himself of the advantage which such unguarded expressions afforded him, and began to deny the necessity of revelation, under the pretence that natural religion was sufficient for every purpose. Our divines again took the alarm, and, instead of endeavouring to mark out the precise bounds of reason and revelation, saw no better mode of extricating themselves from the difficulty than by running into the opposite extreme, and decrying natural religion with as much vehemence as their predecessors had extolled it.—To return to Tertullian.

We have seen his opinion respecting the testimony borne by the soul of man to the unity and attributes of God, and to a future state. Let us now examine his sentiments respecting the soul itself, which are detailed in the treatise *de Animâ*.[1] After the body of flesh of Adam[2] had been formed out of the dust of the earth,[3] God breathed into his nostrils the breath of life,[4] and man became a living soul. Man, therefore, is composed of two parts, σάρξ and ψυχὴ, Caro and Anima,[5] flesh and soul; and the term soul, according to Tertullian, includes both the vital and intellectual principles, the latter of which was afterwards distinguished by the name νοῦς, Animus or Mens. He describes νοῦς,[6] or Animus, as coexistent and consubstantial with the soul,

1 We have seen that our author wrote a distinct treatise on the origin of the soul, *de Censu Animæ*, against Hermogenes, who contended that it was formed out of matter. Chap. i. p. 32.

2 C. 3. See, concerning the creation of man, *de Resurrectione Carnis*, cc. 5, 7.

3 Tertullian supposes the earth, out of which man was made, to have been in a humid state, having been lately covered with water. *De Baptismo*, c. 3; *adv. Valentinianos*, c. 24; *adv. Hermogenem*, c. 29. "Qui tunc de *limo* formari habebat." *Adv. Praxeam*, c. 12. "De limo caro in Adam." *De Animâ*, c. 27. For a definition of the body see *de Resurrectione Carnis*, c. 35.

4 This breath Tertullian sometimes calls the substance of God. "A rationali scilicet artifice non tantum factus (homo), sed etiam ex substantiâ ipsius animatus." *Adv. Praxeam*, c. 5. Compare *adv. Marc.* l. ii. cc. 5, 6. "Quoquo tamen, inquis, modo substantia Creatoris delicti capax invenitur, quum afflatus Dei, id est, anima, in homine deliquit," c. 9. The objection here stated was urged not only by the Marcionites, but also by Hermogenes. See *de Animâ*, c. 11.

5 Tertullian sometimes uses the word Spiritus to designate the soul. See *de Baptismo*, cc. 4, 5; *de Pœnitentiâ*, c. 3. "Siquidem et caro et Spiritus Dei res; alia manu ejus expressa; alia afflatu ejus consummata." *De Spectaculis*, c. 2. "Et tamen et corpore et spiritu desciit a suo institutore." In another passage in the same tract, c. 13, Spiritus and Anima are joined together, and appear to be synonymous, unless the former means the breath. "Quæ non intestinis transiguntur, sed in ipso Spiritu et Animâ digeruntur." See also c. 17, *sub fine*, and *de Animâ*, cc. 10, 11. But generally Tertullian uses the word Spiritus to designate the Holy Spirit, the communication of whose influence constitutes the spiritual man, πνευματικὸς, in contradistinction to the animal man, ψυχικὸς. "Qui non tantum animæ erant, verum et spiritûs," c. 26. In c. 41 we find the spirit clearly distinguished from the soul. "Sequitur animam nubentem Spiritui caro, ut dotale mancipium, et jam non animæ famula, sed Spiritûs." Using the word Spiritus in this sense, he calls the soul suffectura Spiritûs ("Quia suffectura est quodammodo Spiritûs Anima," *adv. Marc.* l. i. c. 28), the substance on which the Spirit acts, or its instrument; and in the tract *de Resurrectione Carnis*, c. 40, he says that the inward man is renewed per suggestum Spiritûs. See also *de Monogamiâ*, c. 1.

6 "Proinde et animum, sive mens est, νοῦς apud Græcos, non aliud quid intelligimus, quam suggestum animæ ingenitum et insitum et nativitus proprium, quo agit, quo sapit, quem secum habens ex semetipsâ se commoveat in semetipsâ," c. 12. Again, in the same chapter, near the end: "Nos autem animum

yet distinct from it, as a minister or deputy is from his principal; being the instrument by which the soul acts, apprehends, moves. For that the pre-eminence, principalitas, is in the soul, Anima, not in the mind, Animus, is evident from the language of common life. We say that a rich man feeds so many souls, not so many minds; that a dying man breathes out his soul, not his mind; that Christ came to save the souls, not the minds of men.[1]

"The Scriptures then," Tertullian proceeds, "prove, in opposition to Plato, that the soul has a beginning. They prove also, in opposition to the same philosopher, that the soul is corporeal."[2] On this last point great difference of opinion existed; some philosophers maintaining, with Cleanthes, that as there could be no mutual action of things corporeal and things incorporeal upon each other, and as the soul and body certainly do act upon each other, the soul must be corporeal.[3] Plato, on the contrary, contended that every body must be either animale, animated by a soul, in which case it will be set in motion by some internal action; or inanimale, not animated by a soul, in which case it will be set in motion by some external action; but the soul falls under neither of these classes, being that which sets the body in motion.[4] To this Tertullian replies that undoubtedly the soul can neither be called animale nor inanimale; still it is a body, though sui generis. It is itself set in motion by external action, when, for instance, it is under the influence of prophetic inspiration; and it sets bodies in motion, which it could not do if it were not a body. Plato further argued that the modes in which we arrive at the knowledge of the qualities of things corporeal

ita dicimus animæ concretum, non ut substantiâ alium, sed ut substantiæ officium." Again, in c. 18: "Putabis quidem abesse animum ab animâ, siquando animo ita afficimur, ut nesciamus nos vidîsse quid vel audîsse, quia alibi fuerit animus: adeo contendam, immo ipsam animam nec vidîsse, nec audîsse, quia alibi fuerit cum suâ vi, id est, animo." *De Resurrectione Carnis*, c. 40. "Porro Apostolus interiorem hominem non tam animam, quam mentem atque animum intelligi mavult, id est, non substantiam ipsam, sed substantiæ saporem."

[1] C. 13. [2] C. 4.

[3] C. 5. Tertullian also ascribes a body to the Spirit. "Licet enim et animæ corpus sit aliquod, suæ qualitatis, sicut et spiritûs. *Adv. Marc.* l. v. c. 15. See also c. 10. "Et si habet aliquod proprium corpus anima vel spiritus, ut possit videri corpus animale animam significare, et corpus spiritale spiritum;" and *adv. Praxeam*, c. 7. "Quis enim negabit Deum corpus esse, etsi Deus spiritus est? Spiritus enim corpus sui generis in suâ effigie." He remarks in general, "Omne, quod est, corpus est sui generis; nihil est incorporale, nisi quod non est." *De Carne Christi*, c. 11. "Nisi fallor enim, omnis res aut corporalis aut incorporalis sit necesse est; ut concedam interim esse aliquid incorporale de substantiis duntaxat, quum ipsa substantia corpus sit rei cujusque." *Adv. Hermogenem*, c. 35.

[4] C. 6.

and things incorporeal, are perfectly distinct. The knowledge of the former is obtained through the bodily senses—sight, touch, etc.; of the latter, of benevolence for instance, or malevolence, through the intellectual senses: the soul therefore is incorporeal. Tertullian denies the correctness of this distinction, and contends, on the contrary, that as the soul is advertised of the existence of things incorporeal, of sounds, colours, smells, through the medium of the corporeal senses, the fair inference rather is that the soul is corporeal. "Still, it must be allowed that the soul and body have each its peculiar sustenance; the latter is supported by meat and drink; the former by wisdom and learning." Here Tertullian appeals to medical authority,[1] and contends that corporeal aliment is necessary also to the well-being of the soul, which would sink without it. Study does not feed, it only adorns the soul; not to mention, he adds, that the Stoics affirmed the arts and sciences to be corporeal. His last argument is drawn from the Scriptures, which speak of the torments endured by the soul of the rich man when in a state of separation from the body—in that intermediate state in which the soul remains until the general resurrection.[2] But if the soul can suffer, it must be corporeal; were it not corporeal, it would not have that whereby it could suffer. Nor let it be argued that the soul is incorporeal because it is invisible; all bodies have not the same properties; that of invisibility is peculiar to the soul.[3] But though invisible to the eye of sense, it is visible to the eye of the spirit; for St. John, when in the Spirit, beheld the souls of the martyrs.[4] The specimens already produced will give the reader a sufficiently accurate idea of the arguments by which the parties in this dispute supported their respective opinions; we will therefore proceed at once to state Tertullian's conclusion. He ascribes to the soul[5] a peculiar character or constitution, boundary, length, breadth, height, and figure.[6] This conclusion he confirms by the testimony of a Christian female who was favoured with a vision, in which the soul was exhibited to her in a corporeal shape and appeared a spirit; not, however, an empty illusion, but capable of being grasped by the hand, soft and transparent, and of an

[1] Soranus, the physician whom Tertullian quotes by name, appears to have been a materialist, and to have maintained the mortality of the soul.

[2] C. 7. Compare *de Resurrectione Carnis*, c. 17. There is, however, some variation in Tertullian's language on this subject. In the *Apology*, c. 48, he speaks as if the soul could not suffer when separated from the body: "Ideoque repræsentabuntur et corpora, quia neque pati quicquam potest anima sola sine stabili materiâ, id est, carne." See also *de Testimonio Animæ*, c. 4.

[3] C. 8.

[4] Apoc. vi. 9.

[5] C. 9.

[6] The Latin word is "habitum."

ethereal colour, and in form agreeing exactly with the human form. For when God breathed into Adam the breath of life, that breath, being diffused through every part and member of his body, produced an interior man corresponding in all respects to the exterior.

Having shown that the soul is corporeal, our author proceeds to maintain that it is simple and uncompounded; in opposition to certain philosophers who distinguished between the soul and the spirit, *anima* and *spiritus*, and made the latter a different substance from the former; the soul being, according to them, the vital principle, the principle by which men live—the spirit that by which they breathe.[1] Anatomists, they said, inform us that moths, and ants, and gnats have no organs of respiration; they have the vital without the breathing principle; those principles are consequently distinct. But Tertullian will not allow that we can thus reason from an insect to a human being.[2] In the nature of man, life and breath are inseparable. The distinction, therefore, between *anima* and *spiritus* is only a distinction of words, similar to that between *lux* and *dies*, the light and the day. The spirit or breath is an act or operation of the soul: the soul breathes. We must not, however, be led astray by the mere sound of words, and confound the spirit, which from the very birth of man is inseparably united to his soul, with the Spirit of God and the spirit of the devil, which, though they act upon the soul, are extraneous to it.[3]

The simplicity of the soul necessarily implies that it is indivisible.[4] When, therefore, the philosophers talk of the parts of the soul, they speak inaccurately: they should say powers, or faculties, or operations, as of moving, acting, thinking, seeing, hearing, etc. Because different parts of the body are, as it were, allotted to the different senses, we must not suppose

[1] Cc. 10, 11.

[2] In c. 19, Tertullian distinguishes between the vital principle in man and in all other created things. "Denique arbores vivere, nec tamen sapere, secundum Aristotelem, et si quis alius substantiam animalem in universa communicat, quæ apud nos in homine privata res est, non modo ut Dei opus quod et cætera, sed ut Dei flatus quod hæc sola, quam dicimus cum omni instructu suo nasci."

[3] "Erunt enim et aliæ Spiritûs species, ut ex Deo, ut ex diabolo," c. 10. Compare c. 18. "Ob hæc ergo præstruximus neque animum aliud quid esse, quam animæ suggestum et structum: neque spiritum extraneum quid quam quod et ipsa per flatum. Cæterum accessioni deputandum, quod aut Deus postea, aut Diabolus adspiraret."

[4] C. 14.

that the case is the same with the soul: on the contrary, the soul pervades the whole frame; as in the hydraulic organ of Archimedes one breath pervades the whole machine, and produces a variety of sounds. With respect to the seat of the soul, the part of the body in which the principle of vitality and sensation peculiarly resides, τὸ ἡγεμονικὸν, *principale*, Tertullian places it in the heart; grounding his opinion upon those passages of Scripture in which man is said to think, to believe, to sin, etc. with the heart.[1]

While, however, Tertullian denies that the soul is divisible into parts, he admits Plato's distinction respecting its rational and irrational qualities, though he explains the distinction in a different manner.[2] The soul of Adam, as created by God and in its original and natural state, was rational. The irrational qualities were infused by the devil, when he seduced our first parents into transgression. Plato applied the terms θυμικὸν and ἐπιθυμητικὸν to the irrational qualities of the soul; but, says Tertullian, there is a rational as well as irrational indignation and desire; indignation at sin, and desire of good.

The credit due to the testimony of the senses[3] was a question on which great diversity of opinion existed among the philosophers.[4] The Platonists contended that no credit can be given to them, because in many instances their testimony is at variance with fact. Thus a straight oar immersed in the water appears bent—a parallel row of trees appears to converge to a point—the sky in the horizon appears to be united to the sea. The state of natural philosophy in Tertullian's days did not enable him to give a correct explanation of these appearances, yet he seems to reason correctly when he says that, as causes can be assigned why the appearances should be such as they are, they constitute no ground for rejecting the testimony of the senses. To persons suffering from a redundancy of gall, all things taste bitter; but the true conclusion is that the body is diseased, not that the sense of taste is fallacious. Tertullian,

1 Compare *de Res. Carnis*, c. 15. The ancient anatomists appear to have instituted experiments for the purpose of ascertaining the seat of the soul, by removing those parts of the body in which it has been usually supposed to reside. Their conclusion was that nothing certain could be pronounced upon the subject; since, choose what part you will as the seat of the soul, animals or insects may be found in which the vital principle remains after that part is removed.

2 C. 16.

3 C. 17.

4 In the tract *de Coronâ*, c. 5, Tertullian calls the senses the instruments of the soul, by which it sees, hears, etc. Compare the first *Tusculan*, c. 20, or 46.

however, does not rely solely upon reasoning: he points out the fatal consequences to the gospel which will follow from admitting the notion of the Platonists. If we cannot trust to the testimony of the senses, what grounds have we for believing that Christ either lived, or wrought miracles, or died, or rose again?

Closely connected with this notion respecting the fallacy of the senses[1] was the notion that the soul, so long as it is united to the body, cannot attain to the *knowledge* of the truth;[2] but must be involved in the maze of *opinion* and error. The business, therefore, of the wise man is to abstract the mind from the senses, and to raise it to the contemplation of those invisible, incorporeal, divine, eternal ideas which are the patterns of the visible objects around us. Doubtless, answers Tertullian, the distinction between things corporeal and things spiritual, things visible and things invisible, is just; and the soul arrives at the knowledge of them through different channels, being conversant with the one by means of the senses, with the other by means of the mind or intellect. But the knowledge obtained through the latter source is not more certain than that obtained through the former.

In opposition[3] to those who affirmed that the soul of the infant was destitute of intellect,[4] which they supposed to be subsequently introduced, Tertullian contends that all the faculties of the soul are co-existent with it, though they are afterwards more or less perfectly developed in different individuals, according to the different circumstances of birth, health, education, condition of life.[5] But observing the great variety of intellectual and moral characters in the world, we are apt to conclude that it arises from some difference in the original constitution of the soul; whereas that is always the same, though it is afterwards modified by external circumstances. This remark is particularly directed against the Valentinian notion that different seeds —material, animal, or spiritual—are introduced into the souls of men after their birth;[6] whence arise the diversities of cha-

[1] C. 18.

[2] The distinction between *scientia* and *opinio* must be familiar to all who are acquainted with Cicero's philosophical writings.

[3] Cc. 19, 20, 21.

[4] In other words, that the infant possesses the vital, but not the intellectual principle.

[5] Compare cc. 24 and 38.

[6] Compare c. 11.

racter discernible among them. One necessary inference from this notion is that the character of the individual is immutably determined by the nature of the seed infused into his soul; whether good or bad, it must always remain so. Our author, on the contrary, argues that the character of God alone is immutable, because He alone is self-existent: the character of a created being must be liable to change, and will depend upon the use which he makes of the freedom of his will—a freedom which he derives from nature. Tertullian, however, was far from intending to assert the sufficiency of man to form within himself by the mere exercise of his free-will a holy temper and disposition; he expressly states that the freedom of the will is subject to the influence of divine grace.[1] The following may be taken as a correct representation of his meaning. The character of man is not irrevocably fixed, as the Valentinians affirm, by any qualities infused into his soul subsequently to his birth. The diversities of character observable in different individuals, and in the same individual at different times, must be referred to the operation of external circumstances, and to the different degrees in which divine grace influences the determinations of the will.

Tertullian now recapitulates all that he has said on the subject of the soul;[2] and affirms that it derives its origin from the breath of God—that it is immortal;[3] corporeal; that it has a figure; is simple in substance; possessing within itself the principle of intelligence; operating in different ways (or through different channels); endued with free-will; affected by external circumstances, and thus producing that infinite variety of talent and disposition observable among mankind; rational; designed to rule the whole man; possessing an insight into futurity.[4] Moreover, the souls of all the inhabitants of the earth are derived from one common source, the soul of Adam.

1 "Hæc erit vis divinæ gratiæ, potentior utique naturâ, habens in nobis subjacentem sibi liberam arbitrii potestatem, quod αὐτεξούσιον dicitur, quæ quum sit et ipsa naturalis atque mutabilis, quoquo vertitur, naturâ convertitur. Inesse autem nobis τὸ αὐτεξούσιον naturaliter, jam Marcioni ostendimus et Hermogeni," c. 21.

2 C. 22. "Definimus Animam, Dei flatu natam, immortalem, corporalem, effigiatam, substantiâ simplicem, de suo sapientem, variè procedentem, liberam arbitrii, accidentiis obnoxiam, per ingenia mutabilem, rationalem, dominatricem, divinatricem, ex unâ redundantem."

3 Immortal in its own nature. Compare *de Res. Carnis*, cc. 18, 34, 35.

4 Tertullian here speaks of a natural insight into futurity; not of the spirit of prophecy, which is derived from the grace of God. See cc. 24, 41.

This last point he proceeds to establish by first refuting Plato's notions respecting the origin and pre-existence of the soul.[1] According to him, Plato said that the souls of men are continually passing to and fro between heaven and earth; that they originally existed in heaven with God, and were there conversant with those eternal ideas of which the visible things below are only the images. Hence during their residence on earth they do not acquire any new knowledge, but merely recall to their recollection what they knew in heaven, and forgot in their passage from heaven to earth. Plato further argued that the heavenly powers, the progeny of God,[2] who were entrusted by Him with the creation of man, and received for that purpose an immortal soul, froze around it a mortal body.[3] In refuting these notions, Tertullian argues principally upon the inconsistency of Plato, who, at the same time that he makes the soul self-existent, and places it almost on an equality with the Deity, yet supposes it capable of forgetting what passed in a previous state.[4] He alludes also to another philosophical notion that the soul is introduced into the fœtus after its birth, being inhaled as it were when the infant first draws breath, and exhaled when man dies.[5] This notion he conceives to be sufficiently refuted by the experience of every pregnant woman.[6] His own opinion is, that the soul and body are conceived together; the womb of the mother being impregnated at the same time by the respective seeds, which, though different in kind, are from the first inseparably united. I must omit the arguments by which he supports this opinion. They are of such a nature that he feels himself obliged to apologise for them by saying that, as the business of a controversialist is to establish his point, he is sometimes under the necessity of sacrificing modesty to truth. The conclusion is, that when God formed Adam out of the dust of the earth, and breathed into his nostrils the breath of life, the seeds of the body and soul were inseparably united together in him, and have been derived, in the same state of union, from him to his posterity. Thus Tertullian establishes his position that the souls of all

[1] C. 23.

[2] "Genimina Dei.

[3] "Mortale ei circumgelaverint corpus."

[4] C. 24.

[5] C. 25. "Perinde animam, extraneam alias et extorrem uteri, primâ aspiratione nascentis infantis adduci, sicut exspiratione novissimâ educi."

[6] "Respondete matres, vosque prægnantes, vosque puerperæ; steriles et masculi taceant; vestræ naturæ veritas quæritur, vestræ passionis fides convenitur, an aliquam in fœtu sentiatis vivacitatem alienam de vestro? de quo palpitent ilia, micent latera, tota ventris ambitio pulsetur, ubique ponderis regio mutetur?" etc.

mankind are derived from one common source, the soul of Adam.

Quitting Plato,[1] Tertullian now passes to the Pythagorean doctrine of the metempsychosis. I will mention one of his arguments against this doctrine, on account of the information which it supplies respecting the height to which cultivation and civilization were then carried. "If the doctrine of the metempsychosis," he says, "is true, the numbers of mankind must always remain the same; there can be no increase of population; whereas we know the fact to be otherwise. So great is the increase that, although we are continually sending out colonies, and penetrating into new regions, we cannot dispose of the excess. Every country is now accessible to the traveller and the merchant. Pleasant farms now smile where formerly were dreary and dangerous wastes—cultivated fields now occupy the place of forests—flocks and herds have expelled the wild beasts—sands are sown—rocks are planted—marshes are drained—and where once was a single cottage is now a populous city. We no longer speak with horror of the savage interior of the islands, or of the dangers of their rocky coasts; everywhere are houses, and inhabitants, and government, and civilized life. Still our population continually increases, and occasions fresh grounds of complaint; our numbers are burthensome to the world, which cannot furnish us with the means of subsistence. Such is our state that we no longer look upon pestilence, and famine, and wars, and earthquakes as positive evils, but as remedies provided by Providence against a greater calamity—as the only means of pruning the redundant luxuriance of the human race."[2] Professor Malthus himself could not have lamented more feelingly the miseries resulting from an excess of population, or have pointed out with greater acuteness the natural checks to that excess.

I shall omit Tertullian's[3] other arguments against the doctrine of the metempsychosis, as well as his observations respecting the difference of the sexes in the human species;[4] the state of the fœtus in the womb;[5] the growth of the soul to maturity;[6] and the corruption of human nature.[7] To his remarks, however, on

[1] C. 28.
[2] C. 30.
[3] He occupies eight chapters, from c. 28 to c. 36, in the discussion of this doctrine, and in proving that Simon Magus and Carpocrates founded some of their heretical notions upon it.
[4] C. 36.
[5] C. 37.
[6] C. 38.
[7] Cc. 39, 40, 41.

the last of these topics I shall hereafter have occasion to refer. The next subject of which he treats is sleep.[1] Having stated the opinions of the different philosophers, he prefers that of the Stoics, who defined sleep—a temporary suspension of the activity of the senses.[2] Sleep he conceives to be necessary only to the body; the soul, being immortal, neither requires nor even admits a state of rest.[3] In sleep, therefore, when the body is at rest, the soul, which never rests, being unable to use the members of the body, uses its own, and the dreamer seems to go through all the operations necessary to the performance of certain acts, though nothing is performed.[4] Tertullian[5] admits that there are well-authenticated accounts of persons who never dreamed in the course of their lives. Suetonius[6] says that this was the case with Nero; and Theopompus,[7] with Thrasymedes. Our author mentions also the story of Hermotimus;[8] of whom it was recorded that, when he slept, his soul entirely abandoned and wandered away from his body. In this state (his wife having revealed the secret) his body was seized by his enemies, who burned it, and his soul, returning too late, found itself deprived of its habitation. Tertullian does not attempt to reconcile these phenomena with his theory of the perpetual activity of the soul, but says that we must receive any solution of them rather than admit that the soul can be separated from the body except by death; or that the soul can sink into a state of absolute rest, which would imply its mortality.[9] We have seen that Tertullian applies the word ecstasies—which he interprets "Excessus sensûs amentiæ instar"[10]—to the state of the prophet's mind when under the influence of inspiration. He applies the same term to the state of the soul when dreaming, and evidently supposes that the knowledge of future events was frequently communicated to it in dreams.[11] Some dreams,[12] he adds, proceed from God;

[1] Cc. 42, 43.

[2] "Resolutionem sensualis vigoris."

[3] Compare *de Res. Carnis*, c. 18. "Arctius dicam, ne in somnum quidem cadit Anima cum corpore, ne tum quidem sternitur cum carne. Etenim agitatur in somnis et jactitatur; quiesceret autem si jacaret."

[4] C. 45. We have seen in what sense Tertullian ascribes members to the soul.

[5] C. 44.

[6] In *Nerone*, c. 46.

[7] See Plutarch, *de defectu Oraculorum*, c. 50.

[8] See Pliny, *Hist. Nat.* l. vii. c. 52. Plutarch, *de Dæmonio Socratis*, c. 22, calls him Hermodorus.

[9] He says that the effect of fasting upon himself was, not to make him sleep without dreaming (such an admission would have been fatal to his theory), but to make him so dream that he was not conscious of having dreamed. "Jejuniis autem nescio an ego solus plurimum ita somniem, ut me somniâsse non sentiam," c. 48—a subtle distinction.

[10] C. 45.

[11] C. 46.

[12] C. 47.

others from demons; others are suggested by intense application of the mind to a particular subject; others again are so utterly wild and extravagant that they can scarcely be related, much less accounted for or interpreted. These last are to be ascribed peculiarly to the ecstatic influence.

From sleep, the image of death, Tertullian passes to death itself, which he defines the separation of the soul from the body.[1] "When we say," he continues, "that death is natural to man, we speak with reference not to his original nature as given him by his Maker, but to his actual nature as polluted by sin. Had Adam continued in his state of innocence, this separation of the soul from the body would never have taken place. Sin introduced death, which even in its mildest form is a violence done to our nature; for how can the intimate union between the body and soul be dissolved without violence?"[2] After this separation from the body, the souls of the mass of mankind descend to the parts below the earth, there to remain until the day of judgment.[3] The souls of the martyrs alone pass not through this middle state, but are transferred immediately to heaven.

Tertullian proceeds to inquire whether the soul, after it has once passed into the lower parts of the earth, can leave them and revisit these upper regions.[4] This question he determines in the negative, arguing principally from the parable of the rich man and Lazarus. But the demons who are continually labouring to seduce us into error, though they cannot call up the soul after death, yet can practise illusions upon the senses; and by presenting themselves under human forms, persuade men that they are the ghosts of persons deceased. Thus Saul was persuaded that he saw and conversed with Samuel. In like manner, Tertullian refers to the agency of demons the deceptions practised by the dealers in magic who generally affected to call up the spirits of such persons as had come to an untimely end; taking advantage of the popular superstition that the souls of men, cut off by a violent death, hover about the earth until the period has elapsed to which, had they not been so cut off, their lives would have been extended.

But in what state, it may be asked, does the soul remain during its abode in the lower parts of the earth?[5] Does it sleep?

[1] Cc. 50, 51. [2] C. 52. [3] C. 55. [4] Cc. 56, 57.
[5] C. 58. Compare *de Res. Carnis*, c. 17, and the 40th of King Edward's

"We have seen," answers Tertullian, "that sleep is an affection of the body, not of the soul. When united to the body, the soul does not sleep; much less when separate from the body. No: the righteous judgments of God begin to take effect in this intermediate state. The souls of the good receive a foretaste of the happiness, and the souls of the wicked of the misery, which will be assigned them as their everlasting portion at the day of final retribution."

Such are Tertullian's speculations upon the origin, nature, and destiny of the soul. Should the examination of them have appeared somewhat minute and tedious, it must be remembered that the only mode of putting the reader in possession of the state of philosophy in any age is to exhibit to him the questions which formed the subjects of discussion, and the manner in which they were discussed. The result of the examination must, we think, be deemed favourable to our author's character for talent and ingenuity. Many of the questions proposed may appear trifling—many of his arguments weak and inconclusive; the questions, however, are not more trifling, or the arguments more inconclusive, than those which occur in the writings of the most celebrated philosophers of antiquity. It would be the extreme of absurdity to compare the writings of Plato and Tertullian as compositions; but if they are considered as specimens of philosophical investigation, of reasoning and argument, he who professes to admire Plato will hardly escape the charge of inconsistency if he thinks meanly or speaks contemptuously of Tertullian.

In further illustration of our author's philosophical opinions, we shall proceed briefly to state his notions respecting the nature of angels and demons. He asserts, in the first place, that there are spiritual substances, or material spirits—this is not denied even by the philosophers.[1] These spiritual or angelic substances

Articles." "Qui animas defunctorum prædicant usque ad diem judicii absque omni sensu dormire, aut illas asserunt unâ cum corporibus mori, et extremo die cum illis excitandas, ab Orthodoxâ Fide, quæ nobis in Sacris Literis traditur, prorsus dissentiunt."

[1] *Apology*, c. 22. "Atque adeo dicimus esse *substantias* quasdam *Spiritales*; nec nomen novum est. Sciunt dæmones Philosophi, Socrate ipso ad dæmonii arbitrium expectante . . . dæmones sciunt Poetæ; et jam vulgus indoctum in usum maledicti frequentat . . . Angelos quoque etiam Plato non negavit." See also *adv. Marcionem*, l. ii. c. 8. "Sed adflatus Dei generosior *Spiritu Materiali*, quo Angeli constiterunt." *Apology*, c. 46. "Quum secundum Deos Philosophi Dæmones deputent." *De Animâ*, c. 1.

were originally created to be the ministers of the Divine will, but some were betrayed into transgression.[1] Smitten with the beauty of the daughters of men, they descended from heaven,[2] and imparted many branches of knowledge, revealed to themselves, but hitherto hidden from mankind—the properties of metals, the virtues of herbs, the powers of enchantment, and the arts of divination and astrology.[3] Out of complaisance also to their earthly brides, they communicated the arts which administer to female vanity—of polishing and setting precious stones, of dyeing wool, of preparing cosmetics.

From these corrupt angels sprang demons, a still more corrupt race of spirits, whose actuating principle is hostility against man, and whose sole object is to accomplish his destruction.[4] This they attempt in various ways, but as they are invisible to the eye, their mischievous activity is known only by its effects. They nip the fruit in the bud; they blight the corn; and, as through the tenuity and subtlety of their substance, they can operate on the soul as well as the body; while they inflict diseases on the one, they agitate the other with furious passions and ungovernable lust. By the same property of their substance they cause men to dream.[5] But their favourite employment is to draw men off from the worship of the true God to idolatry.[6] For this purpose they lurk within the statues of deceased mortals;[7] practising illusions upon weak minds, and seducing them into a belief in the divinity of an idol.[8] In their attempts to deceive mankind, they derive great assistance from the rapidity with which they transport themselves from one part of the globe to another.[9] They are thus enabled to know and to declare

[1] "Nos officia divina Angelos credimus." *De Animâ*, c. 37; *Apology*, c. 22; *de Idololatriâ*, c. 4.

[2] In proof of the alleged intercourse between the angels and the daughters of men, Tertullian appeals to Genesis vi. 2, *de Virgin. vel.* c. 7, and to the apocryphal book of Enoch. *De Cultu Fœminarum*, l. i. c. 3.

[3] *De Cultu Fœminarum*, l. i. c. 2; l. ii. cc. 4, 10. *De Idololatriâ*, c. 9. *Apology*, c. 35.

[4] *Apology*, c. 22. Compare *de Spectaculis*, c. 2.

[5] *De Animâ*, cc. 47, 49. *Apology*, c. 23.

[6] *Apology*, cc. 23, 27. Compare *de Idololatriâ*, cc. 3, 4, 15.

[7] *De Spectaculis*, cc. 10, 12, 13, 23, where Tertullian ascribes the invention of the games and scenic exhibitions to the demons.

[8] The illusions practised by the professors of magic were, according to our author, peculiarly the work of demons; when, for instance, the object of the incantation was to raise a dead man from the grave, a demon presented himself under the figure of the deceased. *De Animâ*, c. 57, where the miracles performed by Pharaoh's magicians are mentioned. See p. 51.

[9] *Apology*, c. 22.

what is passing in the most distant countries, so that they gain the credit of being the authors of events of which they are only the reporters. It was this peculiarity in the nature of demons which enabled them to communicate to the Pythian priestess what Crœsus was at that very moment doing in Lydia. In like manner, as they are continually passing to and fro through the region of the air, they can foretell the changes of the weather, and thus procure for the idol the reputation of possessing an insight into futurity. When by their delusions they have induced men to offer sacrifice, they hover about the victim, snuffing up with delight the savoury steam, which is their proper food.[1] The demons employed other artifices in order to effect the destruction of man. As during their abode in heaven they were enabled to obtain some insight into the nature of the divine dispensations, they endeavoured to preoccupy the minds of men, and to prevent them from embracing Christianity, by inventing fables bearing some resemblance to the truths which were to become the objects of faith under the gospel.[2] Thus they invented the tales of the tribunal of Minos and Rhadamanthus in the infernal regions; of the river Pyriphlegethon, and the Elysian Fields, in order that when the doctrines of a future judgment, and of the eternal happiness and misery prepared for the good and wicked in another life, should be revealed, the common people might think the former equally credible, the philosopher equally incredible with the latter.

As the purpose for which the angels were created was to execute the commands of God,[3] they who retain their original purity still occupy themselves in observing the course of human affairs, and fulfilling the duties allotted them;[4]—thus, one angel

[1] "Hæc enim dæmoniorum pabula sunt." *Ad Scapulam*, c. 2.

[2] *Apology*, c. 22. "Dispositiones etiam Dei, et *tunc Prophetis concionantibus* exceperunt et *nunc lectionibus resonantibus* carpunt." C. 21. "Sciebant qui penes vos *fabulas* ad destructionem veritatis istius *æmulas* præministraverunt." C. 47. "Omnia adversus veritatem de ipsâ veritate constructa sunt, operantibus æmulationem istam Spiritibus erroris. Ab his adulteria hujusmodi salutaris disciplinæ subornata; ab his quædam etiam fabulæ immissæ, quæ de similitudine fidem infirmarent veritatis, vel eam sibi potius evincerent: ut quis ideo non putet Christianis credendum, quia nec Poetis nec Philosophis: vel ideo magis Poetis et Philosophis existimet credendum, quia non Christianis," etc. See also *de Præscriptione Hæreticorum*, c. 40, and some very fanciful instances in the tract *de Spectaculis*, c. 23.

[3] See note 1, p. 107. The word angel, as Tertullian remarks, is descriptive, not of a nature, but an office. "Angelus, id est, nuntius; officii, non naturæ vocabulo." *De Carne Christi*, c. 14.

[4] *De Spectaculis*, c. 27. "Dubitas enim illo momento, quo in Diaboli Ecclesiâ fueris, omnes Angelos prospicere de cœlo, et singulos denotare, etc.?"

is especially appointed to preside over prayer;[1] another over baptism;[2] another to watch over men in their dying moments, and as it were to call away their souls;[3] another to execute the righteous judgments of God upon wicked men.[4] Tertullian states also, on the authority of Scripture, that it is a part of their office to appear occasionally to men; in which case, according to him, they assume not only the human form but the human body itself, by a peculiar privilege of their nature, which enables them to create it out of nothing.[5] It is worthy of observation that Tertullian, while he assigns to each angel a particular office or department—as prayer, baptism—uses a different language with respect to demons, assigning to each individual his attendant demon;[6] thus he accounts for the story of the Dæmon of Socrates.[7]

I will conclude this chapter by a few remarks on Gibbon's representation of the opinions entertained by the primitive Christians respecting demons. "It was," he says, "the universal sentiment both of the Church and of heretics, that the demons were the authors, the patrons, and the objects of idolatry."[8] That Tertullian ascribed to them the two former characters is manifest from the foregoing statement of his opinions. They were the authors of idolatry, because every evil deed, every evil thought of man is the result of their corrupt suggestions; and it was consequently by their instigation that he was first drawn aside from his allegiance to the one true God, and induced to offer his adorations to the creature instead of the Creator. They were the patrons, because they promoted its cause by practising illusions upon the senses of mankind, and thus confirming their belief in the divinity of the idol. But they were not, at least in Tertullian's estimation, the objects. He

[1] "Angelo adhuc Orationis astante." *De Oratione*, c. 12.

[2] "Angelus Baptismi Arbiter." *De Baptismo*, c. 6.

[3] "De ipsius statim Angeli facie, Evocatoris animarum, Mercurii Poetarum." *De Animâ*, c. 53, *sub fine.*

[4] "Et judex te tradat Angelo Executionis, et ille te in carcerem mandet infernum." *De Animâ*, c. 35.

[5] *Adv. Marcionem*, l. iii. c. 9. *De Carne Christi*, cc. 3, 6. "Igitur quum relatum non sit unde sumpserint carnem, relinquitur intellectui nostro non dubitare, hoc esse proprium Angelicæ potestatis ex nullâ materiâ corpus sibi sumere."

[6] "Nam et suggessimus nullum pene hominem carere dæmonio." *De Animâ*, c. 57.

[7] *Apology*, c. 46. "Sane Socrates facilius diverso Spiritu agebatur; si quidem aiunt dæmonium illi a puero adhæsisse, pessimum revera pædagogum." *De Animâ*, c. 1. See also cc. 25, 39.

[8] Chap. xv. p. 463, ed. 4to.

expressly says that the objects of idolatry were dead men, who were conceived to be gods, on account of some useful invention by which they had contributed to the comfort and well-being of man in his present life.[1] The demons were content to lead man into error, and to feed upon the savoury steam arising from the sacrifices, without attempting to propose themselves as the immediate objects of worship.[2]

---

## CHAPTER IV.

### ON THE GOVERNMENT OF THE CHURCH.

FOLLOWING Mosheim's arrangement, we now proceed to inquire what information can be derived from the writings of Tertullian respecting the government and discipline of the Church in his day. The edict of Trajan,[3] already alluded to, proves the extreme jealousy with which all associations were regarded by the Roman Emperors. We cannot, therefore, be surprised that the intimate union which subsisted between the professors of Christianity rendered them objects of suspicion and distrust. One point at which Tertullian aims in his *Apology* is to convince the governors whom he is addressing of the injustice of their suspicions, by explaining the nature and purposes of the Christian assemblies. "We form,"[4] he says, "a body, being joined together by a community of religion, of discipline, and of hope. In our assemblies we meet to offer up our united supplications to God, to read the Scriptures, to deliver exhortations, to pronounce censures, cutting off from communion in prayer and in every holy exercise those who have been guilty of any flagrant

[1] "Quando etiam error orbis propterea Deos præsumpserit, quos homines interdum confitetur, quoniam aliquid ab unoquoque prospectum videtur utilitatibus et commodis vitæ." *Adv. Marcionem*, l. i. c. 11. See also the *Apology*, cc. 10, 11; *de Idololatriâ*, c. 15.

[2] See *de Coronâ*, c. 10, where Tertullian is exposing the absurdity of placing crowns on the heads of idols. "Sed vacat totum, et est ipsum quoque opus mortuum, quantum in idolis; vivum plane quantum in dæmoniis, ad quæ pertinet superstitio." To crown an idol, the ostensible object of worship, is useless, since it can have no enjoyment of the fragrance or beauty of the flowers. The demons alone (who lurk within the idols) profit by these superstitious practices.

[3] See chap. ii. p. 58, note 4.

[4] C. 39.

offence. The older members, men of tried piety and prudence, preside; having obtained the dignity, not by purchase, but by acknowledged merit. If any collection is made at our meetings, it is perfectly voluntary: each contributes according to his ability, either monthly or as often as he pleases. These contributions we regard as a sacred deposit; not to be spent in feasting and gluttony, but in maintaining or burying the poor, and relieving the distresses of the orphan, the aged, or the shipwrecked mariner. A portion is also appropriated to the use of those who are suffering in the cause of religion; who are condemned to the mines, or banished to the islands, or confined in prison."

In this brief account of the Christian assemblies, Tertullian appears to speak of the Presidentship as conferred solely in consideration of superior age and piety.[1] It has therefore been inferred either that the distinction between the clergy and the laity was not then generally acknowledged in the Church, or at least that its validity was not recognised by our author. Attempts have been made to support the latter inference by an appeal to other passages of his works, the full force of which can only be perceived by viewing them in connexion with the subjects of which he is treating.

We have already noticed,[2] and shall again have occasion to notice, Tertullian's sentiments respecting a second marriage. They who maintained its lawfulness alleged the passages[3] in the

[1] Tertullian's words are: "Præsident *probati quique Seniores*, honorem istum non pretio, sed testimonio adepti"—which Bingham translates, *The bishops and presbyters*, who preside over us, are advanced to that honour only by public testimony, l. iv. c. 3, sect. iv. He assigns no reason for thus translating the words *probati quique Seniores.* I am far from intending to say that the presidents were not bishops and presbyters; on the contrary, the following passage in the first tract *ad Uxorem*, c. 7, when compared with 1 Tim. iii. 2 and Titus i. 6, appears to limit the presidency to them:—"Quantum detrahant fidei, quantum obstrepant sanctitati nuptiæ secundæ, disciplina Ecclesiæ et præscriptio Apostoli declarat, quum digamos non sinit præsidere." Compare also *de Idololatriâ*, c. 7, with *de Coronâ*, c. 3; *de Jejuniis*, c. 17, with 1 Tim. v. 17. But Bingham ought surely to have explained why he affixed a sense to the words so foreign from their literal meaning; especially as in another place, l. ii. c. 19, sect. xix., he speaks of certain *seniores ecclesiæ* who were not of the clergy, yet had some concern in the care of the Church.

[2] Chap. i. p. 9.

[3] 1 Tim. iii. 2, 12; Titus i. 6. Bishops and priests who contracted a second marriage were sometimes degraded. "Usque adeo quosdam memini digamos loco dejectos." *De Exhort. Castit.* c. 7. Compare *de Monogamiâ*, c. 11. Our author, however, complains that there was great laxity of discipline on this point. "Quot enim et digami præsident apud vos, insultantes utique Apostolo?" *De Monogamiâ*, c. 12.

Epistles to Timothy and Titus, in which St. Paul enjoins that bishops, priests, and deacons shall be μιᾶς γυναικὸς ἄνδρες—that is, according to the interpretation generally received in Tertullian's time, men who had been only once married. They contended, therefore, that as this restriction applied only to the clergy, laymen were at liberty to contract a second marriage. To evade this inference, Tertullian has recourse to the following argument:[1]—"Do not," he says, "suppose that what is forbidden to the clergy is allowed to the laity. All Christians are priests, agreeably to the words of St. John in the Book of Revelation—'Christ has made us a kingdom and a priesthood to God and His Father.' The authority of the Church and its honour, which derives sanctity from the assembled clergy, has established the distinction between the clergy and laity. In places where there are no clergy, any single Christian may exercise the functions of the priesthood, may celebrate[2] the eucharist, and baptize. But where three, though laymen, are gathered together, there is a Church. Every one *lives by his own faith, nor is there respect of persons with God; since not the hearers, but the doers, of the law are justified by God*, according to the apostle. If, therefore, you possess within yourself the right of the priesthood to be exercised in cases of necessity, you ought also to conform

[1] *De Exhort. Cast.* c. 7, referred to in chap. i. p. 4, note 1. I now give the whole passage. "Vani erimus, si putaverimus, quod Sacerdotibus non liceat, Laicis licere. Nonne et Laici Sacerdotes sumus? Scriptum est, *Regnum quoque nos et Sacerdotes Deo et Patri suo fecit.* Differentiam inter Ordinem et Plebem constituit Ecclesiæ autoritas, et honor per Ordinas consessum sanctificatus." (There is an ambiguity in the latter clause of this sentence, which must be differently translated, according as *honor* is referred to *Ecclesiæ* or to *Differentia inter Ordinem et Plebem.* I have adopted the former sense, though by no means certain of its correctness. I conceive the allusion to be to the higher seats occupied by the clergy, apart from the laity, in the places of religious assembly. In the tract *de Fugâ in Persecutione*, c. 11, Tertullian makes a distinction between Christians *majoris et minoris loci;* apparently meaning the clergy by the former, and the laity by the latter. So in the tract *de Baptismo*, c. 17. "Sed quanto magis Laicis disciplina verecundiæ et modestiæ incumbit, quum ea *majoribus* competant.") "Adeo ubi Ecclesiastici Ordinis non est consessus, et offers, et tinguis, et sacerdos es tibi solus. Sed ubi tres, ecclesia est, licet laici; unusquisque enim *suâ fide vivit, nec est personarum acceptio apud Deum.* Quoniam non *auditores legis* justificabuntur à Deo, sed *factores,* secundum quod et Apostolus dicit. Igitur si habes jus sacerdotis in temetipso, ubi necesse est, habeas oportet etiam disciplinam sacerdotis, ubi necesse sit habere jus sacerdotis. Digamus tinguis? digamus offers? quanto magis Laico digamo capitale est agere pro sacerdote, qûum ipsi sacerdoti digamo facto auferatur agere sacerdotem? Sed necessitati, inquis, indulgetur. Nulla necessitas excusatur, quæ potest non esse. Noli denique digamus deprehendi, et non committis in necessitatem administrandi quod non licet digamo. Omnes nos Deus ita vult dispositos esse, ut ubique Sacramentis ejus obeundis apti simus." Bennet, in his *Rights of the Clergy*, etc., has bestowed a whole chapter on this passage.

[2] So the word *offers* must, I think, be translated in this passage.

yourself to the rule of life prescribed to those who engage in the priesthood, the rights of which you may be called to exercise. Do you, after contracting a second marriage, venture to baptize or to celebrate the eucharist? How much more heinous is it in a layman who has contracted a second marriage to exercise the functions of the priesthood, when a second marriage is deemed a sufficient ground for degrading a priest from his order? But you will plead the necessity of the case as an apology for the act. The plea is invalid, because you were not placed under the necessity of marrying a second time. Do not marry again, and you will not run the hazard of being obliged to do that which a digamist is not allowed to do. It is the will of God that we should at all times be in a fit state to administer His sacraments if an occasion should arise." We are very far from meaning to defend the soundness of Tertullian's argument in this passage. We quote it because it is one of the passages which have been brought forward to prove that *he* did not recognise the distinction between the clergy and the laity; whereas a directly opposite inference ought to be drawn. He limits the right of the laity to exercise the ministerial functions to extraordinary cases—to cases of necessity. Were they to assume it in ordinary cases, they would be guilty of an act of criminal presumption, as he indirectly asserts in the tract *de Monogamiâ*, where he pursues the very same train of reasoning in refutation of the same objection.[1] That he recognised the distinction between the clergy and laity is further proved by the fact that, among other accusations which he urges against the heretics, he states that they conferred orders without making strict inquiry into the qualifications of the candidates; and that they not only allowed but even enjoined the laity to assume the sacerdotal office and administer the ceremonies of religion.[2] In showing that the distinction was recognised by Tertullian, we have incidentally shown that it was generally recognised in the Church. This, indeed, is implied in the very words *clerus* and *ordo ecclesiasticus*, which frequently occur.

[1] "Sed quum *extollimur et inflamur adversus Clerum*, tunc unum omnes sumus: tunc omnes Sacerdotes, quia *Sacerdotes nos Deo et Patri fecit*; quum ad peræquationem disciplinæ sacerdotalis provocamur, deponimus infulas, et impares sumus." *De Monogamiâ*, c. 12. We may, however, infer from this passage that in Tertullian's day the validity of the distinction was occasionally questioned.

[2] "Ordinationes eorum temerariæ, leves, inconstantes. Nunc neophytos conlocant, nunc seculo obstrictos, nunc Apostatas nostros." *De Præscriptione Hæreticorum*, c. 41; and in the same chapter, "Nam et Laicis sacerdotalia munera injungunt." In the tract *de Idololatriâ*, c. 7, Tertullian complains that the artificers of idols were admitted into orders; "Adleguntur in Ordinem Ecclesiasticum Artifices Idolorum."

But what, it may be asked, is Tertullian's meaning when he says that the distinction between the clergy and the laity is established by the authority of the Church? Before we can answer this question we must ascertain what was his notion of the Church; and for this purpose we will turn to the tract *de Præscriptione Hæreticorum*, in which he takes a rapid survey of its origin and progress. "Christ," he says, "during His residence on earth, declared the purposes of His mission, and the rule of faith and practice, either publicly to the people or privately to the disciples, of whom He attached twelve more immediately to His person, intending that they should be the teachers of the Gentiles.[1] One of them betrayed Him; but the remaining eleven He commanded to go and instruct all nations, and to baptize them in the name of the Father, Son, and Holy Ghost. These eleven, having added to their number a twelfth, in the room of him who had been cut off, and having received the promised effusion of the Holy Spirit, by which they were endowed with supernatural powers, first preached the gospel and founded churches in Judæa: they then went forth to the Gentiles, preaching in like manner and founding churches in every city. From these churches others were propagated and continue to be propagated at the present day, which are all reckoned in the number of apostolic churches, inasmuch as they are the offspring of apostolic churches. Moreover, all these churches constitute one Church,[2] being joined together in the unity of faith and in the bond of peace." In conformity with this view of the origin of the Church, Tertullian never fails, when arguing upon any disputed point of doctrine or discipline, to appeal to the belief or practice of those churches which had been actually founded by the apostles; on the ground that in them the faith taught and the institutions established by the apostles were still preserved. When, therefore, he says that the authority of the Church made the distinction between the clergy and laity, the expression, in his view of the subject, is manifestly equivalent to saying that the distinction may be traced to the apostles, the founders of the Church. Thus he

[1] C. 20. Compare cc. 32, 36. "Si hæc ita se habent, ut veritas nobis adjudicetur quicunque in eâ regulâ incedimus quam Ecclesia ab Apostolis, Apostoli a Christo, Christus a Deo tradidit," c. 37.

[2] On the Unity of the Church, see c. 32, and *de Virgin. vel.* c. 2. This Church Tertullian calls the house of God. *De Pudicitiâ*, c. 7. In it were preserved the authentic rule of faith and discipline, and the genuine Scriptures. *De Præscript. Hæreticorum*, cc. 21, 37, *et passim.* With respect to particular churches, Tertullian admits by implication that they may fall into error, c. 27.

contends that all virgins should be compelled to wear veils;[1] because such was the practice in those churches which had been founded either by the apostles or by apostolic men; and consequently the probable inference was that it was of apostolic institution. It is true that, after his separation from the Church, he held a different language. He then began to contend, as we have already seen,[2] that wherever three, though laymen, were gathered together, there was a church; and in the tract *de Pudicitiâ*,[3] he says that any number of individuals, who meet together under the influence of the Spirit, constitute a church; which is not a number of bishops, but is the Spirit itself acting through the instrumentality of a spiritual man (πνευματικὸς as opposed to ψυχικὸς)—that is, of a man who believed in the revelations and prophecies of Montanus.

At the same time that Tertullian bears testimony to the existence of a distinction between the clergy and laity, he bears testimony also to the existence of a distinction of orders among the clergy. One of his charges against the heretics is that they neglected this distinction. "With them," he says, "one man is a bishop to-day, another to-morrow; he who is to-day a deacon will be to-morrow a reader; he who is a priest to-day will to-morrow be a layman."[4] In the tracts *de Baptismò*[5] and *de Fugâ in Persecutione*,[6] the three orders of bishops, priests, and deacons are enumerated together; and in the former the superior authority of the bishop is expressly asserted.

The episcopal office, according to Tertullian, was of apostolic institution. In the tract *de Præscriptione Hæreticorum*, he throws

[1] *De Virginibus vel.* c. 2.

[2] Chap. i. p. 30.

[3] "Nam et Ecclesia propriè et principaliter ipse est Spiritus, in quo est Trinitas unius Divinitatis, Pater et Filius et Spiritus Sanctus. Illam Ecclesiam congregat, quam Dominus in tribus posuit. Atque ita exinde etiam numerus omnis qui in hanc fidem conspiraverint, Ecclesia ab auctore et consecratore censetur, et ideo Ecclesia quidem delicta donabit: sed Ecclesia Spiritus per Spiritalem hominem non Ecclesia numerus Episcoporum," c. 21. Compare *de Pœnitentiâ*, c. 10. "In uno et altero Ecclesia est; Ecclesia vero Christus." *De Fugâ in Persecutione*, c. 14. "Sit tibi in tribus Ecclesia." Pamelius, as we observed in chapter i. p. 30, note 5, supposes without sufficient grounds that, in the tract *de Pudicitiâ*, c. 21, by the three who were to constitute a church, Tertullian meant Montanus and his two prophetesses. There is no necessity to invent absurdities for our author, who has to answer for so many of his own. Again, in the tract *de Baptismo*, c. 6, "Quoniam ubi tres, id est, Pater et Filius et Spiritus Sanctus, ibi Ecclesia quæ trium corpus est."

[4] "Itaque alius hodie Episcopus, cras alius: hodie Diaconus, qui cras Lector: hodie Presbyter, qui cras Laicus." *De Præscript. Hæreticorum*, c. 41.

[5] C. 17.

[6] C. 11. See also *de Præscript. Hæreticorum*, c. 3.

out the following challenge to the heretics.[1] "Let them show," he says, "the origin of their churches; let them trace the succession of their bishops, and thus connect the individual who first held the office, either with some apostle, or some apostolic man who always remained in communion with the Church. It is thus that the apostolic churches show their origin. That of Smyrna traces its bishops in an unbroken line from Polycarp, who was placed there by St. John; that of Rome from Clemens, who was placed there by St. Peter:[2] and every other church can point out the individual to whom the superintendence of its doctrine and discipline was first committed by some one of the apostles." The same statement is repeated in the fourth book *against Marcion*.[3]

But how clearly soever the distinction between the bishops and the other orders of clergy may be asserted in the writings of Tertullian, they afford us little assistance in ascertaining wherein this distinction consisted. In a passage to which we have just referred, the right of the priests and deacons to baptize is said to be derived entirely from the authority of the bishop, who is styled *Summus Sacerdos*, the Supreme Priest.[4] Bingham says that Tertullian commonly gives to bishops the title of presidents or provosts of the Church;[5] but the passages to which he refers scarcely bear him out in the assertion. One of them we have already considered.[6] In another, Tertullian says

[1] C. 32. See also the tract *de Fugâ in Persecutione*, c. 13. "Hanc Episcopatui formam Apostoli providentius condiderunt."

[2] Irenæus, l. iii. c. 3, says that Linus was the first bishop of Rome, Anacletus the second, and Clemens the third; and that the Church of Rome was founded jointly by St. Peter and St. Paul. Bingham reconciles this difference by supposing that Linus and Anacletus died whilst St. Peter lived, and that Clemens was also ordained their successor by St. Peter. L. ii. c. 1. sect. iv. Had the works of Irenæus and Tertullian proceeded from Semler's Roman Club, this apparent contradiction would probably have been avoided.

[3] C. 5, *sub in.* Among other statements contained in the passage is the following: "Habemus et Ioannis alumnas Ecclesias. Nam etsi Apocalypsin ejus Marcion respuit, *ordo tamen Episcoporum ad originem recensus in Ioannem stabit Auctorem.* Sic et cæterarum (Ecclesiarum) generositas recognoscitur." The words in italics Bingham has translated, "The *order of bishops*, when it is traced up to its original, will be found to have St. John for one of its authors." L. ii. c. 1. sect. iii. We do not deny that this inference may be legitimately drawn from Tertullian's words. But by the expression *Ordo Episcoporum* he did not mean the *order of bishops*, as distinct from priests and deacons, but the *succession* of bishops in the churches founded by St. John.

[4] See note 5 on p. 115. "Dandi (baptismum) quidem habet jus summus Sacerdos, qui est Episcopus; dehinc Presbyteri et Diaconi, non tamen sine Episcopi auctoritate, propter Ecclesiæ honorem." *De Baptismo*, c. 17.

[5] L. ii. c. 2, sect. v.

[6] In note 1, p. 111. The passage is in the *Apology*, c. 39.

that the communicants received the eucharist only from the hands of the presidents;[1] and in a third, that a digamist was not allowed to preside in the church.[2] But in neither case is it certain that Tertullian meant to speak exclusively of bishops, since priests might administer the sacraments; and he says that he had himself known instances of *priests* who had been degraded for digamy.[3] The bishops, doubtless, presided when they were present; but in their absence the office devolved upon one of the presbyters. The regulation of the internal economy of each particular church was certainly vested in the hands of the bishop.[4] He appointed, for instance, days of fasting, whenever the circumstances of the church appeared to call for such marks of humiliation.[5]

The passages already alleged sufficiently prove that, in Tertullian's estimation, all the apostolic churches were independent of each other, and equal in rank and authority.[6] He professes, indeed, a peculiar respect for the Church of Rome; not, however, because it was founded by St. Peter, but because both that apostle and St. Paul there sealed their testimony to the gospel with their blood, and St. John was there thrown into the cauldron of burning oil.[7] From a passage in the tract *de Pudicitiâ* it appears that the words of our Saviour to St. Peter—"On this rock I will build my Church," and "I will give unto thee the keys of the kingdom of heaven"—were not supposed *at that time* to refer exclusively to the Church of Rome, but generally to all the churches of which St. Peter was the founder.[8] Tertullian himself contends that they were spoken by our Saviour with a

[1] *De Coronâ Militis*, c. 3. "Eucharistiæ Sacramentum nec de aliorum manu quam de Præsidentium sumimus."

[2] *Ad Uxorem*, l. i. c. 7, also quoted in note 1, p. 111. "Quum digamos non sinit præsidere."

[3] *De Exhort. Castit.* c. 7, quoted in note 1, p. 112. "Quum ipsi Sacerdoti Digamo facto auferatur agere Sacerdotem."

[4] *De Virginibus velandis*, c. 9.

[5] "Benè autem quod et Episcopi universæ plebi mandare jejunia assolent, non dico de industriâ stipium conferendarum ut vestræ capturæ est, sed interdum et ex aliquâ solicitudinis Ecclesiasticæ causâ." *De Jejuniis*, c. 13.

[6] We have seen that in one sense our author called all orthodox churches apostolic.

[7] *De Præscriptione Hæreticorum*, c. 36.

[8] C. 21. "De tuâ nunc sententiâ quæro unde hoc jus Ecclesiæ usurpas. Si quia dixerit Petro Dominus: *Super hanc petram*, etc., idcirco præsumis et ad te derivâsse solvendi et alligandi potestatem, id est, ad omnem Ecclesiam Petri propinquam, qualis es evertens atque commutans manifestam Domini intentionem personaliter hoc Petro conferentem? Super *te*, inquit, ædificabo Ecclesiam meam, et dabo *tibi* claves, non *Ecclesiæ*; et quæcunque *solveris* vel *alligaveris*, non quæ *solverint* vel *alligaverint*. Sic enim et exitus docet. In ipso Ecclesia extructa

personal reference to St. Peter, in whom they were afterwards fulfilled. "For he it was who first put the key into the lock, when he preached the gospel to the assembled Israelites on the day of Pentecost. He it was who opened to them the kingdom of heaven, by baptizing them with the baptism of Christ, and thereby loosing them from the sins by which they had been bound; as he afterwards bound Ananias by inflicting upon him the punishment of death. He it was who, in the discussion at Jerusalem, first declared that the yoke of circumcision ought not to be imposed on the necks of the Gentile brethren, thereby loosing them from the observance of the ceremonial, and binding them to the observance of the moral law." There is, however, in the *Scorpiace* a passage in which Tertullian appears at first sight to admit that Christ had transmitted the power of the keys through Peter to His Church.[1] "Nam etsi adhuc clausum putas cœlum, memento claves ejus hic Dominum Petro, et per eum Ecclesiæ reliquisse, quas hic unusquisque interrogatus atque confessus ferat secum." But the concluding words show his meaning to have been, not that the power of the keys was transmitted to the Church as a society, but to each individual member who confessed, like St. Peter, that Jesus was Christ, the Son of the living God; or as he expresses himself in the tract *de Pudicitiâ*, to the spiritual Church of Montanus.[2] For the *Scorpiace* was, as we have seen, written after he had recognised the divine inspiration of Montanus, though probably before he actually seceded from the Church.

In opposition to the opinion above expressed respecting the independence of the Christian Churches, a passage has been quoted from which it is inferred that even at that early period the Bishop of Rome had assumed to himself the titles of Pontifex Maximus and Episcopus Episcoporum.[3] Allix indeed affirms that our author is speaking of an edict promulgated, not by the

est, id est, per ipsum; ipse clavem imbuit; vides quam—*Viri Israelitæ, auribus mandate quæ dico: Iesum Nazarenum, virum a Deo vobis destinatum*, et reliqua." (Acts ii. 22.) "Ipse denique primus in Christi baptismo reseravit aditum cœlestis regni, quo solvuntur alligata retro delicta, et alligantur quæ non fuerint soluta secundum veram salutem, et Ananiam vinxit vinculo mortis," etc. Compare *de Præscriptione Hæreticorum*, c. 22. "Latuit aliquid Petrum ædificandæ Ecclesiæ *petram* dictum, claves regni cœlorum consecutum, et solvendi et alligandi in cœlis et in terris potestatem."

[1] C. 10. [2] See the passage quoted in note 2, p. 115 of this chapter.

[3] "Audio etiam edictum esse propositum, et quidem peremptorium, *Pontifex* scilicet *Maximus, Episcopus Episcoporum* dicit—'Ego et mœchiæ et fornicationis delicta pœnitentiâ functis dimitto.'" *De Pudicitiâ*, c. 1.

Roman Pontiff, but by the Bishop of Carthage.[1] In the remarks prefixed to the opinions delivered by the bishops at the Council of Carthage on the subject of heretical baptism, Cyprian asserts the perfect equality of all bishops, and uses the following remarkable expressions:—"Neque enim quisquam *nostrûm* Episcopum se Episcoporum constituit, aut tyrannico terrore ad obsequendi necessitatem collegas suos adigit." That this remark is aimed at some bishop who had called himself *Episcopus Episcoporum*, cannot, we think, be doubted. The majority of writers apply it to Stephen, Bishop of Rome, from whom Cyprian differed on the point in question. Allix, on the other hand, supposes that Cyprian, having Tertullian's words in his mind, alluded to the pretensions of his predecessor in the see of Carthage, for the express purpose of disclaiming them. He infers also, from a passage in a letter of Cyprian to Antonianus, that the controversy respecting the re-admission of adulterers to the communion of the Church was confined to Africa, and that the Roman Pontiff took no share in it.[2] The statements of both parties in this question must be received with some degree of caution, for each writes with a view to a particular object. The Romanists contend that although Tertullian, then a Montanist, denied the supremacy of the Roman pontiffs, his words prove that it was openly asserted by them in his day—an inference which Allix was naturally anxious to controvert, since he maintained that the jurisdiction of the bishops of Rome did not at that period extend beyond the limits of their own diocese. With respect to the titles then given to bishops, we may observe that Bingham has produced instances of the application of the title, Summi Pontifices, to ordinary bishops.[3]

The word Papa occurs in the tract *de Pudicitiâ*, and being coupled with the epithet benedictus, is generally supposed to mean a bishop,[4] and according to the Romanists, the bishop of Rome.[5] But whatever may be its meaning in this particular passage, it is certain that the title of Papa was at that period given to bishops in general.[6] After Tertullian's secession from

[1] C. 8.

[2] Ep. 55, ed. Fell. "Et quidem apud antecessores nostros quidam de Episcopis istic in Provinciâ nostrâ dandam pacem mœchis non putaverunt, et in totum pœnitentiæ locum contra adulteria clauserunt."

[3] L. ii. c. 3, sect. vi.

[4] "Bonus Pastor et benedictus Papa concionaris," c. 13.

[5] The Romanists cite the following words from the tract *de Præscriptione Hæreticorum*, c. 30, in confirmation of their interpretation:—"Sub Episcopatu Eleutherii benedicti."

[6] See Cyprian's works. *Cler. Rom. ad Cler. Carthag.* Epp. 8, 23, 31, 36.

the Church, his respect for the episcopal office, or rather perhaps for the individuals who were in his day appointed to it, appears to have undergone a considerable diminution. He insinuates that they were actuated by worldly motives, and ascribes to their anxiety to retain their power and emoluments a practice, which had been introduced into some churches, of levying contributions upon the members for the purpose of bribing the governors and military to connive at the religious meetings of the Christians.[1]

Besides bishops, priests, and deacons, Tertullian mentions an order of readers, Lectores, whose office it was to read the Scriptures to the people.[2] He speaks also of an order of Widows, and complains that a bishop, in direct violation of the discipline of the Church, had admitted into that order a virgin who had not attained her twentieth year.[3] The third book of the *Apostolic Constitutions* is entitled περὶ χηρῶν—and it is here directed, in conformity to the injunction of St. Paul, that no widow shall be appointed who has not attained the age of sixty.[4] She was moreover to have been only once married—a restriction also founded on St. Paul's injunction.[5] Widows who had brought up families appear to have been preferred, because their experience in the different affections of the human heart rendered them fitter to give counsel and consolation to others, and because they had passed through all the trials by which female virtue can be proved. The duty of the widows consisted in administering to the wants of the poor; in attending upon the sick; in instructing the younger females of the community, in watching over their conduct and framing their morals. They

[1] "Hanc Episcopatui formam Apostoli providentius condiderunt, ut regno suo securi frui possent sub obtentu procurandi: scilicet enim talem pacem Christus ad Patrem regrediens mandavit a militibus per Saturnalitia redimendam." *De Fugâ in Persecutione*, c. 13.

[2] "Hodiè Diaconus, qui cras Lector. *De Præscript. Hæret*, c. 41." See Bingham, l. iii. c. 5.

[3] "Plane scio alicubi Virginem in Viduatu ab annis nondum viginti collocatam; cui si quid refrigerii debuerat Episcopus, aliter utique salvo respectu disciplinæ præstare potuisset." *De Virginibus vel.* c. 9. See also *de Monogamiâ*, c. 16. "Habet Viduam utique, quam adsumat licebit;" and *de Exhortatione Castitatis*, c. 12. "Habe aliquam uxorem spiritalem, adsume de Viduis."

[4] 1 Tim. v. 3–11. Titus ii. 3.

[5] So Tertullian, *ad Uxorem*, l. i. c. 7. "Quum Viduam allegi in ordinem nisi univiram non concedit;" and *de Monogamiâ*, c. 11, *sub in. De Virginibus vel.* c. 9. "Ad quam sedem præter annos sexaginta non tantum univiræ, id est, nuptæ, aliquando eliguntur, sed et matres et quidem educatrices filiorum: scilicet, ut experimentis omnium affectuum structæ facile norint cæteras et consilio et solatio juvare, et ut nihilominus ea decucurrerint, per quæ fœmina probari potest."

were not allowed to perform any of the ministerial functions; to speak in the church, to teach, to baptize, etc.[1] They were maintained out of the common stock, and had a higher place allotted them in the public assemblies. St. Paul appears to speak of widows in the strict sense of the word; subsequently the name was given to females who had led a life of celibacy, and generally to the order of deaconesses.[2] According to Hammond, there were two sorts of χηραὶ—that is, as he translates the word, lone women—deaconesses, who were for the most part unmarried females, and widows properly so called, who, being childless and helpless, were sustained by the Church;—he supposes St. Paul to speak of the latter.[3] Suicer, on the contrary, says that the deaconesses were originally widows, and that the admission of unmarried females was of a subsequent date.[4] The reader will find in Bingham all the information which ecclesiastical antiquity supplies on the subject.[5]

In addition to the notices which may be collected from the writings of Tertullian respecting the constitution of each particular church, and the distinction of orders in it, we learn from them that synods were in his time held in Greece, composed of deputies from all the churches,[6] who might be considered as representing the whole body of Christians dispersed throughout Greece. These meetings were always preceded by solemn fasts, and opened with prayer. In them all the more important questions which arose from time to time were discussed;[7] and thus the unity of doctrine and discipline was preserved. Baronius supposes that Tertullian alludes to particular councils which were convened at that time by Zephyrinus,

1 "Non permittitur mulieri *in ecclesiâ loqui* (1 Cor. xiv. 34), sed nec docere, nec tinguere, nec offerre, nec ullius virilis muneris, nedum sacerdotalis officii sortem sibi vindicare." *De Virgin. vel.* c. 9. One of Tertullian's charges against the heretics is, that they allowed their females to perform these various acts. *De Præscriptione Hæretic.* c. 41. Compare *de Baptismo*, c. 1, *sub fine*, c. 17. Females, however, might prophesy, agreeably to St. Paul's direction, 1 Cor. xi. 5. "Cæterum prophetandi jus et illas habere jam ostendit, quum mulieri etiam prophetanti velamen imponit." *Adv. Marcionem*, l. v. c. 8.

2 *Ignatius ad Smyrnæos, sub fine.*

3 Note on 1 Tim. v. 3. 4 *Sub voce* διακόνισσα. 5 L. ii. c. 22.

6 "Aguntur præterea per Græcias illa certis in locis concilia *ex universis Ecclesiis*, per quæ et altiora quæque in commune tractantur, et ipsa repræsentatio totius nominis Christiani magnâ veneratione celebratur.—Conventus autem illi, stationibus prius et jejunationibus operati, dolere cum dolentibus, et ita demum congaudere gaudentibus norunt." *De Jejuniis*, c. 13.

7 For instance, it was determined in these councils what writings were, and what were not, to be received as genuine parts of Scripture. *De Pudicitiâ*, c. 10.

Bishop of Rome, for the purpose of condemning the Montanists; others suppose that he alludes to councils held by the Montanists themselves—a supposition which in my opinion is at variance with the whole context. He appears to me to speak without reference to any particular council, and to describe a general custom.

As the converts from heathenism, to use Tertullian's expression, were not born, but became Christians, they went through a course of instruction in the principles and doctrines of the gospel, and were subjected to a strict probation, before they were admitted to the rite of baptism.[1] In this stage of their progress they were called catechumens; of whom, according to Suicer,[2] there were two classes—one called audientes, who had only entered upon their course, and begun to hear the word of God; the other συναιτοῦντες, or competentes, who had made such advances in Christian knowledge and practice as to be qualified to appear at the font. Tertullian, however, appears either not to have known or to have neglected this distinction, since he applies the names of audientes and auditores indifferently to all who had not partaken of the rite of baptism.[3] When the catechumens had given full proof of the ripeness of their knowledge and of the stedfastness of their faith, they were baptized, admitted to the table of the Lord, and styled Fideles.[4] The importance which Tertullian attached to this previous probation of the candidates for baptism appears from the fact that he founds upon the neglect of it one of his charges against the heretics. "Among them," he says, "no distinction is made between the catechumen and the faithful or confirmed Christian: the catechumen is pronounced fit for baptism before he is

[1] "Fiunt, non nascuntur, Christiani." *Apology*, c. 18.

[2] *Sub voce* κατηχούμενοι.

[3] "An alius est Intinctis Christus, alius Audientibus?" And again, "Itaque Audientes optare Intinctionem, non præsumere oportet." *De Pœnitentiâ*, c. 6. In the same chapter Tertullian speaks of the Auditorum tyrocinia, and applies the title of Novitioli to the catechumens. In the tract *de Idololatriâ*, c. 24, we find the following distinction:—"Hæc *accedentibus ad fidem* proponenda, et *ingredientibus in fidem* inculcanda est;" and the following in the tract *de Spectaculis*, c. 1:—"Cognoscite, qui *quum maxime ad Deum acceditis*, recognoscite, qui *jam accessisse vos testificati et confessi estis*." In the tract *de Præscriptione Hæreticorum*, c. 14, our author distinguishes between doctores and quærentes. "Est utique frater aliquis doctor, gratiâ scientiæ donatus: est aliquis inter exercitatos conversatus; aliquis tecum, curiosius tamen, quærens."

[4] Sometimes, however, the word Fideles included also the catechumens. Thus in the tract *de Coronâ*, c. 2, "Neminem dico Fidelium coronam capite nosse alias, extra tempus tentationis ejusmodi. Omnes ita observant a Catechumenis usque ad Confessores et Martyres, vel Negatores."

instructed; all come in indiscriminately; all hear, all pray together."[1]

The teachers, who undertook to prepare the catechumens for reception at the baptismal font, appear to have pursued the course pointed out by the Baptist and by our blessed Lord. They began by insisting on the necessity of repentance and amendment of life.[2] Unfortunately, the effect of their exhortations upon the minds of their hearers was frequently counteracted by a fatal perversion of the doctrine of the Church respecting the efficacy of baptism.[3] In every age the object of a large portion of those who call themselves Christians has been, to secure the benefits without fulfilling the conditions of the Christian covenant—to obtain the rewards of righteousness without sacrificing their present gratifications. When, therefore, the proselyte was told that baptism conferred upon him who received it the remission of all his former sins, he persuaded himself that he might with safety defer the work of repentance; and passed the time allotted for his probation, not in mortifying his lusts and acquiring a purity of heart and affections suitable to his Christian profession, but in a more unrestrained enjoyment of those worldly and sensual pleasures, in which he knew that, *after baptism*, he could not indulge, without forfeiting his hopes of eternal happiness. So general had this licentious practice become, that Tertullian devotes a considerable portion of the tract *de Pœnitentiâ* to the exposure of its folly and wickedness;[4] and the historian of the Roman Empire might there have found better arguments than those which he has extracted from Chrysostom, against the delay of baptism,[5] though our author's attention was not immediately directed to that subject.

[1] "Inprimis quis Catechumenus, quis Fidelis, incertum est: pariter adeunt, pariter audiunt, pariter orant." And again, "Ante sunt perfecti Catechumeni quam edocti." *De Præscript. Hæretic.* c. 41.

[2] See the first five chapters of the tract *de Pœnitentiâ.*

[3] Tertullian in the following sentence explains the prevalent opinion, at the same time that he points out the qualifications necessary to render baptism efficacious. "Neque ego renuo divinum beneficium, id est, abolitionem delictorum, inituris aquam omnimodo salvum esse; sed ut eo pervenire contingat elaborandum est. Quis enim tibi, tam infidæ pœnitentiæ viro, asperginem unam cujuslibet aquæ commodabit?" *De Pœnitentiâ*, c. 6.

[4] See particularly c. 6, where Tertullian argues that baptism, in order to be effectual to the pardon of sin, pre-supposes a renunciation of all sinful habits on the part of him who is to receive it. Men are admitted to baptism because they have already repented and reformed their lives; not in order that they may afterwards repent and reform. "Non ideo abluimur ut delinquere desinamus, sed quia desiimus."

[5] Chap. xx. note 68.

While the teacher was endeavouring to impress upon the catechumen the necessity of repentance and amendment of life, he would at the same time gradually unfold the great truths which constitute the objects of a Christian's faith; suiting his instructions to the comprehension and previous acquirements of the proselyte, and proceeding from the simpler to the more sublime and mysterious doctrines of the gospel. Of some the communication was postponed until the convert had been baptized, and numbered among the members of the Church. But after that rite was conferred, there was no further reserve, and the whole counsel of God was declared alike to all the faithful. In our account of Montanus, we stated that part of that knowledge, γνῶσις, which, according to Clemens Alexandrinus, had been communicated by the apostles to a select few, and through them handed down to his own time by oral tradition, consisted of mystical interpretations of Scripture.[1] We find occasionally in Tertullian's works, expressions implying that he also admitted the existence of interpretations, the knowledge of which was confined to those whom he terms *the more worthy*.[2] But he condemns, in the most pointed manner, the notion that the apostles had kept back any of the truths revealed to them, and had not imparted them alike to all Christians. He applies to it the name of madness, and considers it as a pure invention of the Gnostics, devised for the purpose of throwing an air of mysterious grandeur around their monstrous fictions, and supported by the grossest misrepresentations of Scripture.[3] Having already delivered our opinion respecting the mischievous consequences which have arisen to the Church from the countenance lent by the writings of Clemens Alexandrinus to the notion of a Disciplina Arcani, we shall now only express our regret that Protestant divines, in their eagerness to establish a favourite point, should sometimes have been induced to resort to it.

In the passage already cited from the *Apology*,[4] Tertullian

[1] Chap. i. p. 16.

[2] Thus in the tract *de Pallio*, where he is speaking of the expulsion of our first parents from Paradise, and of the fig-leaves of which they made aprons, he adds, "Sed arcana ista, nec omnium nôsse," c. 3; and in the tract *de Idololatriâ*, speaking of the brazen serpent set up by Moses in the wilderness, he says, "Sive quæ alia figuræ istius expositio *dignioribus* revelata est," c. 5.

[3] "Sed ut diximus, eadem dementia est, quum confitentur quidem nihil Apostolos ignorâsse, nec diversa inter se prædicâsse; non tamen omnia volunt illos omnibus revelâsse: quædam enim palam et universis, quædam secreto et paucis demandâsse." *De Præscriptione Hæretic.* c. 25. See also c. 26.

[4] See p. 111. The sentence was pronounced by the president. "Quomodo ut

states one purpose of the Christian assemblies to have been the maintenance of discipline by pronouncing censures, according to the circumstances of the offence, against those who had erred either in practice or in doctrine. We have seen that the proselyte, before he was admitted to the baptismal font, was subjected to a strict probation.[1] In baptism he received the remission of all his former transgressions, and solemnly renounced all his former carnal desires and impure habits.[2] If, however, through the weakness of human nature and the arts of his spiritual adversary, he was afterwards betrayed into sin, the door of mercy was not closed against him; he might still be restored to the favour of God and of the Church by making a public confession of his guilt. It was not sufficient that the unhappy offender felt the deepest remorse, and that his peace of mind was destroyed by the remembrance of his transgression: he was required to express his contrition by some public acts, which might at once satisfy the Church of his sincerity, and deter others from similar transgressions. The name given to this public confession of guilt was Exomologesis; and it consisted in various external marks of humiliation. The penitent was clothed in the meanest apparel; he lay in sackcloth and ashes; he either fasted entirely, or lived upon bread and water; he passed whole days and nights in tears and lamentations; he embraced the knees of the presbyters as they entered the church, and entreated the brethren to intercede by their prayers in his behalf.[3] In this state of degradation and exclusion from the communion of the faithful he remained a longer or a shorter period, according to the magnitude of his offence; when that period was expired, the bishop publicly pronounced his absolution, by which he was restored to the favour of God and to the communion of the Church.[4] Such is the account given by Tertullian of the Exomologesis, or public confession enjoined by the Church for sins committed after baptism. Its benefits could be obtained only once;[5] if the penitent relapsed, a place of repentance was

auferatur de medio illorum? Non utique ut extra Ecclesiam detur; hoc enim non a Deo postularetur quod erat in Præsidentis officio." *De Pudicitiâ*, c. 14.

1 P. 122.

2 See the tract *de Pœnitentiâ*, cc. 7, 9.

3 Compare *de Pudicitiâ*, c. 5, *sub fine*, c. 13. "Et tu quidem pœnitentiam mœchi ad exorandam fraternitatem," etc.

4 See the passage quoted from the tract *de Pudicitia*, c. 13, in note 4. p. 124, and c. 18 *sub fine*. "Salvâ illâ pœnitentiæ specie post Fidem, quæ aut levioribus delictis veniam ab Episcopo consequi poterit, aut majoribus et irremissibilibus a Deo solo."

5 "Collocavit in vestibulo pœnitentiam secundam, quæ pulsantibus patefaciat; sed jam semel, quia jam secundo; sed amplius nunquam, quia proximè frustra." *De Pœnitentiâ*, c. 7. See also c. 9.

no longer open to him. Although, however, he could not be reconciled to the Church in this world, we must not infer that Tertullian intended to exclude him from all hope of pardon in the next. They indeed who, through false shame or an unwillingness to submit to the penance enjoined them, desperately refused to reconcile themselves to the Church by making a public confession, would be consigned to eternal misery.[1] But our author expressly distinguishes between remission of sins by the Church and by God; and affirms that the sincere penitent, though he may not by his tears and lamentations obtain re-admission into the Church, may yet secure his reception into the kingdom of heaven.[2]

In our attempts to distinguish between the works composed by Tertullian before and after his adoption of the opinions of Montanus, we remarked that the tract *de Pœnitentiâ* belonged to the former class;[3] and that he there spoke as if all crimes, committed after baptism, might once, though only once, be pardoned upon repentance.[4] But in the tract *de Pudicitiâ*, which was written after he had seceded from the Church, we find him drawing a distinction between greater and less offences—between those which could not, and those which could be pardoned by the Church.[5] If, for instance, a Christian had been excommunicated for being present at a chariot race, or a combat of gladiators, or a dramatic representation, or any gymnastic exercise;[6] for attending any secular game or entertainment, or working at any trade which ministered to the purposes of idolatry,

[1] *De Pœnitentiâ*, cc. 10, 11, 12.

[2] See *de Pudicitiâ*, c. 3. "Et si pacem hic non metit, apud Dominum seminat." Tertullian reasons throughout the tract on the supposition that the more heinous offences, *majora delicta*, can be pardoned by God alone. See cc. 11, 18, *sub fine*.

[3] See chap. i. p. 22.

[4] See particularly the commencement of c. 8. But at other times Tertullian speaks as if idolaters, apostates, and murderers were never re-admitted to the communion of the Church. *De Pudicitiâ*, cc. 5, 9, 12, *sub fine.* "Hinc est quod neque Idololatriæ neque sanguini pax ab Ecclesiis redditur." Crimes against nature were also under the same irremissible sentence of exclusion. "Reliquas autem libidinum furias impias et in corpora et in sexus ultra jura naturæ, non modo limine, verum omni Ecclesiæ tecto submovemus; quia non sunt delicta, sed monstra," c. 4. See Bingham, l. xviii. c. 4.; l. xvi. c. 10, sect. ii.

[5] *De Pudicitiâ*, cc. 1, 2. "Secundum hanc differentiam delictorum pœnitentiæ quoque conditio discriminatur. Alia erit, quæ veniam consequi possit, in delicto scilicet remissibili; alia quæ consequi nullo modo potest, in delicto scilicet irremissibili," c. 18, *sub fine.* "Hæc ut principalia penes Dominum delicta." *De Patientiâ*, c. 5.

[6] "Ita licet dici perisse quod salvum est. Perit igitur et fidelis elapsus in spectaculum quadrigarii furoris, et gladiatorii cruoris, et scenicæ fœditatis, et xysticæ vanitatis, in lusus, in convivia secularis solennitatis; in officium, in

or using any expression which might be construed into a denial of his faith or into blasphemy against Christ; or if from passion or impatience of censure he had himself broken off his connexion with the Church,—still his guilt was not of so deep a dye but that he might, upon his public confession, be again received into its communion. In a subsequent passage he classes among the venial sins—being angry without a cause, and allowing the sun to go down upon our wrath, acts of violence, evil-speaking, rash swearing, non-performance of contracts, violations of truth; and among the heinous sins—homicide, idolatry, fraud, denial of Christ, blasphemy, adultery, and fornication.[1] Of these he says that there is no remission, and that even Christ will not intercede for those who commit them. Such were the severe notions of discipline entertained by Tertullian after he became a Montanist. In his tract *de Pudicitiâ* he applies them to adulterers and fornicators in particular, and even extends them to those who contract a second marriage;[2] branding the orthodox,[3] who recommended a milder course, with the name of ψυχικοὶ, *animales*, that is, men possessing indeed the *anima* which God breathed into Adam, thereby constituting him a living soul, but strangers to the influence of that Spirit by which the disciples of the Paraclete were inspired.

We may take this opportunity of observing that Tertullian's

ministerium alienæ idololatriæ aliquas artes adhibuit curiositatis; in verbum ancipitis negationis aut blasphemiæ impegit; ob tale quid extra gregem datus est, vel et ipse forte irâ, tumore, æmulatione, quod denique sæpe fit dedignatione castigationis abrupit; debet requiri atque revocari." *De Pudicitiâ*, c. 7.

[1] "Cui enim non accidit aut irasci iniquè et ultra solis occasum, aut et manum immittere, aut facilè maledicere, aut temerè jurare, aut fidem pacti destruere, aut verecundiâ aut necessitate mentiri? in negotiis, in officiis, in quæstu, in victu, in visu, in auditu quanta tentamur! ut si nulla sit venia istorum, nemini salus competat. Horum ergo erit venia per exoratorem Patris, Christum. Sunt autem et contraria istis, ut graviora et exitiosa, quæ veniam non capiant, homicidium, idololatria, fraus, negatio, blasphemia, utique et mœchia et fornicatio, et si qua alia violatio templi Dei. Horum ultra exorator non erit Christus," c. 19. In the fourth book *against Marcion*, the enumeration of the *delicta majora* is somewhat different. "Quæ septem maculis capitalium delictorum inhorrerent, idololatriâ, blasphemiâ, homicidio, adulterio, stupro, falso testimonio, fraude," c. 9. On other occasions Tertullian appears to overlook the distinction between greater and lesser offences. "Quum—omne delictum voluntarium in Domino grande sit." *Ad Uxorem*, l. ii. c. 3.

[2] "Et ideo durissime nos, infamantes Paracletum disciplinæ enormitate, *Digamos* foris sistimus, eundem limitem liminis *mœchis* quoque et *fornicatoribus* figimus, jejunas pacis lachrymas profusuris, nec amplius ab Ecclesiâ quam publicationem dedecoris relaturis." *De Pudicitiâ*, c. 1, *sub fine*.

[3] See chap. i. note 1, p. 15. The tract *de Pudicitiâ* was directed against an edict, published by a bishop (probably of Rome), and allowing adulterers and fornicators to be re-admitted to the communion of the Church upon repentance. See p. 118.

works contain no allusion to the practice of auricular confession.

At the end of the chapter on the Government of the Church, Mosheim gives a short account of the ecclesiastical authors who flourished during the century of which he is treating. The notices which the writings of Tertullian supply on this point are very few in number. He alludes to the *Shepherd of Hermas* in a manner which shows that it was highly esteemed in the Church, and even deemed by some of authority; for he supposes that a practice, which appears to have prevailed in his day, of sitting down after the conclusion of the public prayers, owed its origin to a misinterpretation of a passage in that work.[1] In his later writings, when he had adopted the rigid notions of Montanus respecting the perpetual exclusion of adulterers from the communion of the Church, he speaks with great bitterness of the *Shepherd of Hermas* as countenancing adultery;[2] and states that it had been pronounced apocryphal by every synod of the orthodox Churches. Yet the opinions expressed in the treatise *de Pœnitentiâ*, written before Tertullian became a Montanist, appear to bear something more than an accidental resemblance to those contained in the *Shepherd of Hermas*.[3]

We have seen that Tertullian mentions Clemens Romanus as having been placed in the see of Rome by St. Peter; and Polycarp in that of Smyrna, by St. John.[4]

In speaking of the authors who had refuted the Valentinian heresy,[5] he mentions Justin, Miltiades,[6] and Irenæus. To them he adds Proculus, supposed by some eminent critics to be the same as Proclus, who is stated by the author of the brief *Enumeration of Heretics*,[7] subjoined to Tertullian's treatise *de Præscriptione Hæreticorum*, to have been the head of one of the two sects into which the Cataphrygians or Montanists were

[1] *De Oratione*, c. 12.

[2] "Sed cederem tibi, si Scriptura Pastoris, quæ sola mœchos amat, divino instrumento meruisset incidi; si non ab omni Concilio Ecclesiarum etiam vestrarum inter Apocrypha et falsa judicaretur; adultera et ipsa et inde patrona sociorum." *De Pudicitiâ*, c. 10. Again in c. 20: "Illo Apocrypho Pastore mœchorum."

[3] Compare *de Pœnitentiâ*, cc. 7, 8, 9, with the *Shepherd of Hermas*, Mand. iv. c. 3.

[4] *De Præscriptione Hæreticorum*, c. 32, quoted in p. 116.

[5] *Adversus Valentinianos*, c. 5.

[6] See Eusebius, *Eccl. Hist.* l. v. c. 17.

[7] C. 52.

divided. He appears to have made a distinction between the Holy Ghost and the Paraclete; the former inspired the apostles, the latter spoke in Montanus, and revealed through him more numerous and more sublime truths than Christ had delivered in the gospel. Proclus did not, however, like Æschines, the head of the other division of the Cataphrygians, confound the Father and the Son. Eusebius,[1] and after him Jerome [2] and Photius,[3] mention a Proclus or Proculus, who was a leader of the sect of Cataphrygians, and held a disputation at Rome with Caius, a distinguished writer of that day. There is therefore no doubt, as Lardner justly observes,[4] that a Montanist of the name of Proculus or Proclus lived at the beginning of the third century; but whether he was the author mentioned by Tertullian has been doubted. The expression Proculus *noster*, which is applied to him, inclines me to think that he was. Tertullian speaks of Tatian as one of the heretics who enjoined abstinence from food,[5] on the ground that the Creator of this world was a Being at variance with the Supreme God, and that it was consequently sinful to partake of any enjoyments which this world affords.

From the manner in which Tertullian speaks of the visions seen by the martyr Perpetua, I infer that a written account of her martyrdom had been circulated among the Christians.[6] Some have supposed that Tertullian was himself the author of the account still extant of the *Passion of Perpetua and Felicitas*.[7]

—o—

## CHAPTER V.

### ON THE DOCTRINE OF THE CHURCH.

We now come to a more important and more extensive branch of our inquiries—to the information which the writings of Tertullian supply respecting the doctrine of the Church in his day.

1 *Eccl. Hist.* l. vi. c. 20.
2 *Catalogus Scriptorum Ecclesiasticorum.* Caius.
3 *Bibliotheca*, Cod. 48.
4 *Credibility of the Gospel History*, c. 40.
5 *De Jejuniis*, c. 15.
6 *De Animâ*, c. 55. "Quomodo Perpetua, fortissima Martyr, sub die passionis in revelatione Paradisi, solos illic commartyres suos vidit?"
7 Lardner, *Credibility*, c. 40.

In treating this part of our subject, we do not think that we can adopt a better course than to consider the different doctrines in the order in which they occur in the Articles of the Church of England. For the present, however, we shall pass over the first and second Articles, which relate to the Trinity and to the person and offices of Christ, because a more convenient opportunity for considering them will present itself when we come to the last of Mosheim's divisions—the heresies which disturbed the peace of the Church during the latter part of the second and the earlier part of the third century. With respect to that portion of the first Article which asserts the unity of God, and describes His nature and attributes, the reader will find a statement of Tertullian's faith in a passage already quoted from the seventeenth chapter of the *Apology*.[1]

Let us therefore proceed to the third Article, the subject of which is Christ's descent into hell.

In order to put the reader in possession of our author's opinion on this Article, it is necessary to premise that he speaks of four different places of future happiness or misery—the Inferi, Abraham's Bosom, Paradise, and Gehenna.

The Inferi he defines to be a deep and vast recess in the very heart and bowels of the earth.[2] He sometimes distinguishes between the Inferi and Abraham's Bosom;[3] at others,[4] includes under the name of Inferi both the place in which the souls of the wicked are kept in a state of torment until the day of judgment, and Abraham's Bosom, the receptacle prepared for the souls of the faithful, where they enjoy a foretaste of the happiness which will afterwards be their portion in heaven. For neither can the

1 See chap. iii. note 4, p. 89.

2 "Nobis Inferi, non nuda cavositas nec subdivalis aliqua mundi sentina creduntur; sed in fossâ terræ, et in alto vastitas, et in ipsis visceribus ejus abstrusa profunditas." *De Animâ*, c. 55.

3 "Aliud enim Inferi, ut puto, aliud quoque Abrahæ sinus." *Adv. Marcionem*, l. iv. c. 34.

4 "Cæterum vester Christus pristinum statum Judæis pollicetur ex restitutione terræ; et post decursum vitæ, apud Inferos, in sinu Abrahæ, refrigerium." *Adv. Marcionem*, l. iii. c. 24. This passage applies to the peculiar notions of Marcion. See note 7 on opposite page. "Igitur si quid tormenti sive solatii anima præcerpit in carcere seu diversorio Inferûm, in igne, vel in sinu Abrahæ." *De Animâ*, c. 7. "Nam et nunc animas torqueri foverique penes Inferos, licet nudas, licet adhuc exules carnis, probabit Lazari exemplum." *De Res. Carnis*, c. 17. See also *de Idololatriâ*, c. 13; *de Animâ*, c. 9, *sub fine*.

full reward of the good be conferred, nor the full punishment of the wicked inflicted, until the soul is re-united to the body at the day of judgment.[1] There is, however, as we shall hereafter have occasion to observe, some inconsistency in Tertullian's language respecting the purposes for which the soul is kept in a separate state *apud Inferos*.[2] The Bosom of Abraham, though not in heaven, was yet elevated far above the place in which the souls of the wicked were confined.[3]

Tertullian defines Paradise to be a place of divine pleasantness, appointed for the reception of the spirits of the saints.[4] While the souls of the rest of mankind were detained *apud Inferos*, in the intermediate state just described, it was the peculiar privilege of the martyrs that their souls were at once transferred to Paradise;[5] for St. John, in the Apocalypse, saw the souls of the martyrs, and of the martyrs only, under the altar.[6] According to Marcion, they who lived under the law were consigned to the Inferi, there to receive their reward or punishment; while heaven was reserved to the followers of Christ.[7]

Gehenna is,[8] as Tertullian expresses himself, a treasure of sacred fire beneath the earth, destined for the punishment of the wicked.

These preliminary observations will enable us fully to compre-

1 See *de Res. Carnis*, c. 17, quoted in the preceding note, where Tertullian says that the soul suffers the punishment of evil thoughts and desires in the intermediate state.

2 See *de Animâ*, c. 58, and *de Res. Carnis*, c. 42. "Ne Inferos experiatur, usque novissimum quadrantem exacturos."

3 "Eam itaque regionem sinum dico Abrahæ, etsi non cœlestem, sublimiorem tamen Inferis, interim refrigerium præbituram animabus justorum, donec consummatio rerum resurrectionem omnium plenitudine mercedis expungat." *Adv. Marcionem*, l. iv. c. 34.

4 "Et si Paradisum nominemus, locum divinæ amœnitatis recipiendis Sanctorum spiritibus destinatum, maceriâ quâdam igneæ illius zonæ a notitiâ orbis communis segregatum." *Apology*, c. 47. Tertullian appears to identify it with the Paradise in which Adam and Eve were placed. *De Res. Carnis*, c. 26, *sub fine*.

5 *De Animâ*, c. 55; *de Res. Carnis*, c. 43. "Nemo enim peregrinatus a corpore statim immoratur penes Dominum nisi ex martyrii prærogativâ, scilicet Paradiso, non Inferis deversurus."

6 C. 6, v. 9.

7 "Sed Marcion aliorsum cogit" (Tertullian is speaking of the parable of Lazarus); "scilicet utramque mercedem Creatoris, sive tormenti, sive refrigerii, apud Inferos determinat iis positam, qui Legi et Prophetis obedierint; Christi vero et Dei sui cœlestem definit sinum et portum." *Adv. Marcionem*, l. iv. c. 34.

8 "Gehennam si comminemur, quæ est ignis arcani subterraneus ad pœnam thesaurus." *Apology*, c. 47. See *de Pœnitentiâ*, cc. 5, 12; *de Res. Carnis*, cc. 34, 35.

hend Tertullian's notions respecting Christ's descent into hell. We have seen that he defines death to be the separation of the soul from the body.[1] Christ really died:[2] His soul was therefore separated from His body; and as the soul does not sleep but remains in a state of perpetual activity, in the interval between Christ's crucifixion and resurrection, *His* soul descended to the general receptacle of departed souls, and there rendered the patriarchs and prophets capable of sharing in the benefits which His mission was designed to communicate. Pearson, in his remarks upon the fifth Article of the Creed, has correctly stated Tertullian's opinion; but has not explained how it is to be deduced from the passage which he quotes, and in which there is no mention of the soul of Christ. That which Pearson proposes as the second end of Christ's descent into hell is stated by Tertullian in the form of an objection to his own opinions. "Sed in hoc, inquiunt, Christus Inferos adiit, ne nos adiremus."[3] Pearson's words are—"Secondly, by the descent of Christ into hell all those which believe in Him are secured from descending thither: He went into those regions of darkness that our souls might never come into those torments which are there."

Tertullian's opinions respecting Christ's resurrection, the subject of our fourth Article, may be learned from the treatise entitled *de Carne Christi*, which he wrote in confutation of certain heretics, who denied the reality of Christ's flesh, or at least its identity with human flesh.[4] They were apprehensive that if they admitted the reality of Christ's flesh, they must also admit His resurrection in the flesh, and consequently the resurrection of the human

[1] Chap. iii. p. 105.

[2] "Quid est autem illud quod ad inferna transfertur post divortium corporis, quod detinetur illic, quod in diem judicii reservatur, ad quod et Christus moriendo descendit, puto, ad animas Patriarcharum?" *De Animâ*, c. 7. "Siquidem Christo in corde terræ triduum mortis legimus expunctum, id est, in recessu intimo, et interno, et in ipsâ terrâ operto, et intra ipsam clauso, et inferioribus adhuc abyssis superstructo. Quod si Christus Deus, quia et homo, mortuus secundum Scripturas, et sepultus secundum easdem, huic quoque legi satisfecit, *formâ humanæ mortis apud Inferos functus*, nec ante ascendit in sublimiora cœlorum, quam descendit in inferiora terrarum, ut illic Patriarchas et Prophetas compotes sui faceret," etc., c. 55. He died according to the fashion of the death of man, in that His soul was separated from His body. Tertullian, therefore, agrees with Pearson respecting the first end of Christ's descent into hell. "I conceive that the end for which He did so was, that He might undergo the condition of a dead man as well as living." P. 250, ed. fol. 1683.

[3] *De Animâ*, c. 55.

[4] "Præterea et nos volumen præmisimus de carne Christi, quo eam et solidam probamus adversum phantasmatis vanitatem, et humanam vindicamus adversus qualitatis proprietatem." *De Res. Carnis*, c. 2.

body after death.[1] Some, therefore, as Marcion, denied the reality both of Christ's birth and of His flesh:[2] others, as Apelles, denied the former, but admitted the latter;[3] contending that, as the angels are recorded in Scripture to have assumed human flesh without being born after the fashion of men, so might Christ, who, according to them, received His body from the stars.[4] Others, again, assigned to Christ an animal flesh, *caro animalis*, or carnal soul, *anima carnalis;* their notion was that the soul, *anima*, being invisible, was rendered visible in the flesh, which was most intimately united with it, or rather absorbed in it.[5] Others affirmed that Christ assumed the angelic substance;[6] Valentinus assigned Him a spiritual flesh;[7] others argued that Christ's flesh could not be human flesh, because it proceeded not from the seed of man;[8] and Alexander, the Valentinian, seems to have denied its reality, on the ground that if it was human flesh, it must also be sinful flesh, whereas one object of Christ's mission was to abolish sinful flesh.[9] Should the reader deem the opinions now enumerated so absurd and trifling as to be altogether undeserving of notice, he must bear in mind that from such an enumeration alone can we acquire an accurate idea of the state of religious controversy in any particular age.

[1] *De Carne Christi*, c. 1. [2] *Ibid.* [3] *Ibid.*

[4] C. 6. Tertullian's answer is, that the angels did not come upon earth like Christ to suffer, be crucified, and die in the flesh; there was consequently no necessity why they should go through the other stages of human being, or why they should be born after the fashion of men.

[5] Cc. 10, 11, 12, 13. The reader will perceive that the word *animal* is not here used in its ordinary sense, but means *that which is animated by a soul.*

[6] Tertullian asks in reply, to what end did Christ assume the angelic substance, since He came not to effect the salvation of angels? c. 14.

[7] C. 15.

[8] Tertullian's answer is, that on the same ground we must deny the reality of Adam's flesh, c. 16, *sub fine.*

[9] I say *seems*, for I am not certain that I understand the objection. The words of Tertullian are, "Insuper argumentandi libidine, ex formâ ingenii hæretici, locum sibi fecit Alexander ille, quasi nos adfirmemus, idcirco Christum terreni censûs induisse carnem, ut evacuaret in semetipso carnem peccati." The orthodox, according to Alexander, affirmed that Christ put on flesh of earthly origin in order that He might in His own person make void or abolish sinful flesh. If, therefore, Alexander contended, Christ abolished sinful flesh in Himself, His flesh could no longer be human flesh. Tertullian answers, We do not say that Christ abolished sinful flesh, *carnem peccati*, but sin in the flesh, *peccatum carnis:* it was for this very end that Christ put on human flesh, in order to show that He could overcome sin in the flesh; to have overcome sin in any other than human flesh would have been nothing to the purpose. Tertullian, referring to St. Paul, says of Christ, "Evacuavit peccatum in carne;" alluding, as I suppose, to Rom. viii. 3. But the corresponding Greek in the printed editions is κατέκρινε τὴν ἁμαρτίαν ἐν τῇ σαρκί. Had Tertullian a different reading in his Greek MSS.? or did he confound Rom. viii. 3 with Rom. vi. 6, ἵνα καταργηθῇ τὸ σῶμα τῆς ἁμαρτίας? Jerome translates the Greek καταργέω by *evacuo*, c. 16. See *adv. Marcionem*, l. v. c. 14.

In opposition to these various heretical notions, our author shows that Christ was born,[1] lived, suffered, died, and was buried in the flesh. Hence it follows that He also rose again in the flesh. "For the same substance which fell by the stroke of death and lay in the sepulchre was also raised.[2] In that substance Christ now sits at the right hand of the Father,—being man, though God;[3] the last Adam, though the primary Word; flesh and blood, though of a purer kind than those of men,—and according to the declaration of the angels, He will descend at the day of judgment, in form and substance the same as He ascended, since He must be recognised by those who pierced Him. He who is called the Mediator between God and man is entrusted with a deposit from each party. As He left with us the earnest of the Spirit, so He took from us the earnest of the flesh, and carried it with Him into heaven, to assure us that both the flesh and the Spirit will then be collected into one sum."

Towards the end of the treatise, Tertullian mentions various strange notions respecting the session of Christ at the right hand of God.[4] Some heretics supposed that His flesh sat there, devoid of all sensation, like an empty scabbard; others that His human soul sat there without the flesh; others His flesh and human soul, or in other words, His human nature alone.

On account of the intimate connexion between the doctrine of the resurrection of the body and that of Christ's resurrection, we will take this opportunity of giving a short account of Tertullian's treatise *de Resurrectione Carnis*. The heretics,

[1] Tertullian contends that, if Christ's birth from the Virgin is once proved, the reality of His flesh follows as a necessary consequence; it being impossible otherwise to assign any reasonable cause why He should be born. See cc. 2, 3, 4, 5, 20, 21, 22, 23.

[2] "Ipsum enim quod cecidit in morte, quod jacuit in sepulturâ, hoc et resurrexit, non tam Christus in carne, quam caro in Christo." *De Res. Carnis*, c. 48.

[3] *De Carne Christi*, c. 16; *de Res. Carnis*, c. 51. "Quum illic adhuc sedeat Iesus ad dexteram Patris; homo, etsi Deus; Adam novissimus, etsi Sermo primarius; caro et sanguis, etsi nostris puriora; idem tamen et substantiâ et formâ quâ ascendit talis etiam descensurus, ut Angeli affirmant (Acts i. 11) agnoscendus scilicet iis, qui illum convulneraverunt. Hic, *sequester Dei atque hominum* appellatus (1 Tim. ii. 5), ex utriusque partis deposito commisso sibi, carnis quoque depositum servat in semetipso, arrabonem summæ totius. Quemadmodum enim nobis arrabonem Spiritûs reliquit, ita et a nobis arrabonem carnis accepit et vexit in cœlum pignus totius summæ, illuc quandoque redigendæ." We shall see what our author meant by flesh and blood of a purer kind than those of men when we speak of the tract *de Resurrectione Carnis*.

[4] C. 24. "Ut et illi erubescant, qui affirmant carnem in cœlis vacuam sensu, ut vaginam, exempto Christo sedere; aut qui carnem et animam tantundem; aut tantummodo animam; carnem vero non jam." See Pearson, Article vi. p. 272.

against whom it is directed, were the same who maintained that the Demiurge, or God who created this world and gave the Mosaic dispensation, was opposed to the Supreme God. Hence they attached an idea of inherent corruption and worthlessness to all His works—among the rest, to the flesh or body of man; affirming that it could not rise again, and that the soul alone was capable of inheriting immortality.[1] Tertullian, therefore, in the first place endeavours to prove that God cannot deem that flesh beneath His notice, or unworthy to be raised again, "which He framed with His own hands in the image of God;—which He afterwards animated with His own breath, communicating to it that life, of which the principle is within Himself;—which He appointed to inhabit, to enjoy, to rule over His whole creation; —which He clothes with His sacraments and His discipline, loving its purity, approving its mortifications, and ascribing a value to its sufferings."[2]

Having thus removed the preliminary objections founded on the supposed worthlessness of the flesh, our author proceeds to prove that the body will rise again;[3] and first asserts the power of God to rebuild the tabernacle of the flesh, in whatever manner it may be dissolved. If we suppose even that it is annihilated, He who created all things out of nothing can surely raise the dead body again from nothing. Nor is there any absurdity in supposing that the members of the human body, which may have been destroyed by fire or devoured by birds or beasts, will nevertheless at the last day be re-united to it.[4] Such a supposition, on the contrary, is countenanced by Scripture.[5] Ter-

[1] Cc. 4, 5. The reader will find what appears to be more than an accidental resemblance between this treatise and the fragments of a tract on the same subject, ascribed to Justin Martyr. See Grabe's *Spicilegium*, tom. ii.

[2] See c. 9, where Tertullian sums up the arguments advanced in the preceding chapters. "Igitur ut retexam, quam Deus manibus suis ad imaginem Dei struxit —quam de suo adflatu ad similitudinem suæ vivacitatis animavit—quam incolatui, fructui, dominatui totius suæ operationis præposuit—quam sacramentis suis disciplinisque vestivit—cujus munditias amat—cujus castigationes probat—cujus passiones sibi adpreciat—hæccine non resurget, totiens Dei?" Tertullian's notion was, that when God said, "Let us make man *in our image*," He alluded to the form which Christ was to bear during His abode on earth. "Quodcunque enim limus exprimebatur, Christus cogitabatur homo futurus, quod et limus, et Sermo caro, quod et terra tunc. Sic enim præfatio Patris ad Filium, *Faciamus hominem ad imaginem et similitudinem nostram. Et fecit hominem Deus.* Id utique quod finxit, ad imaginem Dei fecit illum, scilicet Christi," c. 6. Compare *adv. Praxeam*, c. 12.

[3] C. 11. Compare the *Apology*, c. 48.

[4] C. 32. Compare Pearson, Article xi. p. 374.

[5] Tertullian's words are, "Sed ne solummodo eorum corporum resurrectio videatur prædicari quæ sepulchris demandantur, habes *scriptum*;" then follows a

tullian further contends that the doctrine of the resurrection of the body is rendered credible by innumerable instances of a resurrection in the natural world.[1] The passage has been translated and adopted by Pearson in his *Exposition of the Eleventh Article of the Creed.*[2] He does not, indeed, appear to have been aware that some of the instances alleged are nothing to the purpose—such as the changes of day and night, of summer and winter. If any inference is to be drawn from them, it would rather be in favour of an alternate dissolution and restoration of the same bodies. Among other illustrations, the instance of the phœnix is brought forward, of which the early Fathers appear to have been fond.[3]

Having established the power of God to raise the dead body, Tertullian next inquires whether any reasons exist which should induce Him to exert that power.[4] As He intends to judge mankind, and to reward or punish them according to their conduct in this life, it is evident that the ends of justice will not be attained, unless men rise again with the same bodies which they had when living.[5] The body co-operated with the soul in this world; it carried into effect the good or evil designs which the soul conceived; it ought therefore to be associated with the soul in its future glory or misery. Tertullian further contends that the very term *resurrection* implies a resurrection of the body: for that alone can be raised which has fallen, and it is the body, not the soul, which falls by the stroke of death.[6] The same inference may be drawn from the compound expression *resurrectio mortuorum;* "for man," as Pearson,[7] who urges both this argument and the preceding, paraphrases the words, "man dieth, not in reference to his soul, which is immortal, but his body."

The arguments of the heretics against the resurrection of the body were deduced either from general reasoning or from passages of Scripture. Of the former description were the following. "The body, you say, in the present life is the receptacle or instrument of the soul by which it is animated.

passage which in Semler's Index is stated as a quotation from Revelation xx. 13; but if our author had that passage in view, he has strangely altered it.

1 C. 12. Compare the *Apology*, c. 48.

2 P. 376.

3 C. 13.

4 Cc. 14, 15.

5 Compare *Apology*, c. 48. Pearson, Article xi. p. 376. *Adv. Marcionem*, l. v. c. 12.

6 C. 18. Compare *adv. Marcionem*, l. v. cc. 9, 14.

7 Article xi. p. 382.

It has itself neither will, nor sense, nor understanding. How then can it be a fit subject of reward or punishment? or to what purpose will it be raised? Why may not the soul exist in the next world, either wholly divested of a body, or clothed in an entirely different body?"[1] Tertullian replies that, although the principle of action is in the soul, it can effect nothing without the body.[2] It thinks, wills, disposes; but in order to carry its designs into execution, it needs the assistance of the body, which is also the medium of sensation. The soul, it is true, might by means of its corporeal substance suffer the punishment due to sinful desires; but unless it shall hereafter be reunited to the body, sinful actions will remain unpunished.

"If then," the heretics rejoined, "the body is to be raised, is it to be raised with all the infirmities and defects under which it laboured on earth? Are the blind, the lame, the deformed, those especially who were so from their birth, to appear with the same imperfections at the day of judgment?"[3] "No," replies Tertullian: "the Almighty does not His work by halves. He, who raises the dead to life, will raise the body in its perfect integrity. This is part of the change which the body will undergo at the resurrection. For though the dead will be raised in the flesh, yet they who attain to the resurrection of happiness will pass into the angelic state and put on the vesture of immortality;[4] according to the declaration of St. Paul, that 'this corruptible must put on incorruption, and this mortal must put on immortality'—and again, that 'our vile bodies will be changed that they may be fashioned like unto the glorious body of Christ.'" We must not, however, suppose that this change is incompatible with the identity of the body.[5] Continual changes take place in the substance of man from his birth to his death: his constitution, his bulk, his strength is perpetually changing; yet he remains the same man. So, when after death he passes into a state of incorruption and immortality, as the mind, the memory, the conscience which he now has will not be done away,[6] so neither will his body. Otherwise he would suffer in a different body from that in which he sinned; and the dispensations of God would appear to be at variance with His justice, which evidently requires that the same soul should be re-united to the same body at the last day. Never-

[1] Cc. 16, 17.
[2] Compare *adv. Marcionem,* l. i. c. 24; l. v. c. 10.
[3] Cc. 4, 57.
[4] Compare cc. 36, 42, and 55.
[5] Cc. 55, 56.
[6] The corresponding Latin word is *aboleri,* c. 56.

theless, in consequence of this change, the flesh will no longer be subject to infirmities and sufferings, or the soul be disturbed by unruly passions and desires.[1]

"The body, therefore," the heretics replied, "after it is risen will be subject to no sufferings, will be harassed by no wants; what, then, will be the use of those members which at present administer to its necessities? what offices will the mouth, the throat, the teeth, the stomach, the intestines have to perform, when man will no longer eat and drink?"[2] We have said, answers Tertullian, that the body will undergo a change; and as man will then be free from the wants of this life, so will his members be released from many of their present duties. But it does not therefore follow that they will be wholly without use: the mouth, for instance, will be employed in singing praises to God. Nor will the final retribution be complete, unless the whole man stands before the judgment-seat of God—unless man stands there with all his members perfect.

When the heretics argued from Scripture, they sometimes said in general that "the language of Scripture is frequently figurative, and ought to be so considered in the present instance.[3] The resurrection of which it speaks is a moral or spiritual resurrection—a resurrection of the soul from the grave of sin—from the death of ignorance to the light of truth and to the knowledge of God.[4] Man, therefore, rises again, according to the meaning of Scripture, in baptism." Aware, however, that they might shock the feelings of those whom they wished to convert by an abrupt and total denial of the resurrection, they practised a verbal deception, and affirmed that every man must rise again, not in *the* flesh generally, *in carne*, but in *this* flesh, *in hâc carne;* tacitly referring to their moral resurrection, and meaning that man must in this life be initiated into their extravagant mysteries. Others again, in order to get rid of the

[1] C. 57. "Ita manebit quidem caro etiam post resurrectionem, eatenus passibilis qua ipsa, qua eadem; ea tamen impassibilis qua in hoc ipsum manumissa a Domino, ne ultra pati possit," etc.

[2] Cc. 60, 61, 62, 63.

[3] C. 19.

[4] Pearson calls this a Socinian notion. Article xi. p. 382. One of King Edward's Articles, entitled "Resurrectio mortuorum nondum est facta," is directed against it. "Resurrectio mortuorum non adhuc facta est, quasi tantum ad *animum* pertineat, qui per Christi gratiam a morte peccatorum excitetur." The article then proceeds, in exact conformity with our author's opinion, to state that the souls of men will be re-united to their bodies at the last day, in order to receive the final sentence of God.

resurrection of the flesh, interpreted the resurrection to mean the departure of the soul either from this world, which they called the habitation of the dead, that is, of those who know not God; or from the body, in which, as in a sepulchre, they conceived the soul to be detained. These objections afford Tertullian an opportunity of making some pertinent observations upon the marks by which we must determine when the language of Scripture is to be figuratively understood.[1] In this case, he says, we cannot so understand it, because the whole Christian faith hinges upon the doctrine of a future state; and surely God would not have made the gospel rest upon a figure.[2] Christ, moreover, in the prophecy in which He at once predicted the destruction of Jerusalem and the final consummation of all things, connected the resurrection with His second coming;[3] and we trace the same connexion in many passages of St. Paul's Epistles,[4] as well as in the Apocalypse. What, then, becomes of those figurative interpretations, according to which the resurrection is already past?[5] At least, Tertullian adds, the heretics ought to be consistent with themselves, and not to put a figurative construction on all that is said of the body, while they interpret literally whatever is said of the soul.[6] Our author, however, is not content with proving the figurative interpretation to be inapplicable in the present instance: he is determined to fight his adversaries with their own weapons, and produces passages of Scripture, equally or even more inapplicable, in which he finds the resurrection prefigured and typified.[7] He dwells particularly on the vision of dry bones in Ezekiel, and urges it in proof of the resurrection of the body.[8] By the heretics it was referred to the captivity of the Jews, and their subsequent restoration to their native land.[9] We learn incidentally from Tertullian's interpretation, that in his opinion the doctrine of the resurrection had been previously revealed to the Jews, and that the design of the vision was to confirm their wavering belief.[10]

[1] C. 20. In c. 33 are some good remarks upon the mode of distinguishing between what is to be understood literally, and what to be regarded as mere illustration in our Saviour's parables.

[2] C. 21. [3] C. 22. [4] Cc. 23, 24, 25.

[5] 2 Tim. ii. 18. [6] C. 32.

[7] Cc. 26, 27, 28. See, for instance, the interpretation of Isaiah lviii. 8. in c. 27.

[8] C. 29. In speaking of this chapter of Ezekiel (xxxvii.), Tertullian falls into a chronological error: he supposes that Ezekiel prophesied before the Captivity, c. 31.

[9] C. 30. Pearson appears to have thought that the vision had no reference to the resurrection of the body. Article xi. p. 372.

[10] C. 31. Compare c. 39.

The passages of Scripture on which Tertullian rests his proof of the resurrection of the body are such as the following. Christ said that He came to save what was lost.[1] What, then, was lost? The whole man, both soul and body. The body, therefore, must be saved as well as the soul; otherwise the purpose of Christ's coming will not be accomplished. Christ also, when He enjoined His hearers to fear *Him* only who can destroy both soul and body in hell, evidently assumed the resurrection of the body;[2] as well as in His answer to the question of the Sadducees respecting the woman who had been seven times married.[3] Of the other arguments urged by Tertullian, I will mention only one, which possesses at least the merit of ingenuity. The Athenians, he observes, would not have sneered at St. Paul for preaching the doctrine of the resurrection, in case he had maintained a mere resurrection of the soul, since that was a doctrine with which they were sufficiently familiar.[4]

Both parties appealed to the miracle performed by Christ in raising Lazarus.[5] Tertullian contended that He performed it in order to confirm the faith of His disciples, by exhibiting the very mode in which the future resurrection would take place. The heretics described it as a mere exercise of power, which could not have been rendered cognizable by the senses had not the body of Lazarus been raised as well as the soul.

"St. Paul," the heretics further argued, "speaks of an outward man that perishes, and of an inward man that is renewed from day to day, evidently alluding to the body and soul, and intimating that the latter alone will be saved."[6] Tertullian answers that this passage is to be understood of what takes place, not in a future, but in the present life—of the afflictions to which the bodies of Christians are subjected in consequence of their profession of the gospel, and of their daily advancement in faith and love through the inspiration of the Holy Spirit. In like manner when St. Paul distinguished between the old and the new man, expressions which the heretics also interpreted of the body and soul, he meant to speak of a difference, not of substance, but of character.[7] The old man was the Jew or Gentile, who walked in the lusts of the flesh; the new man the Christian, who, being renewed in the spirit of his mind, led a life of purity and holiness.

[1] C. 34. Luke xix. 10. [2] C. 35. Matt. x. 28. [3] C. 36. [4] C. 39.
[5] Cc. 39, 53. [6] Cc. 40, 41, 42, 43, 44. 2 Cor. iv. 16.
[7] Cc. 45, 46, 47. Eph. iv. 22.

So, when the apostle says that they who are in the flesh cannot please God,[1] he condemns not the flesh, but the works of the flesh; for he shortly afterwards adds that they who by the Spirit mortify the deeds of the flesh, shall live.[2]

But the passage on which the heretics principally relied was the declaration of St. Paul, that flesh and blood cannot inherit the kingdom of heaven.[3] "Here," they said, "is no figure, but a plain and express assertion that the body cannot be saved." To this objection Tertullian gives a variety of answers. He first states the circumstances which led the apostle into that particular train of thought, and shows very satisfactorily that, as St. Paul makes Christ's resurrection the foundation of our hope of a resurrection, the necessary inference is that we shall rise as He did, that is, in the flesh. He then borrows a weapon from the armoury of his opponents, and says that the expression *flesh and blood* is figurative, and means carnal conversation, which certainly excludes man from the kingdom of heaven.[4] "But if," he proceeds, "the expression is understood literally, still it contains no direct denial of the resurrection of the body.[5] We must distinguish between the resurrection of the body and its admission into the kingdom of heaven. The same body is raised in order that the whole man may stand before the judgment-seat of God; but before he can be received into the kingdom of heaven, he must be changed[6]—must be made partaker of the vivifying influence of the Spirit, and put on the vesture of incorruption and immortality. Death is the separation of the soul from the body: the body crumbles in the dust, the soul passes to the Inferi, where it remains in a state of imperfect happiness or misery according to the deeds done in the flesh. At the day of judg-

[1] Rom. viii. 8.

[2] Rom. viii. 13.

[3] C. 48. 1 Cor. xv. 50. Some in Tertullian's day appear to have interpreted the expression *flesh and blood* in this passage, as well as in Gal. i. 16, of Judaism, c. 50.

[4] C. 49. Compare *adv. Marcionem*, l. v. c. 10.

[5] Cc. 50, 51, 42.

[6] Compare the *Apology*, c. 48. "Superinduti substantiâ propriâ æternitatis." The substance of the glorified body will be, according to Tertullian, the same as that of the angels. *De Cultu Fœminarum*, l. i. c. 2, *sub fine; ad Uxorem*, l. i. c. 1; *ad Martyres*, c. 3. *de Animâ*, c. 56. "Ad Angelicæ plenitudinis mensuram temperatum." Our Saviour's declaration, that in the resurrection, men will be as the angels of God, appears to have given rise to this notion respecting the angelic substance. The change which will take place in the body of man is urged by Tertullian in answer to another heretical argument, founded upon the difference between this world and the next: "whatever belongs to the latter is immortal, and cannot therefore be possessed by 'flesh and blood,' which are mortal," c. 59.

ment it will be reunited to the body, and man will then receive his final sentence: if of condemnation, he will suffer eternal punishment in hell; if of justification, his body will be transformed and glorified, and he will thus be fitted to partake of the happiness of heaven. They who shall be alive on earth at the day of judgment will not die, but will at once undergo the change above described."

"But does not St. Paul say, 'That which thou sowest, thou sowest not that body which shall be, but bare grain'? and does not this comparison necessarily imply that man will be raised in a different body from that in which he died?"[1] Tertullian answers, by no means; for though there may be a difference of appearance, the body remains in kind, in nature, in quality the same. If you sow a grain of wheat, barley does not come up; or the converse. The apostle's comparison leads to the inference that a change will take place in the body, but not such a change as will destroy its identity.

The heretics grounded an argument upon another passage in the same chapter;[2] but in order to understand it we must turn to the original Greek. The words are, σπείρεται σῶμα ψυχικὸν, *seminatur corpus animale*, which in our version are rendered, *it is sown a natural body*.[3] The heretics affirmed σῶμα ψυχικὸν to be merely a periphrasis for ψυχὴ, and σῶμα πνευματικὸν for πνεῦμα. St. Paul, therefore, by omitting all mention of the flesh, evidently intended to exclude it from all share of the resurrection. In our account of the treatise *de Animâ*, we stated that our author conceived God to have given a soul to Adam, when the breath of life was breathed into his nostrils. He argues, therefore, that as σῶμα ψυχικὸν means a body animated by a soul, σῶμα πνευματικὸν means the same body, now become the habitation of the Spirit, and thus imbued with the principle of immortality. The pas-

[1] C. 52. 1 Cor. xv. 37. In interpreting St. Paul's words, "*There is one kind of flesh of men, another flesh of beasts, another of fishes, another of birds*," our author understands *men* to mean servants of God, *beasts* the heathen, *birds* martyrs who essay to fly up to heaven, *fishes* the mass of Christians, those who have been baptized. So in a subsequent passage, "*There is one glory of the sun, and another glory of the moon, and another glory of the stars*," the *sun* means Christ, the *moon* the Church, the *stars* the seed of Abraham, whether Jews or Christians.

[2] C. 53. 1 Cor. xv. 44. Compare *adv. Marcionem*, l. v. c. 10.

[3] Our translators, though they have not rendered the word ψυχικὸν literally, appear correctly to have represented St. Paul's meaning. Ὁ ἄνθρωπος ψυχικὸς is, as Tertullian expresses himself, *homo solius carnis et animæ*, the natural man—as opposed to ὁ ἄνθρωπος πνευματικὸς, the man who has received the Holy Spirit.

sage, far from subverting, establishes the doctrine of the resurrection of the body.

We will conclude this analysis of Tertullian's tract with observing that he alludes to the passage respecting the baptism for the dead in the fifteenth chapter of the First Epistle to the Corinthians, and speaks of it as if St. Paul had referred to a superstitious practice prevalent in his days, of baptizing a living person as a proxy for the dead.[1] But in the fifth book *against Marcion*, he ridicules this as an idle fancy,[2] on which it was unlikely that St. Paul should found an argument; and interprets the words *for the dead* to mean *for the body*, which is declared to be dead in baptism.

Passing over for the present the fifth Article of our Church, for the same reasons which induced us to omit the first and second, we proceed to the sixth.[3] The first question which presents itself for our consideration is, whether Tertullian uniformly speaks of the Scriptures as containing the whole rule to which the faith and practice of Christians must be conformed in points necessary to salvation. To this inquiry his pointed condemnation, already quoted,[4] of the Valentinian notion that the apostles had not communicated to mankind, publicly and indifferently, all the truths imparted to them by their heavenly Master, appears to furnish a satisfactory answer. So great indeed is the weight which he is on some occasions disposed to ascribe to the authority of Scripture, that he goes the length of denying the lawfulness of any act which is not permitted therein;[5] and even of asserting that whatever is not there related, must be supposed not to have happened.[6] We mean not to defend this extravagant

[1] "Si autem et baptizantur quidam pro mortuis (videbimus an ratione?) certe illâ præsumptione hoc eos instituisse contendit, quâ alii etiam carni, ut vicarium baptisma, profuturum existimarent ad spem resurrectionis, quæ nisi corporalis, non alias hic baptismate corporali obligantur," c. 48.

[2] "*Quid*, ait, *facient qui pro mortuis baptizantur, si mortui non resurgunt?* Viderit institutio ista; Calendæ si forte Februariæ respondebunt illi, pro mortuis petere. Noli ergo Apostolum novum statim auctorem aut confirmatorem ejus denotare, ut tanto magis sisteret carnis resurrectionem, quanto illi, qui vanè pro mortuis baptizarentur, fide resurrectionis hoc facerent. Habemus illum alicubi unius baptismi definitorem. Igitur et pro mortuis tingui pro corporibus est tingui: mortuum enim corpus ostendimus," c. 10.

[3] P. 262.

[4] Chap. iv. p. 250.

[5] "Immo prohibetur, quod non ultro permissum est." *De Coronâ*, c. 2, *sub fine*. Tertullian, however, appears himself to have been conscious of the weakness of the reasoning. See also *ad Uxorem*, l. ii. c. 2, *sub fine*.

[6] "Negat Scriptura quod non notat." *De Monogamiâ*, c. 4. Scripture

language, but produce it in order to show what were his opinions on the subject.

But does Tertullian always speak the same language? Does he not on other occasions appeal to tradition? Does he not even say, in his tract *de Præscriptione Hæreticorum*, that in arguing with the heretics no appeal ought to be made to the Scriptures; and that they can only be confuted by ascertaining the tradition which has been preserved and handed down in the Apostolic Churches? Undoubtedly he does. But in order to understand the precise meaning of Tertullian's appeal to tradition, we must consider the object which he had immediately in view. "In disputing with the heretics," he says, "it is necessary, in the very outset, to except against all arguments urged by them out of Scripture.[1] For as they do not acknowledge all the books received by the Church, and have mutilated or corrupted those which they do acknowledge, and have put their own interpretations upon the passages respecting the genuineness of which both parties are agreed, the first point to be determined is, which of the two is in possession of the genuine Scriptures, and of their true interpretation.[2] How, then, is this point to be determined? By inquiring what doctrines are held, and what Scriptures received, by the Apostolic Churches; for in them is preserved the truth, as it was originally communicated by Christ to the apostles, and by the apostles, either orally or by letter, to the Churches which they founded; so that whatever doctrines and Scriptures are so held and received must be deemed orthodox and genuine." Tertullian's opponents do not appear to have objected to the correctness of this mode of reasoning, but to have denied the premises. They contended either that the apostles were not themselves fully instructed in the truth, or that they did not communicate to the Churches all the truths which had been revealed to them.[3]

In support of the former assertion they alleged the reproof given by St. Paul to St. Peter, which they conceived to imply a defect of knowledge on the part of the latter.[4] Tertullian justly observes in reply, that the controversy between those two apostles related not to any fundamental article of faith, but to a

mentions the polygamy of Lamech, but of no other individual; he was therefore, according to Tertullian, at that period the only polygamist.

[1] C. 15. See also c. 37.

[2] C. 17.

[3] Cc. 19, 20, 21. See also cc. 37, 38. Compare *adv. Marcionem*, l. i. c. 21.

[4] C. 22.

question of practice—whether St. Peter had not been guilty of inconsistency in his conduct towards the Gentile brethren.

In support of the second assertion, they quoted St. Paul's exhortations to Timothy:[1] "Keep that which is committed to thy trust"—"That good thing which was committed to thee, keep;" interpreting these expressions of certain doctrines which St. Paul had secretly communicated to Timothy; though, as Tertullian well remarks, St. Paul's design was merely to caution Timothy against allowing any new doctrine to creep in, different from that in which he had been instructed.[2]

"But may not," the heretics asked, "may not the Churches in process of time have perverted the doctrine originally delivered to them by the apostles?[3] May they not all have wandered from the truth?" "Such an inference," our author answers, "is contrary to all experience. Truth is uniform and consistent; but it is of the very essence of error to be continually assuming new shapes. If the Churches had erred, they would have erred after many different fashions; whence then arises this surprising agreement in error? The single fact, that the same doctrine is maintained by so many different Churches situated in distant quarters of the globe, affords a strong presumption of its truth." I need scarcely observe that the force of this argument was much greater in Tertullian's time, when all the Churches were independent, than in after ages when the bishops of Rome assumed the right of prescribing the rule of faith to the whole Christian community. In this part of his argument our author clearly shows his opinion to be, that the promise of the Holy Spirit, made by Christ to the Church, precludes the possibility of an universal defection from the true faith.[4]

The superior antiquity of the doctrine maintained in the Church furnishes Tertullian with another argument in favour of its truth.[5] As truth necessarily precedes error, which is, as it were, its image or counterfeit, that must be the true doctrine which was prior in time; that which was subsequent, false: and it may be easily shown that the origin of the heretical sects was posterior to the foundation of the Apostolic Churches.

[1] C. 23. Compare *adv. Marcionem,* l. iv. c. 3.
[2] Cc. 25, 26; 1 Tim. vi. 20; 2 Tim. i. 14.
[3] Cc. 27, 28.
[4] See the commencement of c. 28.
[5] Cc. 29, 30, 31, 32. Compare the *Apology,* c. 47.

The circumstance, however, most to our present purpose is, that Tertullian, when he comes at last to examine and confute the heretical doctrines, appeals to the apostolic writings, and shows that St. Paul had, as it were by anticipation, condemned many of those doctrines.[1] If he had not condemned all, it was simply because all were not then in existence; his very silence, therefore, proves the novelty, and consequently the falsehood of the heretical opinions which he did not notice. Tertullian alleges as an instance the heretical notion that the Demiurge who gave the law was not only a distinct being from the Supreme God who gave the gospel, but at variance with Him. "If this opinion existed in the days of St. Paul, how comes it that he never alludes to it in his Epistles? The questions which he discusses relate to meats offered to idols, to marriage, to the introduction of fables and endless genealogies, and to the resurrection. Much of his labour is employed in proving that the observance of the Mosaic ritual is no longer obligatory on the conscience.[2] Surely he would not have taken this unnecessary trouble if the heretical doctrine now alluded to had been then received, since he might at once have put an end to the controversy by saying that the law and the gospel did not proceed from the same author."

If, then, we closely attend to the object which Tertullian had in view, we shall be led to the conclusion that the tract *de Præscriptione Hæreticorum*, far from lending any sanction, is directly opposed to the Roman Catholic notion respecting tradition—to the notion that there are certain doctrines, of which the belief is necessary to salvation, and which rest on the authority, not of Scripture, but of unwritten tradition. Tertullian, it is true, refuses to dispute with the heretics out of the Scriptures; not, however, because he was not persuaded that the Scriptures contained the whole rule of faith, but because the heretics rejected a large portion of the sacred writings, and either mutilated or put forced and erroneous interpretations upon those parts which they received. Before, therefore, an appeal could be made to the Scriptures, it was necessary to determine which were the genuine Scriptures, and what the true interpretation of them. The first of these questions was purely historical; to be determined by ascertaining what books had from the earliest

[1] Cc. 33, 34. See also c. 38, in which Tertullian asserts in the strongest terms the genuineness and integrity of the Scriptures used in the Church.

[2] See *adv. Marcionem*, l. v. c. 2.

times been generally received by the Apostolic Churches; and, with respect to the second, though interpretations which had received the sanction of the Church were not to be lightly rejected, yet the practice of Tertullian himself proves that he believed every Christian to be at liberty to exercise his own judgment upon them.[1] The language of Tertullian corresponds exactly with that of the Church of England in the twentieth Article. According to him, the Church is the witness and keeper of Holy Writ; but so far is he from thinking that the Church can either decide anything against Scripture, or prescribe anything not contained in it, as necessary to salvation, that he uniformly and strenuously insists *upon the exact agreement* between the tradition preserved in the Church and the doctrine delivered in Scripture.[2]

[1] Respecting the degree of authority ascribed by our Church to tradition, in the interpretation of Scripture, see some excellent remarks of Bishop Jebb in the Appendix to his Sermons.

[2] See *de Præscript. Hæretic.* c. 38. While the first edition of the present work was passing through the press, I received a copy of the translation of Dr. Schleiermacher's *Critical Essay on the Gospel of St. Luke.* In a learned and ingenious Introduction, the translator has made some remarks on the superiority ascribed by Tertullian to tradition over Scripture, with a particular reference to the tract *de Præscriptione Hæreticorum.*[1] He admits that "Tertullian's argument is perfectly consistent with Protestant principles;" and that "the tradition which is the subject of controversy between Roman Catholics and Protestants is very different from the *Traditio Apostolorum* spoken of by Tertullian" (*de Præscr. Hæret.* c. 21). But he afterwards states "what he conceives to be an incontestable fact, that the maxims of the Protestant Church with respect to the use of the Scriptures are as different from those which prevailed in all ages, from the time of Tertullian down to the Reformation, as from those which now prevail in the Roman Catholic Church." As I had myself expressed a different opinion, viz. that Tertullian's language respecting tradition corresponds exactly with that of the Church of England—one, and certainly not the least important branch of the Protestant Church—I was induced by the learned translator's remark to reconsider the subject; and I must confess that, after having again perused the tract *de Præscriptione Hæreticorum,* I discover no reason for coming to a different conclusion from that which I had before formed.

From the commencement of the treatise it appears that the minds of many members of the Church were disquieted by the rapid progress of heresy. They were surprised and scandalized at the divisions which prevailed among those who called themselves Christians; and their surprise was increased by observing that men of high reputation for wisdom and piety from time to time quitted the Church, and attached themselves to one or other of the heretical sects. Tertullian, therefore, in the first four chapters of the tract, contends that the existence and prevalence of heresy ought not to be a matter of surprise, since Christ had predicted that heresies would arise, and St. Paul had affirmed that the very purpose of their existence was to prove the faith of Christians.

In the fifth and sixth chapters he appeals to the authority of the same apostle, in proof of the mischievous nature of heresy; and in the seventh, traces the tenets of the different sects to the Grecian philosophy. In the eighth he states that the heretics gained many converts to their opinions by persuading men that it was the duty of every Christian to search the Scriptures. "*Seek,*" they said, "*and you*

[1] P. cxxxv. *et seq.*

If we mistake not the signs of the times, the period is not far distant when the whole controversy between the English and

*shall find; knock, and it shall be opened unto you*, are the injunctions of Christ Himself." Tertullian, in reply, first contends that those injunctions were delivered in the very outset of Christ's ministry, and addressed especially to the Jews, who, by searching their Scriptures—those of the Old Testament—might have learned that He was the Messiah predicted by the prophets. "But grant," Tertullian continues, "that the injunction was addressed indiscriminately to all mankind, still it is evident that Christ intended to propose some definite object of search; and when that was attained, to release His followers from the labour of further inquiry. He could not mean that they were to go on searching for ever. They were to inquire what was the doctrine which He had actually delivered; and when they had found it, they were to believe. If, after having been once satisfied that they have found the truth, Christians are to recommence their inquiries as often as a new opinion is started, their faith can never be settled or stedfast. At least it must be allowed to be absurd and useless to seek the truth among the heretics, who differ as widely from each other as they do from the Church; or among those who, having believed as we do, have deserted their original faith, and having been once our friends, are now our enemies."[1]

In the thirteenth chapter Tertullian lays down what he calls the rule of faith, *Regula Fidei;* and promises to prove that it was delivered by Christ.[2] In the fourteenth he says that all our inquiries into Scripture should be conducted with reference and in subordination to that rule. But as the heretics rested their whole cause upon an appeal to Scripture, asserting that their doctrine was derived from it, and that the rule of faith could only be found *ex litteris fidei*, in those books which are of the faith, Tertullian proceeds, in the fifteenth and following chapters, to assign the reasons of which we have just given a sketch, why, in arguing with the heretics, he declined all appeal to the Scriptures.

Now, whatever may be the case with other Protestant Churches, I see nothing in Tertullian's reasoning at variance with the maxims of the Church of England respecting the use of the Scriptures. Tertullian, according to the learned translator, appeals to apostolic tradition—to a rule of faith, not *originally* deduced from Scripture, but delivered by the apostles orally to the Churches which they founded, and regularly transmitted from them to his own time. How, I would ask, is this appeal inconsistent with the principles of the Church of England, which declares *only* that Holy Scripture contains all things necessary to salvation? Respecting the source from which the rule of faith was *originally* deduced, our Church is silent. The framers of our Articles meant not to deny that the rule of faith might, independently of the Scriptures, have been faithfully transmitted in the Apostolic Churches *down to Tertullian's time.* What they meant to assert was, that the rule, so transmitted, contained no article which was not either expressed in Scripture, or might not be proved by it; and that the peculiar doctrines, in support of which the Roman Catholics appealed to tradition, formed no part of the apostolic rule.

With respect also to the motives of Tertullian's appeal to apostolic tradition, I cannot think that the learned translator is warranted in saying that Tertullian considered it as the only sure foundation of Christian faith, and appealed to it as an authority paramount to Scripture. To me he appears to have appealed to it from necessity, because he could not, from the nature of the dispute in which he was engaged, directly appeal to Scripture. The heretics with whom he was contending not only proposed a different rule of faith, but in defence of it produced a different set of Scriptures. How, then, was Tertullian to confute them? By showing that the faith which he professed, and the Scriptures to which he appealed, were, and had always been, the faith and Scriptures of those Churches of which the origin could be traced to the apostles—the first depositaries of the faith. In

[1] Cc. 9, 10, 11, 12.

[2] He fulfils this promise in cc. 20, 21.

Romish Churches will be revived, and all the points in dispute again brought under review. Of those points none is more important than the question respecting tradition; and it is therefore most essential that they who stand forth as the defenders of the Church of England should take a correct and rational view of the subject—the view, in short, which was taken by our divines at the Reformation. Nothing was more remote from their intention than indiscriminately to condemn all tradition. They knew that, in strictness of speech, Scripture is tradition — written tradition.[1] They knew that, as far as external evidence is concerned, the tradition preserved in the Church is the only ground on which the genuineness of the books of Scripture can be established. For though we are not, upon the authority of the Church, bound to receive as Scripture any book which contains internal evidence of its own spuriousness—such as discrepancies,

this case Tertullian had no alternative: he was *compelled* to appeal to apostolic tradition. But when he is contending against Praxeas, a heretic who acknowledged the Scriptures received by the Church, though he begins with laying down the rule of faith nearly in the same words as in the tract *de Præscriptione Hæreticorum*, yet he conducts the controversy by *a constant appeal to Scripture*. Why, indeed, did Marcion think it necessary to compile a gospel, if it was not usual for the contending parties even in his time to allege the authority of the written word in support of their respective tenets? Let it be observed also that in Tertullian's view of the subject the genuine Scriptures evidently formed a part of the apostolic tradition.[1]

When, again, the learned translator says that Tertullian dissuades his believing brother from entering into any scriptural researches, he appears to me not to make due allowance for the vehemence of Tertullian's temper, and his disposition always to use the strongest expressions which occurred to him at the moment. In the place referred to, he is manifestly addressing himself to ordinary Christians—to those who are unfitted by their talents and acquirements to engage in theological controversy.[2] To them he says, "Adhere closely to the creed in which you have been instructed. If you read the Scriptures, and meet with difficulties, consult some doctor of the Church who has made the sacred volume his peculiar study; or if you cannot readily have recourse to such a person, be content to be ignorant. It is faith that saves you, not familiarity with the Scriptures. At any rate, do not go for a solution of your doubts to the heretics, who confess by their continual inquiries that they are themselves in doubt." Tertullian's object in this passage manifestly is to deter the unlearned Christian from curious researches which may lead him into error; and, as his custom is, he employs very strong language. But a writer, whose works teem with scriptural quotations, could not deliberately intend to disparage scriptural knowledge.

[1] Tertullian uses the expression *Scripta Traditio. De Coronâ*, c. 3. In the tract *de Carne Christi*, c. 2, speaking of the history of our Saviour's life and actions as delivered in Scripture, he says, "Si tantum Christianus es, crede quod traditum est;" and again, "Porro quod traditum erat, id erat verum, ut ab iis traditum quorum fuit tradere."

[1] See *adv. Marcionem*, l. iv. c. 5, the whole object of which is to prove by an appeal to the tradition preserved in the Apostolic Churches, that the Gospel of St. Luke used by the orthodox was genuine, that of Marcion spurious.

[2] *De Præscriptione Hæreticorum*, c. 14.

contradictions of other portions of Scripture, idle fables, or precepts at variance with the great principles of morality—yet no internal evidence is sufficient to prove a book to be Scripture, of which the reception, by a portion at least of the Church, cannot be traced from the earliest period of its history to the present time. What our reformers opposed was the notion that men must, upon the mere authority of tradition, receive, as necessary to salvation, doctrines not contained in Scripture. Against this notion in general they urged the incredibility of the supposition that the apostles, when unfolding *in their writings* the principles of the gospel, should have entirely omitted any doctrines essential to man's salvation. The whole tenor, indeed, of those writings, as well as of our blessed Lord's discourses, runs counter to the supposition that any truths of fundamental importance would be suffered long to rest upon so precarious a foundation as that of oral tradition. With respect to the particular doctrines, in defence of which the Roman Catholics appeal to tradition, our reformers contended that some were directly at variance with Scripture; and that others, far from being supported by an unbroken chain of tradition from the apostolic age, were of very recent origin, and utterly unknown to the early Fathers. Such was the view of this important question taken by our reformers. In this, as in other instances, they wisely adopted a middle course; they neither bowed submissively to the authority of tradition, nor yet rejected it altogether. We in the present day must tread in their footsteps and imitate their moderation, if we intend to combat our Roman Catholic adversaries with success. We must be careful that, in our anxiety to avoid one extreme, we run not into the other by adopting the extravagant language of those who, not content with ascribing a paramount authority to the written word on all points pertaining to eternal salvation, talk as if the Bible—and that too the Bible in our English translation—were, independently of all external aids and evidence, sufficient to prove its own genuineness and inspiration, and to be its own interpreter.

To return to Tertullian. In the passage to which reference has just been made,[1] he speaks both of written and unwritten tradition; but the cases in which he lays any stress upon the authority of the latter are precisely those which our reformers allowed to be within its province—cases of ceremonies and ritual observances.[2] Of these he enumerates several, for which no

[1] In the preceding note, from the tract *de Coronâ Militis*, c. 3.

[2] It is important to distinguish between traditional doctrines and traditional

express warrant can be found in Scripture, and which must consequently have been derived solely from tradition ; the forms, for instance, observed in baptism, in the administration of the Lord's Supper, and in public prayer.[1] Even in these cases he seems to have deemed it essential to the validity of a traditional observance, that some satisfactory reason should be assigned for its original institution ;[2] and when different observances have prevailed in different Churches, it is our duty, he says,[3] to inquire which of the two is more agreeable to the rule of life laid down by Scripture. In relation to the subject now treated of, there is only one point in which I discover any difference of opinion between Tertullian and the framers of our Articles. He sometimes appears to contend that an uniformity of ceremonies ought to be maintained in all the particular Churches, of which the visible Church is composed ;[4] and that any Church which breaks this uniformity divides the body of Christ. Our Church,[5] on the contrary, though it asserts that every individual member of a Church is bound to comply with the observances ordained in it by competent authority, yet, availing itself of that liberty in things indifferent which the apostle of the Gentiles allows, declares that "traditions and ceremonies need not be in all places one and utterly like, but may be changed according to the diversities of countries, times, and men's manners," with this single proviso, "that nothing be ordained against God's Word." Our author, however, is not always consistent with himself, for in another place he speaks as if it were lawful, not merely for every

practices. Our Church receives no traditional doctrines—no doctrines necessary to salvation, preserved through several ages by oral tradition, and afterwards committed to writing ; but it has a respect for traditional practices : not, however, such a respect as to preclude it from examining their original reasonableness, and their suitableness to existing manners and circumstances.

1 *De Coronâ*, cc. 3, 4.

2 "Rationem traditioni, et consuetudini, et fidei patrocinaturam aut ipse perspicies, aut ab aliquo qui perspexerit disces : interim nonnullam esse credes, cui debeatur obsequium." *De Coronâ*, c. 4. "Sed quia eorum quæ ex traditione observantur tanto magis dignam rationem afferre debemus, quanto carent Scripturæ auctoritate." *De Jejuniis*, c. 10. "Non exploratis rationibus Traditionum." *De Baptismo*, c. 1.

3 "Tamen hic, sicut in omnibus variè institutis et dubiis et incertis fieri solet, adhibenda fuit examinatio, quæ magis ex duabus tam diversis consuetudinibus disciplinæ Dei conveniret." *De Virginibus velandis*, c. 2.

4 "Non possumus respuere consuetudinem, quam damnare non possumus, utpote non extraneam, quia non extraneorum, cum quibus scilicet communicamus jus pacis et nomen fraternitatis. Una nobis et illis fides, unus Deus, idem Christus, eadem spes, eadem lavacri Sacramenta. Semel dixerim, una Ecclesia sumus. Ita nostrum est quodcunque nostrorum est. Cæterum dividis corpus." *De Virginibus velandis*, c. 2.

5 Article 34.

Church, but for every Christian, to appoint observances, if they are but agreeable to the Word of God, tend to promote a Christian temper and life, and are profitable unto salvation.[1] Before we quit the subject of tradition, we must, in justice to Tertullian, remark that when, in opposition to the tradition of the Church, he contended for the reception of the new discipline of Montanus, he was not chargeable with inconsistency; since, conceiving as he did, that Montanus was divinely inspired, he conceived him to possess at least equal authority with the apostles themselves.

We will now proceed to inquire what information the writings of Tertullian supply respecting the canon of Scripture. His quotations include all the books of the Old Testament, excepting Ruth, the two Books of Chronicles, the Book of Nehemiah, and the prophecies of Obadiah and Haggai. Of the apocryphal books he quotes Judith, Wisdom, Ecclesiasticus, Baruch under the name of Jeremiah,[2] the Song of the Three Children under the name of Daniel,[3] the Stories of Susannah[4] and of Bel and the Dragon,[5] and the first Book of Maccabees. He quotes all the books of the New Testament,[6] excepting the Second Epistle of St. Peter, the Third of St. John, and perhaps the Epistle of St. James;[7] for we concur in Lardner's opinion that there is sufficient ground for believing some words to have dropped out towards the conclusion of the fifth book *against Marcion* which contained a reference to the Epistle to Philemon.[8] The reader will find in the fourth book *against Marcion* some valuable remarks upon the genuineness and integrity of the Gospels.[9] Tertullian states

[1] "Annon putas *omni fideli* licere concipere et constituere, duntaxat quod Deo congruat, quod disciplinæ conducat, quod saluti proficiat? dicente Domino, *cur autem non et a vobis ipsis quod justum est judicatis?* et non de judicio tantum, sed de omni sententiâ rerum examinandarum." *De Coronâ*, c. 4. Tertullian in this passage could scarcely mean to assert that observances appointed by one individual were obligatory upon others.

[2] "*Scorpiace*, c. 8. The quotation is from the sixth chapter, which is called in our Bibles the Epistle of Jeremiah.

[3] "Cui etiam inanimalia et incorporalia laudes canunt apud Danielem." *Adv. Hermogenem*, c. 44.

[4] *De Coronâ*, c. 4.

[5] *De Idololatriâ*, c. 18; *de Jejuniis*, c. 7, *sub fine*.

[6] In the *Index locorum ex Scripturis Sacris*, annexed to the Paris edition, the second (or fourth) Book of Esdras and the second Book of Maccabees occur; but the supposed quotations are of a very doubtful character. The former is probably referred to in the first book *de Cultu Fœminarum*, c. 3.

[7] See Lardner, *Credibility*, c. 27, sect. XI.

[8] *Credibility of the Gospel History*, c. 27. Rigault thinks that there is an allusion to the Epistle to Philemon in the following passage from the tract *adv. Valentinianos*, "Et forsitan parias aliquem Onesimum Æonem," c. 32. St. Paul speaks of Onesimus as his son, begotten by him, v. 10.

[9] Cc. 2, 3, 4, 5. In c. 5, the Apocalypse is ascribed to St. John.

St. Luke to have been the author of the Acts of the Apostles.[1] The account which Tertullian gives of the Septuagint translation is, that Ptolemy Philadelphus, at the suggestion of Demetrius Phalereus, obtained a copy of the Hebrew Scriptures in order to place it in his library, and afterwards caused it to be translated by seventy-two interpreters, who were sent to him by the Jews for that purpose. This Tertullian states on the authority of Aristæus or Aristeas; and adds that the Hebrew copy was preserved in his own time in the temple of Serapis at Alexandria.[2] He evidently supposed that the translators executed their work under the influence of divine inspiration. It is unnecessary to detail the reasons which have induced the majority of learned men to treat the narrative of Aristæus as a fable. We will content ourselves with observing that Tertullian, in quoting the Old Testament, appears either himself to have translated from the Greek, or to have used a Latin version made from the Greek, not from the Hebrew.[3]

Tertullian quotes, more than once, the prophecy of Enoch.[4] In one place he admits that it was not received into the Jewish canon; but supposes that the Jews rejected it merely because they were unable to account for its having survived the deluge.[5] He argues, therefore, that Noah might have received it from his great-grandfather Enoch, and handed it down to his posterity; or if it was actually lost at the deluge, Noah might have restored it from immediate revelation, as Ezra restored the whole Jewish Scripture.[6] "Perhaps," he adds, "the Jews reject it because it contains a prediction of Christ's advent; at any rate, the reference to it made by the apostle Jude ought to quiet all our doubts respecting its genuineness." For a more detailed

[1] "Porro quum in eodem commentario Lucæ." *De Jejuniis*, c. 10. The allusion is to the second chapter of Acts.

[2] Tertullian must have been mistaken in conceiving that the Hebrew copy was extant in his day, if, as Gibbon tells us, the *old* library of the Ptolemies was *totally* consumed in Cæsar's Alexandrian war. Chap. xxviii. note 41.

[3] Thus in citing Isaiah v. 18. Tertullian, *de Pænitentiâ*, c. 11, reads, "Væ illis qui delicta sua velut procero fune nectunt;" conformably to the Septuagint, *οὐαὶ οἱ ἐπισπώμενοι τὰς ἁμαρτίας ὡς σχοινίῳ μακρῷ.* Jerome in agreement with the Hebrew reads, "Væ qui trahitis iniquitatem in funiculis vanitatis."

[4] *De Idololatriâ*, c. 15; *de Cultu Fæminarum*, l. ii. c. 10.

[5] "Scio Scripturam Enoch, quæ hunc ordinem Angelis dedit, non recipi a quibusdam, quia nec in armarium Judaicum admittitur." *De Cultu Fæminarum*, l. i. c. 3.

[6] We are not certain whether Tertullian borrowed this statement respecting the restoration of the Hebrew Scriptures from the apocryphal book of Esdras xiv. 21, or drew an inference from Nehemiah viii.

account of this book we refer the reader to the Dissertation, prefixed by Dr. Laurence[1] to his translation of the book of Enoch the Prophet, from an Ethiopic MS. in the Bodleian Library.

Such of our readers as are acquainted with the late Professor Porson's letters to Archdeacon Travis will remember the archdeacon's interpretation of an expression used by Tertullian, when speaking of the Apostolic Churches. "Percurre Ecclesias Apostolicas, apud quas ipsæ adhuc Cathedræ Apostolorum suis locis præsident, apud quas ipsæ Authenticæ Literæ eorum recitantur, sonantes vocem et repræsentantes faciem uniuscujusque."[2] By the words *authenticæ literæ* the archdeacon understood Tertullian to mean the autographs of the apostles. If, however, we turn to the tract *de Monogamiâ*,[3] we find our author, after he has given the Latin version of a passage, stating that it was differently read *in Græco authentico;* that is, in the original Greek, as contradistinguished from a translation. In like manner he uses the expressions *originalia instrumenta Christi; originale instrumentum Moysi;*[4] meaning, of course, not an autograph either of Christ or Moses, but the Gospels and the Pentateuch, as they were originally written. Berriman, therefore, and others, suppose that Tertullian by the words *authenticæ literæ* meant only the genuine unadulterated Epistles.[5] Lardner conceives that our author intended to appeal, not to the Epistles which St. Paul addressed to the particular Churches mentioned by Tertullian, but to *all* the Scriptures of the New Testament, of which the Apostolic Churches were peculiarly the depositaries.[6] But Lardner's argument is, in my opinion, founded on a misapprehension of Tertullian's immediate object in the passage in question. He there appeals to the Apostolic Churches as bear-

[1] Now Lord Archbishop Cashel. The work was published at Oxford in 1821.

[2] *De Præscriptione Hæreticorum*, c. 36.

[3] C. 11. The passage is 1 Cor. vii. 39. The MSS. now extant lend no countenance to Tertullian's assertion. Does not, however, the assertion prove that a Latin version was actually extant in his time, in opposition to Semler's notion stated in chap. ii. note 38? See Lardner, *Credibility*, c. 27, sect. xix. The following passage in the tract *against Praxeas* seems to remove all doubts on the subject: "Ideoque jam in usu est nostrorum, per simplicitatem interpretationis, *Sermonem* dicere *in primordio apud Deum fuisse*," c. 5.

[4] *De Carne Christi*, c. 2. *Adv. Hermogenem*, c. 19.

[5] Tertullian says of Valentinus, "De Ecclesiâ *authenticæ* regulæ abrupit," he separated himself from the Church which possessed the genuine rule of life. *Adv. Valentinianos*, c. 4. In another place he says of our Saviour, "Ipse *authenticus* Pontifex Dei Patris." He was the true, the original Priest, of whom the priests under the Mosaic law were only copies. *Adv. Marcionem*, l. iv. c. 35.

[6] *Credibility of the Gospel History*, c. 27.

ing witness, not to the genuineness and integrity of the Scriptures, but to the true and uncorrupted doctrine of the gospel. For this he tells us that we must look to those Churches which were founded by the apostles, and were able to produce the authority of epistles addressed to them by the apostles. The words *literæ authenticæ* may therefore mean epistles possessing authority. It is, however, of little consequence to which of the above meanings we give the preference, since the whole passage is evidently nothing more than a declamatory mode of stating the weight which Tertullian attached to the authority of the Apostolic Churches. To infer from it that the very chairs in which the apostles sat, or that the very Epistles which they wrote, then actually existed at Corinth, Ephesus, Rome, etc., would be only to betray a total ignorance of Tertullian's style.

Tertullian expressly ascribes the Epistle to the Hebrews to Barnabas:[1] he does not say that it was universally received in the Church, but that it was more generally received than the *Shepherd of Hermas.* He mentions also a work falsely ascribed to St. Paul,[2] but composed by an Asiatic presbyter, who was impelled, as he himself confessed, to commit the pious fraud by admiration of the apostle. The work appears to have been quoted in defence of a custom which had crept in of allowing females to baptize.

In speaking of the mode in which the canon of the New Testament was formed, Lardner says that it was not determined by the authority of councils.[3] This may in one sense be true. Yet it appears from a passage in the tract *de Pudicitiâ*, referred to in a former chapter,[4] that in Tertullian's time one part of the business of councils was to decide what books were genuine, and what spurious; for he appeals to the decisions of councils

[1] *De Pudicitiâ,* c. 20. "Extat enim et Barnabæ titulus ad Hebræos: adeo satis auctoritatis viro, ut quem Paulus juxta se constituerit in abstinentiæ tenore: *aut ego solus et Barnabas non habemus hoc operandi potestatem?* Et utique receptior apud Ecclesias Epistola Barnabæ illo apocrypho Pastore mœchorum." Tertullian then proceeds to quote a passage from the sixth chapter of the Epistle to the Hebrews. Lardner thinks it doubtful whether Tertullian's works contain any other allusion to the Epistle.

[2] *De Baptismo,* c. 17, *sub fine.* Jerome, *Catalogus Scriptorum Ecclesiasticorum* under St. Luke. He appears to have supposed that the work in question was entitled the *Travels of Paul and Thecla.*

[3] *History of the Apostles and Evangelists,* c. 3.

[4] Chap. iv. p. 121, note 17. "Sed cederem tibi, si Scriptura Pastoris, quæ sola mœchos amat, divino instrumento meruisset incidi: si non ab omni concilio Ecclesiarum etiam vestrarum inter apocrypha et falsa judicaretur," c. 10.

in support of his rejection of the *Shepherd of Hermas.* We have seen that Tertullian appeals to the original Greek text of the First Epistle to the Corinthians.[1] This fact appears to militate strongly against the theory of the author of a recent work entitled *Palæoromaica,* who asserts that the said Epistle, as well as the greater part of the New Testament, was originally written in Latin.

When we contrast the acuteness which the anonymous author of that work occasionally, and the extensive reading which he always displays, with the extraordinary conclusions at which he arrives, we are strongly tempted to suspect that he is only playing with his readers, and trying how far intrepid assertion will go towards inducing men to lend a favourable ear to the most startling paradoxes. To take a single instance from the Epistle just mentioned. His solution of the celebrated difficulty respecting the power which, according to St. Paul,[2] a woman ought to have on her head, is—that in the original Latin the word was *habitus,* which the ignorant translator rendered etymologically ἐξουσία.[3] In support of this fancy he quotes the following words from Tertullian's treatise *de Virginibus velandis,* c. 3: "O sacrilegæ manus, quæ dicatum Deo *habitum* (the veil) detrahere potuerunt!"—meaning his readers to infer that Tertullian found *habitus* in the verse in question, but omitting to inform them that it is twice quoted by Tertullian in this very tract, and that in both instances the reading is *potestas.*[4] That the omission proceeded, not from inadvertence, but design, is, we think, rendered certain by the still more extraordinary solution subjoined by the author, that *vestitus* was the original reading; which, when pronounced by a Jew, might easily be confounded with *potestas.* It is impossible that the author could be serious in throwing out either of these conjectures.

We will mention one other argument of a more plausible character, alleged by the author in support of his theory. The author contends that the very titles of the existing Greek Gospels, τὸ εὐαγγέλιον κατὰ Ματθαῖον, κατὰ Λοῦκαν, prove them to be translations.[5] The version of the Septuagint was called κατὰ τοὺς Ἑβδομήκοντα, that of Aquila κατὰ Ἀκυλάν. But why does

[1] See p. 154, note 3.

[2] 1 Cor. xi. 10.

[3] Supplement to *Palæoromaica,* p. 61, note 5. The author does not inform us how the word *habitus* came to be translated etymologically ἐξουσία; does he mean that the translator confounded ἕξις and ἐξουσία?

[4] Cc. 7, 17.

[5] Supplement to *Palæoromaica,* p. 3, note 2.

he stop short in his inference? If the argument proves anything, it proves, not merely that the existing Greek Gospels were translations, but also that Matthew, Luke, etc., were the translators. The true answer, however, is that the force of the preposition *κατὰ* depends entirely upon the word with which it is connected. The title *τὸ εὐαγγέλιον κατὰ Ματθαῖον* means "the glad tidings of salvation as delivered by St. Matthew;" or as paraphrased by Hammond, "That story of Christ which Matthew compiled and set down." For though the word *εὐαγγέλιον* was employed at a very early period to signify a written book,[1] yet it continued to be used in its primitive meaning; as by Tertullian, when he calls St. Matthew, *fidelissimus Evangelii commentator*, the most faithful expositor of the life and doctrine of Christ.[2] We will take this opportunity of remarking that our author, in speaking of the Scriptures, sometimes calls them Instrumentum, sometimes Testamentum;[3] but says on one occasion that the latter term was in more general use.[4] He calls them also Digesta.[5]

Some learned men have contended that the Epistle, which in our Bibles is inscribed to the Ephesians, should be entitled to the Laodiceans.[6] Tertullian in one place says that the heretics alone gave it that title;[7] in another,[8] that Marcion had at one time manifested an intention to alter the title of the Epistle. Semler's inference is that some of the Epistles were without inscriptions, and received in consequence a variety of titles.

There are in Tertullian, as well as in the other Fathers, quotations purporting to be taken from Scripture, but which cannot be found in our present copies. Thus in the tract *de Idololatriâ*,

1 See *de Res. Carnis*, c. 33: *de Carne Christi*, c. 7: *adv. Marcionem*, l. i. c. 1; l. iv. cc. 1, 3; l. v. 1: *Scorpiace*, c. 2.

2 *De Carne Christi*, c. 22. See also *de Res. Carnis*, c. 33. The word *commentator* is similarly used, *adv. Marcionem*, l. iv. c. 2.

3 "Vetus Instrumentum." *Apology*, c. 47. "Ex instrumento divinarum Scripturarum." *Adv. Judæos*, c. 1. The two words are joined together, *adv. Praxeam*, c. 20. "Instrumentum utriusque testamenti."

4 "Alterum alterius instrumenti, vel (quod magis usui est dicere) testamenti." *Adv. Marcionem*, l. iv. c. 1.

5 "Et inde sunt nostra digesta." *Adv. Marcionem*, l. iv. c. 2. "Si quid in sanctis offenderunt digestis." *Apology*, c. 47.

6 Lardner, *History of the Apostles and Evangelists*, c. 13.

7 "Prætereo hic et de aliâ epistolâ, quam nos ad Ephesios perscriptam habemus; Hæretici vero ad Laodicenos." *Adv. Marcionem*, l. v. c. 11.

8 "Ecclesiæ quidem veritate, Epistolam istam ad Ephesios habemus emissam, non ad Laodicenos: sed Marcion ei titulum aliquando interpolare gestiit, quasi et in isto diligentissimus explorator." *Adv. Marcionem*, l. v. c. 17.

c. 20, "Nam sicut scriptum est *ecce homo et facta ejus*, ita, *ex ore tuo justificaberis*."[1] The commentators have not been able to trace the former of the two quotations, and some suppose it to have been taken from the book of Enoch. On three different occasions Tertullian quotes the words *Dominus regnavit a ligno* as a portion of the tenth verse of the 95th (or 96th) Psalm;[2] from which, according to Justin Martyr, the words corresponding to *a ligno* had been erased by the Jews. In the tract *de Carne Christi*, c. 23, we find the following sentence: "Legimus quidem apud Ezechielem de vaccâ illâ, *quæ peperit et non peperit*;" the words are also quoted by Clemens Alexandrinus,[3] but he does not refer to any particular portion of Scripture. In the tract *de Exhortatione Castitatis*,[4] Tertullian says, "Cautum in Levitico, *Sacerdotes mei non plus nubent*;" but the prohibition,[5] as it stands in our Bibles, is that a priest shall not marry a widow or divorced female. Tertullian's writings afford many exemplifications of the justice of Porson's remarks respecting the want of correctness and precision observable in the quotations of the Fathers from the Scriptures. He sometimes refers his readers to one part of Scripture for passages which belong to another; and he so mixes up the quotations with his own words, that it is difficult to distinguish between them.[6] The consequence has been that his inferences and explanations have been mistaken for various readings,[7] and have in some instances found their way into the text of the sacred volume.[8]

We proceed to the seventh Article, on which it will be sufficient to remark that, as the heretical opinions of Marcion were founded on the notion that the God who created the world and gave the law was opposed to the Supreme God, he maintained as a necessary consequence that the Old Testament was contrary to the New. Our author, therefore, who undertakes to confute

[1] Matt. xii. 37.

[2] *Adv. Judæos*, cc. 10, 13. *Adv. Marcionem*, l. iii. c. 19. See Thirlby's note on *Justin Martyr against Trypho*, p. 298 D.

[3] *Strom.* l. vii. p. 890, ed. Potter. See Porson's *Letters to Travis*, p. 275.

[4] C. 7. Compare *de Monogamiâ*, c. 7.

[5] Lev. xxi. 7, 13, 14.

[6] Thus in the *Scorpiace*, c. 13, a passage extant in the first chapter of the Epistle to the Philippians, is quoted as from the Epistles to the Thessalonians.

[7] See an instance in Porson's *Letters to Travis*, p. 273, or in Semler's *Dissertation*, sect. ix.

[8] The author might have produced numerous other instances in confirmation of the statements made in this paragraph, but he was unwilling to swell the bulk of the volume.

him, must have held that the two Testaments were not at variance.[1]

We have seen that Tertullian,[2] when arguing against the heretics, uniformly represents the rule of faith maintained in the Apostolic Churches to be the same which the apostles originally delivered. He does not indeed state that they compiled any creed or public declaration of belief, to which all the members of the Church were bound to give their assent. But in the commencement of the tract *de Virginibus velandis*,[3] he describes what he calls the one fixed, unchangeable rule of faith, which will be found to contain nearly all the articles of what is now termed the Apostles' Creed. Those which are there wanting may be supplied, either from another summary of faith in the second chapter of the tract *against Praxeas*,[4] or from detached passages of our author's writings. Thus the conception by the Holy Ghost is stated in the treatise *against Praxeas*, c. 27: "Certè enim de Spiritu Sancto Virgo concepit;" and we have seen in our remarks on the third Article that Tertullian believed the doctrine of Christ's descent into hell. Schlitingius indeed contended, on the authority of the passage just quoted from the tract *de Virginibus velandis*, that a belief in the Holy Ghost formed no part of the faith required from a Christian in the time of Tertullian;[5] but the whole tenor of the tract *against Praxeas* confutes the assertion, and proves that the divinity of the Holy Ghost was then received as one of the doctrines of the Church. With

[1] See particularly *adv. Marcionem*, l. iv. c. 11, where are some judicious observations respecting the relation in which the Law stands to the Gospel.

[2] Chap. iv. p. 114, note 2.

[3] "Regula quidem fidei una omnino est, sola immobilis et irreformabilis, credendi scilicet in unicum Deum omnipotentem, mundi conditorem, et Filium ejus Iesum Christum, natum ex Virgine Mariâ, crucifixum sub Pontio Pilato, tertio die resuscitatum a mortuis, receptum in cœlis, sedentem nunc ad dexteram Patris, venturum judicare vivos et mortuos per carnis etiam resurrectionem." Compare *de Præscriptione Hæreticorum*, c. 13.

[4] "Nos vero, et semper, et nunc magis ut instructiores per Paracletum, deductorem scilicet omnis veritatis, unicum quidem Deum credimus; sub hâc tamen dispensatione, quam οἰκονομίαν dicimus, ut unici Dei sit et filius, Sermo ipsius, qui ex ipso processerit, *per quem omnia facta sunt et sine quo factum est nihil.* Hunc missum a Patre in Virginem, et ex eâ natum, hominem et Deum, filium hominis et filium Dei, et cognominatum Iesum Christum. Hunc passum, hunc mortuum et sepultum secundum Scripturas, et resuscitatum a Patre, et in cœlos resumptum, sedere ad dexteram Patris, venturum judicare vivos et mortuos. Qui exinde miserit, secundum promissionem suam, a Patre Spiritum Sanctum Paracletum, Sanctificatorem fidei eorum, qui credunt in Patrem et Filium et Spiritum Sanctum. Hanc regulam ab initio Evangelii decucurrisse," etc. See also cap. ult. "Si non exinde Pater et Filius et Spiritus Sanctus, tres crediti, unum Deum sistunt."

[5] Pearson *On the Creed*, Article viii. p. 307.

respect to the next clause—the Holy Catholic Church—by which I understand, with Pearson, a visible Church on earth,[1] Tertullian repeatedly speaks of a Church which was founded by the apostles,[2] especially by St. Peter,[3] according to the promise made by Christ to him, and is composed of all the Christian communities throughout the world, which are united by the profession of a common faith, by the same hope in Christ Jesus, and by the same sacrament of baptism.[4] To this Church Tertullian applies also the term *Catholica*.[5] Of the doctrine contained in the next clause of the Apostles' Creed—the Communion of Saints—as it is explained by Pearson, I find no traces in Tertullian's writings; and with respect to the remission of sins, we have seen that, though after he became a Montanist he denied to the Church the power of forgiving certain sins in this life, he still supposed that the offender might, through the blood of Christ, upon sincere repentance, obtain pardon in the life to come.[6] The inference, therefore, to be drawn from a comparison of different passages scattered through Tertullian's writings is, that the Apostles' Creed in its present form was not known to him as a summary of faith, but that the various clauses of which it is composed were generally received as articles of faith by orthodox Christians. When we come to speak of the tract *against Praxeas*, we shall have an opportunity of ascertaining how far the opinions of our author coincided with the language employed in the Nicene and Athanasian Creeds.

We proceed to the ninth Article of our Church—on original sin—a subject on which we must not expect Tertullian to speak with the same precision of language which was used by those who wrote after the Pelagian controversy had arisen. In describing the cause and consequences of Adam's fall, he says that our first parent, having been seduced into disobedience by Satan, was delivered over unto death, and transmitted his

[1] Article ix. p. 339. Tertullian, however, speaks sometimes of a heavenly or invisible Church. "Emissa de cœlis, ubi Ecclesia est arcâ figurata." *De Baptismo*, c. 8. "Una Ecclesia *in cœlis*," c. 15. "Jam tunc de mundo in Ecclesiam," *Adv. Marcionem*, l. ii. c. 4. Here, however, the expression is ambiguous; it may mean the transition from Paganism to Christianity. "Apud Veram et Catholicam Hierusalem," etc., l. iii. c. 22.

[2] "In Ecclesiam, quam nondum Apostoli struxerant." *De Baptismo*, c. 11.

[3] "In ipso Ecclesia extructa est, id est, per ipsum." *De Pudicitiâ*, c. 21.

[4] "Una nobis et illis fides, unus Deus, idem Christus, eadem spes, eadem lavacri Sacramenta." *De Virginibus velandis*, c. 2.

[5] *De Præscriptione Hæreticorum*, cc. 26, 30.

[6] Chap. iv. p. 127.

condemnation to the whole human race, which was infected from his seed.[1] The effect of this condemnation was to involve mankind in sin as well as in punishment. In our account of the treatise *de Animâ*, we stated that our author expressed his approbation of the Platonic division of the soul into rational and irrational.[2] According to him, the rational was its natural, original character, as it was created by God; the irrational was introduced by Satan, and has since been wrought so completely into the soul as to have become as it were its natural character. In the same tract he says also that every soul is numbered in Adam, until, being born of water and the Spirit, it is numbered anew in Christ.[3] He does not, however, appear to have admitted a total corruption of man's nature. "Besides the evil," he says, "which the soul contracts from the intervention of the wicked spirit, there is an antecedent, and in a certain sense natural evil, arising from its corrupt origin. For, as we have already observed, the corruption of our nature is another nature; having its proper god and father, namely the author of that corruption. Still there is a portion of good in the soul; of that original, divine, and genuine good, which is its proper nature. For that which is derived from God is rather obscured than extinguished. It may be obscured, because it is not God; but it cannot be extinguished, because it emanates from God. As, therefore, light, when intercepted by an opaque body, still remains, though it is not seen, so the good in the soul, being weighed down by the evil, is either not seen at all, or is partially and occasionally visible. Men differ widely in their moral characters, yet the souls of all form but one genus: in the worst there is something good; in the best there is something bad.[4] For God alone is without sin; and the only man without sin is Christ, since Christ is God. Thus the divine nature of the soul bursts forth in prophetic anticipations, the consequences of its original good; and conscious of its origin it bears testimony to God,

1 "Per quem (Satanam) homo a primordio circumventus ut præceptum Dei excederet, et propterea in mortem datus, exinde totum genus de suo semine infectum suæ etiam damnationis traducem fecit." *De Testimonio Animæ*, c. 3. "Homo damnatur ad mortem ob unius arbusculæ delibationem, et exinde proficiunt delicta cum pœnis, et pereunt jam omnes, qui Paradisi nullum cespitem nôrunt." *Adv. Marcionem*, l. i. c. 22.

2 C. 16. Compare c. 11, where Tertullian speaks of Adam's soul.

3 "Ita omnis anima eo usque in Adam censetur, donec in Christo recenseatur," c. 40. In the tract *de Patientiâ*, c. 5, Tertullian says that the sin of Adam consisted in impatience, *i.e.* under the commandment of God; but in the tract *de Pudicitiâ*, c. 6, he ascribes the fall to what the apostle terms the lust of the eye (1 John ii. 16).

4 Compare *adv. Marcionem*, l. ii. c. 23.

its author, in exclamations like these—*Deus bonus est, Deus videt, Deo commendo.* As no soul is without sin, neither is any without the seeds of good. Moreover, when the soul embraces the true faith, being renewed in its second birth by water and the power from above, then the veil of its former corruption being taken away, it beholds the light in all its brightness. As in its first birth it was received by the unholy, in its second it is received by the Holy Spirit. The flesh follows the soul now wedded to the Spirit, as a part of the bridal portion; no longer the servant of the soul, but of the Spirit. O happy marriage, if no violation of the marriage vow takes place!"[1]

The language of the passages now cited appears to differ little from that of our Article. The original state of Adam was a state of righteousness:[2] in his nature, as he was created, good was the pervading principle, good immediately derived from God and akin to the divine goodness; or, as Tertullian expresses himself on another occasion, the original righteousness of Adam consisted in a participation in the Spirit of God, which he lost by his transgression.[3] The effect of his transgression has been to make his offspring the heirs of his condemnation—to entail upon them a corruption of nature, from which no man born into the world is exempt, and for which there is no other remedy than to be born again by water and the Holy Spirit.[4] Although, therefore, Tertullian denies that the corruption of man's nature is total, and that the seeds of good are altogether extinguished in it, yet he expressly states that man cannot by his own efforts restore himself to the favour of God, but requires that his soul should be renewed by grace from above. Had our author admitted the total corruption of human nature—had he used

[1] *De Animâ,* c. 41.

[2] *De Pudicitiâ,* c. 9. Tertullian speaking of the prodigal son says, "Recordatur Patris Dei, satisfacto redit, vestem pristinam recipit, statum scilicet eum quem Adam transgressus amiserat." Compare *de Monogamiâ,* c. 5.

[3] "Recipit enim illum Dei Spiritum, quem tunc de afflatu ejus acceperat, sed post amiserat per delictum." *De Baptismo,* c. 5. Tertullian's notion here seems to be that God made man *in His image,* that is, in the form which Christ was to bear during His residence on earth; this image man retained after the fall. (Compare *adv. Marcionem,* l. v. c. 8, *sub in.*) But God also made man after His likeness, that is, immortal; this likeness man lost at the fall, but it is restored to him in baptism through the Holy Spirit. In the second book *against Marcion,* c. 2, Tertullian applies to Adam at the time of his transgression the term *homo animalis,* that is, without the Spirit of God, as opposed to *spiritalis.*

[4] See *de Jejuniis,* c. 3, where, speaking of the effects of Adam's fall, Tertullian says, "In me quoque cum ipso genere transductam." So in the tract *de Exhortatione Castitatis,* c. 2, "Semini enim tuo respondeas necesse esse." See also *de Pudicitiâ,* c. 6.

the language which is sometimes used in our own day, that man is wholly the offspring of the devil—his adversary Marcion might have turned round upon him and said, "This is my doctrine, for I affirm that man was made by a being distinct from the supreme God and at variance with Him."

It must, however, be admitted that there is, in the tract *de Baptismo*, a passage which seems to imply a denial of the doctrine of original sin.[1] Tertullian recommends delay in administering the rite of baptism, particularly in the case of children; and asks, "Why should the *age of innocence* (infancy) be in haste to obtain the remission of sins?"[2] Here is an evident inconsistency. The passages which we have already cited, prove that our author was strongly impressed with the conviction that baptism is necessary in order to relieve mankind from the injurious consequences of Adam's fall.[3] We might therefore reasonably have expected to find him a strenuous advocate of infant baptism. As we shall have occasion to recur to this passage when we come to treat of the rites and ceremonies of the Church, we shall say nothing more respecting it at present.

We will take this opportunity of noticing two strange opinions of Tertullian. One is, that the prohibition given to Adam in Paradise contained in it all the precepts of the decalogue;[4] the other, that Eve was a virgin when tempted by the serpent[5]—an assertion which he does not attempt to reconcile with the divine blessing, "Be fruitful and multiply." It marks, however, his strong disposition to exaggerate the merit of a life of celibacy.

Tertullian's notions on free-will—the subject of the tenth Article of our Church—may be collected from a passage in his treatise *de Animâ*.[6] He is arguing against the Valentinians, who maintained that men were of three kinds—spiritual, animal, and terrestrial—and that, as this distinction took place at their birth, it was consequently immutable: as a thorn cannot produce figs,

[1] C. 18.

[2] The expression *innocens ætas* occurs again in the fourth book *against Marcion*, c. 23. See also *de Animâ*, c. 56, *sub fine*.

[3] See particularly the passage quoted on p. 161, note 3.

[4] *Adv. Judæos*, c. 2.

[5] *De Carne Christi*, c. 17. Compare *de Monogamiâ*, c. 5. "Christus innuptus in totum, quod etiam primus Adam ante exilium."

[6] C. 21, partly quoted in chap. iii. note 2, p. 101.

or a thistle grapes, an animal man cannot produce the works of the Spirit; or the contrary. "If this were so," answers Tertullian, "God could neither out of stones raise up sons to Abraham, nor could the generation of vipers bring forth the fruits of repentance; and the apostle was in error when he wrote, *Ye were once darkness, and we also were once by nature the children of wrath, and ye were of the same number, but now ye have been washed.* The declarations of Scripture are never at variance with each other: a bad tree will not produce good fruit, unless a graft is made upon it; and a good tree will bring forth bad fruit, unless it is cultivated; and stones will become the sons of Abraham, if they are formed into the faith of Abraham; and the generation of vipers will bring forth the fruits of repentance, if they cast out the poison of a malignant nature. Such is the power of divine grace; being stronger than nature, and having subject to itself the free power of the will within us, which the Greeks call αὐτεξούσιον.[1] This power is natural and changeable; consequently in what direction soever it turns, the nature (of man) turns in that direction with it. For we have already shown that man possesses by nature freedom of will." On another occasion, Tertullian is disputing with Marcion, who contended that the fall of Adam was irreconcilable with the attributes of God; who must be deemed deficient either in goodness if He willed, in prescience if He did not foresee, or in power if He did not prevent it.[2] Our author answers that the cause of Adam's fall must be sought, not in the attributes of God, but in the condition and nature of man. Adam was created free; for God would not have given him a law and annexed the penalty of death to transgression, unless it had been in his power either to obey or disobey. Precepts, threats, and exhortations all proceed upon the assumption that man acts freely and according to his will. "But did not God foresee that Adam would make an ill use of his freedom? how then can we reconcile it to His goodness that He should have bestowed a gift which He foresaw that Adam would abuse?" To this question Tertullian replies in a laboured argument, the object of which is to prove that God, having determined to create man after His own image and likeness, and consequently to make him a free agent, could not consistently

[1] Tertullian appears not to have held the notion of a self-determining power of the will; for he speaks of it as determined by something extraneous. "Nam et voluntas poterit necessitas contendi: habens scilicet unde cogatur." *De Coronâ*, c. 11.

[2] *Adv. Marcionem*, l. ii. cc. 5, 6, 7, 8. Compare cc. 10, 25.

interpose to prevent him from using his freedom as he pleased. We must observe that throughout this passage Tertullian is speaking of the original state of Adam; not of his state after the fall, or of the state in which all men are born into the world. Before man in his present state can repent and do that which is good, his will must be brought under subjection to the grace of God. The great object of Tertullian is to vindicate the dealings of God with man, and to prove that, when men sin, the guilt is strictly and properly their own.[1] Adam sinned voluntarily; the tempter did not impose upon him the inclination to sin, but afforded him the means of gratifying the inclination which already existed. We may think Tertullian's reasoning incorrect, and deny that his solution of the difficulties connected with the questions of the divine agency and the freedom of man is satisfactory: where, indeed, are we to look for a satisfactory solution? But it is evident that nothing could be more remote from his intention than *so* to assert the freedom of man's will as either to deny the necessity or to detract from the efficacy of divine grace; from the sole operation of which he conceived patience and the other moral graces to take their origin.[2]

What I remarked with respect to the doctrine of original sin is equally applicable to that of justification, the subject of the eleventh Article of our Church. No controversy on the subject existed in Tertullian's time. That which occupied so large a portion of St. Paul's attention, the dispute respecting the necessity of observing the Mosaic ritual as a means of justification, appears to have died away immediately after the expulsion of the Jews by Adrian. We must not therefore expect in Tertullian's language, when he speaks on this subject, the precision of controversy. He describes, however, the death of Christ as the whole weight and benefit of the Christian name, and the foundation of man's salvation.[3] He says in one place that we are

[1] Compare *de Monogamiâ*, c. 14. "Nec ideo duritia imputabitur Christo de arbitrii cujuscunque liberi vitio. 'Ecce, inquit, posui ante te bonum et malum.' Elige quod bonum est; si non potes, quia non vis (posse enim te, si velis, ostendit, quia tuo arbitrio utrumque proposuit) discedas oportet ab eo cujus non facis voluntatem."

[2] "Nisi quod bonorum quorundam, sicuti et malorum, intolerabilis magnitudo est, ut ad capienda et præstanda ea sola gratia divinæ inspirationis operetur. Nam quod maximè bonum, id maximè penes Deum, nec alius id quam qu possidet dispensat, ut cuique dignatur." *De Patientiâ*, c. 1.

[3] "Totum Christiani nominis et pondus et fructus, mors Christi, negatur, quam tam impressè Apostolus demandat, utique veram, summum eam fundamentum Evangelii constituens, et salutis nostræ, et prædicationis suæ: *Tradidi enim*

redeemed by the blood of God;[1] in another, by the blood of the Lord and the Lamb.[2] He asserts that such is the efficacy of the blood of Christ, that it not only cleanses men from sin and brings them out of darkness into light, but preserves them also in a state of purity if they continue to walk in the light.[3] He speaks of a repentance which is justified by faith, *pœnitentiam ex fide justificatam;*[4] and of justification by faith without the ordinances of the law.[5] If, therefore, on other occasions we find him dwelling in strong terms on the efficacy of repentance, we ought in fairness to infer that he did not mean to represent it as of itself possessing this efficacy, but as deriving its reconciling virtue from the sacrifice of Christ.[6] In the same sense we must understand other passages, in which he ascribes to bodily mortifications a certain degree of merit, and the power of appeasing the divine displeasure.[7] The case in which Tertullian's language approaches most nearly to the Roman Catholic doctrine of merit, is that of martyrdom. To this undoubtedly he ascribed the power of washing away guilt; still, we conceive, under the restriction under which he ascribes the same power to baptism.[8] The efficacy which martyrdom possessed was derived solely from the death of Christ. This at least is certain, that he positively denied all superabundance of merit in the martyr. "Let it suffice," he says, speaking of the custom then prevalent of restoring penitents to the communion of the Church at the intercession of martyrs, "let it suffice to the martyr to have

inquit, *vobis in primis, quod Christus mortuus sit pro peccatis nostris,*" etc. *Adv. Marcionem,* l. iii. c. 8. See also l. ii. c. 26. "Christum—oblatorem animæ suæ pro populi salute;" and the *Scorpiace,* c. 7, "Christus est qui se tradidit pro delictis nostris." *De Idololatriâ.* "Quum Christus non aliâ ex causâ descenderit, quam liberandorum peccatorum."

1 "Non sumus nostri, sed pretio empti; et quali pretio? sanguine Dei." *Ad Uxorem,* l. ii. c. 3.

2 "Itaque si exinde quo statum vertit (caro) et in Christum tincta induit Christum, et magno redempta est, sanguine scilicet Domini et Agni." *De Pudicitiâ,* c. 6.

3 "Hæc est enim vis Dominici Sanguinis, ut quos jam delicto mundârit, et exinde in lumine constituerit, mundos exinde præstet, si in lumine incedere perseveraverint." *De Pudicitiâ,* c. 19.

4 *Adv. Marcionem,* l. iv. c. 18, *sub fine.*

5 "Ex fide jam justificandos sine ordine legis." *Adv. Marcionem,* l. iv. c. 35.

6 See *de Pœnitentiâ,* cc. 4, 9.

7 "In primis adflictatio carnis hostia Domino placatoria per humiliationis sacrificium," etc. *De Patientiâ,* c. 13; *de Res. Carnis,* c. 9. "Quo plenius id quod de Evâ trahit (ignominiam, dico, primi delicti et invidiam perditionis humanæ) omni satisfactionis habitu expiaret." *De Cultu Fœminarum,* l. i. c. 1. *De Jejuniis,* cc. 3, 4, 7, *et passim.*

8 "Ubi accessit, pati exoptat, ut Dei totam gratiam redimat, ut omnem veniam ab eo compensatione sanguinis sui expediat? Omnia enim huic operi (martyrio) delicta donantur." *Apology, sub fine.*

washed away his own sins. It is a mark of ingratitude or presumption in him to scatter profusely upon others that which he has himself acquired at a great price. For who but the Son of God can by His own death relieve others from death? He indeed delivered the thief at the very moment of His passion; for He had come for this very end, that being Himself free from sin and perfectly holy, He might die for sinners. You then who imitate Christ in pardoning sins, if you are yourself sinless, suffer death for me. But if you are yourself a sinner, how can the oil out of your cruse suffice both for you and me?"[1]

We have observed nothing in Tertullian's works which bears upon the twelfth Article of our Church; but with reference to the thirteenth—which involves the question respecting the nature of heathen virtue—he is supposed by his editor Rigault, in a passage in the tract *de Spectaculis*,[2] to express a doubt whether a heathen can be actuated by a really virtuous principle; literally, whether a heathen has any savour of that which is good. In the tract *ad Martyres*,[3] a distinction is made between the principles in which the fortitude of a Christian and of a heathen originates. But in neither case is the language of that clear and express character which will warrant us in building any decided conclusion upon it. The fair inference, however, from the general tenor of Tertullian's writings is, that he deemed all heathen virtue imperfect, and could not therefore ascribe to it any merit of congruity.[4]

From the passage which has been just quoted from the tract *de Pudicitiâ*, it is manifest that Tertullian entirely rejected, with our fourteenth Article, the notion of works of supererogation;[5] and in the same passage, the reader would remark that, in agreement with our fifteenth Article, he declared Christ alone to be without sin. The same statement is repeated in various

[1] *De Pudicitiâ*, c. 22.

[2] "Quam melius ergo est nescire quum mali puniuntur, ne sciam et quum boni pereunt, *si tamen bonum sapiunt*," c. 19.

[3] C. 4, *sub fine*.

[4] "Quia nihil verum in his (fœminis) quæ Deum nesciunt Præsidem et Magistratum veritatis." *De Cultu Fœminarum*, l. ii. c. 1. "Igitur ignorantes quique Deum, rem quoque ejus ignorent necesse est." *De Pœnitentiâ*, c. 1. "Philosophi quidem qui alicujus sapientiæ *animalis* deputantur." *De Patientiâ*, c. 1. "Cui enim veritas comperta sine Deo? Cui Deus cognitus sine Christo? Cui Christus exploratus sine Spiritu Sancto?" etc. *De Animâ*, c. 1.

[5] C. 22.

parts of his writings;[1] and it is amusing to observe the anxiety of several of the Romish commentators to limit its application, and to assure us that the Virgin is not to be included in this general charge of sinfulness. All the other descendants of Adam contract guilt; and that, too, after they have received marks of the divine favour.[2] In proof of this assertion, our author appeals to the cases of Saul, and David, and Solomon. "These," he says, "are they who soil their wedding garment, and provide no oil in their lamps, and having strayed from the flock must be sought in the mountains and woods, and be brought back on the shoulders of the Shepherd."[3]

With respect to the recovery of those who fall into sin after baptism—the subject of the sixteenth Article—we have seen that the opinions of Tertullian underwent a material alteration;[4] and that, after he had adopted the notions of Montanus in all their rigour, he allowed a place of repentance only to those who fell into venial transgressions; maintaining that the stain of mortal sin after baptism could only be washed away by martyrdom, by the baptism of the sinner in his own blood.[5] Of the sin against the Holy Ghost he makes no express mention. With respect to perseverance, Tertullian appears to have thought that the true Christian will either persevere to the end, or will only fall into those lighter offences from which no man is free.[6] He who does not persevere never was a Christian;[7] so that if, in order to accommodate Tertullian's language to the controversies of later times, we substitute the word elect for Christian, perseverance, according to him, is the evidence of election; though he did not think that Christians can be assured of their final perseverance.[8] On comparing, therefore, the *later* opinions of Tertullian with the doctrine of the Church of England in its

[1] *De Oratione*, c. 7; *de Animâ*, c. 41; *de Carne Christi*, c. 16; *de Præscriptione Hæreticorum*, c. 3.

[2] *De Præscriptione Hæreticorum*, c. 3.

[3] "Prospexerat et has Deus imbecillitates conditionis humanæ, adversarii insidias, rerum fallacias, seculi retia, etiam post Lavacrum periclitaturam fidem, perituros plerosque rursum post salutem: qui vestitum obsoletâssent nuptialem, qui faculis oleum non præparâssent, qui requirendi per montes et saltus, et humeris essent reportandi." *Scorpiace*, c. 6.

[4] Chap. iv. p. 126.

[5] "Posuit igitur secunda solatia et extrema præsidia, dimicationem martyrii, et lavacrum sanguinis exinde securum." *Scorpiace*, c. 6.

[6] *De Pudicitiâ*, c. 19, *prope finem*.

[7] "Nemo autem Christianus, *nisi qui ad finem usque perseveraverit*." *De Præscriptione Hæreticorum*, c. 3.

[8] "Optantes perseverare id in nobis, non tamen præsumentes." *De Cultu Fœminarum*, l. ii. c. 2.

sixteenth Article, we find that they are directly opposed to each other. He regards perseverance as the evidence that a man is a Christian; or in the language of the Article, that he has received the Holy Ghost. But when he says that *he* alone is a Christian who perseveres to the end, his words seem to imply that he who does not persevere never was a Christian—had never received grace; whereas the express declaration of the Article is, that a man *may* receive grace and afterwards fall from it; and such indeed is the declaration of our author himself, in the passage which has been just quoted respecting the defection of Saul, David, and Solomon.[1] This apparent contradiction leads me to observe, that in reading the works of the Fathers we should be careful to distinguish between incidental or general remarks, and remarks made with reference to the particular controversies then subsisting. In the former they must not be supposed to speak with the same precision as in the latter. There was no controversy in Tertullian's day on the subject of perseverance; we must therefore not construe his expressions too strictly.

Of Predestination, as the term is defined in our seventeenth Article, we find no trace in the writings of Tertullian. The doctrine, as proposed in the Article, is the result of a number of texts of Scripture, describing the various steps of a true believer's progress towards salvation. What Tertullian says on the subject has a closer connexion with the questions agitated in the schools of philosophy, respecting fate and free-will, than with the Scriptures. His controversies with the heretics of his time, who appear to have lost their way in the vain search after a solution of the difficulties respecting the origin of evil, frequently oblige him to speak of the purpose or will of God in the natural and moral government of the world; and to contend that this purpose or will is not inconsistent with human liberty. "Some," he says, "argue that whatever happens, happens by the will of God; for if God had not willed, it would not have happened. But this is to strike at the root of all virtue, and to offer an apology for every sin. The sophistry, moreover, of the argument is not less glaring than its pernicious tendency. For if nothing happens but what God wills, God wills the commission of crime; in other words, He wills what He forbids. We must not therefore *so* refer all events to the will of God as to leave nothing in the power of man. Man has also a will,

[1] See p. 168, note 3. Compare *de Pœnitentiâ*, c. 7.

which ought always to conspire with the will of God, but is often at variance with it."[1] In the chapter which immediately follows, our author distinguishes between the will by which God ordains, and the will by which He permits; calling the former *pura voluntas*, the latter *invita voluntas*. Yet at other times he seems to have been aware that this in the case of the Almighty is a verbal, not a real distinction; for in reasoning upon the apostle's declaration, that "there must be heresies that they which are approved may be made manifest,"[2] he says that the very purpose of heresies being to try the faith of Christians, they must necessarily pervert those whose faith is not well grounded and stedfast. For that which is ordained to be (for instance, heresies), as it has a cause or purpose on account of which it is (the trial of the faith of Christians), so it must also possess a power by which it is, and cannot but be what it is (cannot but be subversive of the faith of unstable Christians); as in the case of fevers and other mortal diseases, which are ordained as modes of removing men from this world, and must therefore possess the power of effecting the end for which they were ordained—that of killing. Here our author evidently supposes that the existence of heresy is not merely permitted, but ordained for a particular end. Still he is careful to add that, if any individuals are perverted, the fault is their own. Had their faith been of a firmer character, which depended upon themselves, they would not have fallen away. We may further observe that Tertullian appears to have considered foreknowledge as the consequence of predestination; or that events are foretold because they are pre-ordained. For in assigning the reason why

[1] *De Exhortatione Castitatis*, c. 2. Compare *adv. Praxeam*, c. 10, *sub fine.*

[2] "Conditio præsentium temporum etiam hanc admonitionem provocat nostram, non oportere nos mirari super Hæreses istas, *sive quia sunt: futuræ enim prænuntiabantur: sive quia fidem quorundam subvertunt; ad hoc enim sunt, ut fides, habendo tentationem, habeat etiam probationem.* Vanè ergo et inconsideratè plerique hoc ipso scandalizantur, quod tantum Hæreses valeant. Quantum si non fuissent? quum quod sortitum est ut omni modo sit, sicut *causam accipit ob quam* sit, sic *vim consequitur per quam sit, nec esse non possit.*" (We have adopted in part the reading of Semler's edition.) "Febrem denique, inter cæteros mortificos et cruciarios exitus, erogando homini deputatam, neque quía est miramur; est enim; neque quia erogat hominem; ad hoc enim est." *De Præscriptione Hæreticorum*, cc. 1, 2.

Tertullian seems also to have been aware that election implied reprobation ("Prælatio alterius sine alterius contumeliâ non potest procedere, quia nec Electio sine Reprobatione," *Apology*, c. 13. Again, *adv. Marcionem*, l. iv. c. 23: "Nam sicut ad salutem vocat, quem non recusat vel etiam quem ultro vocat; ita in perditionem damnat, quem recusat"), as well as of the futility of the distinction which is attempted to be drawn, when it is said that God does not positively reprobate, but only does not elect or passes by. *Adv. Marcionem*, l. iv. 29.

in the prophetic writings future events are frequently spoken of as if they had already happened, he says that there is no distinction of time in the divine mind.[1] God regards that which He has decreed to do as if it were already done.

We have seen that Tertullian was inclined to ascribe a certain degree of divine inspiration to the philosophers who had ridiculed the absurdities of the national polytheism.[2] With respect, however, to the Gentile world in general, his opinion was that it was under the dominion of the powers of darkness, and consequently in a state of alienation from God.[3] The question which is involved in the eighteenth Article of our Church—whether a heathen, who framed his life according to the light of nature, could be saved?—appears never to have presented itself to Tertullian's mind. Had it been proposed to him, entertaining the opinions which he did respecting the necessity of baptism to salvation, he must have replied in the negative.

Having already laid before the reader all the information which the writings of our author supply respecting the Church and its authority, and the authority of general councils, the subjects of our nineteenth, twentieth, and twenty-first Articles,[4] we proceed to the twenty-second, entitled of Purgatory.

The Roman Catholic commentators, as we might naturally expect, are extremely anxious to discover their doctrine of Purgatory in the writings of Tertullian. In our review of his tract *de Animâ*, we stated his opinion to be, that the souls of ordinary Christians, immediately after death, are transferred to a place to which he gives the name of *Inferi*, and there remain until the general resurrection, when they will be re-united to their respective bodies—that while they remain there, the souls of the good

[1] "Nam et divinitati competit, quæcunque decreverit, ut perfecta reputare, quia non sit apud illam differentia temporis, apud quam uniformem statum temporum dirigit æternitas ipsa: et divinationi propheticæ magis familiare est id quod prospiciat, dum prospicit, jam visum atque ita jam expunctum, id est, omni modo futurum demonstrare." *Adv. Marcionem*, l. iii. c. 5.

[2] *Ad Nationes*, l. i. c. 10, quoted in chap. iii. note 1, p. 87.

[3] See the passages quoted in note 4, p. 167, particularly the commencement of the tract *de Pœnitentiâ*, and that from the second tract *de Cultu Fœminarum*, in which Tertullian says that the Gentiles, though they might not be devoid of *all* feelings of remorse or of *all* sense of modesty, yet could not possibly comprehend the true notion of repentance and chastity. See also *ad Nationes*, l. ii. c. 2. "Quis autem sapiens expers veritatis, qui ipsius sapientiæ ac veritatis patrem et dominum Deum ignoret?"

[4] Chap. iv. pp. 114–121. Chap. v. pp. 150–155.

enjoy a foretaste of the happiness, and the souls of the wicked of the misery, which will be their eternal portion—and that, until the soul is re-united to the body, the work of retribution cannot be complete.[1] We need scarcely observe that this opinion, which makes the final state of man a continuation only of the intermediate state just described, is directly opposed to the doctrine of Purgatory. It must, however, be admitted that there are in Tertullian's writings passages which seem to imply that, in the interval between death and the general resurrection, the souls of those who are destined to eternal happiness undergo a purification from the stains which even the best men contract during their lives.[2] Though he was, as we have seen,[3] fully aware of the mischief which had arisen from blending the tenets of philosophy with the doctrines of the gospel, he was unable to keep himself entirely free from the prevalent contagion; for there can be no doubt that the notion of a purification, which is necessary to the soul before it can be admitted to the happiness of heaven, is of Platonic origin.[4]

[1] Chap. iii. p. 105. "Omnes ergo animæ penes Inferos, inquis. Velis ac nolis, et *supplicia jam illic et refrigeria;* habes pauperem et divitem——Cur enim non putes animam et puniri et foveri in Inferis interim sub expectatione utriusque judicii in quâdam usurpatione et candidâ ejus?—Delibari putes judicium, an incipi? præcipitari, an præministrari? Jam vero quam iniquissimum etiam apud Inferos, si et nocentibus adhuc illic bene est, et innocentibus nondum." *De Animâ*, cap. ult.

[2] Thus, in the very chapter of the tract *de Animâ* to which we have just referred, "In summâ, quum carcerem illum, quem Evangelium demonstrat" (see Matt. v. 25 or Luke xii. 58). "Inferos intelligamus, et novissimum quadrantem, modicum quodque delictum morâ resurrectionis illic luendum interpretemur, nemo dubitabit animam aliquid pensare penes Inferos, salvâ resurrectionis plenitudine per carnem quoque." Again, in c. 35: "Et Judex te tradat Angelo executionis, et ille te in carcerem mandet infernum, unde non dimittaris, nisi modico quoque delicto morâ resurrectionis expenso." See also *de Res. Carnis*, c. 42: "Ne inferos experiatur, usque novissimum quadrantem exacturos;" and *de Oratione*, c. 7. See Bingham, l. xv. c. 3, sect. 16. Perhaps the correct statement of Tertullian's opinion, after he became a Montanist, is, that he conceived the souls of the wicked to remain in a state of suffering *apud Inferos* till the general judgment; the souls of the saints to be reunited to their bodies, not at once, but at different times, according to their different merits, *pro meritis maturius vel tardius resurgentium*, in the course of the thousand years during which the reign of the saints on earth was to last. At the end of those thousand years the general judgment would take place. The souls of the wicked being re-united to their bodies, they would be consigned to eternal misery; while the bodies of the saints, who had already risen, would undergo the transformation mentioned in our account of the tract *de Res. Carnis*. See this chapter, p. 141, and note 4, p. 181. According to this opinion, the souls even of the saints require purification, though in different degrees, *apud Inferos*.

[3] Chap. iii. p. 87.

[4] Our author, however, refers the origin of the notion to the revelations of the Paraclete. "Hoc etiam Paracletus frequentissimè commendavit." *De Animâ*, cap. ult.

Of Pardons, in the sense in which the word is used in our twenty-second Article, there is no mention in Tertullian's writings.

The same remark applies to image-worship and to the invocation of saints.[1] It is, however, impossible to read our author's animadversions on the Gentile idolatry, without being convinced that he would have regarded the slightest approach to image-worship with the utmost abhorrence.

On the other hand, we find more than one allusion to the practice of praying and offering for the dead,[2] and of making oblations in honour of the martyrs on the anniversary of their martyrdom.[3]

We may take this opportunity of observing that Pearson [4] maintains the perpetual virginity of the mother of our Lord, on the ground that it has been believed by the Church of God in all ages. He admits, indeed, that Tertullian had been appealed to as an assertor of the opposite opinion; and that Jerome,[5] instead of denying the charge, had contented himself with replying that Tertullian was a separatist from the Church;—but he thinks, though he does not state the grounds of his opinion, that Jerome might have denied the charge. There is, however, a passage in the tract *de Monogamiâ* [6] which, though not entirely free from ambiguity, appears to be inconsistent with the notion of the perpetual virginity.

1 "Ut quem (Deum) ubique audire et videre fideret, ei soli religionem suam offerret." *De Oratione*, c. 1. This remark would scarcely have been made by one who allowed the invocation of saints.

2 "Neque enim pristinam (uxorem) poteris odisse, cui etiam religiosiorem reservas affectionem, ut jam receptæ apud Deum, *pro cujus Spiritu postulas*, pro quâ *oblationes annuas* reddis?" *De Exhortatione Castitatis*, c. 11. "Enimvero et pro animâ ejus orat, et refrigerium interim adpostulat ei, et in primâ resurrectione consortium, et offert annuis diebus dormitionis ejus." *De Monogamiâ*, c. 10.

3 "Oblationes pro defunctis, pro natalitiis, annuâ die facimus." *De Coronâ*, c. 3. In one place Bingham speaks as if this practice applied to the dead generally, b. xv. c. 3, sect. 15; in another, as if it had been confined to martyrs, b. xiii. c. 9, sect. 5.

4 Article iii. p. 173.

5 *Adversus Helvidium*, Ep. 53. "Et de Tertulliano quidem nihil amplius dico, quam Ecclesiæ hominem non fuisse."

6 C. 8. "Et Christum quidem virgo enixa est, semel nuptura *post* partum, ut uterque titulus sanctitatis in Christi censu dispungeretur, per matrem et virginem et univiram." But Semler instead of *post* reads *ob*. See also *de Carne Christi*, c. 23: "Et virgo, quantum a viro; non virgo, quantum a partu."

What has been already stated respecting Tertullian's notion of the Church sufficiently proves that, in agreement with our twenty-third Article, he considered no one at liberty to preach the Word of God without a regular commission.[1] The apostles, he says, were appointed by our Lord to the office of preaching the gospel throughout the world.[2] They appointed persons to preside in the different Churches which they founded; and thus an uninterrupted succession of bishops had been kept up to the very time at which he wrote. We have seen also that, among other charges which he brought against the heretics, he particularly alleged that they made no sufficient inquiry into the qualifications of the persons whom they ordained, and that they even enjoined laymen to perform the sacerdotal functions.[3] Those passages of his writings in which he appears to claim for Christians in general the right of administering the sacraments, on the ground that the priestly character is, if I may use the term, inherent equally in all Christians, refer only to cases of necessity.[4]

The prevalent, perhaps the universal, opinion of the early Christians was, that baptism was absolutely necessary to salvation. This opinion they grounded upon the words of Christ to Nicodemus—"Except a man be born of water and the Spirit, he cannot enter into the kingdom of God." In those days cases must frequently have occurred in which persons suffering under severe illness, and expecting the near approach of death, were anxious to receive baptism, but could not procure the attendance of a regularly ordained minister. What, then, was to be done? The answer of reflecting men at the present day would probably be, that when a sincere desire exists to receive baptism, as well as the devout frame of mind necessary to its worthy reception, the unavoidable omission of the outward act will never constitute, in the sight of a merciful God, a reason for excluding a believer from the benefits of the Christian covenant. But Tertullian and the Christians of his day reasoned otherwise,—they were impressed with the belief that the external rite was absolutely necessary to

[1] Chap. iv. p. 114.

[2] "Cum Discipulis autem quibusdam apud Galilæam, Judææ regionem, ad quadraginta dies egit, docens eos quæ docerent: dehinc ordinatis iis ad officium prædicandi per orbem, circumfusâ nube in cœlum ereptus est." *Apology*, c. 21. See also *de Præscriptione Hæreticorum*, c. 32, referred to in chap. iv. note 1, p. 114.

[3] *De Præscriptione Hæreticorum*, c. 41, quoted in chap. iv. note 2, p. 113.

[4] See *de Baptismo*, c. 17; *de Exhortatione Castitatis*, c. 7, quoted in chap. iv. note 1, p. 112; *de Monogamiâ*, c. 12, quoted in the same chapter, note 1, p. 113.

salvation. In cases, therefore, such as I have now described, they thought it better that the rite should be performed by a layman, than that it should not be performed at all; and they justified this deviation from the established discipline of the Church, by the notion that the priestly character is impressed upon all Christians indifferently at their baptism. Still our author's reasoning clearly proves his opinion to have been, that this latent power, if it may so be termed, was only to be called into actual exercise in cases of necessity. Laymen who in the present day take upon themselves to administer the rite of baptism in cases in which the attendance of a regularly ordained minister can be procured, must not appeal to the authority of Tertullian in defence of their rash assumption of the sacred office.

Were it not for a passage in the tract *de Baptismo*,[1] in which the inherent right of the laity to baptize is expressly asserted, we should have been inclined to regard Tertullian's reasoning as an argument *ad hominem* of the following kind :—" It is a favourite notion with you (laymen) that all Christians are priests, and may consequently exercise the sacerdotal functions. Be consistent with yourselves. If you assume the power of the clergy, conform yourselves to the rule of life prescribed to them. Do not say, the clergy may not contract a second marriage, but the laity may. The distinction between the clergy and laity is a distinction of office, and does not affect the relation in which they stand to the great rules of morality. These they are both alike bound to observe; and what is criminal in the clergy is also criminal in the laity." Viewed in this light, Tertullian's reasoning is correct, though it proceeds upon the erroneous assumption that a second marriage is forbidden to the clergy.

With regard to the twenty-fourth Article, although our author does not expressly tell us in what language the service of the Church was performed, the necessary inference from his writings is, that it was performed in a language with which the whole congregation was familiar. In order to remove the distrust with which the Roman governors regarded the Christian assemblies, he states, in the *Apology*, the object of those meetings.[2] " We

[1] C. 17.

[2] " Corpus sumus de conscientiâ religionis, et disciplinæ unitate, et spei fœdere. Coimus ad Deum, ut *quasi manu factâ* precationibus ambiamus. Hæc vis Deo grata est. Oramus etiam pro imperatoribus, pro ministris eorum ac potestatibus, pro statu

form," he says, "a body, being joined together by a community of religion, discipline, and hope. We come together for the purpose of offering our prayers to God, and as it were extorting by our numbers and united supplications a compliance with our desires. Such violence is pleasing to God. We pray also for the emperors, for their officers, for all who are in authority; we pray that the course of this world may be peaceably ordered, and the consummation of all things be deferred. We come together for the purpose of reading the Holy Scriptures, when the circumstances of the times appear to call for any particular admonitions, or for the careful discussion of any particular topics. Of this at least we are sure, that our faith will be nourished, our hope elevated, our confidence confirmed, by listening to the words of Scripture; and that the Christian rule of life will be impressed upon us with increased effect, through the inculcation of holy precepts." It is evident that none of the objects which Tertullian here enumerates could have been attained if the prayers had been offered, or the Scriptures read, in a tongue to which the majority of the persons assembled were strangers.

We now proceed to the twenty-fifth Article—De Sacramentis. The controversy between the Romish and English Churches respecting the number of sacraments seems in a great measure to have arisen from the laxity with which the Latin Fathers used the word *sacramentum*.[1] In classical writers *sacramentum* means an oath or promise, ratified by a sacred or religious ceremony. Thus the oath taken by the military was called *sacramentum;* and in this sense the word is frequently used by Tertullian.[2] In strict conformity with this its original signification, it is used to express the promise made by Christians in baptism.[3] From the

seculi, pro rerum quiete, pro morâ finis. Coimus ad Literarum Divinarum commemorationem, si quid præsentium temporum qualitas aut præmonere cogit aut recognoscere. Certè fidem sanctis vocibus pascimus, spem erigimus, fiduciam figimus, disciplinam præceptorum nihilominus inculcationibus densamus," c. 39, quoted in chap. iv. p. 110. The expression *quasi manu factâ precationibus ambiamus*, implies that all present joined in prayer. The passage in the second tract *ad Uxorem*, c. 6, relates rather to family devotion. "Quæ Dei mentio? quæ Christi invocatio? ubi fomenta fidei de Scripturarum interjectione? ubi Spiritus? ubi refrigerium? ubi divina benedictio?"

[1] Now that the word *sacrament* has been strictly defined, the case is very different; and the question between the two Churches respecting the number of sacraments becomes of great importance.

[2] "Nemo in castra hostium transit, nisi projectis armis suis, nisi destitutis signis et Sacramentis Principis sui." *De Spectaculis*, c. 24; *de Idololatriâ*, c. 19; *de Coronâ*, c. 11; *Scorpiace*, c. 4; *de Jejuniis*, c. 10; *ad Martyres*, c. 3.

[3] "De ipso Sacramento nostro interpretaremur nobis, adversas esse fidei ejusmodi artes. Quomodo enim renuntiamus Diabolo et Angelis ejus, si eos facimus."

oath the transition was easy to the ceremony by which it was ratified. Thus *sacramentum* came to signify any religious ordinance,[1] and in general to stand for that which in the Greek is expressed by the word *μυστήριον*—any emblematical action of a sacred import; any external rite having an internal or sacred meaning. By a similar transition, the word was also used to express that which the convert promised to observe—the whole Christian doctrine and rule of life.[2]

With respect to baptism and the Eucharist, Tertullian calls the former Sacramentum Aquæ,[3] Lavacri,[4] Fidei;[5] the latter, Sacramentum Eucharistiæ.[6] In the tract *de Baptismo* we find the expression, *sacramentum sanctificationis;*[7] which, though not applied to the external rite of baptism, conveys the idea contained in the definition of a sacrament given in our Catechism—"an outward and visible sign of an inward and spiritual grace." Notwithstanding the laxity with which Tertullian uses the word, I do not find it applied to any of the five Romish sacraments, excepting marriage, and then with a particular reference to Ephesians v. 32, where he renders the words *μέγα μυστήριον*, *magnum sacramentum.*[8] In the tract *against Praxeas*[9] I find the expression *unctionis sacramentum;* but Tertullian is there speaking of the anointing of our Saviour by the Holy Ghost.

Soon after the time of Tertullian, a controversy arose respecting the validity of heretical baptism. Cyprian contended that it was invalid, and that all persons so baptized, if they wished afterwards to become members of the Church, must be re-baptized.

*De Idololatriâ*, c. 6. "Semel jam in Sacramenti testatione ejeratæ." *De Coronâ*, c. 13.

[1] *Apology*, cc. 7, 47; *ad Nationes*, l. i. c. 16, *sub fine; de Præscriptione Hæreticorum*, c. 26, "Dominus palam edixit, sine ullâ significatione alicujus tecti Sacramenti," c. 40, *et passim.*

[2] "Hoc prius capite, et omnem hic *Sacramenti nostri* ordinem haurite." *Apology*, c. 14, *sub fine,* compared with c. 16, *sub fine.* "Quæ omnia, conversi jam ad demonstrationem *religionis nostræ*, repurgavimus." So in c. 19, "In quo videtur thesaurus collocatus totius Judaici Sacramenti, et inde etiam nostri." See also *de Præscriptione Hæreticorum*, c. 20, *sub fine.* "Addita est ampliatio *Sacramento.*" *De Baptismo*, c. 13, *et passim.*

[3] *De Baptismo*, cc. 1, 12.

[4] *De Virginibus velandis*, c. 2.

[5] *De Animâ*, c. 1.

[6] *De Coronâ*, c. 3.

[7] C. 4. "Igitur omnes aquæ de pristinâ prærogativâ Sacramentum sanctificationis consequuntur, invocato Deo." All water acquires from ancient prerogative (because the Spirit of God moved upon the face of the waters, Gen. i. 2), the sacramental power of sanctification ("vim sanctificandi," as Tertullian afterwards expresses himself), through prayer to God.

[8] *De Jejuniis*, c. 3.

[9] C. 28, *sub initio.*

Stephen, the Bishop of Rome, thought otherwise; and the Church, though long divided on the subject, appears finally to have adopted his opinion. All baptism by water performed in the name of the Holy Trinity, by whomsoever administered, was deemed to be valid and not to be repeated.[1] Had the dispute existed in our author's time, it is evident, from the general tenor of his writings, that he would have sided with Cyprian.[2] On one occasion he denies that heretics are entitled to the name of Christians; they could not possibly possess that priestly character which he supposed all Christians to receive at their baptism.[3] It is indeed probable that in this instance, as in others, Cyprian formed his opinion from the perusal of *his master's* works. The case which was discussed in Cyprian's day differed in one material point from that contemplated by our twenty-sixth Article. The disqualification in the minister, which was supposed to affect the validity of the sacraments when administered by him, existed *ab initio;* he was not a member of the true Church. The case which our Article has in view is that of a minister regularly ordained, who after ordination falls into gross immoralities; and the question arising out of it is, whether his profligacy vitiates the sacraments. This question does not appear to have presented itself to our author, nor could it frequently happen in those days, when the discipline of the Church was still maintained in its original purity and vigour. An openly vicious minister would then have been immediately degraded, and cut off from the communion of the Church. Standing, therefore, on the footing of a heathen, he would have been deemed incapable of administering any of the rites of the Church.

We shall defer the consideration of the Articles relating to baptism and the Lord's Supper until we come to speak of the rites and ceremonies of the Church. Indeed, we observe nothing in Tertullian's works which bears upon the twenty-ninth or thirty-first Article. We proceed therefore to the thirty-second Article, De Conjugio Sacerdotum. That the clergy in Tertullian's time were not obliged to lead a life of celibacy, must be admitted by every person who has perused his writings. Yet the austerity of his character would certainly have impelled him to impose

1 Hooker, *Ecclesiastical Polity*, l. v. sect. 62.

2 See particularly *de Baptismo*, c. 15. We should, however, bear in mind that the heretics, whom Tertullian had in view, were the Marcionites, Valentinians, etc., who denied that the God of the Old Testament was the Supreme God.

3 "Si enim Hæretici sunt, Christiani esse non possunt." *De Præscriptione Hæreticorum*, c. 37. See also c. 16,

upon them this restriction, could he have discovered any plausible pretence for doing it.[1] He remarks with evident satisfaction, that of all the apostles, as far as his researches extended, St. Peter alone was married,[2]—and having admitted in the tract *de Exhortatione Castitatis* that the apostles were allowed to carry about their wives with them,[3] he afterwards, in the tract *de Monogamiâ*,[4] gives a different interpretation of the passage, and asserts that the females there spoken of were not wives, but women who ministered to the apostles, as Martha and others had done to Christ. The arguments, however, by which he endeavours to prove that laymen ought not to contract a second marriage, show that the clergy were at liberty to marry once;[5] and his interpretation of the texts in the Epistles to Timothy and Titus leads to the same conclusion.[6] We know also that he was himself married; but the Romish commentators attempt to get rid of this perplexing fact by saying that, when he became a priest, he ceased to cohabit with his wife.[7]

In our observations upon the government of the Church,[8] we referred to a passage in the *Apology*, in which Tertullian says, that in the assemblies of the Christians censures were pronounced and offenders cut off from the communion of the Church.[9] It may, however, be inferred from his words, that Excommunication, the subject of our thirty-third Article, did not then imply an interruption of all civil intercourse with the offending party, but only an exclusion from all participation in religious exercises—"a communicatione orationis, et conventûs, et omnis sancti commercii."

1 "Quanti igitur et quantæ *in Ecclesiasticis Ordinibus* de continentiâ censentur, qui Deo nubere maluerunt, qui carnis suæ honorem restituerunt, quique se jam illius ævi filios dicaverunt, occidentes in se concupiscentiam libidinis, et totum illud quod intra Paradisum non potuit admitti." *De Exhortatione Castitatis*, cap. ult. *sub fine*. This passage proves that, although many ecclesiastics led a life of celibacy, it was not required of all.

2 *De Monogamiâ*, c. 8.

3 C. 8.

4 C. 8, 1 Cor. ix. 5. This change of opinion seems to confirm the statement made in chap. i. p. 30, that Tertullian, when he wrote the tract *de Exhortatione Castitatis*, had not embraced the tenets of Montanus in all their rigour.

5 See *de Exhortatione Castitatis*, c. 7; *de Monogamiâ*, c. 12, quoted in chap. iv. note 1, p. 113.

6 1 Tim. iii. 2; Titus i. 6.

7 The reader will find in the *Life of Tertullian*, by Pamelius, under the year 201, the reasons alleged by that commentator in support of the opinion mentioned in the text; and in Allix's *Dissertation*, c. 2, reasons for doubting its correctness. If Tertullian and his wife had separated by mutual consent, it seems scarcely necessary for him to have cautioned her against contracting a second marriage after his death.

8 Chap. iv. p. 125.

9 C. 39.

The thirty-fourth Article of our Church is entitled De Traditionibus Ecclesiasticis; but in our remarks upon the sixth Article we have already laid before our readers all the information which the writings of Tertullian supply with respect both to traditional doctrines and practices.

Passing over the thirty-fifth and thirty-sixth Articles,[1] we proceed to the thirty-seventh, De Civilibus Magistratibus. It is evident, from various passages of Tertullian's works, that he deemed the exercise of the functions of the magistracy incompatible with the profession of Christianity, not merely on account of the danger to which, under a pagan government, a magistrate was continually exposed of being betrayed into some idolatrous act,[2] but also because the dress and other insignia savoured of those pomps and vanities, those works of the devil, which Christians renounce at their baptism.[3] He does not expressly say that capital punishments are prohibited by the gospel;[4] but he certainly thought that Christians ought not to sit as judges in criminal causes,[5] or attend the amphitheatre, or be present at an execution.[6]

In the treatise *de Coronâ* he enters into a regular discussion of the question, whether it is allowable for a Christian to engage in the military profession.[7] This question he determines in the negative, for reasons sufficiently weak and frivolous.[8] It might, he was aware, be objected that neither did John the Baptist command the soldiers who came to his baptism, nor Christ the

[1] *De Homiliis*, and *de Episcoporum et Ministrorum Consecratione*.

[2] "Et enim nobis ab omni gloriæ et dignitatis ardore frigentibus nulla est necessitas cœtûs, nec ulla magis res aliena, quam publica." *Apology*, c. 38. See also cc. 31 and 46. "Si de modestiâ certem, ecce Pythagoras apud Thurios, Zeno apud Prienenses tyrannidem affectant: Christianus vero nec ædilitatem."

[3] *De Spectaculis*, c. 12. But see particularly *de Idololatriâ*, cc. 17, 18, where the question is regularly discussed.

[4] "Nec isti porro exitus violenti, quos justitia decernit, *violentiæ vindex*." *De Animâ*, c. 56.

[5] "Jam vero quæ sunt potestatis, neque judicet (Christianus) de capite alicujus vel pudore (feras enim de pecuniâ), neque damnet, neque prædamnet, neminem vinciat, neminem recludat, aut torqueat." *De Idololatriâ*, c. 17. Tertullian calls the judicial proceedings of the magistrates *justitiam seculi*, an expression which implies an indirect condemnation. *De Animâ*, c. 33. Compare *de Spectaculis*, c. 15, "Seculum Dei est, secularia autem diaboli;" and *de Idololatriâ*, c. 18, "Nam Dæmonia magistratus sunt seculi."

[6] *De Spectaculis*, c. 19.

[7] C. 11. Compare *de Idololatriâ*, c. 19.

[8] For instance, that a Christian, who has pledged his allegiance to Christ in baptism, cannot afterwards take the military oath to a mortal monarch.

centurion, to renounce the military life; but he gets rid of this objection by drawing a distinction between the case of one who is actually a soldier when he embraces Christianity, and that of a Christian who becomes a soldier. In the *Apology*,[1] however, where our author's object is to prove that Christians are not unprofitable to the State, he says that they were to be found in the Roman armies; and this fact is necessarily assumed in the celebrated story of the Thundering Legion.

We find nothing in Tertullian's works from which it can be inferred that he maintained the doctrine—against which the thirty-eighth Article is directed—of a community of goods among Christians, *as touching the right, title, and possession of the same*, though he describes them as contributing without reserve from their own substance towards the relief of their brethren, and living as if there was no distinction of property among them.[2]

With respect to oaths—the subject of the thirty-ninth Article—he appears to have understood our Saviour's injunction, "Swear not at all," literally, and to have thought that an oath was not under any circumstances allowable.[3]

Among King Edward's Articles is one against the millenarians. In my account of Tertullian I stated that he had adopted the notion of a millennium,[4] and referred to a story in the third

1 "Navigamus et nos vobiscum, et vobiscum militamus," c. 42.

2 "Itaque qui animo animâque miscemur, nihil de rei communicatione dubitamus; omnia indiscreta sunt apud nos, præter uxores." *Apology*, c. 39.

3 "Taceo de perjurio, quando ne jurare quidem liceat." *De Idololatriâ*, c. 11. "Ne juret quidem," c. 17. See also c. 23.

4 Chap. i. p. 9. We will give the passage at full length. *Adv. Marcionem*, l. iii. c. 24. "De restitutione vero Judææ, quam et ipsi Judæi ita ut describitur sperant, locorum et regionum nominibus inducti, quomodo *allegorica interpretatio*" (compare *de Res. Carnis*, c. 62) "in Christum et in Ecclesiam et habitum et fructum ejus *spiritaliter* competat, et longum est persequi, et in alio opere digestum, quod inscribimus *De Spe Fidelium*; et in præsenti vel eo otiosum, quia non de terrenâ, sed de cœlesti promissione sit quæstio." (Compare l. iii. c. 16.) "Nam et confitemur *in terrâ nobis regnum repromissum*, sed ante cœlum, sed alio statu, utpote post resurrectionem, in mille annos, in civitate divini operis, Hierusalem, cœlo delatâ, quam et Apostolus matrem nostram sursum designat, et πολίτευμα nostrum, id est, municipatum, in cœlis esse pronuntians, alicui utique cœlesti civitati eum deputat. Hanc et Ezechiel novit, et Apostolus Ioannes vidit, et qui apud fidem nostram est Novæ Prophetiæ Sermo testatur, ut etiam effigiem civitatis ante repræsentationem ejus conspectui futuram in signum prædicaret. Denique proxime expunctum est Orientali Expeditione. Constat enim, Ethnicis quoque testibus, in Judæâ per dies quadraginta matutinis momentis civitatem de cœlo pependisse, omni mœniorum habitu, evanescentem de profectu diei et alias de proximo nullam. Hanc dicimus excipiendis resurrectione Sanctis et refovendis

book *against Marcion* of a city which had been seen in Judæa suspended in the air for forty successive days during the early part of the morning. This city, according to him, was the image of the New Jerusalem, destined for the reception of the saints during their reign of a thousand years on earth, in the course of which their resurrection will be gradually effected according to their different degrees of merit, and which is to be followed by the conflagration of the world and the general judgment. Tertullian states, however, that the enjoyments and delights of this New Jerusalem will be purely, or as Mosheim understands the passage, chiefly spiritual. In the tract *de Pudicitiâ* he connects the hope of Christians with the restoration of the Jews.[1] We may take this opportunity of observing that he notices and ridicules the Platonic or Pythagorean notion that, after an interval of a thousand years had elapsed, the dead are recalled to life, and again run their course on earth.[2]

Another of King Edward's Articles was directed against those who maintained that all men, even the most impious, after suffering punishment for a certain time, would be finally saved. Tertullian appears to have coincided in opinion with the framers of this Article. He asserts distinctly that all men will not be saved,[3] and maintains that the punishments of the wicked will endure for ever.[4]

In the early ages of the Church,[5] a notion was very generally prevalent among its members that the end of the world was at hand; and sceptical writers have insinuated that the apostles

omnium bonorum *utique spiritalium* copiâ, in compensationem eorum quæ in seculo vel despeximus vel amisimus, a Deo prospectam. Siquidem et justum et Deo dignum illic quoque exsultare famulos ejus, ubi sunt et afflicti in nomine ipsius. Hæc ratio regni terreni: post cujus mille annos, intra quam ætatem concluditur Sanctorum resurrectio pro meritis maturius vel tardius resurgentium, tunc et mundi destructione et judicii conflagratione commissâ, demutati in atomo in angelicam substantiam, scilicet per illud incorruptelæ superindumentum, transferemur in cœleste regnum." See Mosheim, "De Rebus Christianis ante Constantinum." *Seculum tertium*, c. 38.

[1] "Christianum enim restitutione Judæi gaudere et non dolere conveniet; siquidem tota spes nostra cum reliquâ Israelis expectatione conjuncta est," c. 8.

[2] *De Animâ*, c. 30, *sub fine*.

[3] "Non enim omnes salvi fiunt." *Adv. Marcionem*, l. i. c. 24.

[4] *De Animâ*, c. 33, *sub fine*; *Apology*, cc. 48, 49.

[5] *Ad Uxorem*, l. i. c. 5, *sub fine*; *de Exhortatione Castitatis*, c. 6, from 1 Cor. vii. 29; *de Monogamiâ*, c. 16; *de Fugâ in Persecutione*, c. 12. "Antichristo jam instante." In the two passages last cited, Tertullian speaks of the near approach of the dreadful persecutions which were to follow the appearance of Antichrist. *De Pudicitiâ*, c. 1, *sub initio*; *de Jejuniis*, c. 12, *sub initio*.

themselves were not entirely exempt from this erroneous persuasion. That the notion took its rise from expressions in the apostolic writings may be admitted; but that it existed in the minds of the writers themselves is far from certain, since the passages may very reasonably be supposed to refer to the capture of Jerusalem by the Romans, and the total subversion of the Jewish polity. The general belief, as stated by Tertullian, was that the end of the world would immediately follow the downfall of the Roman Empire, which was conceived to be the obstacle mentioned by St. Paul to the revelation of the man of sin.[1] Our author urges this belief as a reason why the Christians, far from entertaining hostile designs against the empire, prayed earnestly for its continuance and prosperity.[2] He is not, however, always consistent with himself; for we have seen that in the tract *de Oratione* he condemns those who pray for the longer continuance of the present world, on the ground that such a petition is at variance with the clause in the Lord's Prayer, *Thy kingdom come.*[3]

Having now gone through the Articles of our Church, and laid before the reader such passages of Tertullian's works as appeared to throw any light upon the doctrines contained in them, we will briefly compare the result of our inquiries with the account given by Mosheim of the doctrines of the Church in the second century. His first remark is, that in this century the simplicity of the gospel began to be corrupted and its beauty to be impaired by the misguided diligence of men, who endeavoured to explain and define the Christian system by a reference to the tenets of pagan philosophy.[4] We have seen [5] that Tertullian was not insensible to the mischief which had arisen from this cause, although, with respect to the particular instance alleged by Mosheim in illustration of the above remark, he appears himself to have been in some degree liable to censure. "Plato," says Mosheim,

[1] 2 Thess. ii. 6. "Quis? nisi Romanus status, cujus abscessio in decem reges dispersa Antichristum superducet." *De Res. Carnis*, c. 24.

[2] "Est et alia major necessitas nobis orandi pro Imperatoribus, etiam pro omni statu imperii rebusque Romanis, qui vim maximam universo orbi imminentem, ipsamque clausulam seculi acerbitates horrendas comminantem, Romani imperii commeatu scimus retardari; itaque nolumus experiri, et dum precamur differri, Romanæ diuturnitati favemus." *Apology*, c. 32. See also c. 39, *pro morâ finis. Ad Scapulam*, c. 2. "Cum toto Romano imperio, quousque seculum stabit; tamdiu enim stabit."

[3] C. 5. Compare *de Res. Carnis*, c. 22, *sub initio*, referred to in chap. i. p. 10, note 4.

[4] *Century* ii. chap. iii. sect. 2, 3.

[5] Chap. iii. p. 86.

"had taught that the souls of heroes, of illustrious men, and eminent philosophers alone ascended after death into the mansions of light and felicity; while those of the generality, weighed down by their lusts and passions, sunk into the infernal regions, whence they were not permitted to emerge before they were purified from their turpitude and corruption. This doctrine was seized with avidity by the Platonic Christians, and applied as a commentary upon that of Jesus. Hence a notion prevailed that the *martyrs* only entered upon a state of happiness immediately after death; and that for the rest a certain obscure region was assigned, in which they were to be imprisoned until the second coming of Christ, or at least until they were purified from their various pollutions." Our author cannot with propriety be denominated a Platonic Christian, yet he certainly entertained the opinion on which Mosheim here animadverts. In this instance, as in many others, there appears to have been a process of the following kind. The tenets of the philosophers were first employed in illustration or amplification of the doctrines of the gospel; and passages of Scripture were afterwards perverted, in order to defend the notions which resulted from this mixture of heathenism and Christianity. The Platonic fancy described by Mosheim gave rise to the notion that martyrs alone were admitted to an immediate participation in the happiness of heaven; and this notion was confirmed by an appeal to the Book of Revelation, in which St. John is represented as having seen the souls of none but martyrs under the altar.[1]

Mosheim's second remark relates to the veneration with which the Scriptures were regarded by the early Christians.[2] Tertullian's numerous quotations from them afford sufficient evidence that his mind was deeply impressed with this feeling of reverence. We shall perhaps recur hereafter to his quotations and expositions of Scripture. For the present, therefore, we shall content ourselves with observing that, although of a very different school of divines from that to which Clemens Alexandrinus belonged, he is by no means exempt from the fault which Mosheim imputes to the latter author—of dealing in forced and extravagant and mystical interpretations.

Mosheim remarks thirdly, that no attempts had yet been made to exhibit the Christian doctrines in a systematic form;[3] or,

[1] C. 6. v. 9. See *de Animâ*, c. 55.
[2] *Ubi supra*, sect. 4, 5.
[3] Sect. 6, 7, 8.

at least, no such attempts have come to our knowledge. The latter part of the remark is undoubtedly true; for the *Apologies* which were published from time to time were, as we have seen, designed rather to repel the calumnious accusations brought against the Christians, than to give a connected view either of the evidences or doctrines of the gospel. But we know that the catechumens passed through a course of instruction before their admission to the baptismal font; and this fact seems almost necessarily to imply that the instruction was communicated upon some regular and systematic plan. When we come to the consideration of Tertullian's controversial writings, we shall find that his reasonings, on the particular points of doctrine which he undertook to maintain against the heretics, are neither deficient in perspicuity nor in force. Mosheim indeed has spoken in the most contemptuous terms of the reasoning powers and controversial qualifications of the early Fathers. Two of his observations may be thought more particularly applicable to Tertullian. "One," he says, "laying aside the sacred writings, from which all the weapons of religious controversy ought to be drawn, refers to the decisions of those bishops who ruled the Apostolic Churches. Another thinks that the antiquity of a doctrine is a mark of its truth, and pleads prescription against his adversary, as if he was maintaining his property before a civil magistrate; than which method of disputing nothing can be more pernicious to the cause of truth." To the reader who remembers our remarks upon the subject of tradition, it can scarcely be necessary to observe that this statement of Mosheim is a most unfair and erroneous representation of the line of argument pursued by Tertullian in his tract *de Præscriptione Hæreticorum.* So far is he from laying aside the sacred writings, that his main charge against the heretics is, that they had substituted the tenets of the heathen philosophers in the place of the doctrines of the gospel; and, in order to effect their purpose, had corrupted the sacred volume, or perverted its meaning by forced and unnatural interpretations.[1] Tertullian uniformly insists that Christ had delivered one, and only one rule of faith—the rule which was to be found in the Scriptures.[2] But here commenced the difference between himself and his opponents: they rejected several books of Scripture which he deemed genuine, and put different interpretations upon those portions of Scripture which they, as well as he, received. On both these points Tertullian appealed to the authority of the

[1] *De Præscriptione Hæreticorum,* cc. 6, 7.

[2] *Ibid.* cc. 9, 13, 14.

Church;[1] contending that in it as well the genuine Scriptures as their genuine interpretation had been preserved; and further contending that it was useless to seek the true interpretation among the heretics, since they differed from each other as widely as they did from the Church.[2] When, therefore, Tertullian refers to those bishops who ruled the Apostolic Churches, he does it, not for the purpose of laying aside the sacred writings, but of establishing their authority; and it is with the same view that he urges the plea of prescription. He contends that the doctrines which had always been maintained, and the Scriptures which had always been received, in those Churches which were founded by the apostles, were more likely to be true and genuine than the doctrines and Scriptures of the heretics, whose origin was known to be of very recent date. Wherein, let me ask, consists the fallacy of this mode of reasoning? or how can it possibly be injurious to the cause of truth? If I can, through independent channels, trace back a doctrine to the age of the apostles, and at the same time show that it is contained in those Scriptures which have always been recognised as authentic by the Apostolic Churches, I have surely done much, not only towards proving its truth, but also towards confirming the genuineness of the Scriptures themselves.

Mosheim places the rise of the ascetics in the second century;[3] and says that they were produced by the double doctrine of certain Christian moralists who laid down two different rules of life, the ordinary and the extraordinary,—the one adapted to the general mass of Christians, the other to those only of a more sublime and exalted character. To the former class of doctrines they gave the name of *precepts*, which were obligatory upon all orders of men; to the latter, that of *counsels*, which were voluntarily obeyed by such Christians as aimed at higher degrees of virtue. Mosheim traces the origin of this double doctrine to the Platonic and Pythagorean schools of philosophy, which taught that the continual aim of him who aspired to the envied title of the *sage* or *truly wise* must be to abstract his mind

[1] *De Præscriptione Hæreticorum*, c. 36.

[2] C. 10. Another argument urged by Tertullian is founded on the nature of faith; which must, he says, have some ascertained truths for its object: those truths we must seek, and having found, must acquiesce in them. There must be a point at which inquiry ceases and faith begins. But with the heretics it is one interminable search: they never attain to the truth; and consequently, having no fixed object of faith, have in reality no faith. Cc. 10, 14.

[3] *Ubi supra*, sect. 11, 12, 13, 14.

from the senses, and to raise it above the contagious influence of the body, which he was in consequence to extenuate by severe discipline and a spare diet. With the same view he was to withdraw himself from the world, and to affect a life of solitude and contemplation. In our account of the tenets of Montanus, we observed that Clemens Alexandrinus was the earliest Christian writer in whose works this distinction between the ordinary and the extraordinary rules of life is expressly laid down.[1] Tertullian drew a distinction of a different kind, between spiritual and animal Christians—between those who received, and those who rejected, the prophecies of Montanus. Yet in the second tract *ad Uxorem* we find him also distinguishing between precepts and counsels;[2] or, to use his own language, between *jussa* and *suasa*, and grounding the distinction upon St. Paul's expressions in 1 Cor. vii. Although, however, it is certain that the discipline of Montanus was of an ascetic character, and that great stress was laid in it upon fasts and other mortifications, we discover nothing in the writings of Tertullian from which we should infer that either the monastic or the eremitical mode of life was practised in his day. There is in the *Apology* a passage which would rather lead to the opposite conclusion.[3]

The rise of pious frauds is also placed by Mosheim in the second century, and in like manner ascribed to the pernicious influence of the Platonic philosophy.[4] Tertullian has recorded a fraud of this kind, practised by a presbyter, who endeavoured to palm upon the Christian world a spurious work under the name of St. Paul.[5] As he pronounces no severe condemnation upon the offender, it may be thought that he did not look upon the offence as of a very heinous character. Yet his writings appear to us to furnish no ground for affirming that he is himself

[1] Chap. i. p. 16.

[2] "Quanto autem nubere *in Domino* perpetrabile est uti nostræ potestatis, tanto culpabilius est non observare quod possis. Eo accedit, quod Apostolus, de Viduis quidem et Innuptis, ut ita permaneant *suadet*, quum dicit, *Cupio autem omnes meo exemplo perseverare;* de nubendo vero *in Domino* quum dicit, *tantum in Domino*, jam non *suadet*, sed exertè *jubet*. Igitur in ista maximè specie, nisi obsequimur, periclitamur. Quia *suasum* impunè quis negligat, quam *jussum;* quod illud de *consilio* veniat et voluntati proponatur, hoc autem de potestate descendat et necessitati obligetur: illic libertas, hic contumacia delinquere videatur," c. 1.

[3] "Sed alio quoque injuriarum titulo postulamur, et infructuosi in negotiis dicimur. Quo pacto? homines vobiscum degentes, ejusdem victûs, habitûs, instructûs, ejusdem ad vitam necessitatis? neque enim Brachmanæ, aut Indorum Gymnosophistæ sumus, silvicolæ, et exules vitæ," c. 42.

[4] *Ubi supra*, sect. 15.

[5] See p. 155, note 2.

justly liable to the charge of practising similar deceptions. We can perceive in him extreme reluctance to admit any fact which militates against the cause which he is defending, and equal readiness to adopt without due examination whatever tends to promote his immediate purpose. But the same dispositions are discernible in the controversialists of all ages; and to make them the pretence for refusing credit to the Fathers in particular, is to display a great deficiency either in information or in candour.

In his chapter on the doctrine of the Church,[1] Mosheim gives a short account of what he calls its penitential discipline. Having already discussed this subject in our account of the government of the Church, under which head it appeared more properly to fall, we shall now only remark that we have found in Tertullian's writings no confirmation of Mosheim's assertion that the Christian discipline began, even at that early period, to be modelled upon the forms observed in the heathen mysteries.

In his strictures upon the qualifications of the Fathers of the second century as moral writers,[2] Mosheim alludes to the controversy between M. Barbeyrac and the Père Cellier on that subject. On no one of the Fathers has M. Barbeyrac animadverted with greater severity than on our author; and an examination of his charges will enable us to form a tolerably accurate estimate of the degree of deference which ought to be paid to the decisions of the Fathers in general upon questions of morals.

But before we enter upon this examination, we must in justice to the early Fathers remark that nothing can be more unfair or more unreasonable than to require in them that perspicuity of arrangement, or that precision of language which we find in the moral writers of modern times. They never studied morality as a system, nor did they profess to teach it systematically. We ought also, before we censure them too harshly for their errors, duly to weigh the circumstances under which they wrote.[3] What we observed with respect to the extravagant terms in which

[1] *Ubi supra*, sect. 17.

[2] Sect. 10, note.

[3] The just and candid mode of estimating the works of the Fathers, when not directly controversial, is to consider them, not as argumentative treatises, but as popular discourses, in which the author is less solicitous to reason accurately, than to say what is striking and calculated to produce an effect upon his readers. Were we to subject many popular treatises on religion published at the present day to the same severe scrutiny to which M. Barbeyrac has subjected the works of Tertullian, the illustrations, I fear, would sometimes be found as impertinent, the premises as unsound, and the conclusions as illogical.

they speak of the merit of martyrdom, is no less applicable to the present subject.[1] They lived at a time when the path of the professor of Christianity was beset with dangers; when he might at any moment be called to suffer privation, pain, or even death, on account of his faith. It was of the utmost importance to the cause of the gospel that he should betray no unmanly fear in the hour of trial—no weak desire to consult his safety by the sacrifice of his principles. Nor was it less important that his moral character should be free from stain—that he should prove himself no less superior to the seductions of pleasure than to the terrors of persecution. Yet instances of human frailty would frequently occur, and the Fathers would be compelled to bewail the apostacy or the immorality of their brethren. Hence, in their anxiety to avert the evil consequences to the Church, which must result from the weakness and vices of its members, they would, especially if, like Tertullian, they were men of austere tempers, be liable to run into extremes,—to imagine that the most effectual mode of preventing the convert from indulging in criminal gratifications was to persuade him that he must debar himself even of those which are innocent; and that the most effectual mode of preparing him for the trials to which his profession might expose him, was to accustom him to a life of voluntary hardship and mortification.[2] Let it not be supposed that we mean by these remarks to justify the extravagances of which the Fathers were guilty; we offer them only in extenuation.

We proceed to M. Barbeyrac, who grounds his first charge on the unqualified manner in which our author condemns every art and profession connected even in the most remote degree with the heathen idolatry.[3] It cannot be denied that in some instances Tertullian's zeal carries him beyond all reasonable bounds; as when he involves in the guilt of idolatry the unhappy trader in frankincense, because it was burned on the altars of the idols.[4]

[1] Chap. ii. p. 77. [2] See the tract *de Spectaculis*, c. 1.

[3] *Traité de la Morale des Pères*, c. 6, sect. 5.

[4] *De Idololatriâ*, c. 11. See the *Apology*, c. 42. The trades and occupations which Tertullian in his treatise *de Idololatriâ* states to be incompatible with the profession of the gospel, are those of the makers of idols (c. 4–8); of those who build, or in any way adorn their temples or altars (c. 8); of astrologers (c. 9); of schoolmasters, among other reasons, because they taught the heathen mythology (c. 10); of merchants, who deal in any article used in the worship of idols, as in frankincense (c. 11). According to Tertullian, no Christian could, without contracting guilt, pay or receive money on the legal days, because they were sacred to some heathen god (c. 13); or suspend lamps or garlands at his door (c. 15). He was also guilty of idolatry if he either swore or allowed himself to be adjured or blessed by the name of any heathen god (cc. 20–22).

He seems not to have perceived the clear distinction between the case of the artificer who formed the idols, and of the merchant who dealt in any of the articles employed in idolatrous worship. An idol is made in order that it may be worshipped, that is, for a forbidden purpose; the very use for which it is designed is unlawful. But frankincense may be employed, as our author himself admits, on many occasions not only innocently, but beneficially.[1] To burn it on the altar of an idol is not to use, but to abuse it; and the guilt of the abuse must rest with the purchaser: to make the seller accountable for the purpose to which the buyer applies it is contrary to every principle of reason and of justice. That Tertullian should have overlooked this distinction is the more remarkable, because in the same treatise he has recourse to one nearly similar. He says[2] that a Christian may, without incurring guilt, be present, *as a spectator*, at the sacrifices with which it was customary to celebrate the assumption of the toga virilis, a marriage, or the naming of a child; because in these cases he is not invited expressly to attend the sacrifice, but to join in a ceremony which has in it nothing of an idolatrous character. Before, however, we proceed too severely to censure Tertullian for the error, which is the subject of M. Barbeyrac's animadversion, let us endeavour for a moment to put ourselves in his place. For this purpose we must imagine to ourselves the feelings with which the primitive Christians regarded the worship paid to the gods of the nations; the pious horror which they felt when they saw the homage, due only to the Creator, transferred to an idol, the work of man's hands.[3] They were, moreover, aware of the strong hold which idolatry possessed upon mankind, through the gratifications which it afforded to their sensual appetites; and were, therefore, desirous to place the convert as far as possible out of the reach of its temptations. Sometimes, in their anxiety to guard themselves and others from pollution, they might perplex their minds with unfounded scruples, or subject themselves to unnecessary restraints.[4] But we shall perhaps be induced to think more favourably even of their discretion, when we reflect that, had their descendants persisted in the same stedfast determination to hold no inter-

[1] *De Coronâ*, c. 10. "Et si me odor alicujus loci offenderit, Arabiæ aliquid incendo; sed non eodem ritu, nec eodem habitu, nec eodem apparatu, quo agitur apud idola."

[2] *De Idololatriâ*, c. 16. Compare *de Spectaculis*, c. 8.

[3] See *ad Martyres*, c. 2; *de Coronâ*, c. 10.

[4] On the subject of intercourse with Gentiles and compliance with Gentile customs, see *de Idololatriâ*, c. 14, and *de Cultu Fœminarum*, l. ii. c. 11.

course with idolatry, neither would the friends of the gospel have occasion to lament that, for a long series of years, a gaudy ritual, calculated only to affect the senses, was substituted almost universally in the place of its pure and spiritual worship; nor would its enemies be enabled to object that the mythology and superstitious practices of pagan Rome still subsist, changed only in name, throughout the larger portion of Christendom.

M. Barbeyrac's second charge relates to Tertullian's notions respecting the incompatibility of a military life with the profession of Christianity.[1] Having in our remarks upon the thirty-seventh Article of our Church [2] exposed the weakness of the grounds on which he maintained this opinion, we have now nothing further to add on the subject.

The treatise *de Coronâ Militis* [3] furnishes M. Barbeyrac with matter for another charge against Tertullian. When the Emperors distributed largesses to the army,[4] it was customary for the soldiers to appear with crowns of laurel on their heads. A Christian soldier on an occasion of this kind, instead of wearing the crown upon his head, bore it in his hand. Being questioned why he was guilty of this breach of discipline, he replied that his religion would not allow him to wear a crown. Persisting in his refusal to place it on his head, he was thrown into prison and sentenced to death. His conduct appears to have been disapproved by the majority of his Christian brethren. The warm and vehement temper of Tertullian led him to view it in a very different light. He regarded the soldier's refusal as an act of truly Christian heroism and self-devotion, and imputed the censures which were cast upon it to the lukewarmness and pusillanimity of the censurers. The reasons by which he justifies the act are not, it is true, of the most satisfactory nature. He admits that the Scriptures are silent on the subject, but says that it was not customary for Christians to wear crowns; and urges this fact as a proof that the tradition of the Church was unfavourable to such a practice.[5] He next contends that flowers, of which crowns were for the most part composed, were intended to gratify the senses of sight and smell; consequently, to weave them into garlands and to wear them on the head is to pervert them from their natural use, by placing them in a situation in

[1] *Ubi supra*, sect. 6, *et seq.*

[2] P. 180.

[3] *Ubi supra*, sect. 14, *et seq.*

[4] *De Coronâ Militis*, c. 1.

[5] Cc. 2, 3, 4. Compare *Apology*, c. 42. "Non emo capiti coronam," etc.

which they can neither be seen nor smelt.[1] But as this argument would apply only to crowns composed of flowers, he proceeds to enumerate the different heathen gods to whom the invention of the different crowns was ascribed.[2] Ornaments, originally suggested by demons, and still consecrated to their service, could not be fit for the head of a Christian. "We find," he continues, "no evidence in the Old Testament that crowns were ever worn by the prophets or priests, or suspended in the temple, or placed upon the ark or altar, or upon any part of the furniture of the sacred edifice."[3] He inquires lastly into the occasions on which crowns were worn, and discovers that the practice was always connected either with some idolatrous observance, or some secular art, or profession, or employment, which was forbidden to Christians.[4] The point upon which the whole question really turned—whether, in the particular case under consideration, to have worn a crown would have implied a participation in an idolatrous act—is scarcely touched by Tertullian. He calls it indeed an idolatrous act, but does not state wherein the idolatry consisted.[5] For further information on this point, the reader may consult Bingham,[6] who says that it was purely a civil act, performed in honour of the Emperors on such days as they gave their largesses or donations to the soldiers. Milner regards it in the same light, and pronounces an unqualified condemnation of the opinions advanced by Tertullian in this treatise.[7]

Among our author's works is a tract written for the express purpose of proving that a Christian could not, without incurring a certain degree of guilt, attend any of the public games. The principal reason which he assigns is, that all those games—having been originally instituted, and continuing to be celebrated in honour of some god—must be regarded as idolatrous ceremonies; all, therefore, who attended them were necessarily involved in the guilt of idolatry.[8] This, however, is not his only argument. He reasons also upon the moral effect of the games, and upon the tumult of passions which they were calculated to excite in the bosom of the spectator; who could scarcely fail to be transported as it were out of himself, and

[1] Cc. 5, 6. [2] Cc. 7, 8. [3] C. 10. [4] C. 11, *et seq.*
[5] See c. 12. [6] L. xvi. c. 4, sect. 8. [7] Vol. i. 315.
[8] *De Spectaculis*, c. 4. The strange application of Ps. i. in c. 3 is deserving of notice, as a specimen of the mode in which the Fathers wrested Scriptures to their purpose. Compare the *Apology*, c. 38, where all the arguments, urged in the tract *de Spectaculis*, are comprised in two sentences.

to give way by turns to hope and fear, to sorrow and resentment.[1] On two passages of this tract Gibbon has conferred celebrity by his animadversions. We shall offer a few remarks upon one of them, as it illustrates an opinion to which we shall hereafter have occasion to allude. Gibbon says that Tertullian "is particularly offended at the dress of the actors, who by the use of the buskin impiously endeavoured to add a cubit to their stature."[2] Now in the passage alluded to, our author is establishing the point on which his whole argument turns—the connexion of all the public games, and among the rest of the theatrical exhibitions, with idolatry. He had previously traced their origin to Satan; he now proceeds to show that the author of evil suggested the pomp and circumstance of the public exhibitions—the chariot race—the various gymnastic exercises—the dress of the actors, the buskin, the mask, etc. In all these devices Satan availed himself of the partial discoveries which he had been able to make, of what Christ would say, and do, and suffer, on earth; accommodating his suggestions to those discoveries—sometimes deceiving mankind by an imitation of Christian rites—at others betraying them into a violation of the precepts of the gospel.[3] Thus, anticipating as it were Christ's declaration, that no man can add a cubit to his stature, he invented the buskin; in order that, through the medium of the actors who wore it, he might practically make Christ a liar.[4] Gibbon's remark scarcely conveys a correct notion of Tertullian's object; which is to caution men against taking part in the theatrical exhibitions, lest they should unconsciously render themselves the instruments of the devil. The other passage, quoted by Gibbon, is from the concluding chapter of the tract, and is a striking specimen of Tertullian's vehemence and proneness to exaggeration.[5]

Having already considered,[6] what is sufficiently obnoxious to censure, Tertullian's notion that Christians ought neither to aspire to, nor to accept any civil office, we shall proceed to his condemnation of second marriages, which furnishes M. Barbeyrac with ample matter of animadversion.[7] On this subject, as we

[1] C. 15.
[2] Chap. xv. note 41. See Barbeyrac, *Traité de la Morale des Pères*, c. 6, sect. 20.
[3] Compare *ad Uxorem*, l. i. c. 7, *sub fine.*
[4] "Sic et tragœdos cothurnis extulit (Diabolus) quia nemo potest adjicere cubitum unum ad staturam suam. Mendacem facere vult Christum."
[5] Chap. xv. p. 474, ed. 4to.
[6] P. 180.
[7] *Ubi supra*, sect. 30, *et seq.*

have before observed, we find a gradually increasing severity in our author's opinions. In our brief notice of the two tracts *ad Uxorem*, we stated that in the former Tertullian dissuades his wife, in case she should survive him, from contracting a second marriage; in the latter, fearful that she might be unwilling to impose upon herself so great a restraint, he cautions her at least not to marry a heathen.[1] Such a marriage he brands with the name of adultery; appealing, in support of this harsh sentence, to 1 Cor. vii. 39, where the apostle says that a widow may marry whom she will, "*tantum in Domino*," *only in the Lord*, that is, according to our author's interpretation, only a Christian.[2]

In the treatise *de Exhortatione Castitatis*, written after he had become a Montanist, but probably before he had adopted the opinions of Montanus in all their rigour, he proceeds a step further. The name of adultery, which he had before applied to a marriage contracted with a heathen, he now applies to second marriages in general; and that for reasons, some of which, as he himself admits, are equally applicable to a first marriage.[3] The object of the treatise is to dissuade a Christian brother, who had lost his wife, from marrying again. "There are," Tertullian says, "three degrees of holiness:—the first exists in those who have continued chaste from their birth; the second in those who have continued chaste from their second birth, that is, their baptism—either separated from their wives, if living, by mutual compact, or remaining single if they have lost their wives; the third in those who, having been once married (after baptism), do not marry again." [4] One of the arguments urged in this treatise affords a striking example of the fallacious reasoning by which Tertullian occasionally imposed upon himself. "You have lost your wife," he says; "it was therefore the will of God that you should become a widower; by marrying again you cease to be a

[1] Chap. i. p. 24.

[2] *Ad Uxorem*, l. ii. cc. 2, 3. "Hæc quum ita sint, Fideles Gentilium matrimonia subeuntes stupri reos esse constat et arcendos ab omni communicatione fraternitatis, ex literis Apostoli dicentis, *cum ejusmodi nec cibum sumendum.*" Compare *adv. Marcionem*, l. v. c. 7; *de Monogamiâ*, cc. 7, 11.

[3] "Si penitus sensus ejus interpretemur, non aliud dicendum erit secundum matrimonium, quam species stupri—Ergo, inquis, jam et primas, id est, unas nuptias destruis; nec immerito: quoniam et ipsæ ex eo constant quo et stuprum," c. 9. See also c. 4.

[4] C. 1. It is worthy of remark that M. Barbeyrac agrees with Tertullian in asserting that a person who has once been married has a stronger inducement to contract a second marriage, than an unmarried person has to marry. Compare *ad Uxorem*, l. i. c. 8, and *de Virgin. vel.* c. 10, with the *Traité de la Morale des Pères*, c. 4, sect. 30.

widower, and thereby strive against the will of God."[1] A considerable portion of the tract is occupied by a commentary on the seventh chapter of the First Epistle to the Corinthians; the design of which is to show that when St. Paul asserted, as a reason for allowing a second marriage, that "it is better to marry than burn," he evidently regarded such a marriage merely as the less of two evils.[2] In the course of this commentary, Tertullian alludes to the distinction made by the apostle between that which he delivered from himself, and that which he delivered from the Lord. In the latter case he thinks that St. Paul spoke from the extraordinary inspiration which was peculiar to him as an apostle; in the former, only as an ordinary Christian, possessing the ordinary gifts of the Spirit. I notice this circumstance because the late Mr. Rennell, in his *Proofs of Inspiration*, etc., has referred to this passage of Tertullian in a manner which may lead his readers to form a very erroneous notion of its real purport. Mr. Rennell[3]—whose object is to prove that what St. Paul delivered as from himself was equally the dictate of divine inspiration with that which he delivered as from the Lord—says that "the apostle decided the question concerning virgins, in 1 Cor. vii. 25, not as an ordinary man, but as one *who had obtained mercy to be faithful;* by which expression he meant to assert the grace and authority of an inspired minister and apostle." Let us now turn to Tertullian, who begins his remarks with the following words:—"In primis autem non videbor irreligiosus, si, quod ipse profitetur, animadvertam, omnem illum indulgentiam nuptiarum de suo, id est, de humano sensu, non de divino præscripto induxisse."[4] He then proceeds to comment upon several verses of the chapter, and concludes with the passage, part of which has been quoted by Mr. Rennell:—"Sed ecce rursus, mulierem marito defuncto dicit nubere posse, si cui velit, *tantum in Domino. Atenim felicior erit*, inquit, *si sic permanserit secundum meum consilium. Puto autem, et ego Dei Spiritum habeo.* Videmus duo consilia, quo supra nubendi veniam facit, et quo postmodum continentiam nubendi indicit. Cui ergo, inquis, adsentabimur? Inspice et lege. Quum veniam facit, *hominis prudentis consilium* adlegat. Quum continentiam indicit, *Spiritûs Sancti consilium* adfirmat. Sequere admonitionem cui divinitas patrocinatur. Spiritum quidem Dei etiam *fideles* habent, sed non *omnes fideles* Apostoli.

1 C. 2. Compare *ad Uxorem*, l. i. c. 7; *de Monogamiâ*, c. 9.
2 C. 3. Compare *ad Uxorem*, l. i. c. 3.
3 P. 28, with the note. The part quoted by Mr. Rennell is from "Quum continentiam indicit" to "fastigium redderet."
4 C. 3.

Quum ergo qui se *fidelem* dixerat, adjicit postea *Spiritum Dei se habere*, quod nemo dubitaret etiam de *fideli*, idcirco id dixit, ut sibi Apostoli fastigium redderet. *Propriè* enim Apostoli Spiritum Sanctum habent in operibus prophetiæ, et efficaciâ virtutum, documentisque linguarum; non *ex parte*, quod cæteri."[1] Now it must be evident to every person who reads the above extract, that Tertullian agrees with Mr. Rennell only in one particular—that in the expression, *I think that I have the Spirit of God*, St. Paul meant to assert his own inspiration.[2] On two important points our author is directly opposed to Mr. Rennell.[3] In the first place, Tertullian makes a decided distinction between the advice given by St. Paul as a prudent or sagacious man, and that given by him at the suggestion of the Holy Spirit. In the second, so far was he from thinking that the apostle, when he spoke of himself as one *who had obtained mercy to be faithful*, meant to assert the grace and authority of an inspired minister and apostle; that by the word *Fideles* he understood an ordinary Christian, as contra-distinguished from an apostle, who was endowed with extraordinary gifts. Let me here observe that I am not contending for the accuracy of Tertullian's interpretation: I am only anxious that his testimony, if urged at all, should be correctly stated.

But to proceed to the tract *de Monogamiâ*, in which Tertullian pursues nearly the same line of argument as in the tract *de Exhortatione Castitatis*, but with greater extravagance both of sentiment and language, because he was then in a state of avowed separation from the Church. He affirms, for instance, that in point of criminality it is immaterial whether a man has two wives at the same time, or marries a second wife after the death of the first.[4] He urges also the example of Christ, who

[1] Does Tertullian here mean to assert that none but the apostles possessed miraculous gifts? or that all those gifts were united in the apostles, which other Christians possessed only in part, with reference to 1 Cor. xii. 4, etc.?

[2] Compare *de Pudicitiâ*, c. 16; *de Monogamiâ*, c. 3.

[3] There is in the tract *de Coronâ* a passage in which Tertullian makes a nearer approach to Mr. Rennell's opinion. "Dicit et Apostolus, *si quid ignoratis, Deus vobis revelabit*, solitus et ipse consilium subministrare, quum præceptum Domini non habebat, et *quædam edicere a semetipso, sed et ipse Spiritum Dei habens deductorem omnis veritatis*. Itaque consilium et edictum ejus divini jam præcepti instar obtinuit, de rationis divinæ patrocinio," c. 4. In this passage our author's object is to place observances, for which no written command could be produced from Scripture, on the same footing with those for which such command could be produced, on the ground that they were probably enjoined by the apostles, and were consequently to be deemed of divine origin. His language varies with the object which he has in view.

[4] "Neque enim refert duas quis uxores singulas habuerit, an pariter singulæ

was unmarried in the flesh. If, therefore, we aim at His perfection, we must also remain unmarried; but if the infirmity of our flesh will not allow this, we must follow in the flesh the example which He has set us in the spirit.[1] He has one spiritual spouse, the Church; we, therefore, must be content with a single marriage. In our remarks upon the thirty-second Article of our Church, we noticed the different interpretations of 1 Cor. ix. 5 given by Tertullian in the tracts *de Exhortatione Castitatis* and *de Monogamiâ*. Towards the conclusion, however, of the latter tract, a suspicion appears to cross his mind that his expositions of St. Paul are far-fetched, and may not be satisfactory to his readers. In order, therefore, to silence all gainsayers, he adds that, as Christ took away the liberty of divorce in which Moses had indulged the Jews on account of the hardness of their hearts, so the Paraclete now takes away that liberty of contracting a second marriage, which St. Paul had allowed the members of the infant Church of Corinth on account of the infirmity of their flesh.[2]

The train of reasoning, if it may be so called, which conducted the early Fathers to these strange conclusions, was, according to M. Barbeyrac,[3] somewhat of the following kind. They observed that men were impelled to the commission of many irregularities and crimes by the desire of gratifying certain appetites which constitute a part of human nature. They could not condemn the appetites themselves without at the same time condemning the author of nature; they hit, therefore, upon another expedient. They said that those appetites were given us for particular ends; the appetite of hunger, for instance, in order to preserve the life of man; the sexual appetite, in order to ensure the continuance of the human species. So long, then, as the acts which originate in those appetites are performed solely with reference to the ends for which the appetites were given, all is right. But the instant that we annex the idea of pleasure to the act, and perform it with a view to the gratification which we shall derive from it, then it becomes sinful. That this is a correct account of the mode in which many of the Fathers reasoned may be true, and we may discern some traces of it in Tertullian's writings. But it is

duas fecerint. Idem numerus conjunctorum et separatorum. Semel tamen vim passa institutio Dei per Lamech constitit postea in finem usque gentis illius," c. 4.

1 "Quando novissimus Adam, id est Christus, innuptus in totum, quod etiam primus Adam ante exilium," c. 5. He applies the name *Spado* to Christ (see also c. 3), as well as to St. Paul (*ibid.*) and to John the Baptist (c. 17), but evidently not in the literal sense of the word.

2 C. 14.

3 C. 4, sect. 34, 35.

certain that he also attached a degree of impurity to the act itself, without any reference to the purpose for which it was performed,—a certain incompatibility with the perfection of the Christian character.[1] He regards marriage as only allowed under the gospel, in condescension to human infirmity. "The union of the sexes was, it is true, in the beginning blessed by God; being devised for the purpose of peopling the earth, and on that account permitted.[2] The patriarchs were even allowed to have a plurality of wives. Then came the law, and afterwards the gospel, which restrained the licence before given, and confined a man to one wife. Lastly, the apostle, as speaking to those upon whom the ends of the world were come, did not indeed forbid marriage, lest man should be tempted to sin, but recommended a life of celibacy, as best suited to the situation of Christians in seasons of difficulty and persecution." [3] The inference which our author draws from this historical sketch is, that the apostle's permission to marry was not willingly given, but extorted by necessity.

But though Tertullian attached a degree of impurity even to the married state, and would certainly have enforced a total abstinence from marriage if the human species could have been continued without it, as he would have prohibited eating and drinking if the life of man could have been sustained without food,[4] yet we find occasionally in his writings passages of a different complexion. In the second tract *ad Uxorem* he breaks out into a glowing description of the blessedness of that marriage, in the celebration of which none of the forms required by the Church has been omitted;[5] and in other places he speaks of the married state, not only as pure, but even honourable.[6] As

[1] Speaking of the intercourse between the sexes even in the married state, he uses the expressions "contumeliam communem," *de Virg. vel.* c. 10; "Dedecoris voluptuosi," *ad Uxorem*, l. i. c. 1. He argues also that it unfits the soul for devotional exercises. *De Exhortatione Castitatis*, cc. 9, 10. He calls it on one occasion "permissam voluptatem," *de Cultu Fœminarum*, l. ii. c. 9.

[2] *Ad Uxorem*, l. i. cc. 2, 3. See also c. 4; *de Exhortatione Castitatis*, cc. 5, 6; *de Monogamiâ*, c. 3.

[3] We have seen that in the tract *de Monogamiâ*, cc. 2, 3, 14, Tertullian states that it was reserved for the Paraclete to prohibit second marriages. During the ministry of our Blessed Lord, men were not yet able to bear so severe a restraint.

[4] "Nos quoque, ut possumus, os cibo excusamus," etc. *De Res. Carnis*, c. 61. Compare *de Jejuniis*, c. 3.

[5] "Unde sufficiamus ad enarrandam felicitatem ejus matrimonii, quod Ecclesia conciliat?" etc., c. 9.

[6] "Natura veneranda est, non erubescenda. Concubitum libido, non conditio fœdavit. Excessus, non status, est impudicus. Siquidem benedictus status apud Deum: *Crescite et in multitudinem proficite.* Excessus vero maledictus—adulteria,

we remarked with reference to another subject, Tertullian's language varies with the object which he has in view.[1] When he speaks his genuine sentiments, he exaggerates the merit of celibacy, and speaks of the married state as rather permitted than approved by God. But when he is contending against Marcion and the other heretics, who condemned marriage altogether, as an institution of the Demiurge who was opposed to the Supreme God, he stands forth in its defence, though he still asserts the superior purity of a life of celibacy.[2]

We will take this opportunity of introducing two observations in some measure connected with the subject immediately before us. The first is, that in Tertullian's time the practice of making vows of continence had already commenced,[3] and had been found to be productive of evil consequences.[4] The females who made such vows were called *Brides of Christ.*[5] The second observation is, that the Roman Catholic notion of the indissolubility of marriage was then unknown. Tertullian on all occasions

et stupra, et lupanaria." *De Animâ*, c. 27. "Sanctitas—quæ non matrimonium excludat, sed libidinem—quæ vas nostrum in honore matrimonii tractet." *Adv. Marcionem*, l. v. c. 15.

[1] See note 3, p. 196.

[2] *De Monogamiâ, sub initio. Adv. Marcionem*, l. i. c. 29. "Sine dubio ex damnatione conjugii ista institutio" (the Marcionite custom of refusing baptism to married persons) "constabit. Videamus, an justâ: non quasi destructuri felicitatem sanctitatis, ut aliqui Nicolaitæ, assertores libidinis atque luxuriæ; sed qui sanctitatem sine nuptiarum damnatione noverimus, et sectemur, et præferamus, non ut malo bonum, sed ut bono melius; non enim projicimus, sed deponimus nuptias; nec præscribimus, sed suademus sanctitatem; servantes et bonum et melius pro viribus cujusque sectando: tunc denique conjugium exertè defendentes, quum inimicè accusatur spurcitiæ nomine in destructionem Creatoris, qui proinde conjugium pro rei honestate benedixit in crementum generis humani, quemadmodum et universum conditionis in integros et bonos usus. Non ideo autem et cibi damnabuntur, quia operosius exquisiti in gulam committunt; ut nec vestitus ideo accusabuntur, quia pretiosius comparati in ambitionem tumescunt. Sic nec matrimonii res ideo despuentur, quia, intemperantius diffusæ in luxuriam inardescunt. Multum differt inter causam et culpam, inter statum et excessum. Ita hujusmodi non institutio, sed exorbitatio, reprobanda est, secundum censuram institutoris ipsius, cujus est tam, *Crescite et multiplicamini*, quam et, *Non adulterabis, et uxorem proximi tui non concupisces.*" Here we find an approach to the mode of reasoning which M. Barbeyrac imputes to the Fathers.

[3] "Viderit et ipsum continentiæ votum." *De Virgin. vel.* c. 11.

[4] See *de Virgin. vel.* c. 14.

[5] "Quot Virgines Christo maritatæ?" *de Res. Carnis*, c. 61; "Malunt enim Deo nubere, Deo speciosæ, Deo sunt puellæ," etc., *ad Uxorem*, l. i. c. 4. Generally, however, such expressions as "Christi solius ancillæ," *de Virgin. vel.* c. 3; "Dei ancillæ," *de Cultu Fœminarum*, l. i. c. 4, l. ii. cc. 1, 11; "Nuptæ Christo," *de Virgin. vel.* c. 16; "Benedictæ," *de Cultu Fœminarum*, l. ii. c. 5; "filiæ sapientiæ," *ibid.* c. 6; "Fœminæ ad Deum pertinentes," *ad Uxorem*, l. i. c. 1, mean only Christian females, as "ancilla Diaboli," *de Cultu Fœm.* l. ii. c. 11, means a heathen female, and "Angeli Dei," *ibid.* c. 3, Christians in general.

affirms that it may be dissolved on account of adultery;[1] and though his peculiar tenets would naturally lead him to deny to either party the liberty of marrying again, yet he admits that such marriages actually took place in the Church.[2]

Two charges which M. Barbeyrac brings against Tertullian remain to be mentioned. One is, that, in opposition to our Saviour's express injunction, he passes a sentence of condemnation upon all who in time of persecution consult their safety by flight. The other, that he advances opinions so extravagant and irrational on the subject of Christian patience that, were they generally adopted, the effect must be to place the honest and peaceable part of the community at the mercy of the robber and ruffian. In our remarks upon the External History of the Church we gave an account of Tertullian's opinions on the former of those points;[3] and with respect to the latter, it will be sufficient to observe that his error appears to have arisen partly from too close an adherence to the letter of our Saviour's injunctions, and partly from a strange misapprehension of their meaning.[4]

We will conclude our review of M. Barbeyrac's animadversions by observing that he seems to have overlooked a passage in the fourth book *against Marcion*;[5] in which Tertullian argues, from a passage in Ezekiel, that no interest ought be taken for the loan of money.

[1] *Ad Uxorem*, l. ii. c. 2; *de Monogamiâ*, c. 9. "Tam repudio matrimonium dirimente quam morte." *De Patientiâ*, c. 12.

[2] *Ad Uxorem*, l. ii. c. 1. "Quarundam exemplis admonentibus, quæ divortio vel mariti excessu oblatâ continentiæ occasione," etc.

[3] Chap. ii. p. 74.

[4] See the tract *de Patientiâ*, cc. 7, 8, 10. In this tract, which is a panegyric upon patience, Tertullian exhorts his readers to the practice of that virtue, by setting forth the forbearance which God at all times exerts towards sinful man, and the patience exhibited by Christ in taking upon Him human flesh, and submitting to every indignity during His residence on earth. There are, however, some passages not unworthy of attention, as c. 9, in which Tertullian enforces the duty of patience under the loss of relations and friends.

[5] C. 17. There is an ambiguity in Tertullian's expressions, but we believe that we have given the true meaning.

——o——

## CHAPTER VI.

### ON THE CEREMONIES USED IN THE CHURCH.

MOSHEIM,[1] in the beginning of his chapter on the Ceremonies of the Church in the Second Century, observes that "in this century many unnecessary ceremonies were added to the Christian worship, the introduction of which was extremely offensive to wise and good men." In support of this statement, he refers to a passage in the tract *de Oratione*, in which Tertullian complains that various forms and observances had been introduced into the Christian worship, of which some bore too close a resemblance to the customs and practices of the Gentiles. Of these observances he specifies several,—the practice, for instance, of washing the hands, or even the whole body, before the commencement of prayer, which he calls a superstitious practice, originally suggested by the act of Pilate when he delivered up Christ to the Jews, and, consequently, unfit to be adopted by Christians;[2] and that of putting off the cloke before the commencement of prayer, which he disapproves because the heathens had a similar custom.[3] He assigns the same reason for objecting to the practice of sitting down after the conclusion of the public prayers; though he supposes its introduction into the Church to have arisen from a misapprehension of a passage in the *Shepherd of Hermas.*

From the passage just alluded to, and from other passages of Tertullian's works, it appears that in the act of prayer, the early Christians raised their hands to heaven, and expanded them in imitation of the mode in which our Saviour's arms were stretched upon the cross.[4] They usually prayed in a kneeling posture,[5] excepting on the Lord's day, and in the interval between Easter

[1] *Century* ii. part ii. chap. iv.

[2] *De Oratione*, c. 11. Compare *de Baptismo*, c. 9, *sub fine*. "Quum deditur in crucem, aqua intervenit; sciunt Pilati manus."

[3] C. 12.

[4] "Nos vero non attollimus tantum, sed etiam expandimus, a dominicâ passione modulantes." *De Oratione*, c. 11, *sub fine*. *Apology*, c. 30, "Manibus expansis." *Ad Marcionem*, l. i. c. 23, *sub fine*.

[5] *De Coronâ*, c. 3; *ad Scapulam*, c. 4. "Quando non geniculationibus et jejunationibus nostris etiam siccitates sunt depulsæ?" In the second tract *ad Uxorem*, c. 9, we find the word *volutari* applied to the act of prayer. "Simul orant, simul volutantur." Compare Pseudo-Justinus, *Quæstiones ad Orthodoxos*, c. 115.

and Whitsunday: they then prayed standing, in commemoration of the resurrection of our Lord from the dead. The men prayed with the head uncovered.[1] With respect to the women, different customs appear to have prevailed in different churches: in some even the virgins were unveiled; but in the tract *de Virginibus velandis*, Tertullian inveighs vehemently against the indecency and irreverence of this practice.[2] It was customary also, in the act of prayer, to turn the face towards the east[3]—a practice borrowed, according to Mosheim, from the eastern nations, who conceived light to be the essence of the Supreme, and therefore worshipped the sun as the image of His glory.[4] We have seen that this practice gave rise to a very general persuasion among the Gentiles that the Christians worshipped the sun.[5] After the prayers were concluded, the persons present usually saluted each other with the kiss of peace, excepting on Good Friday, which was observed as a solemn fast by every member of the Church.[6] Tertullian censures the affectation of those who, at other seasons, refused the kiss of peace, on the ground that they had kept a fast.

Having alluded to the tract *de Oratione*, we will take this opportunity of mentioning that the greater part of it is occupied by a commentary on the Lord's Prayer.[7] After some preliminary remarks on the injunctions to pray in secret and not to use long prayers, by which the Lord's Prayer is introduced in the gospel, Tertullian observes that this form, concise as it is, contains an epitome of the whole Christian doctrine. In commenting upon the different clauses, our author displays an extensive knowledge of Scripture, but for the most part little judgment in the application. He concludes with stating that, although in our devotions we must on no account omit this

[1] "Capite nudo." *Apology*, c. 30.

[2] C. 2. See *de Coronâ*, c. 4.

[3] *Apology*, c. 16; *ad Nationes*, l. i. c. 13.

[4] *Century* ii. part ii. chap. iv. sect. 7. There is in the tract *against the Valentinians*, c. 3, the following remark:—"Amat figura Spiritûs Sancti (Columba) Orientem, Christi figuram," referring perhaps to Zechariah iii. 8: *I will bring forth my Servant the Branch.* The word corresponding to *branch* in the Septuagint is ἀνατολήν.

[5] Chap. ii. p. 62.

[6] "Alia jam consuetudo invaluit; jejunantes habitâ oratione cum fratribus, subtrahunt osculum pacis, quod est signaculum orationis." *De Oratione*, c. 14. "Jam vero alicui fratrum ad osculum convenire." *Ad Uxorem*, l. ii. c. 4. From the latter quotation we might infer that the Christian mode of salutation was by a kiss.

[7] There are also some remarks on the Lord's Prayer in the fourth book *against Marcion*, c. 26.

prayer, yet we may add to it such petitions as are suitable to our particular circumstances;[1] remembering always that, in order to render our prayers acceptable to God, we must approach Him in a right frame of mind—with hearts free from anger and every other evil passion.[2] In addition to these remarks upon the spirit in which men ought to pray, he offers some cautions against all extravagance of gesture in putting up our prayers to the throne of grace.[3] Our gesture and countenance ought to bespeak humility and modesty. He says also that we should be careful not to pray in so loud a tone of voice as to disturb the devotions of those near us. It is not by reason of the strength of our lungs that our prayers reach the ear of the Almighty.

In speaking of the Christian assemblies, Mosheim gives the following account of the purposes for which they were held.[4] "During the sacred meetings of the Christians, prayers were repeated, the Holy Scriptures were publicly read, select discourses upon the duties of Christians were addressed to the people, hymns were sung, and a portion of the oblations presented by the faithful was employed in the celebration of the Lord's Supper and the feast of charity." We need scarcely remind the reader that this account is merely an epitome of a passage in the *Apology*,[5] which was given in the chapter on the Government of the Church.

There is, however, in the *Apology*, an expression which has been urged by those who object to the use of set forms of prayer, in confirmation of their opinion. Tertullian, speaking of the primitive Christians, says "that they prayed for the Emperor without a prompter, because they prayed from the heart."[6] From the words "without a prompter" it has been

[1] C. 9. [2] C. 10.

[3] C. 13. In Semler's edition, the tract *de Oratione* contains nine additional chapters, which were published by Muratori; of these the first two relate to the question whether virgins ought to wear veils in the church, and are little else than an epitome of the tract *de Virginibus velandis;* the third, to the practice of kneeling in the act of prayer; the fourth, to the place, the fifth, to the hour of prayer; the sixth, to the propriety of not allowing a Christian brother to quit the house without joining in prayer; the seventh, to the custom of saying Halleluiah at the conclusion of our prayers; in the eighth, prayer is stated to be the spiritual sacrifice, by which the ancient sacrifices were superseded; the ninth relates to the efficacy of prayer. From the style and tone of these additional chapters, I should infer that they were not written by Tertullian.

[4] *Century* ii. part ii. chap. iv. sect. 8. [5] C. 39 in chap. iv. p. 110.

[6] C. 30. "Denique sine monitore, quia de pectore oramus." See Bingham, l. xiii. c. 5, sect. 5.

inferred that their prayers were on all occasions extemporaneous effusions. But the context clearly shows that Tertullian merely intended to contrast the cordial sincerity of their prayers for the safety and prosperity of the emperors, with the forced and hollow exclamations of the heathen populace, who required to be bribed with largesses, and even to be prompted before they would cry out in the accustomed form, "De nostris annis tibi Jupiter augeat annos."[1]

From incidental notices scattered over Tertullian's works we collect that Sunday, or the Lord's Day, was regarded by the primitive Christians as a day of rejoicing; and that to fast upon it was deemed unlawful.[2] The word Sabbatum is always used to designate, not the first, but the seventh day of the week; which appears in Tertullian's time to have been also kept as a day of rejoicing. Even the Montanists—anxious as they were to introduce a more rigorous discipline in the observance of fasts—when they kept their two weeks of Xerophagiæ, did not fast on the Saturday and Sunday.[3] The Saturday before Easter day was, however, an exception; that *was* observed as a fast.[4] The custom of observing every Saturday as a fast, which became general throughout the western Church, does not appear to have existed in Tertullian's time.[5] That men who, like our author, on all occasions contended that the ritual and ceremonial law of Moses had ceased, should observe the seventh day of the week as a festival, is perhaps to be ascribed to a desire of conciliating the Jewish converts.

We find in Tertullian's works no notice of the celebration of our Lord's nativity, although the festivals of Easter and Whitsuntide are frequently mentioned; with reference to which it should be observed, that the word Pascha was not used to signify merely the day of our Lord's resurrection, but also the day of His passion, or rather the whole interval of time from His crucifixion

[1] Compare c. 35.

[2] Tertullian uses both names; that of Sunday, when addressing the heathens. *Apology*, c. 16. "Æque si diem Solis lætitiæ indulgemus," etc. *Ad Nationes*, l. i. c. 13; that of the Lord's Day, when writing to Christians. *De Coronâ*, c. 3. "Die Dominico jejunium nefas ducimus." *De Jejuniis*, c. 15; *de Idololatriâ*, c. 14; *de Animâ*, c. 9. "Inter Dominica Solennia." *De Fugâ in Persecutione*, c. 14. We are not, however, certain that Tertullian uniformly observes this distinction. Bingham thinks that he does. L. xx. c. 2, sect 1.

[3] *De Jejuniis*, c. 15. The Gentiles feasted on a Saturday. *Apology*. c. 16.

[4] *De Jejuniis*, c. 14.

[5] See Bingham, l. xx. c. 3.

to His resurrection.[1] In like manner the word Pentecost signified, not merely Whitsunday, but also the fifty days which intervened between Easter and Whitsunday.[2] Tertullian makes no allusion to the paschal controversy—a controversy which was carried on with great bitterness towards the middle of the second century, respecting the days on which the death and resurrection of Christ ought to be commemorated. He says only in general terms that they were always commemorated in the first month of the year.[3]

We have already had occasion to allude to the custom of making offerings at the tombs of the martyrs on the anniversary of their martyrdom.[4] To the anniversary itself was given the name of Natalitium or Natalis Dies, on the ground that it was the day of their birth into eternal life. Some of the commentators fancy that they discover, in a passage in the tract *de Coronâ*, an allusion to the practice of noting down the days on which the martyrs suffered—in other words, of composing martyrologies; but the passage is not of that decided character on which an inference can be safely built.[5]

After Tertullian became a Montanist, he wrote his tract *de Jejuniis*, the object of which was to defend the number, length, and severity of the fasts described by the founder of the sect. In order to refute the notion that the season of our Saviour's Passion was the only season at which Christians were positively bound to fast, he undertakes to establish the general obligation of fasting. With this view he goes back to Adam's transgression.[6] Adam was forbidden to eat of the fruit of the tree of knowledge; he ate and fell. As, therefore, he fell by yielding to his appetite, it follows that the sure way for man to regain the favour of God is to mortify his appetite. Adam offended by eating; we must remedy the evil consequences of the offence by fasting. Our author refers also to various instances, both in the Old and New Testaments, in which punishment had been averted, and spiritual

[1] *De Coronâ*, c. 3; *ad Uxorem*, l. ii. c. 4. "Quis denique solemnibus Paschæ abnoctantem securus sustinebit?" Bingham supposes that our author here speaks of the Paschal Vigil or Easter Eve. (L. xiii. c. 9, sect. 4; or l. xxi. c. 1, sect. 32.) *De Baptismo*, c. 19; *ad Marcionem*, l. iv. c. 40.

[2] *De Coronâ*, c. 3; *de Idololatriâ*, c. 14, *sub fine; de Baptismo*, c. 19; *de Jejuniis*, c. 14.

[3] *De Jejuniis*, c. 14.

[4] Chap. v. note 3, p. 173. Compare the *Scorpiace*, c. 15. "Tunc Paulus civitatis Romanæ consequitur nativitatem, quum illic martyrii renascitur generositate."

[5] C. 13. "Habes tuos census, *tuos fastos*."

[6] C. 3.

and temporal blessings obtained, by fasting.[1] God, moreover, by testifying His favourable acceptance of fasts observed in consequence of voluntary vows, thereby declared His will, and rendered such fasts obligatory in future.[2] This favourable acceptance supplied the place of a positive command. Tertullian, however, is met in the very outset by a perplexing objection.[3] "If fasting was designed to be the means of recovering God's favour, how came it to pass that, after the deluge, the liberty respecting food was not curtailed but extended? That man, who was originally confined to a vegetable diet, was then allowed to eat flesh?" To this question Tertullian returns an answer, for which few of his readers could, we think, have been prepared. At first the liberty respecting food was enlarged, in order that man might have an opportunity of evincing a greater desire to please God, by a voluntary abstinence from those kinds of food which he was permitted to take.[4] Afterwards, when the law was given, a distinction was made between clean and unclean animals, for the purpose of preparing mankind for the fasts which in due season they would be required to observe under the gospel.[5] One argument urged by Tertullian in favour of fasting is, that it fitted the Christian to encounter the bodily hardships to which the profession of his faith exposed him.[6] Another is grounded on the natural tendency of fasting to render the intellectual and moral faculties vigorous and active; whereas a full stomach weighs down the soul, rendering it unfit for contemplation, and devotional exercises, and intercourse with heaven.[7] This remark our author confirms by the examples of Moses and Elias, who fasted forty days and forty nights, when they were admitted to the divine presence.[8]

From this treatise, and from other parts of Tertullian's writings, we learn that the fasts observed by the Church in his day were—(1) The Paschal Fast, which consisted in a total abstinence from food (*jejunium*) during the interval between Christ's passion and resurrection.[9] This was considered as obligatory upon all Christians. (2) Stationary days, Dies Stationarii, Wednesday and Friday in every week, on which a half-fast (*semi-jejunium*)

[1] Cc. 7, 8. Compare *de Patientiâ*, c. 13. [2] C. 11. [3] C. 4.
[4] Compare *de Cultu Fœminarum*, l. ii. c. 10; *de Exhortatione Castitatis*, c. 8.
[5] C. 5. Compare *adv. Marcionem*, l. ii. c. 18. [6] C. 12. [7] C. 6.
[8] Compare *de Res. Carnis*, c. 61.
[9] "Certe in Evangelio illos dies jejuniis determinatos putant, in quibus ablatus est sponsus (Matt. ix. 15), et hos esse jam solos legitimos jejuniorum Christianorum, abolitis legalibus et propheticis vetustatibus." *De Jejuniis*, c. 2. Compare c. 13, *sub in.*, c. 14; *de Oratione*, c. 14.

was kept, terminating at three in the afternoon.[1] These were voluntary fasts, and observed on the authority of tradition; Wednesday being selected, because on that day the Jews took counsel to destroy Christ; and Friday, because that was the day of His crucifixion.[2] The reason assigned for terminating the Statio at the ninth hour was,[3] that Peter is said in the Acts of the Apostles to have gone with John into the temple at that hour.[4] "But whence," asks Tertullian, who contended that the Statio ought to be prolonged till the evening, "whence does it appear that the apostles had on that day been keeping a fast? The example of St. Peter might be more plausibly alleged for terminating the fast at the sixth hour; for in another chapter we are told that he went up to pray at that hour, and became very hungry, and would have eaten."[5] (3) Xerophagiæ, days on which it was usual to abstain from flesh and wine, in imitation, perhaps, of the restraint which Daniel is stated to have imposed upon himself.[6] These fasts were not enjoined by the Church, but were voluntary exercises of piety on the part of individuals;[7] and some of the orthodox appear to have objected to them altogether, on the ground that they were borrowed from the heathen superstitions.[8]

The difference between the orthodox and Montanists, on the subject of fasting, appears to have consisted in the following particulars. With respect to the Jejunium, or total abstinence from food, the former thought that the interval between our Saviour's death and resurrection was the only period during which the apostles observed a total fast, and consequently the only period during which fasting was of positive obligation upon all Christians. At other times it rested with themselves to

[1] "Cur Stationibus quartam et sextam Sabbati dicamus?" *De Jejuniis*, c. 14. "Sic et Apostolos observâsse, nullum aliud imponentes jugum certorum et in commune omnibus obeundorum jejuniorum; proinde nec stationum, quæ et ipsæ suos quidem dies habeant, quartæ feriæ et sextæ; passivè tamen currant, neque sub lege præcepti; neque ultra supremam diei, quando et orationes fere hora nona concludat, de Petri exemplo, quod Actis refertur," c. 2. See also *de Oratione*, c. 14, where our author supposes the word *statio* to be borrowed from the military art. "Si statio de militari exemplo nomen accipit; nam et militia Dei sumus." Tertullian uses the expression "trium hebdomadum statione" in speaking of Daniel's fast (c. 10). *De Animâ*, c. 48.

[2] See *de Jejuniis*, c. 13, *sub in.* Bingham, l. xxi. c. 3, sect. 2, from Augustine, ep. 86 or 36 *ad Casulanum.*

[3] *De Jejuniis*, c. 10.

[4] C. 3, v. 1.

[5] C. 10, v. 9.

[6] C. 10, v. 3.

[7] *De Jejuniis*, c. 13.

[8] "Xerophagias vero novum affectari officii nomen et proximum Ethnicæ superstitioni, quales castimoniæ Apim, Isidem, et Magnam Matrem certorum eduliorum exceptione purificant." *De Jejuniis*, c. 2. See also c. 16.

determine whether they would fast or not. The Montanists, on the contrary, contended that there were other seasons during which fasting was obligatory, and that the appointment of those seasons constituted a part of the revelations of the Paraclete.[1] With respect to the Dies Stationarii, the Montanists not only pronounced the fast obligatory upon all Christians, but prolonged it until the evening, instead of terminating it, as was the orthodox custom, at the ninth hour.[2] In the observance of the Xerophagiæ the Montanists abstained—not only from flesh and wine, like the orthodox—but also from the richer and more juicy kinds of fruit, and omitted all their customary ablutions.[3] Montanus appears to have enjoined only two weeks of Xerophagiæ in the year;[4] but his followers were animated by a greater love of fasting than their master, for Jerome says that, in his day, the Montanists kept three Lents, one of them after Whitsunday.[5]

We have already observed that, in Tertullian's time, the bishops exercised the power of appointing days of fasting, whenever the circumstances of the Church seemed to require such outward marks of sorrow and humiliation; and that the councils or general assemblies, which were held in Greece for the purpose of regulating the affairs of the Church, were opened by a solemn fast.[6]

Ecclesiastical history abounds with proofs of the tendency of mankind to run into extremes; and thus to convert institutions, which in their original design and application were beneficial and salutary, into sources of the most pernicious errors and abuses. Were we required to produce an instance in confirma-

[1] *De Jejuniis*, cc. 1, 13.

[2] *De Jejuniis*, c. 1. "Quod Stationes plerumque in vesperam producamus."

[3] *De Jejuniis*, c. 1. "Quod etiam Xerophagias observemus, siccantes cibum ab omni carne, et omni jurulentiâ, et vividioribus quibusque pomis, ne quid vinositatis vel edamus vel potemus. Lavacri quoque abstinentiam, congruentem arido victui." See also cc. 9, 10, where Tertullian defends the practice of the Montanists as strictly conformable to the practice of holy men under the Mosaic and Christian dispensations. The Marcionites appear to have deemed fish a holy diet. *Adv. Marcionem*, l. i. c. 14.

[4] "Duas in anno hebdomadas Xerophagiarum, nec totas, exceptis scilicet Sabbatis et Dominicis, offerimus Deo." *De Jejuniis*, c. 15.

[5] "Illi tres in anno faciunt quadragesimas, quasi tres passi sint Salvatores." *Ad Marcellam*, ep. 54. "Et ex hujus occasione testimonii Montanus, Prisca, et Maximilla, etiam post Pentecosten faciunt quadragesimam, quod, ablato sponso, filii sponsi debeant jejunare." In Matt. ix. Bingham infers that each of these Lent fasts continued for two weeks. L. xxi. c. 1, sect. 15.

[6] Chap. iv. note 5, p. 117. *De Jejuniis*, c. 13.

tion of the truth of this remark, we should without hesitation refer the reader to the subject which we have been now considering. Fasting, as it was originally practised in the Church, was regarded as a means to a moral end: as a means, peculiarly fitted both to the circumstances and to the nature of man, of nourishing in him those feelings of contrition and self-abasement, and of enabling him to acquire that mastery over his sensual appetites which are essential elements in the composition of the Christian character. When, at the season appointed by the Church for the commemoration of the Passion of Christ, its members, amongst other external observances—designed to express their lively sense of their own unworthiness, and of the deadly nature of sin which could be expiated only by so great a sacrifice—abstained also from their customary meals and recreations; surely the most enlightened reason must approve the motive of their abstinence, and admit as well its suitableness to the fallen condition of man, as its tendency to encourage a devout and humble temper. To these considerations we may add that, from the mixed constitution of man's nature and the intimate union which subsists between his soul and body, the occasional restraints, which the primitive Christians voluntarily imposed upon themselves in respect of food and amusement, could scarcely fail to have a beneficial operation upon their character; were it only by interrupting for a time their ordinary habits, and reminding them that the objects of sense possessed neither the sole, nor the principal, claim to their attention. A life of habitual indulgence, even when that indulgence leads not to positive excess, is favourable neither to intellectual nor spiritual improvement. It enfeebles our mental powers; it deadens our moral perceptions; it tends especially to render us selfish and regardless of the wants and feelings of others. But when experience also tells us that such a course of life terminates almost invariably in excess, no further argument can be wanting to prove the reasonableness and utility of occasional abstinence—if used only as a means to an end—to invigorate the moral principle within us, and to promote humility of temper and purity of heart. Unhappily, however, for the Church, from the propensity of the human mind to run into extremes—from an increasing fondness for the tenets of the Platonic philosophy—and an indiscriminate imitation of what is recorded in Scripture of holy men, who, being placed in extraordinary circumstances, were never designed to be held up as examples, in all points of their conduct, to ordinary Christians—from the combined operation of all these causes, fasting, instead of being considered as a salutary discipline, or as a means to holiness, came to be regarded as holiness itself. The piety of men was estimated by the frequency and severity of their fasts. In proportion as they subjected themselves to greater privations and hardships, they acquired a higher reputation for sanctity. A species of rivalry was thus excited; new and strange methods were invented of macerating and torturing their bodies, till at length extravagance in practice led to error in doctrine; fasts and mortifications were regarded as meritorious in themselves—as procuring by their intrinsic efficacy remission of sin and restoration to the favour of God.

To the same causes, which led men into the errors now described respecting the merit of fasting, may be traced the erroneous opinions which were gradually introduced, respecting the superior sanctity of the monastic and eremitical modes of life. No man, who has reflected upon the constitution of his own nature and believes that he is destined to exist in a purer and more spiritual state, can doubt the utility, or rather necessity, of occasional retirement and seclusion, for the purposes of self-examination, and of securing to religion that paramount influence over the thoughts and affections which is liable to be weakened, or even destroyed, by a constant intercourse with the world. Here, then, was a reasonable motive to induce Christians, wisely anxious for their own salvation, to withdraw themselves, at stated intervals, from worldly pleasures, and cares, and occupations. The frequency with which those intervals recurred would depend in each case upon the temper of the individual. Men of an austere and unsocial, as well as those of an enthusiastic character, would naturally run into excess, and contend that, if *occasional* seclusion was thus favourable to the growth of religion in the soul, the benefits to be derived from *total* seclusion must be proportionally greater;—in a word, that the most effectual mode of securing their virtue against the temptations of the world was to quit it altogether. The deference paid in the Church to the authority of Plato contributed to give currency and weight to these opinions. One principle of his philosophy was, that the visible things around us are only the fleeting and fallacious images of those eternal, immutable ideas which alone possess a real existence. The business, therefore, of *him*, who wishes to arrive at the knowledge of the truth, and to elevate his nature to the perfection of which it is capable, must be to abstract his mind from his senses—entirely to exclude from his observation those forms of perishable matter which serve only to bewilder and lead him astray—and to give himself up to the contemplation of the ideal world. These speculative notions, originally derived from the Platonic school, no sooner gained a footing in the Church, than they were reduced to practice Men began to affect a life of solitude and contemplation, and to deem all intercourse with the world a positive hindrance to the attainment of that spiritual elevation at which the Christian ought to aim. Overlooking the clear intimations supplied by the constitution of their own nature, that man is designed for society—overlooking the express declarations of Scripture and the example of our Blessed Lord, whose ministry was one continued course of active benevolence—they took Elias and the Baptist for their models, without reflecting for a moment either upon the peculiar circumstances in which those holy men were placed, or the peculiar objects which they were appointed to accomplish. Thus, while they passed their hours in a state of indolent abstraction—discharging no one social duty, and living as if they were alone in the world—they succeeded in persuading themselves and others that they were treading the path which leads to Christian perfection, and pursuing the course most pleasing in the sight of God—that they were the especial objects of His regard, were holding habitual intercourse with Him, and enjoying a foretaste of that ineffable bliss which would be their portion, when removed from this world of sin and misery to His immediate presence. Hence the stories of dreams and visions which occur so frequently in the lives of the saints, and have been too hastily stigmatized as the offspring of deliberate fraud; whereas they were in most instances the creations of a distempered mind, cut off from the active pursuits in which it was designed to be engaged, and supplying their place by imaginary scenes and objects. It forms no part of our plan to enter into a minute detail of the follies and extravagances which were the natural fruits of the eremitical and monastic modes of life. Let it suffice to have pointed out the sources from which they took their rise, and to have exposed the mischievous consequences of setting up any one mode of life as pre-eminently pure and holy—as rendering those who adopt it the peculiar favourites of heaven.

To return to our author. In refuting the calumnious accusations of the pagans, he speaks of the Agape, or feast of charity. "Its object," he says, "is evident from its name, which signifies love.[1] In these feasts, therefore, we testify our love towards our poorer brethren, by relieving their wants. We commence the entertainment by offering up a prayer to God; and after eating and drinking in moderation, we wash our hands, and lights being introduced, each individual is invited to address God in a psalm, either taken from the Scriptures or the produce of his own meditations. The feast concludes, as it began, with prayer." Tertullian does not expressly say, but it may be fairly inferred, that the materials of the feast were furnished out of the oblations made at the Eucharist; a portion of which appears also to have been allotted to the support of the martyrs in prison.[2] When we read the above description of the Agape, we cannot but participate in the regret expressed by Dr. Hey, that scandal should have occasioned the discontinuance of an entertainment so entirely consonant to the benevolent spirit of the gospel.[3] If, however, we may believe Tertullian, the grossest abuses were introduced into it even in his time; for we find him, in the tract *de Jejuniis*,[4] charging the orthodox with the very same licentious practices in their feasts of charity which the pagans were in the habit of imputing—and according to the statement in the *Apology*, falsely imputing—to the whole Christian body. On these contradictory assertions of our author, we may remark that the truth probably lies between them. Abuses did exist, but neither so numerous, nor so flagrant, as the enemies of the gospel, and Tertullian himself, after he became a Montanist, alleged.

Tertullian speaks both of public and private vigils;[5] and says that it was customary for the Christian females to bring water to wash the feet of the brethren, and to visit the dwellings of the pôor, for the purpose, it may be presumed, of giving them instruction and relieving their wants. The Romish commentators have endeavoured to defend the religious processions of their Church

[1] *Apology*, c. 39.

[2] "Imo et quæ justa sunt caro non amittit per curam Ecclesiæ, agapen fratrum." *Ad Martyres*, c. 2.

[3] Book iv. art. 28, sect. 5.

[4] C. 17. "Sed major his est agape, quia per hanc adolescentes tui cum sororibus dormiunt: appendices scilicet gulæ lascivia atque luxuria." Compare the *Apology*, cc. 7, 8.

[5] "Ita saturantur, ut qui meminerint etiam per noctem adorandum sibi Deum esse." *Apology*, c. 39. "Quis nocturnis convocationibus, si ita oportuerit, a latere suo adimi libenter feret?" *Ad Uxorem*, l. ii. c. 4. "Quum etiam per noctem exsurgis oratum," c. 5. "Aquam sanctorum pedibus offerre," c. 4. "Quis autem sinat conjugem suam, visitandorum fratrum gratiâ, vicatim aliena et quidem pauperiora quæque tuguria circumire?" *Ibid.*

by the authority of Tertullian, who uses the word *Procedendum* in the passage from which the preceding remarks are taken.[1] But if we compare it with another passage in the second tract *de Cultu Fœminarum*,[2] we shall find that the word *procedere* means "to go from home;" which, Tertullian observes, a Christian female ought never to do, excepting for some religious or charitable purpose.[3]

We will now proceed to the rite of baptism, on which Tertullian wrote an express treatise in confutation of a female, named Quintilla, who denied its necessity, affirming that faith alone was sufficient to salvation. In that treatise, as well as in other parts of his works, he speaks in strong terms of the efficacy of baptism. "By it," he says, "we are cleansed from all our sins, and rendered capable of attaining eternal life."[4] By it we regain that Spirit of God which Adam received at his creation, and lost by his transgression."[5] Tertullian connects regeneration with it;[6] calling it our second birth, in which the soul is formed as it were anew by water and the power from above, and the veil of its former corruption being drawn aside, beholds the full refulgence of its native light. In the first book *against Marcion*, he declares the following spiritual blessings to be consequent upon baptism:—Remission of sins, deliverance from death, regeneration, and participation in the Holy Spirit.[7] He calls it the sacrament of washing,[8] the blessed sacrament of water,[9] the laver of regeneration,[10]

1 "Si procedendum erit," etc.

2 C. 11. "Ac si necessitas amicitiarum officiorumque gentilium vos vacat, cur non vestris armis indutæ proceditis?" See also c. 12.

3 "Vobis autem nulla procedendi causa non tetrica; aut imbecillus aliquis ex fratribus visitatur, aut sacrificium offertur, aut Dei verbum administratur," c. 11.

4 See *de Pœnitentiâ*, c. 6; *de Baptismo*, cc. 1, 7.

5 *De Baptismo*, c. 5, *sub fine*. "Recipit enim illum Dei Spiritum, quem tunc de afflatu ejus acceperat, sed post amiserat per delictum." Tertullian usually speaks as if the soul, that is, the vital and intellectual principles, had been communicated when God breathed into the nostrils of Adam the breath of life. Here he appears to confound the soul and spirit. See chap. iii. p. 86; chap. v. note 3, p. 162. "Aquâ signat, Sancto Spiritu vestit." *De Præscriptione Hæreticorum*, c. 36.

6 *De Animâ*, c. 41. See chap. v. p. 162; *de Res. Carnis*, c. 47; *de Pudicitiâ*, cc. 6, 9. We find in the tract *de Carne Christi*, c. 4, the expression "*Cœlestis Regeneratio*," and in the *Scorpiace*, c. 6, "*Secunda Regeneratio;*" but in both cases the allusion seems to be to the change in the body of man, which will take place when it puts on incorruption and immortality.

7 C. 28.

8 "Eadem lavacri Sacramenta." *De Virginibus velandis*, c. 2. See chap. v. p. 162.

9 "Felix Sacramentum aquæ nostræ." *De Baptismo, sub initio.*

10 "Per lavacrum regenerationis." *De Pudicitiâ*, c. 1.

the sacrament of faith,[1] the sign,[2] or seal of our faith.[3] There is an apparent inconsistency in his accounts of the mode in which the spiritual benefits of baptism are conferred. At one time he speaks as if the sanctification of the water used in baptism was effected by the immediate agency of the Holy Spirit, who descended upon it as soon as the prayer of invocation had been addressed to God.[4] At another time he supposes the effect to be produced through the ministry of an angel, whom he terms *Angelus Baptismi Arbiter*.[5] To this angel, who, according to him, is the precursor of the Holy Spirit, as the Baptist was of Christ, belongs the especial office of preparing the soul of man for the reception of the Holy Spirit in baptism. We call the inconsistency of these two statements only an apparent inconsistency, because, occurring as they do not only in the same tract, but even in the same chapter, our author could scarcely have deemed them inconsistent. The latter statement is evidently founded on the narrative in St. John's Gospel respecting the angel who imparted a healing efficacy to the waters of the pool of Bethesda.[6]

In the tract *de Coronâ Militis*, Tertullian gives a summary account of the forms used in administering the rite of baptism.[7] The candidate having been prepared for its due reception by frequent prayers, fasts and vigils,[8] professed, in the presence of the congregation,[9] and under the hand of the president,[10] that he renounced the devil, his pomp, and angels.[11] He was then

1 "Sine Fidei Sacramento." *De Animâ*, c. 1.

2 "In signaculo Fidei." *De Spectaculis*, c. 24; *Signaculi nostri*, c. 4. Speaking of circumcision, Tertullian uses the expression "*Signaculum corporis*." *Apology*, c. 21.

3 In the tract *de Pudicitiâ*, c. 10, Tertullian calls the baptism of John, the washing of repentance.

4 "Igitur omnes aquæ de pristinâ originis prærogativâ Sacramentum sanctificationis consequuntur, invocato Deo. Supervenit enim statim Spiritus de cœlis, et aquis superest, sanctificans eas de semetipso, et ita sanctificatæ vim sanctificandi combibunt." *De Baptismo*, c. 4, quoted in chap. v. note 7, p. 177. See also c. 8.

5 "Igitur medicatis quodammodo aquis per Angeli interventum, et Spiritus in aquis corporaliter diluitur, et caro in iisdem spiritaliter mundatur," c. 4. Again in c. 6: "Non quod in aquis Spiritum Sanctum consequimur, sed in aquâ emundati sub Angelo Spiritui Sancto præparamur. Hic quoque figura præcessit. Sic enim Ioannes ante præcursor Domini fuit, præparans vias ejus; ita et Angelus Baptismi arbiter superventuro Spiritui Sancto vias dirigit ablutione delictorum." See chap. iii. note 2, p. 109.

6 C. 5.

7 C. 3.

8 *De Baptismo*, c. 20.

9 The expression is "*in Ecclesiâ*," which Bingham translates *in the Church*. The translation may be correct, for in the same tract, c. 13, the word *Ecclesia* seems to mean the place of assembly. "Et ipsum curiæ nomen Ecclesia est Christi."

10 "Sub Antistitis manu."

11 Compare *de Spectaculis*, c. 4; *de Idololatriâ*, c. 6; *de Cultu Fœminarum*, l. i. c. 2.

plunged into the water three times, in allusion to the Three Persons of the Holy Trinity,[1] making certain responses which, like the other forms here mentioned, were not prescribed in Scripture, but rested on custom and tradition.[2] He then tasted a mixture of milk and honey[3]—was anointed with oil,[4] in allusion to the practice under the Mosaic dispensation of anointing those who were appointed to the priesthood, since all Christians are in a certain sense supposed to be priests—and was signed with the sign of the cross.[5] Lastly followed the imposition of hands, the origin of which ceremony is referred by our author to the benediction pronounced by Jacob upon the sons of Joseph.[6] With us the imposition of hands is deferred till the child is brought to be confirmed; but in Tertullian's time, when a large proportion of the persons baptized were adults, confirmation immediately followed the administration of baptism, and formed a part of the ceremony. It was usual for the baptized person to abstain, during the week subsequent to his reception of the rite, from his daily ablutions.[7] Some also contended that baptism ought to be followed by fasting, because our Lord immediately after His baptism fasted forty days and forty nights.[8] But our author replies that baptism is in fact an occasion of joy, inasmuch as it opens to us the door of salvation. Christ's conduct in this instance was not designed to be an example for our imitation, as it had a particular reference to certain events which took place under the Mosaic dispensation. In commenting upon the parable of the Prodigal Son, Tertullian calls the ring which the father directed to be put upon his hand, the seal of baptism; by which the Christian, when interrogated, seals the covenant of his faith.[9] The natural inference from these words appears to be that a ring used to be given in baptism; but I have found no other trace of such a custom.

Tertullian alludes to the custom of having sponsors, who made,

[1] "Nam nec semel, sed ter, ad singula nomina in personas singulas tingimur." *Adv. Praxeam*, c. 26.
[2] "In aquam demissus, et inter pauca verba tinctus." *De Baptismo*, c. 2.
[3] *Adv. Marcionem*, l. i. c. 14.
[4] *De Baptismo*, c. 7; *de Res. Carnis*, c. 26.
[5] *De Res. Carnis*, c. 8.
[6] *De Baptismo*, c. 8; *de Res. Carnis*, c. 8.
[7] *De Coronâ*, c. 3.
[8] *De Baptismo*, c. 20. But compare *de Jejuniis*, c. 8. "Ipse mox Dominus baptisma suum, et in suo *omnium* jejuniis dedicavit." This variation of opinion affords an additional presumption that the tract *de Baptismo* was written before Tertullian became a Montanist.
[9] "Annulum denuo signaculum lavacri." *De Pudicitiâ*, c. 9. "Annulum quoque accepit tunc primum, quo fidei pactionem interrogatus obsignat." *Ibid.*

in the name of the children brought to the font, those promises which they were unable to make for themselves.[1]

From the passages already referred to, and from others scattered through Tertullian's works, it is evident that in his day baptism was administered in the name of the Father, Son, and Holy Ghost;[2] and that the candidate professed his belief in the Three Persons of the Trinity, who were at once the witnesses of his profession and the sponsors for his salvation.[3] We will take this opportunity of observing that, whatever might be the case with the Montanists in after times, the writings of Tertullian afford no ground for supposing that the founder of the sect introduced a new form of baptism.

After enforcing the necessity of baptism by water, and describing and explaining the forms observed in the administration of the rite, Tertullian proceeds, in the remaining chapters of the tract *de Baptismo*, to discuss some other points connected with the subject. He first considers the question proposed by Christ to the Pharisees—"The baptism of John, was it from heaven or of men?"[4] To this Tertullian replies, that it was of divine commandment, because John was sent by God to baptize. So far it was from heaven. But it conveyed no heavenly gift; it conferred neither the remission of sins nor the Holy Spirit. John's was the baptism of repentance, designed to fit men for the reception of that baptism, by which, through the efficacy of the death and resurrection of Christ, they obtain the remission of sins and the sanctifying influences of the Spirit.[5] Until the descent of the Holy Ghost on the day of Pentecost, the disciples of Christ baptized only with the baptism of John, that is, unto repentance.[6] Tertullian's interpretation of the words—"He shall baptize you with the Holy Ghost and with fire"—is, that the baptism with the Holy Ghost applies to those whose faith is sincere and stedfast; the baptism with fire to those whose faith is feigned and unstable, and who are therefore baptized, not to salvation, but to judgment.[7] Our author supposes the Baptist's message to Christ

[1] "Quid enim necesse est sponsores etiam periculo ingeri?" *De Baptismo*, c. 18. See also c. 6.

[2] *De Baptismo*, c. 13.

[3] *De Baptismo*, c. 6.

[4] C. 10. Matt. xxi. 25.

[5] On the subject of John's mission, see *adv. Marcionem*, l. iv. c. 33; l. v. c. 2.

[6] C. 11.

[7] C. 10, *sub fine*. Some in Tertullian's day appear to have contended that there was a contradiction between the Baptist's prediction that Christ would baptize, and St. John's declaration (iv. 2), that He did not baptize, c. 11.

to have originated in the failure of his faith, occasioned by the transfer of the Spirit from him to Christ—a notion founded on John's declaration—"He must increase, and I must decrease."[1]

In the passage just alluded to, Tertullian does not merely assert that the disciples of Christ baptized with the baptism of John, but assigns his reasons for making the assertion.[2] His words are—"Itaque tingebant Discipuli ejus (Christi) ut ministri, ut Ioannes ante præcursor, eodem baptismo Ioannis, ne qui alio putet, quia nec extat alius nisi postea Christi, qui tunc utique a discentibus dari non poterat, utpote nondum adimpletâ gloriâ Domini, nec instructâ efficaciâ lavacri per passionem et resurrectionem." From these words we may fairly infer that Tertullian knew no baptisms connected with the divine dispensations, besides those of John and Christ. Yet Wall, in the introduction to his *History of Infant Baptism*, has quoted a passage from this very tract, to prove that our author was acquainted with the Jewish baptism of proselytes. The passage is in the fifth chapter —"Sed enim nationes, extraneæ ab omni intellectu Spiritalium, Potestatem eâdem efficaciâ suis idolis subministrant, sed viduis aquis sibi mentiuntur. Nam et sacris quibusdam per lavacrum initiantur, Isidis alicujus, aut Mithræ—certè ludis Apollinaribus et Eleusiniis tinguntur. Idque se in regenerationem et impunitatem perjuriorum suorum agere præsumunt—quo agnito, hic quoque studium Diaboli cognoscimus res Dei æmulantis, quum et ipse baptismum in suis exercet." On this passage Wall makes the following remark:—"Now the divine baptism, which he says the devil imitated, must be the Jewish baptism. For the rites of Apollo and Ceres, in which he there instances as those in which the said baptism was used, were long before the times of the Christian baptism." This, however, is by no means a necessary inference. In describing the notions entertained by Tertullian respecting the nature of demons, we mentioned that their chief employment and pleasure was to prevent mankind from embracing the worship of the true God, and that they were assisted in the attainment of this object by the partial knowledge which they had acquired, during their abode in heaven, of the nature of the divine dispensations.[3] Availing themselves of this knowledge, they endeavoured to preoccupy the minds of men by inventing rites, bearing some resemblance to those which were to be observed under the gospel. Thus, by their suggestion, baptism

[1] C. 10. Matt. xi. Compare *de Oratione*, c. 1; *adv. Marcionem*, l. iv. c. 18. John iii. 30.

[2] C. 11.

[3] Chap. iii. p. 107.

was introduced into the Eleusinian mysteries as a mode of initiation, being, if I may use the expression, an imitation by anticipation of Christian baptism.

That this is a correct exposition of our author's meaning will be evident from a comparison of the different passages in which he alludes to the subject. The reader will find some of them quoted at length in chapter iii.;[1] and reference made to a passage in the tract *de Præscriptione Hæreticorum*,[2] which is as follows:—"Tingit et ipse (Diabolus) quosdam, utique credentes et fideles suos: expositionem delictorum de lavacro repromittit: et si adhuc memini, Mithra signat illic in frontibus milites suos; celebrat et panis oblationem, et imaginem resurrectionis inducit, et sub gladio redimit coronam." Here we find that not merely baptism, but also the custom of marking the forehead with the sign of the cross, and the consecration of the bread in the Eucharist, were imitated in the mysteries of Mithra. Are we therefore to conclude that the latter were also Jewish customs? I am aware that there are writers who answer this question in the affirmative, and among them Bishop Hooper in his *Discourse on Lent*, part ii. c. 3, sect. 1, c. 6, sect. 5. But I must confess that the learned prelate's arguments appear to me only to prove that, when our author has once taken up an hypothesis, he will never be at a loss for reasons wherewith to defend it. Wall's conclusion is founded entirely on the assumption that the imitation of divine rites, which Tertullian ascribed to the devil, was necessarily an imitation of rites actually instituted; whereas he held that its very purpose was to anticipate their institution. This is not the proper place for inquiring whether baptism was practised by the Jews before our Saviour's advent as an *initiatory* rite, or only as a mode of *purification*. Be this as it may, Tertullian's express declaration, that besides the baptisms of Christ and John there was no other baptism, renders him but an indifferent voucher for its use among the Jews as an *initiatory* rite.

To proceed with the tract *de Baptismo*. The next question discussed by our author is, whether the apostles were baptized—and if not, whether they could be saved, since our Saviour declared to Nicodemus that, "unless a man is born of water and the Spirit, he cannot enter into the kingdom"—a passage which

[1] Note 1, p. 106.

[2] C. 40. See also the instances mentioned in the tract *de Spectaculis*, c. 23, one of which is referred to in chap. v. p. 192.

the ancients uniformly interpreted of baptism.[1] Tertullian admits that St. Paul is the only apostle of whom it is expressly recorded that he was baptized *in the Lord*—that is, with Christian baptism. He shows it, however, to be highly probable that the apostles had received John's baptism, which, as the baptism of Christ was not then instituted, would be sufficient; our Lord Himself having said to Peter, "He that is once washed needs not to be washed again."[2] "But if," Tertullian continues, "we should admit that the apostles were never baptized, theirs was an extraordinary case, and formed an exception to the general rule respecting the necessity of baptism." It is amusing to observe how greatly the ancients were perplexed with this difficulty, and to what expedients they had recourse in order to get rid of it. They argued, for instance, that Peter was baptized when he attempted to walk upon the sea, and the other apostles when the waves broke over the vessel in the storm on the lake of Gennesaret.

They who denied the necessity of baptism alleged the example of Abraham, who pleased God by faith alone, without baptism.[3] "True," replies Tertullian; "but as, since the promulgation of the gospel, additional objects of faith—the birth, death, and resurrection of Christ—have been proposed to mankind, so also a new condition of salvation has been introduced, and faith will not now avail without baptism." He confirms his argument by a reference to our Saviour's injunction to the apostles, "Go and teach all nations, baptizing them in the name of the Father, Son, and Holy Ghost;" and to his favourite passage, the declaration to Nicodemus.

Another argument against the necessity of baptism[4] was founded on the statement of St. Paul in the First Epistle to the Corinthians, that "he was sent to preach, not to baptize."[5] Our author justly remarks, that these words must be understood with reference to the disputes then prevailing at Corinth; not as meant positively to declare that it was no part of an apostle's office to baptize. St. Paul had himself baptized Gaius, and Crispus, and the household of Stephanas.

With respect to the propriety of rebaptizing, Tertullian says

[1] C. 12. See chap. i. note 2, p. 43.
[2] John xiii. 10. The verse is quoted inaccurately.
[3] C. 13. [4] C. 14. [5] C. 1, v. 17.

explicitly that baptism ought not to be repeated; but he considered heretical baptism as utterly null.[1] "As heretics," he argues, "have neither the same God nor the same Christ with us, so neither have they the same baptism. Since, therefore, they never were baptized, they must be cleansed by baptism before they are admitted into the Church." We should, as has been already observed, bear in mind that the heretics, with whom Tertullian had principally to contend, were those who affirmed that the Creator of the world was not the Supreme God.[2]

We have already seen that Tertullian calls martyrdom a second baptism.[3] He says that martyrdom will both supply the want of baptism by water, and restore it to those who have lost it by transgression.[4]

In our remarks on the twenty-third Article of the Church, we alluded to a passage in the tract *de Baptismo*, in which Tertullian ascribes to the laity an inherent right to administer baptism.[5] We should now deem it sufficient to refer the reader to what we have there said had we not observed that the passage has been mistranslated by Dr. Waterland, in his second letter to Mr. Kelsall on lay baptism.[6] The passage is as follows:—"Dandi quidem habet jus summus sacerdos, qui est Episcopus. Dehinc presbyteri et diaconi, non tamen sine Episcopi auctoritate, propter Ecclesiæ honorem, quo salvo salva pax est. Alioquin etiam laicis jus est; quod enim ex æquo accipitur, ex æquo dari potest; nisi Episcopi jam, aut presbyteri, aut diaconi vocantur discentes.[7] Domini sermo non debet abscondi ab ullo; proinde baptismus, æquè Dei census, ab omnibus exerceri potest." Of this passage Dr. Waterland gives the following translation:— "The chief priest, who is the bishop, has power to give (baptism), and next to him the priests and deacons (but not

[1] C. 15. "Hæretici autem nullum habent consortium nostræ disciplinæ, quos extraneos utique testatur ipsa ademptio communicationis. Non debeo in illis agnoscere quod mihi est præceptum, quia nec idem Deus est nobis et illis, nec unus Christus, id est idem." See also *de Pudicitiâ*, c. 19. "Unde et apud nos, ut Ethnico par, immo et super Ethnicum, Hæreticus etiam per baptisma veritatis utroque homine purgatus admittitur." But when the tract *de Pudicitiâ* was written, Tertullian had seceded openly from the Church.

[2] See chap. v. notes 2 and 3, p. 178.

[3] C. 16. See chap. ii. note 2, p. 71.

[4] "Hic est baptismus, qui lavacrum et non acceptum repræsentat, et perditum reddit." Compare *de Pudicitiâ*, c. 13. "Quæ exinde jam perierat baptismate amisso."

[5] C. 17. Chap. v. p. 175.

[6] Waterland's *Works*, vol. x. p. 108.

[7] We believe the true reading to be "vocarentur discentes." Some editions have "vocantur dicentes," which reading Waterland follows.

without the authority of the bishop) *because of their honourable post in the Church*, in preservation of which peace is preserved; otherwise even laymen have a right to give it; for what is received in common, may be given in common. Except then that either bishops, or presbyters, or deacons *intervene*, the ordinary Christians are called to it." Dr. Waterland subjoins the following observation:—"I have thrown in two or three words in the translation, to clear the sense of this passage; I have chiefly followed Mr. Bennet, both as to the sense and to the pointing of them, and refer you to him for their vindication."[1] To us, however, it appears certain that both Dr. Waterland and Mr. Bennet have mistaken the meaning of the passage; which is —"The chief priest, that is, the bishop, possesses the right of conferring baptism. After him the priests and deacons, but not without his authority, *out of regard to the honour* (*or dignity*) *of the Church*, on the preservation of which depends the preservation of peace. Otherwise the laity possess the right: for that which all equally receive, all may equally confer; unless bishops, or priests, or deacons were alone designated by the word *discentes*, *i.e.* disciples.[2] The word of God ought not to be concealed by any; baptism, therefore, which equally (with the word) proceeds from God, may be administered by all." Our author then goes on to say that although the laity possess the right, yet as modesty and humility are peculiarly becoming in them, they ought only to exercise it in cases of necessity, when the eternal salvation of a fellow-creature is at stake. He does not, however, extend the right to women; on the contrary, he stigmatizes the attempt on their part to baptize as a most flagrant act of presumption.[3] In the passage just cited, Tertullian rests the right of the laity to administer baptism on the assumption that a man has the power of conferring upon another whatever he has himself received, and on the comprehensive meaning of the word *disciples* in John iv. 2. On other occasions, as we have seen,[4] he rests it on the ground that all Christians are in fact priests. It is not easy to determine which of the three arguments is the least conclusive.

[1] *Rights of the Clergy*, p. 118. Mr. Bennet does not quote the latter part of the passage.

[2] The allusion is to John iv. 2. *Though Jesus Himself baptized not, but His disciples.* Tertullian frequently uses the word *discentes* in this sense. Thus in c. 11: "Qui tunc utique a *discentibus* dari non poterat." *Adv. Marcionem*, l. iv. c. 22: "Tres de *discentibus* arbitros futuræ visionis, et vocis assumit." See *de Præscriptione Hæreticorum*, cc. 3, 20, 22, 30, 44.

[3] Compare *de Præscriptione Hæreticorum*, c. 41.

[4] Chap. iv. p. 112, note 1.

The next question discussed by Tertullian relates to the persons who may receive the rite of baptism.[1] He says that it must not be hastily conferred; and recommends delay in the case not only of infants, but also of unmarried persons and widows, whom he considers peculiarly exposed to temptation. What he says with respect to the baptism of infants has been already noticed in our remarks on the ninth Article of the Church:[2] we then observed that the recommendation of delay in their case was inconsistent with the conviction, which he manifests on other occasions, of the absolute necessity of baptism to relieve mankind from the injurious consequences of Adam's fall. In the treatise *de Animâ*,[3] alluding to what St. Paul says respecting the holiness of children either of whose parents is a Christian, he supposes the apostle to affirm that the children of believing parents are, by the very circumstances of their birth, marked out to holiness, and, therefore, to salvation. "But," he continues, "the apostle had a particular object in view when he made the assertion; he wished to prevent the dissolution of marriage in cases in which one of the parties was a heathen. Otherwise, he would have borne in mind our Lord's declaration, that *unless a man is born of water and the Spirit, he cannot enter into the kingdom of heaven*, that is, cannot be holy. So that every soul is numbered in Adam, until it is numbered anew in Christ; being, until it is thus numbered anew, unclean, and consequently sinful." It is scarcely possible to conceive words more strongly declaratory of the universality of original sin, or of the necessity of bringing the children of believing parents to the baptismal font, in order that they may become partakers of the holiness for which they are designed at their birth. Some have supposed that Tertullian was led to contend for the expediency of delaying baptism, in consequence of the opinion which he entertained concerning the irremissible character of heinous sins committed after baptism; and the passage in the tract *de Baptismo*, on which we have been remarking, favours the supposition.[4] But, not to detain the reader longer with the consideration of an inconsistency for which we do not undertake to account, we will only add that the anti-pædobaptists lay great stress upon this passage; although, as Wall, who has gone into a detailed examination of it, justly observes, the fair inference from it is, that, whatever might be Tertullian's individual

[1] C. 18.

[2] Chap. v. pp. 160-163.

[3] C. 39. 1 Cor. vii. 14. Compare Hooker's *Ecclesiastical Polity*, book v. c. 60.

[4] Hey's *Lectures*, book iv. article 27, sect. 14.

opinion, the general practice of the Church was to baptize infants.

With respect to the season when baptism might be administered, Tertullian remarks that every day and every hour are alike suited to the performance of so holy a rite.[1] He specifies, however, the interval between Good Friday and Whitsunday as peculiarly appropriate; because in that interval the passion, resurrection, and ascension of Christ, as well as the descent of the Holy Ghost, took place and were commemorated.

We now proceed to the other sacrament of our Church, which is called by Tertullian Eucharistia,[2] Eucharistiæ Sacramentum,[3] Convivium Dominicum,[4] Convivium Dei,[5] Panis et Calicis Sacramentum.[6] The term Sacrificium [7] is also applied to the Eucharist; but in the same general manner in which it is applied to other parts of divine worship, and to other modes of conciliating the divine favour; as to prayer, or fasting, or bodily mortifications.[8] Tertullian says [9] that the Eucharist, which was instituted by our blessed Lord during a meal—the institution being accompanied by a command which applied generally to all present—was in his own day celebrated in the assemblies which were held before daybreak; and received only at the hands of the presidents. He notices also the extreme solicitude of the Christians to prevent any part of the bread and wine from falling to the ground; and speaks of the communicants as standing at the altar of God, when they received the sacrament.[10] It may, however, be doubted whether

[1] C. 19. [2] *De Præscriptione Hæreticorum*, c. 36. "Eucharistia pascit."

[3] *De Coronâ*, c. 3, referred to in chap. v. p. 177, note 6.

[4] *Ad Uxorem*, l. ii. c. 4.

[5] *Ad Uxorem*, l. ii. c. 9. "In convivio Dei;" but Semler reads "In connubio Dei."

[6] "Proinde panis et calicis sacramento, jam in Evangelio probavimus corporis et sanguinis Dominici veritatem, adversus phantasma Marcionis." *Adv. Marcionem*, l. v. c. 8. This title ought to have been added to those mentioned in our remarks on the twenty-fifth Article of the Church. Chap. v. p. 176.

[7] See the tract *de Oratione*, c. 14; *de Cultu Fœminarum*. l. ii. c. 11.

[8] *Adv. Marcionem*, l. iv. c. 1; *de Res. Carnis*, c. 8.

[9] *De Coronâ*, c. 3. "Eucharistiæ sacramentum, et in tempore victûs et omnibus mandatum a Domino, etiam ante lucanis cœtibus, nec de aliorum manibus quam præsidentium sumimus.—Calicis aut panis etiam nostri aliquid decuti in terram anxiè patimur."

[10] "Nonne solennior erit statio tua, si et ad aram Dei steteris?" *De Oratione*, c. 14. Bingham (l. viii. c. 6, sect. 12) refers to a passage in the first tract *ad Uxorem*, c. 7. "Aram enim Dei nundam proponi oportet:" but it is evidently nothing to the purpose. He refers also to the tract *de Exhortatione*

the expression is to be understood literally; or whether we are warranted in inferring from it that altars had at that early period been generally introduced into the places of religious assembly. The kiss of peace appears to have been constantly given at the celebration of the Eucharist. Our author calls it *signaculum orationis*,[1]—an expression from which Bingham infers that, in that age of the Church, it was given after the prayers of consecration;[2] but there appears to be no sufficient reason for understanding the word *orationis* in that restricted sense. We are rather disposed to infer that, at the conclusion of all their meetings for the purposes of devotion, the early Christians were accustomed to give the kiss of peace, in token of the brotherly love subsisting amongst them.[3]

The Roman Catholic commentators on Tertullian are naturally desirous to allege his authority in support of the doctrine of transubstantiation. When, however, the different passages in which he speaks of the body and blood of Christ are compared together, it will be evident that he never thought of any corporeal presence of Christ in the Eucharist. He speaks, indeed, "of feeding on the fatness of the Lord's body, that is, on the Eucharist;"[4] and "of our flesh feeding on the body and blood of Christ, in order that our soul may be fattened of God."[5] These, it must be allowed, are strong expressions; but when compared with other passages in his writings, they will manifestly appear to have been used in a figurative sense. Thus, in commenting upon the clause in the Lord's Prayer, "*Give us this day our daily bread*," he says that we should understand it spiritually.[6] "Christ is our bread; for Christ is life, and bread is life. Christ said, *I am the bread of life;* and a little before, *The word of the living God which descended from heaven, that is bread.* Moreover,

*Castitatis*, c. 10. "Quomodo audebit orationem ducere ad altare?" but the reading *ad altare* is only a conjecture of Rigault.

[1] *De Oratione*, c. 14. [2] L. xv. c. 3, sect. 3.

[3] See *ad Uxorem*, l. ii. c. 4, quoted on p. 202, note 6.

[4] "Atque ita exinde opimitate Dominici corporis vescitur, Eucharistiâ scilicet." *De Pudicitiâ*, c. 9, where the words *Eucharistiâ scilicet* bear the appearance of a gloss. See also *adv. Marcionem*, l. iii. c. 7; *adv. Judæos*, c. 14. "Dominicæ gratiæ quasi visceratione quâdam fruerentur."

[5] "Caro corpore et sanguine Christi vescitur, ut et anima de Deo saginetur." *De Res. Carnis*, c. 8.

[6] "Quanquam *panem nostrum quotidianum da nobis hodie* spiritaliter potius intelligamus. Christus enim panis noster est, quia vita Christus, et vita panis. *Ego sum*, inquit, *panis vitæ*. Et paulo supra: *Panis est sermo Dei vivi, qui descendit de cœlis*." (The words are not accurately quoted.) "Tum quod et corpus ejus in pane censetur, *Hoc est corpus meum*." *De Oratione*, c. 6. Compare *de Res. Carnis*, c. 37.

His body is reckoned (or supposed) to be in the bread, in the words *This is my body.*" It is evident, from the whole tenor of the passage, that Tertullian affixed a figurative interpretation to the words, *This is my body.* In other places he expressly calls the bread the *representation* of the body of Christ;[1] and the wine, of His blood.

There is one passage from which Pamelius has so strangely contrived to extract an argument in favour of transubstantiation, that we cannot forbear referring the reader to it. It is in the treatise *against Praxeas*,[2] where Tertullian is inquiring, "How the Word was made flesh? was He transfigured into flesh, or did He put on flesh?" "Surely, He put it on," is Tertullian's answer, "for as God is eternal, we must also believe that He is immutable, and incapable of being formed (into another substance). But transfiguration is a destruction of that which before existed: whatever is transfigured into another thing ceases to be what it was, and begins to be what it was not." This passage, says Pamelius, makes for transubstantiation. By what process of reasoning he arrived at this conclusion, we are utterly at a loss to conceive. Tertullian evidently means to say that if the Word had been transfigured into flesh, either the divine nature would have been entirely destroyed, and the human alone would have remained, or a third nature have arisen from the mixture of the former two, as the substance called electrum from the mixture of gold and silver.[3] In either case the substance which is transfigured disappears; and that into which it is transfigured is alone

1 "Nec panem, quo ipsum corpus suum *repræsentat.*" *Adv. Marcionem*, l. i. c. 14. "Panem corpus suum appellans, ut et hinc jam eum intelligas, corporis sui *figuram* pani dedisse," l. iii. c. 19. *Adv. Judæos*, c. 10. "Acceptum panem et distributum discipulis, corpus illum suum fecit, *hoc est corpus meum* dicendo, id est *figura* corporis mei—ut autem et sanguinis veterem figuram in vino recognoscas, aderit Esaias." *Adv. Marcionem*, l. iv. c. 40. See also *ad Uxorem*, l. ii. c. 5; *de Animâ*, c. 17. "Alium postea vini saporem, quod in sanguinis sui memoriam consecravit."

2 "Igitur sermo in carne, dum et de hoc quærendum, quomodo sermo caro sit factus, utrumne quasi transfiguratus in carne, an indutus carnem? imo indutus. Cæterum Deum immutabilem et informabilem credi necesse est, ut æternum. Transfiguratio autem interemptio est pristini. Omne enim quodcunque transfiguratur in aliud, desinit esse quod fuerat, et incipit esse quod non erat. Deus autem neque desinit esse, neque aliud potest esse," etc., c. 27. The remark of Pamelius is, "Eacit hic locus pro transubstantione, quam Catholici in Sacramento Eucharistiæ adserunt."

3 "Si enim sermo ex transfiguratione et demutatione substantiæ caro factus est; una jam erat substantia Iesûs ex duabus, ex carne et Spiritu, mixtura quædam, ut electrum ex auro et argento; et incipit nec aurum esse, id est, Spiritus, neque argentum, id est caro; dum alterum altero mutatur, et tertium quid efficitur," c. 27.

cognizable by the senses. Whereas, according to the doctrine of transubstantiation, the bread, the substance which is changed, remains in appearance, while that into which it is changed, the body of Christ, is not seen. Pamelius takes another opportunity of enforcing the doctrine of transubstantiation in commenting on a passage in the first book *against Marcion*, from which an inference directly opposed to it may be fairly drawn.[1] From what has been already said, it is evident that the Roman Catholic custom of withholding the cup from the laity was unknown to Tertullian, and that both the bread and the wine were in his day alike offered to the communicants.[2]

One other rite of the Church still remains to be considered—that of Marriage. Bingham infers,[3] apparently with justice, from a passage in the tract *de Monogamiâ*,[4] that the parties were bound in the first instance to make known their intentions to the Church and obtain the permission of the Ecclesiastical Orders. They were also bound to obtain the consent of their parents.[5] Parties marrying clandestinely ran the hazard of being regarded in the light of adulterers or fornicators.[6] That marriage was esteemed by the Christians a strictly religious contract is evident from a

[1] "Non putem impudentiorem, quam qui in alienâ aquâ alii Deo tingitur, ad alienum cœlum alii Deo expanditur, in alienâ terrâ alii Deo sternitur, super alienum panem alii Deo gratiarum actionibus fungitur, de alienis bonis ob alium Deum nomine eleemosynæ et dilectionis operatur," c. 23, *sub fine*. Tertullian is here contending that, if the doctrine of the Marcionites was true—that the supreme God who sent Christ was not the God who created the world—then it would follow that He had most unjustly appropriated to His own uses the works and productions of another.

[2] A reference should here have been made to the practice of reserving a portion of the consecrated bread, and eating it at home before every other nourishment. "Accepto corpore Domini et *reservato*, utrumque salvum est." *De Oratione*, c. 14. "Non sciet maritus quid secreto ante omnem cibum gustas: et si sciverit panem, non illum credit esse qui dicitur." *Ad Uxorem*, l. ii. c. 5. See Bingham, l. xv. c. 4, sect. 13. This practice, having given occasion to abuses, was forbidden. See the sixth Rubric after the Communion Service.

[3] L. xxii. c. 2, sect. 2.

[4] C. 11. "Qualis es id matrimonium postulans, quod iis a quibus postulas non licet habere—ab Episcopo monogamo, a presbyteris et diaconis ejusdem sacramenti, a viduis quarum sectam in te recusâsti? Et illi plane sic dabunt viros et uxores, quomodo buccellas (Hoc enim est apud illos, *Omni petenti te dabis*), et conjungent vos in Ecclesiâ Virgine, unius Christi unicâ sponsâ."

[5] "Nam nec in terris filii sine consensu patrum rite et jure nubunt." *Ad Uxorem*, l. ii. c. 9.

[6] "Ideo penes nos occultæ quoque conjunctiones, id est non prius apud ecclesiam professæ, juxta mœchiam et fornicationem judicari periclitantur." *De Pudicitiâ*, c. 4. He applies a similar title to marriages contracted by Christians with heathens. "Hæc quum ita sint, fideles gentilium matrimonia subeuntes stupri reos esse constat, et arcendos ab omni communicatione fraternitatis." *Ad Uxorem*, l. ii. c. 3, quoted in chap. v. note 2, p. 194.

passage in the second tract *ad Uxorem*,[1] in which Tertullian expresses his inability to describe the happiness of that marriage, which is cemented by the Church, is confirmed by prayers and oblations, is sealed by a blessing, is announced by angels, and ratified by the Father in heaven. He mentions also the custom of putting a ring on the finger of the female, as a part of the rites, not of marriage, but of espousal, intended as an earnest of the future marriage.[2] He speaks of it as observed by the heathens, but in terms which imply that he deemed it perfectly innocent. In the tract *de Virginibus velandis* the kiss and the joining of hands are noticed as parts of the ceremony.[3]

Tertullian, as we have seen, states that a Christian named Proculus cured the Emperor Severus of a disorder by anointing him with oil.[4] It may be doubted whether we ought to infer from this statement that a practice then subsisted in the Church of anointing sick persons with oil, founded on the injunction in the Epistle of St. James. This, however, is certain, that the practice, if it subsisted, was directly opposed to the Romish sacrament of extreme Unction, which is administered, not with a view to the recovery of the patient, but when his case is hopeless.

We have had frequent occasion to allude to a passage in the tract *de Coronâ*, in which Tertullian mentions a variety of customs resting solely on the authority of tradition.[5] Among them is the practice of making the sign of the cross upon the forehead, which was most scrupulously observed by the primitive Christians: they ventured not to perform the most trivial act, not even to put on their shoes, until they had thus testified their entire reliance upon the cross of Christ. The pagans appear to have regarded this practice with suspicion, as a species of magical superstition.[6]

[1] See chap. v. p. 194. "Unde sufficiamus ad enarrandam felicitatem ejus matrimonii, quod ecclesia conciliat, et confirmat oblatio, et obsignat benedictio, angeli renuntiant, Pater rato habet?" c. 9. The words *ecclesia conciliat* may either mean "when both the parties are Christians," or "when the sanction of the Church has been regularly obtained," or may embrace both meanings.

[2] "Quum aurum nulla norat præter unico digito, quem sponsus oppignerâsset pronubo annulo." *Apology*, c. 6. See also *de Idololatriâ*, c. 16.

[3] "Si autem ad desponsationem velantur, quia et corpore et spiritu masculo mixtæ sunt, per osculum et dexteras," etc., c. 11.

[4] *Ad Scapulam*, c. 4, referred to in chap. i. note 2, p. 27.

[5] C. 3. See the *Scorpiace*, c. 1, quoted in chap. ii. note 1, p. 48, where the practice is described as a protection or remedy against the bite of poisonous animals.

[6] *Ad Uxorem*, l. ii. c. 5.

In our remarks upon the testimony afforded by our author's writings to the existence of miraculous powers in the Church, we said that the only power, of the exercise of which specific instances are alleged, was that of exorcising evil spirits.[1] This power, according to him, was not confined to the clergy or to any particular order of men, but was possessed by all Christians in common.[2] Tertullian mentions also the practice of exsufflation, or of blowing away any smoke or savour which might arise from the victims on the altar, etc., in order to escape the pollution of idolatry.[3]

We will conclude our observations on this branch of the internal history of the Church, by referring the reader to a passage in which there is an allusion to the custom of publicly announcing the third, sixth, and ninth hours.[4]

——o——

## CHAPTER VII.

### CONCERNING THE HERESIES AND DIVISIONS WHICH TROUBLED THE CHURCH.

We now come to the last, and unhappily not the least extensive, of the five branches into which Mosheim divides the internal history of the Church — the heresies by which its repose was troubled during the second century. But before I proceed to consider his enumeration of Christian sects, I must briefly call the reader's attention to Tertullian's tract *against the Jews*. Mosheim, in his chapter on the Doctrine of the Church,[5] has observed "that Justin Martyr and Tertullian embarked in a controversy with the Jews, which it was not possible for them to manage with the highest success and dexterity, as they were very little acquainted with the language, the history, and the learning of the Hebrews, and wrote with more levity and inaccuracy than

[1] Chap. ii. p. 51.

[2] *Apology*, cc. 23, 37, 43; *de Animâ*, c. 57; *de Spectaculis*, c. 26; *de Idololatriâ*, c. 11; *de Coronâ*, c. 11; *de Exhortatione Castitatis*, c. 10.

[3] *De Idololatriâ*, c. 11. "Quo ore Christanus thurarius, si per templa transibit, spumantes aras despuet, et exsufflabit, quibus ipse prospexit?" *Ad Uxorem*, l. ii. c. 5. "Quum aliquid immundum flantis explodis."

[4] *De Jejuniis*, c. 10.

[5] *Century* ii. part ii. c. 3, sect. 7.

such a subject would justify." That Tertullian was unacquainted with the language of the Hebrews may be allowed;[1] but thoroughly conversant as he was with the Septuagint version of the Old Testament, his knowledge of their history could be little inferior to that of the Hebrews themselves. Whether, however, he was well or ill qualified to manage the controversy with them, it must be at once interesting and instructive to inquire in what manner the controversy was actually conducted by the early Christians.

Our author begins his tract *adversus Judæos* with disputing the claim set up by the Jews to be considered exclusively as the people of God.[2] In support of this claim, they alleged, in the first place, that they were the descendants of the younger brother Jacob, of whom it was predicted that he should rule over the elder Esau; in the second, that the law was given to them by Moses. Tertullian contends, on the contrary, that the Christians, inasmuch as they were posterior in time to the Jews, were in fact the descendants of the younger brother; and with respect to the law, he observes that mankind never were without a law. God gave Adam a law, in which were contained all the precepts of the decalogue.[3] Moreover, the written law of Moses was nothing more than a repetition of the natural unwritten law, by obeying which the patriarchs gained the favour of God, although they neither kept the Jewish Sabbath nor practised the Jewish rite of circumcision.

Hence, proceeds Tertullian, it is evident that circumcision does not confer, as the Jews pretend, an exclusive title to the favour of God.[4] Abraham himself pleased God before he was circumcised. Carnal circumcision was designed as a mark, by which the Jews might be distinguished from other nations in all ages—but particularly in these latter days, when the heavy judgments predicted by the prophets are fallen upon them.[5] We may also collect with certainty, from the prophetic writings, that carnal circumcision was not intended to be of perpetual observ-

[1] We have observed that Tertullian sometimes speaks as if he was acquainted with Hebrew. Chap. i. note 6, p. 33.

[2] Cc. 1, 2. See Gen. xxv. 23.

[3] Tertullian points out the manner in which our first parents violated each of the commandments of the decalogue by eating the forbidden fruit, c. 2. See chap. v. p. 163.

[4] C. 3.

[5] Tertullian supposes the prediction in Isaiah i. 7 to have referred to the edict of Adrian, by which the Jews were prevented from setting foot in Jerusalem.

ance. Jeremiah speaks of a spiritual circumcision, as well as of a new covenant which God was to give to His people.[1]

In like manner the observance of the Sabbath was not designed to be perpetual.[2] The Jews indeed say that God sanctified the seventh day from the creation of the world, because on that day He rested from His work. But the sanctification spoken of applies to an eternal, not a temporal Sabbath. For what evidence can be produced that either Adam, or Abel, or Enoch, or Noah, or Abraham, kept the Sabbath? It is evident, therefore, that the circumcision, the Sabbath, and the sacrifices appointed under the Mosaic dispensation were intended to subsist only until a new lawgiver should arise, who was to introduce a spiritual circumcision, a spiritual Sabbath, and spiritual sacrifices.[3]

Having thus shown that the Mosaic dispensation was not designed to be perpetual, but preparatory to another system, Tertullian says that the great point to be ascertained is, whether the exalted personage, pointed out by the prophets as the giver of a new law—as enjoining a spiritual Sabbath and spiritual sacrifices—as the eternal ruler of an eternal kingdom—had yet appeared on earth.[4] "Now it is certain that Jesus, whom we affirm to be the promised Lawgiver, has promulgated a new law, and that the predictions respecting the Messiah have been accomplished in Him. Compare, for instance, the prophecies of the Old Testament, which describe the wide extent of the Messiah's kingdom, with the actual diffusion of Christianity at the present moment.[5] Nations, which the Roman arms have never yet subdued, have submitted themselves to the dominion of Jesus and received the gospel."

"But," proceeds our author, "there is in the prophet Daniel an express prediction of the time when the Messiah was to appear."[6] The numerical errors which have crept into Tertullian's text, joined to his gross ignorance of chronology, render it impossible to unravel the difficulties in which his calculation of the seventy weeks is involved. But the principles of the calculation are, that the commencement of the seventy weeks is to be dated from the first year of Darius, in which Daniel states that

[1] C. iv. ver. 3. [2] C. 4. [3] C. 5. [4] C. 7.

[5] The prophecy particularly selected by Tertullian is from Isaiah xlv. 1. But between his version of the passage and that given in our English Bibles there are important differences. In our translation it seems to apply exclusively to Cyrus.

[6] C. 8.

he saw the vision—that sixty-two weeks and half a week were completed in the forty-first year of the reign of Augustus when Christ was born—and that the remaining seven weeks and half a week were completed in the first year of Vespasian, when the Jews were reduced beneath the Roman yoke. I need scarcely observe that none of the above principles are admitted by the learned men of modern times, who have endeavoured to elucidate the prophecy of the seventy weeks.

Tertullian goes on to show that the prophecies of the Old Testament, which foretold the birth of the Messiah, were accomplished in Jesus.[1] Thus it was predicted by Isaiah that He should be born of a virgin; that His name should be called Emmanuel; and that, before He was able to pronounce the names of His father and mother, He should take of the riches of Damascus and of the spoils of Samaria from the King of Assyria.[2] The Jews, on the contrary, affirmed that no part of this prophecy was fulfilled in Jesus. He was neither called Emmanuel, nor did He take of the spoils of Damascus and Samaria. They affirmed also that the Hebrew word, which we translate "virgin," ought to be translated "a young female." To these objections our author replies, that as the divine and human natures were united in Christ, He was not merely called, but actually was Emmanuel, that is, God with us;—and that with respect to the spoils of Damascus and Samaria, the Jews were misled by their preconceived notions that the Messiah was to be a warlike prince and conqueror; whereas the words of the prophet were accomplished when the Magi brought to the infant Jesus their offerings of gold, and frankincense, and myrrh—the peculiar produce of Arabia and the East. Tertullian admits that, in the Psalms and other parts of the Old Testament, the Messiah is spoken of as a triumphant warrior; but the expressions, he observes, are to be understood of spiritual triumphs achieved over the corrupt hearts and perverse dispositions of man. With respect to the word *virgin*, Tertullian observes that the prophet begins with telling Ahaz that the Lord would give him *a sign*, meaning evidently that some event would take place out of the ordinary course of nature; whereas the pregnancy of a young female is an event of daily occurrence. In order, there-

[1] C. 9.

[2] Tertullian here connects, as Justin Martyr had done before him, Isaiah vii. 14 with viii. 4, and gives a similar explanation of the passage. See the *Dialogue with Trypho*, part ii. p. 303 A, p. 310 C.

fore, to give any consistent meaning to the prophet's words, we must suppose him to have alluded to the pregnancy of a virgin.

One of the objections urged by the Jews was, that in no part of the Old Testament was it predicted that the future deliverer should bear the name of Jesus. To this Tertullian replies, that Joshua was the type of Christ; and that when Moses changed his name from Oshea to Joshua or Jesus, because he was destined to conduct the Israelites into the earthly Canaan, it was manifestly implied that the Messiah, who was to introduce mankind into the heavenly Canaan, would also be called Jesus. Our author then shows from Isaiah xi. 2 that the Messiah was to spring from the seed of David—from Isaiah liii. that He was to undergo severe humiliations and sufferings with the greatest patience—from Isaiah lviii. that He was to be a preacher of righteousness—and from Isaiah xxxv. that He was to work miracles. All these marks, by which the Messiah was to be distinguished, were actually found in Jesus.

But the death of Jesus on the cross constituted, in the opinion of the Jews, the strongest argument against the belief that He was the promised Messiah.[1] It had been expressly declared, in the Mosaic law, that "he who was hanged on a tree was accursed of God."[2] Was it then credible that God would expose the Messiah to a death so ignominious? Nor could any passage of Scripture be produced in which it was predicted that the Messiah was to die on the cross. To the former part of this objection Tertullian replies, that the persons, of whom Moses declared that they were accursed, were malefactors—men who had committed sins worthy of death. How then could the declaration be applicable to Jesus, in whose mouth was no guile, and whose life was one uninterrupted course of justice and benevolence? With respect to the latter part of the objection, Tertullian admits that the particular mode of the Messiah's death is nowhere expressly predicted in the Old Testament, but contends that it is in many places obscurely prefigured—for instance, in the twenty-second Psalm. He then goes on to produce various passages of Scripture, in which he finds allusions to the form of the cross—allusions which were certainly never contemplated by the sacred penman, and are so grossly extravagant that it is difficult to conceive how they could ever enter into the head of any rational being. I know not whether it will be deemed any apology for

[1] C. 10. [2] Deut. xxi. 22.

Tertullian to observe that he was not the inventor of these fancies; for it argues perhaps a more lamentable weakness of judgment to have copied, than to have invented them: most, however, if not all, are to be found in Justin Martyr. In speaking of the circumstances connected with our Saviour's Passion, Tertullian asserts that the preternatural darkness at the crucifixion was predicted by the prophet Amos.[1] "But not only," continues our author, "did the prophets predict the death of the Messiah: they foretold also the dispersion of the Jewish people, and the destruction of Jerusalem."[2] The passages which he alleges in proof of this statement are Ezekiel viii. 12 and Deuteronomy xxviii. 64. "Here, then," he says, addressing the Jews, "we find an additional proof that Jesus was the Christ:—your rejection of Him has been followed by a series of the most grievous calamities that ever befel a nation—your holy temple has been consumed with fire, and you are forbidden to set foot upon the territory of your ancestors. Was it not also foretold of the Messiah that *the Gentiles should be His inheritance, and the ends of the earth His possession?* was He not described as *the light of the Gentiles?* and are not these predictions accomplished in the diffusion of the gospel of Jesus through every part of the known world?"[3]

"We, therefore, do not err when we affirm that the Messiah is already come.[4] The error is yours, who still look for His coming. The Messiah was to be born in Bethlehem of Judah, according to the prophet.[5] But at the present moment no one of the stock of Israel remains at Bethlehem: either, therefore, the prophecy is already fulfilled, or its fulfilment is impossible." Tertullian concludes with pointing out the source of the error of the Jews, who did not perceive that two advents of Christ were announced in Scripture—the first in humiliation, the second in glory.[6] Fixing their thoughts exclusively on the latter, they refused to acknowledge a meek and suffering Saviour.

Such were the arguments by which Tertullian endeavoured to show, in opposition to the objections of the Jews, that Jesus of Nazareth was the promised Messiah. It appears from them that the controversy then stood precisely on the same footing on which it stands in the present day; and that the Jews of his time resorted to the same subterfuges and cavils as the modern

1 C. viii. 9.
2 C. 11.
3 C. 12; Ps. ii. 7; Isa. xlii. 6.
4 C. 13.
5 Micah v. 1.
6 C. 14.

Jews, in order to evade the force of the prophecies which, as the Christians maintained, had been fulfilled in Jesus. If we return to Bishop Pearson, we shall find that the course which he pursues in establishing the truth of the second Article of the Creed, differs not very materially from that of our author.[1] We notice this resemblance for the purpose of removing, at least in part, the unfavourable impression which Mosheim's strictures are calculated to create against this portion of Tertullian's labours. In judging also of the treatise *adversus Judæos*, we should bear in mind that it has come down to us in a corrupt state, some passages bearing evident marks of interpolation.[2] We will conclude our remarks upon it with observing that Tertullian, when he charges the Jews with confounding the two advents of Christ, makes no allusion to the notion of two Messiahs—one suffering, the other triumphant; whence we are warranted in concluding either that he was ignorant of this device, or that it had not been resorted to in his day.

To return to Mosheim. In his enumeration of the heresies which divided the Church in the second century, he first mentions that which originated in a superstitious attachment to the Mosaic law.[3] This heresy is scarcely noticed by Tertullian. There can indeed be little doubt that, after the promulgation of Adrian's edict, those Christians who had united the observance of the Mosaic ritual with the profession of the gospel, fearful lest they should be confounded with the Jews, gradually abandoned the Jewish ceremonies—so that in the time of Tertullian the number of Judaizing Christians had become extremely small.[4] We are now speaking of those whom Mosheim calls Nazarenes—who, though they retained the Mosaic rites, believed all the fundamental articles of the Christian faith.[5] The Ebionites, on the contrary, who also maintained the necessity of observing the ceremonial law, rejected many essential doctrines of Christianity.[6] They are more than once mentioned by Tertullian, who always speaks of them as having received their appellation from their

[1] See p. 76, where he shows that Joshua was a type of Christ. See also article iii. "born of the Virgin Mary," and article iv. "was crucified."

[2] See c. 5 and c. 14, *sub fine*.

[3] *Century* ii. part ii. chap. v.

[4] See Wilson's *Illustration of the Method of Explaining the New Testament*, etc., c. 11, where he enumerates the different causes which contributed to the gradual extinction of the Judaizing Christians, or, as he terms them, Christian Jews.

[5] The Jews, in Tertullian's time, appear to have called Christians in general by the name of Nazarenes. *Adv. Marcionem*, l. iv. c. 8, *sub initio*. *Apud Hebræos Christianos*, l. iii. c. 12.

[6] *De Præscriptione Hæreticorum*, c. 33.

founder Ebion. He did not write any express treatise against them; but we learn from incidental notices in his works that they denied the miraculous conception,[1] and affirmed that Jesus was not the Son of God, but a mere man born according to the ordinary course of nature.[2]

The next heresies of which Mosheim speaks are those which he imagines to have arisen from the attempt *to explain the doctrines of Christianity in a manner conformable to the dictates of the Oriental philosophy concerning the origin of evil.* In every age, both before and since the promulgation of the gospel, this question has been found to baffle the powers of the human understanding, and to involve in an endless maze of error all who have engaged in the unavailing research. Of this Tertullian was fully aware; and he traces the rise of many of the heretical opinions which he combats to the curiosity of vain and presumptuous men venturing to explore the hidden things of God.[3] But though he so far connects philosophy with heresy as to style the philosophers the ancestors of the heretics,[4] yet neither he nor any other of the early Fathers appears to have thought that the heretics derived their notions from the Oriental philosophy.[5] On the contrary, Tertullian repeatedly charges them with borrowing from Pythagoras and Plato and other Greek philosophers.[6] In like manner Irenæus affirms that Valentinus was indebted for his succession of Æons to the Theogonies of the Greek poets.[7] It will be said, perhaps, that the authority of the early Fathers can be of little weight in the determination of this question, on account of their ignorance of the Eastern languages; and that it matters little whether the heretics derived their opinions directly from the East, or indirectly through the medium of Pythagoras and Plato, the germ of whose philosophy is known to have been formed during

[1] "Quam utique virginem constat fuisse, licet Ebion resistat." *De Virginibus velandis*, c. 6.

[2] *De Præscriptione Hæreticorum*, c. 33; *de Carne Christi*, cc. 14, 18, 24.

[3] "Unde malum, et quare? et unde homo, et quomodo? et quod proxime Valentinus proposuit, unde Deus?" *De Præscriptione Hæreticorum*, c. 7.

[4] "Hæreticorum Patriarchæ Philosophi." *Adv. Hermogenem*, c. 8; *de Animâ*, cc. 3, 23. "Ipsi illi sapientiæ professores, de quorum ingeniis omnis hæresis animatur." *Adv. Marcionem*, l. i. c. 13. See also l. v. c. 19.

[5] Mosheim refers to Clemens Alexandrinus, l. vii. c. 17, p. 898, and to Cyprian, ep. 75. But those passages only confirm his statement that Basilides, Cerdo, and the other heretics began to publish their opinions about the time of Adrian: respecting the Oriental origin of the opinions they are silent.

[6] "Ubi tunc Marcion, Ponticus, Nauclerus, Stoicæ studiosus? ubi Valentinus, Platonicæ Sectator?" *De Præscriptione Hæreticorum*, c. 30.

[7] L. ii. c. 19.

their residence in Egypt. The present is not a fit opportunity for inquiring into the reality of this alleged connexion between the Oriental and Platonic philosophies. Our object in the above observations is merely to show that if any weight is to be attached to the opinions of the early Fathers, the heresies which Mosheim calls Oriental ought rather to be denominated Grecian.

Mosheim speaks of two branches into which the Oriental heretics were divided—the Asiatic and the Egyptian branch. Elxai, whom he mentions as the head of the former, appears to have been entirely unknown to Tertullian; nor does Mosheim himself seem to have arrived at any certain conclusion respecting this heretic; for he doubts whether the followers of Elxai were to be numbered among the Christian or Jewish sects. Of Saturninus, whom he also mentions as a leader of the Asiatic branch, the name occurs but once in our author's writings.[1] He is there described as a disciple of Menander, who was himself a disciple of Simon Magus; and he is said to have maintained the following extraordinary doctrine respecting the origin of the human race—that man was formed by the angels, an imperfect image of the Supreme Being—that he crept upon the ground like a worm in a state of utter helplessness and inability to stand upright, until the Supreme Being mercifully animated him with the spark of life, and raised him from the earth—and that at his death this spark will bring him back to the original source of his existence. Of Cerdo, whom Mosheim also numbers among the leaders of the Asiatic sect, Tertullian only states that Marcion borrowed many notions from him.[2] But against Marcion himself our author expressly composed five books, in which he has entered into an elaborate examination and confutation of that heretic's errors.

From various notices scattered over Tertullian's writings we may collect that Marcion was a native of Pontus[3]—that he flourished during the reign of Antoninus Pius and the pontificate of Eleutherius, being originally in communion with the Church at Rome—that he was a man of a restless temper, fond of novelties, by the publication of which he unsettled the faith of

[1] *De Animâ*, c. 23.
[2] *Adv. Marcionem*, l. i. cc. 2, 22, *sub fine;* l. iii. c. 21; l. iv. c. 17.
[3] *De Præscriptione Hæreticorum*, c. 30; *adv. Marcionem*, l. i. cc. 1. 19. Tertullian frequently calls Marcion *Ponticus Nauclerus*, because his countrymen, the natives of Pontus, were chiefly occupied in nautical pursuits, l. i. c. 18, *sub fine;* iii. c. 6.

the weaker brethren, and was in consequence more than once ejected from the congregation—that he afterwards became sensible of his errors, and expressed a wish to be reconciled to the Church—and that his wish was granted, on condition that he should bring back with him those whom he had perverted by his doctrines.[1] He died, however, before he was formally restored to its communion. Tertullian refers in confirmation of some parts of this statement to a certain letter of Marcion, the genuineness of which appears to have been questioned by his followers.[2] Marcion, like many other heretics, was betrayed into his errors and extravagances by the desire of framing a system which would reconcile the existence of evil in the universe with the *perfect* power and wisdom and goodness of the Supreme Being.[3] But the precise nature of his opinions will be best understood from a brief analysis of the five books written by our author against them, and still extant amongst his works.

Tertullian had previously written two works in refutation of Marcion's doctrines. The first was a hurried composition, the defects of which he intended to supply by a second or more perfect treatise.[4] Of the latter a copy was obtained by a person who, having afterwards embraced the opinions of Marcion, published it in a very inaccurate form. Our author was in consequence obliged in self-defence to compose the five books, of which we shall now proceed to give an account.

After an exordium[5]—in which he abuses not only Marcion but also the Pontus Euxinus, because that heretic happened to be born upon its shores—Tertullian proceeds to say that Marcion

[1] *Adv. Marcionem*, l. v. c. 19; l. iv. c. 4, where it is said that Marcion in the first fervour of his faith made a donation of a sum of money to the Church, which was returned to him when he was expelled from its communion. Some learned men doubt the story respecting Marcion's repeated ejections from the Church, and suppose that Tertullian confounded Marcion with Cerdo. Lardner's *History of Heretics*, c. 9, sect. 3.

[2] "Sicut et ipse confiteris in quâdam epistolâ: et tui non negant, et nostri probant." *De Carne Christi*, c. 2. But in the fourth book *against Marcion*, c. 4, we find the following sentence:—"Quid nunc si negaverint Marcionitæ primam apud nos fidem ejus, adversus epistolam quoque ipsius? quid si nec epistolam agnoverint?"

[3] "Languens enim (quod et nunc multi, et maximè hæretici) circa mali quæstionem, Unde malum?" *Adv. Marcionem*, l. i. c. 2.

[4] "Primum opusculum, quasi properatum, pleniore postea compositione resciderarn. Hanc quoque nondum exemplariis suffectam fraude tunc fratris, dehinc apostatæ, amisi, qui forte descripserat quædam mendosissime, et exhibuit frequentiæ. Emendationis necessitas facta est," etc., l. i. c. 1.

[5] C. 1.

held the doctrine of two gods—the one the author of evil, who created the world; the other a deity of pure benevolence, who was unknown to mankind until revealed by Christ.[1] In confutation of this doctrine, Tertullian first observes that in the definition of God are comprised the ideas of supreme power, eternal duration, and self-existence.[2] "The unity of the Deity is a necessary consequence from this definition, since the supposition of two supreme beings involves a contradiction in terms. Nor can this conclusion be evaded by a reference to worldly monarchs, who are as numerous as the kingdoms into which the earth is divided, each being supreme in his own dominions.[3] We cannot thus argue from man to God. Two deities, in every respect equal, are in fact only one deity:—nor, if you introduce two, can any satisfactory reason be assigned why you may not, with Valentinus, introduce thirty.[4] Should Marcion reply that he does not assert the perfect equality of his two deities, he would by that very reply give up the point in dispute.[5] He would admit that the inferior of the two is not strictly entitled to the name of God, since he does not possess the attributes of the Godhead, and that the name is applied to him only in a subordinate sense, in which we find it occasionally used in Scripture."

"How absurd," proceeds Tertullian, addressing the Marcionites, "is the notion that, during the whole interval between the creation and the coming of Christ, the Supreme Being should have remained utterly unknown; while the inferior deity, the Demiurge, received the undivided homage of mankind![5] It would surely be more reasonable to assign the superiority to that Being who had manifested His power in the works of creation, than to him who had not even afforded any evidence of his existence.[6] But, in order to evade the force of this argument, you affect to despise the world in which you live;[7] and notwithstanding the innumerable instances of skill and contrivance which it exhibits

[1] Tertullian supposes Marcion to have adopted this notion of a God of pure benevolence from the Stoics. "Inde Marcionis Deus melior, de tranquillitate, a Stoicis venerat." *De Præscriptione Hæreticorum*, c. 7.

[2] C. 3. "Quantum humana conditio de Deo definire potest, id definio quod et omnium conscientia agnoscet, Deum summum esse magnum, in æternitate constitutum, innatum, infectum, sine initio, sine fine."

[3] C. 4. Tertullian ought rather to have contended that the illustration strengthened his argument. In each kingdom there is only one supreme power; but the universe is God's kingdom; there is therefore only one Supreme Power in the universe.

[4] C. 5. [5] Cc. 6, 7. [6] Cc. 9, 10, 11, 12. [7] Cc. 13, 14.

on every side, you represent it as altogether unworthy to be regarded as the work of the Supreme Being. Yet Christ, whom you suppose to have been sent to deliver man from the dominion of the Demiurge, has been content to allow the use of the elements and productions of this vile world, even in the sacraments which He has instituted—of water, and oil, and milk, and honey in baptism, and of bread in the Eucharist. Nay, you yourselves also, with unaccountable inconsistency, have recourse to them for sustenance and enjoyment. How, moreover, do you account for the fact that, notwithstanding two hundred years have elapsed since the birth of Christ, the old world—the work of the Demiurge—still continues to subsist, and has not been superseded by a new creation proceeding from the Supreme Being, whom you suppose to have been revealed in Christ?"[1] Tertullian here states incidentally that, according to Marcion, the world was created by the Demiurge out of pre-existent matter.[2]

In answer to our author's last question, the Marcionites appear to have affirmed that, as the Supreme Being was invisible, so also were His works; and that the deliverance of man from the dominion of the Demiurge was an incontestable manifestation of His power.[3] "Why, then," rejoins Tertullian, "was the deliverance so long delayed?[4] Why was man left, during the whole interval between the creation and Christ's advent, under the power of a malignant deity? And in what manner was the Supreme Deity at last revealed?[5] We admit two modes of arriving at the knowledge of God—by His works, and by express revelation. But the Supreme Deity could not be known by His works, inasmuch as the visible world in which we live was not made by Him, but by the Demiurge. You will therefore answer that He was made known by express revelation: 'in the fifteenth year of the reign of Tiberius, Christ Jesus, a Spirit of health (Spiritus salutaris), condescended to come down from heaven.'[6] How then happened it that the purpose of His coming was still kept secret from mankind? that the full disclosure of the truth was reserved till the reign of Antoninus Pius,[7] when Marcion first began to teach that the God revealed

[1] C. 15.

[2] "Sed ex materiâ et ille fuisse debebit, eâdem ratione occurrente illi quoque Deo, quæ opponeretur Creatori, ut æque Deo." Compare l. v. c. 19.

[3] C. 16. [4] C. 17. [5] C. 18. [6] C. 19.

[7] Tertullian places an interval of 115 years and 6½ months between Tiberius and Antoninus Pius.

by Christ was a different God from the Creator; and that the Law and the Gospel were at variance with each other?"

Marcion appears to have appealed, in confirmation of his opinions, to the dispute between St. Paul and St. Peter, respecting the observance of the ceremonial law; and to have argued that the part then taken by the former, in denying the necessity of any such observance, implied a conviction in his mind that there was an opposition between the Law and the Gospel.[1] To this argument Tertullian answers that the inference is incorrect, since in the Old Testament, which, according to Marcion, was a revelation from the Demiurge, the cessation of the ceremonial law, and the introduction of a more spiritual system, are clearly predicted. "But," he adds, "if St. Paul had known that Christ came for the purpose of revealing a God distinct from the Creator, that fact alone would have been decisive as to the abolition of the ceremonial law; and he would have spared himself the unnecessary trouble of *proving* that it was no longer obligatory. The real difficulty with which the apostle had to contend arose from the fact that the law and the gospel proceeded from the *same* God; since it thence became necessary to explain why observances, which God had Himself enjoined under the former, were no longer to be deemed obligatory under the latter."[2] Our author then urges the agreement of all the Churches, which traced their descent from the apostles, in the belief that Christ was sent by the Creator of this world, as a proof of the truth of that belief.[3]

Tertullian lastly contends that Marcion's system does not even accomplish the main object which its author had in view—it does not establish the pure benevolence of his supposed Supreme Being.[4] "For how," he asks, "can the goodness of that Being be reconciled with the supposition that a malignant deity was so long permitted to hold the universe in subjection? Goodness, moreover, loses its character if it is not guided by reason and justice; but it was neither reasonable nor just in Marcion's Supreme God to invade as it were the territory of the Creator, and to deprive Him of the allegiance of man—His creature and subject. At best, the goodness of Marcion's God is imperfect:—it neither saves the whole human race, nor even a single individual, fully and completely; since, according to Marcion, the

[1] C. 20.

[2] C. 21. See chap. v. p. 146.

[3] See chap. v. p. 145.

[4] C. 22, *ad finem*.

soul only is saved, while the body is destroyed. Yet Marcion would persuade us that his Supreme Deity is a Deity of pure benevolence and goodness, who neither judges, nor condemns, nor punishes, but is in every respect similar to the listless and indolent gods of Epicurus. Does not, then, the very term *goodness* imply an abhorrence of evil? And what are we to think of a goodness which either does not forbid the commission of evil, or overlooks it when committed? Such doctrines proclaim impunity to every species of profligacy and crime; yet with strange inconsistency the Marcionites profess to believe that evil-doers will finally be punished."[1] While, however, Tertullian asserts that the doctrines of Marcion lead by necessary consequence to the encouragement of vice, he does not appear to charge the Marcionites with actual immorality.

The foregoing sketch of the first book *against Marcion* will give the reader an insight into the nature of the controversy, and the mode in which Tertullian conducted it. With respect to the remaining four books, we shall content ourselves with merely stating the subjects discussed in each. We have seen that the object of the first book was to expose the absurdity of maintaining that there is a Supreme Deity distinct from the Creator of the world. That of the second is to expose the futility of the reasonings by which Marcion endeavoured to prove that the Creator of the world was not the Supreme Deity. It has been already observed that Marcion's errors originated in a desire to reconcile the existence of evil, both in the natural and moral world, with the goodness of God. Whatever exists, exists, if not by the appointment, at least by the permission of God; and a God of infinite power and goodness would not permit the existence of evil. Marcion could devise no better mode of solving this difficulty than by supposing the existence of two deities—one the Creator of the world, the other the Supreme God—a God of pure and absolute benevolence. Tertullian, on the contrary, endeavours to show, in the second book, that the appearances of evil in the world are not inconsistent with the

[1] Their notion seems to have been that bad men would not be punished by the Supreme God—for perfect goodness cannot punish—but would be rejected by Him; and being thus rejected, would become the prey of the fire of the Creator. "Multo adhuc vanius, quum interrogati, 'quid fiat peccatori cuique die illo,' respondent, 'abjici illum quasi ab oculis.' Nonne et hoc judicio agitur? judicatur enim abjiciendus, et utique judicio damnationis: nisi in salutem abjiciatur peccator, ut et hoc Deo optimo competat," c. 27. Again, in c. 28, "Exitus autem illi abjecto quis? ab igne, inquiunt, Creatoris deprehendetur."

perfect goodness of its Author. He expatiates upon the folly and presumption of which a blind, imperfect being, like man, is guilty, in venturing to canvass the divine dispensations.[1] He appeals to the proofs of the divine goodness exhibited in the material world, in the creation of man, and in the law which was given to Adam; the superiority of man to all other animals being evinced by the very circumstance that a law was given him, which he possessed the power either of obeying or disobeying.[2] To the common argument, that the fall of Adam implied a defect either in the goodness, power, or prescience of God, Tertullian replies that, possessing as we do, clear and decisive evidences of the exercise of those attributes, we must not allow our faith to be shaken by any speculative reasoning.[3] God made man in His own image; man was consequently to be endowed with freedom of will: he abused that excellent gift, and fell. His fall, therefore, detracts not from the goodness of God. "But why," rejoined Marcion, "endow him with a gift which God must have foreseen that he would abuse?"[4] "Because," Tertullian answered, "his likeness to his Maker consisted partly in the freedom of his will." Without entering into any further detail of the arguments either of Marcion or Tertullian, we may remark that our author is, as might be expected, far more successful in exposing the errors and inconsistencies of his opponent, than in solving the difficulties in which the question itself is involved.[5] Not that his failure in the latter respect is to be attributed to any want of acuteness or ingenuity on his part, but to the nature of the inquiry, which must ever baffle the powers of human reason.

Having once established that the fall of Adam was the consequence of the abuse of that free-will with which he was endowed at his creation, Tertullian finds no difficulty in proving that the evil, which was introduced into the world by the fall, and still continues to exist, is in no way derogatory from the goodness of God. Marcion appears to have contended that the denunciation and infliction of punishment were inconsistent with perfect goodness. Tertullian, on the contrary, argues that justice is

[1] C. 2.

[2] Cc. 3, 4.

[3] C. 5. See the observations on the tenth Article of our Church, in chap. v. p. 164. Compare also l. iv. c. 41.

[4] Cc. 6, 7, 8.

[5] One of Marcion's arguments is that, since it is the soul which sins in man, and the soul derives its origin from the breath of God, that is, of the Creator, sin must in some degree be ascribed to the nature of the Creator, c. 9, quoted in chap. iii. note 4, p. 95.

inseparable from goodness, and that the punishment of vice is nothing but an exercise of justice.[1] To reckon justice among the attributes of the Deity, and at the same time to affirm that the judgments which He brings upon men on account of their wickedness are at variance with His goodness, is as absurd as to admit on the one hand that the skill of the surgeon is beneficial to society, and, on the other, to accuse him of cruelty because he occasionally causes his patients to suffer pain.[2] Nor must we, when we read in Scripture of the anger, or indignation, or jealousy of God, suppose that those passions exist in Him as they do in man; unless we are also prepared to assert that He has human hands, and eyes, and feet, because those members are ascribed to Him in the sacred writings. "Even the precepts and institutions," Tertullian continues, "which Marcion produces from Scripture as proofs of the harshness and severity of the God who gave the law, will, on examination, be found to tend directly to the benefit of man.[3] Thus the Lex Talionis was a law adapted to the character of the Jewish people, and instituted for the purpose of repressing violence and injustice.[4] The prohibition of certain kinds of food was designed to inculcate self-restraint, and thereby to preserve men from the evil consequences of excess. The sacrifices and other burthensome observances of the ceremonial law, independently of their typical and prophetic meaning, answered the immediate purpose of preventing the Jews from being seduced into idolatry by the splendid rites of their heathen neighbours."

One of the passages of Scripture urged by the Marcionites was that in which God commands the Israelites, previously to their departure from Egypt, to borrow gold and silver of the Egyptians.[5] This Marcion termed a fraudulent command, and denounced it as inconsistent with every idea of goodness. The mode in which Tertullian accounts for it is, that the Egyptians were greatly indebted to the Israelites, and that the gold and silver which the latter obtained, constituted a very inadequate compensation for the toil and labour of the many years during

[1] Something like a fallacy appears to pervade the whole of Tertullian's reasoning on this point, arising out of the double meaning of the word *bonitas*, which he here employs as if it meant goodness, that is, the combination of all those excellences which constitute a perfect moral character; whereas Marcion rather used the word to express kindness or benevolence, as opposed to severity, malice, etc. See c. 12.

[2] C. 19. Compare *de Pudicitiâ*, c. 2.

[3] Cc. 17, 18, 19.

[4] Compare l. iv. c. 16.

[5] C. 20. Compare l. iv. c. 24. *Philo Judæus de Mose*, tom. ii. p. 103, ed. Mangey.

which they had been detained in servitude. The Marcionites also objected to certain contradictions which they pretended to discover in Scripture:[1] for example, between the general command not to perform any manner of work on the Sabbath, and the particular command to bear the ark round the walls of Jericho for seven successive days, one of which must necessarily have been a Sabbath—between the general command not to make any graven image, and the particular command to make the brazen serpent, etc.[2] In like manner, they objected to those passages in which God is said to repent—for instance, of having made Saul king—on the ground that repentance necessarily implies previous error, either of judgment or conduct.[3] Tertullian does not appear to have been aware of the true answer to this objection—that when we speak of the anger, repentance, jealousy of God, we merely mean to say that such effects have been produced in the course of the divine dispensations as would, if they were the results of human conduct, be ascribed to the operation of those passions; and that we use the terms, because the narrowness of human conceptions, and the imperfection of human language, furnish us with no better modes of expressing ourselves. Our author notices various other inconsistencies which the Marcionites professed to find in the Scripture; and concludes this part of his subject with observing, that all the reasons assigned by those heretics, for denying that the God who created the word was the Supreme God, applied with equal force to their own imaginary deity.[4]

Having thus proved, as he thinks satisfactorily, that the notion of two distinct deities, one the Creator of the world, the other Supreme, was a mere fiction, and that the former was indeed the one Supreme God, Tertullian proceeds to refute the notion that Jesus was not sent by the Creator. The mode which he adopts is to compare the predictions in the Old Testament with the actions of Jesus as recorded in the New, and to show that the former were exactly accomplished in the latter. The necessary conclusion is, that Jesus must have been sent by the same Deity who spoke by the prophets under the patriarchal and Mosaic dispensations, that is, by the Creator of the world. It can scarcely be necessary to remark that, in this part of the

[1] C. 21. Tertullian's words are, "Jubentis arcam circumferri per dies octo." Compare l. iv. c. 12, where Rigault, however, reads *septem diebus;* and we find the same reading in the tract *adv. Judæos*, c. 4.

[2] Cc. 22, 23.

[3] C. 24.

[4] C. 25, *ad finem.*

controversy with Marcion, our author is obliged to take precisely the same ground which I have already described him to have taken in his treatise *against the Jews.* But before he enters upon the investigation of particular prophecies, he makes some general observations which are not unworthy of notice. He contends, for instance, that unless the coming of Christ had been predicted, the evidence of His divine mission would have been incomplete.[1] The miracles which He performed were not, as Marcion asserted, alone sufficient to establish the point; it was further necessary that previous intimations of His appearance and character should have been given, in order to furnish a test whereby to ascertain whether He was really the person He professed to be. The conclusion which Tertullian builds upon these premises is, that Jesus must have been sent by the Creator of the world, who foretold His coming, and not by Marcion's supposed Supreme Being, who had given no intimation whatever on the subject. Our author then mentions two circumstances which ought, he says, always to be borne in mind by the reader of the prophetic writings — that in them, future events are frequently spoken of as if they had already happened; and that, as the language of prophecy is frequently figurative, men may be led into great errors by affixing to it too literal a meaning.[2]

His next remark is, that the Marcionites, although in one respect they made common cause with the Jews—namely, by denying that the prophecies of the Old Testament were accomplished in Jesus of Nazareth—were on all other points directly opposed to them.[3] For the Jews alleged the supposed disagreement between the prophecies respecting the Messiah and the history of Jesus as a reason for rejecting the pretensions of the latter; whereas the Marcionites alleged it as a reason for asserting that Jesus was sent by the Supreme God—not by the God of the Old Testament. Tertullian then proceeds, almost in the same words which he has used in his treatise *against the Jews*, to show that they, as well as the Marcionites, had been betrayed into their error by not distinguishing between the two advents of Christ—the one in humiliation, the other in glory.[4] He dwells[5] at some length on the absurd consequences which

[1] L. iii. cc. 2, 3. Lardner (tom. iv. ed. 4to, p. 604), in speaking of this part of Tertullian's work, accuses him of rashness in weakening a very strong, if not the strongest, argument for the truth of the Christian religion; but Lardner's representation scarcely does justice to our author's reasoning on the subject. See chap. ii. note 1, p. 67.

[2] C. 5. [3] C. 6. [4] C. 7. [5] Cc. 8, 9, 10.

necessarily flow from the notion of the Marcionites, that the body of Christ was a mere phantasm, and says that the title of Antichrist might with greater propriety be applied to them than to the heretics mentioned by St. John, who denied that Christ had come in the flesh. To the latter it appeared incredible that God should be made flesh; the former further denied that God was the Creator of man or of the flesh. We learn incidentally that the Marcionites denied the reality of Christ's flesh, because they felt that if they admitted it, they should also be compelled to admit the reality of His birth, and consequently His connexion with the Demiurge, the author of the human body or flesh.[1] The remainder of the third book consists principally of references to the same passages in the Old Testament, which were produced in the treatise *against the Jews*, in order to prove that Jesus was the Messiah predicted by the prophets. We have already noticed the inference deduced by Semler from this resemblance between the two treatises, and assigned what seemed to us satisfactory reasons for thinking the inference unsound.[2]

Marcion appears to have composed a work to which he gave the title of *Antitheses*, because in it he had set, as it were in opposition to each other, passages from the Old and New Testaments, intending his readers to infer, from the apparent disagreement between them, that the law and the gospel did not proceed from the same author.[3] The object of Tertullian's fourth book is to expose the weakness of this attempt. He admits that, as all previous dispensations were only preparatory to the Christian, and were designed to apply to mankind when placed under very different circumstances, the law and the gospel could not but differ in some respects from each other. But he contends that this difference had been clearly pointed out by the prophets, and was therefore an argument that the Creator, who inspired the prophets and gave the law, gave the gospel also. As the genuine Gospels did not suit Marcion's purpose, he compiled a gospel for himself, out of that of St. Luke;[4] which he appears to have

[1] C. 11. Compare l. iv. c. 19. *De Carne Christi*, cc. 1, 2, 3, 5.

[2] Chap. i. p. 43.

[3] L. iv. c. 1. This work seems to have been placed by Marcion in the hands of his followers, for the purpose of instructing them in the principles of his system. Compare l. i. c. 19; l. ii. cc. 28, 29; l. iv. cc. 4, 6.

[4] Cc. 2, 5. Marcion does not appear to have called it St. Luke's Gospel. He cut out from it such passages as he conceived to militate against his own opinions; such as the History of the Temptation, l. v. c. 6. See *de Carne Christi*, c. 7. In speaking of Marcion's gospel, Tertullian calls it Evangelium vestrum, l. iii. cap. ult.; Evangelium ejus, l. iv. c. 1. See also l. iv. c. 3; l. v. c. 16, *sub fine*.

selected because that evangelist was supposed to have written from the preaching and under the direction of St. Paul, who had reproved St. Peter for departing from the truth of the gospel. The conclusion which Marcion meant to draw from this circumstance was that, in order to discover the genuine doctrines of Christianity, recourse must be had to St. Paul, in preference to the other apostles. This conclusion our author overthrows by observing that St. Paul appears, from the Epistle to the Galatians, to have gone up to Jerusalem for the very purpose of ascertaining whether the doctrines which he preached coincided with those preached by Peter, and James, and John. "All the apostles," continues Tertullian, "were equally commissioned by Christ to preach the gospel; all, therefore, preached the genuine doctrine. Instead of setting the authority of St. Paul above that of the rest, Marcion ought rather to contend that the Gospels which the orthodox use, have been adulterated, and that his alone contains the truth."[1] With respect to the Gospel of St. Luke, Marcion contended that it had been adulterated by those Judaizing Christians who were anxious to establish a connexion between the law and the gospel, and that he had restored it to its original integrity.[2] Tertullian here enters into that discussion, respecting the mode of ascertaining the genuineness of the sacred Scriptures, to which we referred in our observations on the sixth Article of our Church.[3]

He next proceeds to state the point actually in controversy, between the orthodox and the Marcionites, respecting Christ.[4] According to the latter, the Christ predicted in the Old Testament had not yet appeared, but was to come at some future period, to restore the Jews to their native land and to their ancient temporal prosperity: whereas the Christ, whose actions are recorded in the New Testament, was sent by the Supreme God to accomplish the salvation of the whole human race. "It would follow," proceeds Tertullian, "from this statement that there ought to be no resemblance, either in character or in the transactions of their lives, between the Christ of the Old and the

On the subject of Marcion's gospel, the reader will find some valuable remarks in the introduction to Dr. Schleiermacher's work to which we have already referred.

[1] C. 3. [2] Cc. 4, 5. [3] See chap. v. p. 54.

[4] Compare l. iii. c. 21. "Nam etsi putes Creatoris quidem terrenas promissiones fuisse, Christi vero cœlestes," l. iv. c. 14, c. 35, *sub fine;* l. iii. c. 24, *sub initio,* quoted in chap. v. note 4, p. 130; whence it appears that, according to Marcion, the Jews were after death to pass to a state of enjoyment in the bosom of Abraham, l. iv. c. 34, quoted in chap. v. note 7, p. 131.

Christ of the New Testament. How then happens it that the latter has carried on the dispensations of the God of the Old Testament—has fulfilled His prophecies—has realized His promises—has confirmed His law—has enforced and perfected the rule of life set forth by Him?" It would be a tedious and not very edifying task to follow our author through all the quotations from Scripture, by which he endeavours to establish the exact correspondence of the actions and sayings of Christ with those ascribed to the promised Messiah by the ancient prophets. It will be sufficient to produce a few examples of the contradictions which Marcion pretended to discover between the Old and New Testaments, and of the mode in which Tertullian accounted for them.

Marcion contended, for instance, that the Lex Talionis, established by Moses, was directly at variance with our Saviour's precept, that we should offer our left cheek to him who smites us on the right.[1] Tertullian replies that, although the Lex Talionis was suited to the temper and moral condition of the Israelites, and at first instituted for the purpose of repressing violence, yet in the prophetic writings we find frequent exhortations to patience under injuries. Those exhortations were inserted in order to prepare the minds of men for that prohibition of all acts of retaliation, and even of angry and revengeful feelings, which the Messiah, one part of whose office would be to perfect the law, would introduce under the gospel.

Another alleged instance of inconsistency was, that Moses voluntarily interfered to put an end to the quarrel between the two Israelites; whereas Christ refused to interfere between the two brethren, one of whom appealed to Him respecting the division of an inheritance.[2] In this case Tertullian has recourse to a most unsatisfactory solution. He says that Christ's refusal was meant to convey a severe reproof of the applicant, by insinuating that, if he were to interfere, He should probably meet with the same ungrateful treatment which Moses experienced from his countryman.

A third instance of contradiction urged by Marcion was that, whereas Moses permitted divorce, Christ prohibited it in every case, excepting that of adultery.[3] Tertullian answers that Christ had Himself furnished a solution of this apparent contradiction

[1] C. 16. See p. 243. [2] C. 28. [3] C. 34.

when He said that from the beginning it was not so, and that Moses had granted the permission to the Jews on account of the hardness of their hearts. He, therefore, who came to take away their stony heart, and to give them a heart of flesh, naturally curtailed the former licence, and restricted divorce to the single case of adultery. Tertullian concludes the fourth book with asserting that he has fully redeemed the pledge which he gave at the commencement, having shown that the doctrines and precepts of Christ coincided so exactly with those delivered by the prophets, and that His miracles, sufferings, and resurrection were so clearly foretold by them as to establish beyond controversy the fact that *their* inspiration and *His* mission originated with the same God—the Creator of the world.

We have observed that Marcion compiled his gospel principally from that of St. Luke, because that evangelist had been the companion of St. Paul.[1] The reason of the preference thus given to the Apostle of the Gentiles was his constant and strenuous opposition to the Judaizing Christians, who wished to re-impose the yoke of the Jewish ceremonies on the necks of their brethren. This opposition the Marcionites wished to construe into a direct denial of the authority of the Mosaic law. They contended also from St. Paul's assertion—that he received his appointment to the apostolic office, not from man, but from Christ—that he alone delivered the genuine doctrines of the gospel. The object, therefore, of Tertullian in the fifth book is to prove, with respect to St. Paul's Epistles, what he had proved in the fourth with respect to St. Luke's Gospel, that, far from being at variance, they were in perfect unison with the writings of the Old Testament. He begins with the Epistle to the Galatians, which was written for the express purpose of confuting the error of those who thought the observance of the Mosaic ritual necessary to salvation.[2] Here he urges an argument to which we have more than once alluded, that the labour bestowed by the apostle was wholly superfluous, in case, as the Marcionites supposed, he had been commissioned to teach that Christ was not sent by the God who gave the Mosaic law.[3] For what need was there, on that supposition, to enter into a long discussion, for the purpose of proving that the gospel had superseded the use of the ceremonial law, when the very fact that they proceeded from different, or, to speak more accurately, from hostile deities, accounted at once for the abolition of the latter? Tertullian examines in like

[1] P. 247. [2] C. 2. [3] Chap. v. pp. 146, 240.

manner the two Epistles to the Corinthians,[1] that to the Romans,[2] which he states to have been grievously mutilated by the Marcionites, the two to the Thessalonians,[3] and those to the Ephesians,[4] Colossians,[5] and Philippians.[6] The same reasons which prevented us from entering into any minute investigation of the quotations from the Gospels, induce us to be equally concise in our notice of the quotations from St. Paul's Epistles. The detail would be extremely tedious, and the information derived from it in no respect proportioned to the time which it would necessarily occupy.

When we examine the opinions of Marcion, whether upon points of faith or practice, we find that they all flowed by natural consequence from the leading article of his creed—that the world was created by a deity distinct from the Supreme Deity, out of pre-existent matter. As the flesh or body of man was the work of the Demiurge, it was held by the Marcionites in abhorrence. Hence their assertion that Christ was neither born of the Virgin Mary,[7] nor passed through the customary stages of infancy and boyhood, but descended at once from heaven a full-grown man,[8] in appearance only, not in reality [9]—hence the opprobrious terms in which they spoke of the body,[10] and their denial of its resurrection [11]—hence their aversion to marriage,[12] which they carried to such a length that they refused to administer the rite of baptism to a married man, or to admit him to the sacrament of the Eucharist, until he had repudiated his wife.[13] We find in Tertullian no mention of that notion respecting an intermediate kind of deity, of a mixed nature, neither perfectly good nor perfectly evil, which Mosheim ascribes to Marcion.[14] Lardner thinks that the distinction which Marcion made between his two deities was, that the one was good, the other just;[15] but in the second chapter of the first book Tertullian expressly says that Marcion conceived the Creator of the world to be the author of evil, and that he was led into that error by misinterpreting certain passages

[1] Cc. 5–13. [2] Cc. 13, 14. [3] Cc. 15, 16. [4] C. 17.
[5] C. 19. [6] C. 20. [7] L. iv. c. 10, *sub fine.*
[8] L. iv. c. 7, *sub in.*, c. 21. *De Carne Christi*, cc. 1, 7.
[9] L. i. cc. 11, 22, *sub in.*, 24; l. ii. c. 28; l. iii. cc. 8, 9, 10; l. iv. cc. 8, 42. *De Res. Carnis*, c. 2; *de Carne Christi*, cc. 4, 6; *de Animâ*, c. 17; *de Præscriptione Hæreticorum*, c. 33.
[10] L. iii. c. 11. *De Carne Christi*, c. 4.
[11] L. i. c. 24; l. iv. c. 37: l. v. c. 10.
[12] L. i. cc. 1, 24, 29; l. iv. c. 11; l. v. c. 7. *Ad Uxorem*, l. 1, c. 3.
[13] L. iv. c. 34.
[14] Cent. ii. par. ii. chap. v. sect. 7.
[15] *History of Heretics*, chap. x. sect. 12.

of Scripture. The other charges brought against him by our author are, that he denied the freedom of the will;[1] and that he rejected some, and mutilated and corrupted other portions of Scripture.[2] His followers were charged with being addicted to astrology.[3] Like other heretical leaders, he appears to have been attended by females, who pretended to great sanctity—a practice probably adopted in imitation of the apostles.[4]

Mosheim speaks of Lucan, Severus, Blastus, and Apelles, as followers of Marcion, who deviated in some respects from the tenets of their master. Lucan is once mentioned by Tertullian as holding the opinion that neither the soul nor the body would rise again, but a sort of third substance—an opinion which our author supposes him to have borrowed from Aristotle.[5] The name of Apelles occurs frequently in Tertullian's writings.[6] He is described as a disciple of Marcion, who endeavoured to improve upon his master's doctrine; and the account given of him is that, being unable to comply with Marcion's strict notions on the subject of continence, he left that heretic and went to Alexandria, where he met with a female named Philumena, who performed various magical illusions by the assistance of an evil spirit.[7] To this woman he attached himself, and under her instruction composed a work called φανέρωσεις, or Revelations. Like his master, he denied the resurrection of the body,[8] and at first prohibited marriage.[9] He affirmed that the souls of men were tempted to come down from the super-celestial regions—the regions above the heavens which invest this earth—by the allurements offered to them by the fiery angel,[10] the God

[1] *De Animâ*, c. 21.

[2] *De Præscriptione Hæreticorum*, c. 38; *adv. Marcionem*, l. i. c. 1. Marcion necessarily rejected the whole of the Old Testament, as proceeding from the Demiurge. *De Præscriptione Hæreticorum*, c. 30. Tertullian mentions also his rejection of St. Matthew's Gospel, l. iv. c. 34; of St. John's Gospel, *de Carne Christi*, c. 3; of the Acts of the Apostles, l. v. c. 2; *de Præscriptione Hæreticorum*, c. 22; of the Apocalypse, l. v. c. 5; of the two Epistles to Timothy and of that to Titus, l. v. cap. ult.; but he appears to have recognised the Epistle to Philemon. The reader will find in Lardner a detailed account of the alterations which Marcion made in St. Luke's Gospel, and in the ten Epistles of St. Paul which he received. *History of Heretics*, chap. x. sect. 35, etc.

[3] L. i. c. 18. [4] L. v. c. 8, *sub fine.* [5] *De Res. Carnis*, c. 2, *sub fine.*

[6] "Hoc meminisse debuerat Apelles, Marcionis de discipulo emendator." *Adv. Marcionem*, l. iv. c. 17; *de Carne Christi*, c. 6, *sub in.*

[7] *De Præscriptione Hæreticorum*, c. 30. See also cc. 6, 10, 37; *de Carne Christi*, c. 24. Lardner questions the story of the incontinence of Apelles. *History of Heretics*, chap. xii. sect. 3.

[8] *De Præscriptione Hæreticorum*, c. 33. [9] *Ibid.*

[10] *De Animâ*, c. 23; *de Carne Christi*, c. 8; *de Res. Carnis*, c. 5.

both of the Israelites and of the Gentiles,[1] who no sooner got them into his power than he surrounded them with sinful flesh. The distinction of sexes existed in these souls previously to their descent upon earth, and was from them communicated to the bodies in which they were clothed.[2] Apelles differed also from his master in admitting the reality of Christ's flesh, though he denied that Christ was born of the Virgin Mary.[3] His notion appears to have been that the flesh of Christ was not given by the fiery angel or god of evil, who clothed the souls which he seduced into these lower regions with sinful flesh,[4] but was a substance brought down originally from the stars by a certain eminent angel, who formed the world, though he afterwards mixed up repentance with his work.[5] Christ's flesh, therefore, was real, but different from human flesh. In the third book *against Marcion*, our author alludes to certain heretics who maintained that the flesh which the angels assumed who are stated in Scripture to have appeared in human shapes, was not human flesh.[6] Pamelius supposes that the heretics here alluded to were the disciples of Apelles. Of Severus and Blastus there is no mention in Tertullian's writings.

The next heretics in Mosheim's catalogue are Bardesanes and Tatian. The former is not even named by Tertullian: of the latter we have already spoken.[7]

[1] Tertullian's expression is, "Ab igneo Angelo, Deo Israelis et nostro." By the word *nostro*, I suppose Tertullian to mean that the fiery angel was not merely the God of the Jews, as some of the heretics supposed with respect to their inferior deity, but also of the Gentiles. But in the tract *de Præscriptione Hæreticorum*, c. 34, Tertullian speaks as if the fiery angel was the God of Israel only: "Apelles Creatorem, Angelum nescio quem gloriosum superioris Dei, faceret Deum Legis et Israëlis, illum igneum affirmans." In c. 7, he traces this notion of a fiery angel to the philosophical tenets of Heraclitus. I conceive it rather to have been derived from the circumstances attending the appearance of God to Moses in the burning bush.

[2] *De Animâ*, c. 36.

[3] "Aut admissâ carne nativitatem negare, ut Apelles discipulus et postea desertor ipsius." *De Carne Christi*, c. 1.

[4] "Nam et Philumena illa magis persuasit Apelli cæterisque desertoribus Marcionis, ex fide quidem Christum circumtulisse carnem, nullius tamen nativitatis, utpote de elementis eam mutuatum." *Adv. Marcionem*, l. iii. c. 11. See *de Res. Carnis*, c. 2; *de Carne Christi*, c. 8.

[5] Tertullian's words are, "Angelum quendam inclytum nominant, qui mundum hunc instituerit, et instituto eo pœnitentiam admiscuerit." *De Carne Christi*, c. 8. Semler for *admiscuerit* reads *admiserit*. If *admiscuerit* is the true reading, I should conjecture the meaning to be that this angel either did not or could not create a perfect world, but introduced into it many things which he afterwards wished to alter.

[6] C. 9. Pamelius refers to the tract *de Carne Christi*, c. 6.

[7] Chap. iv. p. 129.

From the Oriental, Mosheim proceeds to what he terms the Egyptian branch of the Gnostics. In this branch he assigns the first place to Basilides, who is mentioned once, and only once, by our author, in the tract *de Resurrectione Carnis.* He is there stated to have agreed with Marcion in denying the reality of Christ's flesh. Mosheim, however, contends that this opinion is unjustly ascribed to him,[1] though probably held by some of his followers.

We come next to Carpocrates, who is twice mentioned by Tertullian, in the treatise *de Animâ.* In one place he is said to have maintained that *his own* soul and the souls of his followers were derived from a heavenly power, who looked down, as it were from an eminence, upon all the powers of this lower world.[2] He conceived, therefore, both himself and them to be entirely on a level with Christ and the apostles. In the other place, he is accused of holding the doctrine of the metempsychosis;[3] on the ground that the soul must perform all the acts to which it was originally destined, before it can attain to a state of rest. In support of this notion he quoted the words of our Saviour, *Verily thou shalt not depart thence, until thou hast paid the uttermost farthing.* Tertullian remarks incidentally that Carpocrates believed nothing to be evil in itself; good and evil depending entirely on opinion.

Tertullian wrote a treatise expressly against the Valentinians. He speaks of them as a very numerous sect,[4] and ascribes their popularity to the fables with which their theology abounded, and to the air of mystery which they threw around their doctrines. He says that their founder, Valentinus, was a man of ability and eloquence, and flourished in the reign of Antoninus Pius.[5] Being offended because the claim of another to a vacant see was preferred to his own, he quitted the Church in disgust, and formed a system, not indeed entirely new, but founded in some measure upon opinions previously current. Of this system, Tertullian's treatise is a concise account;[6] taken, as he admits, from the writings of Justin, Miltiades, Irenæus,

[1] C. 2. Lardner also thinks that there is reason for doubting whether Basilides denied the reality of Christ's flesh. *History of Heretics,* chap. ii. sect. 6.

[2] C. 23.

[3] C. 35. See Lardner, *History of Heretics,* chap. iii. sect. 11, where he assigns reasons for doubting the truth of many of the charges against the Carpocratians.

[4] *Adv. Valentinianos,* c. 1.

[5] C. 4. Compare *de Præscriptione Hæreticorum,* cc. 29, 30.

[6] Cc. 5, 6.

and Proculus, whom he calls contemporaries of the heresiarchs. It is in fact little more than a translation of the first book of the work of Irenæus against the Gnostics. The whole system is so replete with absurdity, that we should be disposed to pass it over without notice, were not the examination of it necessary to the completion of our plan, which is to place before the reader all the information supplied by our author's writings respecting the history of the Church in his day.

Valentinus, then, supposed a God, self-existent, infinite, invisible, eternal, who dwelt in the very highest regions, living in a state of imperturbable tranquillity, like the gods of Epicurus.[1] To this God he gave the names of *αἰὼν τέλειος*, *προαρχὴ*, *ἀρχὴ*, and with somewhat of inconsistency, *βυθός*. This Deity, however, was not alone, but had with him, or rather within him, another Being to whom the names of *ἔννοια*, *χάρις*, *σιγὴ* were assigned. From the latter, who appears to have been considered as a female, and to have been impregnated by the Sovereign Deity, sprang *νοῦς*,[2] who was in every respect like and equal to his Father, and alone capable of comprehending his Father's greatness. He was regarded as the beginning or origin of all things, and even distinguished by the appellation of Father. He was also called *μονογενὴς*, or only-begotten; notwithstanding that at the same time with him was born a female Æon, called *ἀλήθεια*, or truth.[3] The above four *βυθὸς*, *σιγὴ*, *νοῦς*, and *ἀλήθεια*, constituted the first Tetras or Quaternion, from which the remaining Æons were derived. For from *νοῦς* sprang *λόγος* and *ζωὴ*, the word and life; and from them again *ἄνθρωπος* and *ἐκκλησία*, man and the Church. The last four, added to the first-mentioned four, constituted the *ὀγδοάς*. Again, from *λόγος* and *ζωὴ* were derived ten:—*βυθὸς* (a second of the name, unless we ought rather to read *βύθιος*) and *μίξις*, *ἀγήρατος* and *ἕνωσις*, *αὐτοφυὴς* and *ἡδονὴ*, *ἀκίνητος* and *σύγκρασις*, *μονογενὴς* (a second of the name) and *μακαρία*.[4] From *ἄνθρωπος* and *ἐκκλησία* were derived twelve:—*παράκλητος* and *πίστις*, *πατρικὸς* and *ἐλπὶς*, *μητρικὸς* and *ἀγάπη*, *αἶνος*[5] and *σύνεσις*, *ἐκκλησιαστικὸς* and *μακαριότης*,

[1] C. 7. See *adv. Marcionem*, l. i. c. 5.

[2] In the tract *de Præscriptione Hæreticorum*, c. 33, Tertullian translates the word *νοῦς* by the Latin *sensus*.

[3] Tertullian says that he should rather have been called *πρωτογενὴς*, or first-begotten. Compare *de Animâ*, c. 12.

[4] C. 8. Compare Irenæus, l. i. c. 1. In the *Scorpiace*, c. 10, we find the name *ἐβασκαντὸς* among the Æons of Valentinus.

[5] Irenæus has *ἀείνους*.

θελητὸς[1] and σοφία. In forming these pairs of Æons, it was evidently the intention of Valentinus to couple together a male and a female Æon; a masculine being regularly joined to a feminine noun. Tertullian, therefore, retains the Greek nouns, lest, in translating them into Latin, the distinction should disappear.[2] We have now reached the number of thirty Æons, which constituted what Valentinus called the πλήρωμα, the fulness of the celestial body.

To νοῦς alone, among the derived Æons, was imparted the full knowledge of the Supreme God.[3] He would have communicated it to the rest, but his mother, σιγὴ, interposed to prevent the communication. They, in consequence, pined with the secret desire of being admitted to the knowledge of the Father. This desire at length became so violent in σοφία, the youngest of the family of the Æons, that she would have been destroyed by its very intensity, and thus one of the members of the Pleroma would have been lost, had she not been preserved by ὅρος, who was sent forth from the Father for this very purpose, at the request of νοῦς. The various emotions, however, by which σοφία was agitated during the continuance of her desire, gave rise to new existences; for to them is to be traced the origin of matter, of ignorance, of fear, of grief. The desire itself—called ἐνθύμησις, which the translator of Irenæus interprets *concupiscentia cum passione*—was separated by ὅρος from its parent σοφία, and driven out of the Pleroma. To ὅρος, on account of the part which he had acted in restoring σοφία to the Pleroma, were given the names of μεταγωγεὺς, ὁροθέτης, σταῦρος (or rather, perhaps, σταυρωτὴς, because he had crucified the desire which preyed upon σοφία), λυτρωτὴς or redeemer, and καρπιστὴς or restorer to liberty.

Having thus described the error of σοφία, the last-born Æon, and her recovery from it, Valentinus proceeded to say that νοῦς sent forth another couple of Æons, Christ and the Holy Spirit.[4] The office of Christ was to instruct the Æons in the nature of the union which subsisted between the different pairs in the Pleroma, and in the mode of arriving at the comprehension of the Supreme Father. The office of the Holy Spirit was to render them, after their instruction by Christ, grateful to the Father,

[1] In several instances we find φιλητὸς instead of θελητὸς, probably by the mistake of the transcriber.

[2] C. 6. [3] Cc. 9, 10. [4] C. 11.

and contented with the degree of knowledge which they possessed. Calm and tranquillity being thus restored to the Pleroma by the exertions of Christ and the Holy Spirit, all the Æons, in honour of the Father, contributed, as it were into a common stock, each his most excellent gift.[1] Out of these contributions was formed the brightest star and most perfect fruit of the Pleroma, Jesus; who was also called *σωτὴρ*, *χριστὸς*, *λόγος*, and *πάντα*, because All had contributed to His formation. Angels also were created to be His attendants; but Tertullian says that he could not ascertain whether they were supposed to be of the same substance or essence with their Lord.

So much for the interior of the Pleroma. With respect to what was *without* it,[2] we have seen that the intense desire which agitated *σοφία*—and which Valentinus called sometimes *ἐνθύμησις*, sometimes Achamoth[3]—was driven from the Pleroma, into the outer regions of darkness, where she remained like an abortion, shapeless and imperfect. In this state Christ, at the suggestion of *ὅρος*, regarded her with an eye of pity, and with the assistance of the Holy Spirit gave her a form. She retained in her new condition some savour of her former incorruption; and, sensible of her fall, sought to be readmitted to the regions of light, but was prevented by *ὅρος*. In consequence of her disappointment, she was assailed by those evils which before afflicted her parent, *σοφία*—fear, grief, and ignorance. To these was now added the desire of conversion to Christ, who gave her life. From her various emotions and affections arose all the substances in this material world.[4] From her desire of conversion arose every living soul, even that of the Demiurge, the God of mankind. From her grief and tears, the element of water; from her fear, the corporeal elements; from her smile, which was caused by the recollection of having seen Christ, light. In the extremity of her distress she at length had recourse to prayer to Christ, who sent to her the Saviour Jesus, with His train of attendant angels.[5] The ecstasy into which she was thrown by their appear-

[1] C. 12.

[2] C. 14.

[3] Tertullianus, c. 14, "hoc nomen *ininterpretabile* vocat, et mox addit, *Achamoth unde, adhuc quæritur.* Feuardentius vero recte deducit a חָכְמָה *Sapientia.*" Irenæus, ed. Grabe, p. 19, note 3.

[4] C. 15. The reader will observe that whatever took place *without* the Pleroma was, as it were, a copy of what took place *within* it. Thus the formation of matter here described corresponds to the formation of matter within the Pleroma, mentioned in cc. 9, 10. See c. 23.

[5] C. 16.

ance caused her to produce three different kinds of existences—material, animal, and spiritual.[1] Out of the animal she formed the Demiurge, called also by the Valentinians μητροπατὼρ, and king.[2] The name of Father, which is included in μητροπατὼρ, was applied to him in the case of animal substances, which they placed on the right; that of Demiurge in the case of material substances, which they placed on the left; and that of King indifferently in both cases. The Demiurge created this visible world.[3]

To the devil Valentinus gave the name of κοσμοκρατὼρ or Munditenens, and appeared in some respects to place him above the Demiurge, because the latter was only animal, the former spiritual.[4]

The Demiurge created man, not out of the dust of the earth, but out of some peculiar matter which he animated with his breath; so that man was both material and animal.[5] The Demiurge afterwards drew over him a covering of flesh.[6] Moreover, at the time when the breath of life was breathed into him a portion of the spiritual seed which Achamoth retained was also communicated. To this spiritual seed was given the appellation of ἐκκλησία, in allusion to the Æon so named within the Pleroma.

Corresponding to the three kinds of substances now described, there are three kinds of men—the carnal or material, who are represented by Cain; the animal, who are represented by Abel; and the spiritual, who are represented by Seth: the first are destined to certain perdition, the last to salvation.[7] The final state of the second is uncertain, being determined by their greater *inclination*, either on the one hand to the carnal, or on the other to the spiritual. They in whom is the spiritual seed, being assured of salvation, are exempt from all discipline, and at liberty to live and act as they please; but the animal man is obliged to work out his salvation with care and diligence.[8] One of the consequences which the Valentinians derived from this triple division was, that no credit can be due to the testimony of

[1] C. 17. *De Animâ*, c. 21.
[2] C. 18. See *de Præscriptione Hæreticorum*, cc. 7, 34. The name μητροπατὼρ was applied to him because he was merely the agent of his mother in creating the visible world.
[3] C. 20. [4] C. 22. [5] C. 24. [6] C. 25. Compare *de Animâ*, cc. 11, 23.
[7] C. 26. [8] Cc. 29, 30.

the senses, as they are to be referred to the animal part of man's nature.[1]

With respect to Christ, the Valentinian doctrine was, that the Demiurge sent forth, *protulit*, from himself an animal Christ, who was foretold by the prophets, and passed through the body of the Virgin as through a canal—that at his baptism, the Saviour, who was before described as formed out of the most excellent qualities of all the Æons in the Pleroma, descended upon him in the shape of a dove, but quitted him when he was examined before Pilate—and thus that only the carnal and animal Christ was crucified.[2] It does not exactly appear whence the Christ of the Demiurge obtained His flesh, which Valentinus supposed to be different from human flesh.[3] We may here observe that, in agreement with this supposition, the Valentinians denied the resurrection of the body.

At the final consummation of all things, Achamoth—who occupied the middle space in the universe, immediately below the Pleroma and above this world—will be received into the Pleroma, and become the bride of the Saviour.[4] The Demiurge will be transferred into the vacant habitation of his mother. Those men in whom was only the material seed will be annihilated. Those in whom was the animal seed, and who lived virtuous lives, will be carried up to the Demiurge, in the middle regions. Those in whom was the spiritual seed, laying aside the souls which they had received from the Demiurge, will be taken up into the Pleroma, and become the brides of the angels who attend upon the Saviour.

Such were the extravagant notions of Valentinus, as they are represented by Tertullian. We have aimed at expressing his meaning accurately, but are not certain that we have always succeeded in the attempt. We doubt, indeed, whether he himself thoroughly comprehended the system which he undertook to describe. Mosheim says that some of the moderns have endeavoured to reconcile the Valentinian doctrines with reason —a more arduous or unpromising undertaking cannot well be

[1] *De Animâ*, c. 18. Tertullian remarks that the Valentinians borrowed their notion from Plato. They supposed the five foolish virgins in the parable to mean the five senses.

[2] C. 27.

[3] *De Carne Christi*, cc. 1, 15; *de Res. Carnis*, c. 2.

[4] Cc. 31, 32, 33.

conceived.[1] The design of the heresiarch doubtless was to account for the origin of evil; but in executing this design he appears to have surrendered himself entirely to the guidance of his fancy. His followers, using the same liberty, changed and added to their master's notions at their own discretion; so that, in Tertullian's day, Axionicus of Antioch alone adhered strictly to the doctrines of Valentinus.[2] Ptolemy,[3] one of his most distinguished disciples, differed from him with respect to the names, the number, and the nature of the Æons. Tertullian mentions among his followers, Colarbasus,[4] if the reading is correct; Heracleon;[5] Secundus;[6] Marcus,[7] to whom our author gives the appellation of Magus; Theotimus,[8] who appears to have employed himself in proposing allegorical or figurative expositions of the law; and Alexander,[9] who urged as a reason for denying the reality of Christ's flesh that, if He actually assumed human flesh, He must have assumed sinful flesh; whereas St. Paul says that Christ abolished sin in the flesh. Tertullian mentions certain psalms or hymns of Valentinus.[10] He says also that Valentinus did not, like Marcion, mutilate the Scriptures, but was content to pervert their meaning.[11] In our account of the *Scorpiace*, we stated the grounds on which the Valentinians denied that Christians were under any obligation to encounter martyrdom.[12] One of them, named Prodicus, appears to have taken the lead in asserting this doctrine.[13]

Of the more obscure Gnostic sects enumerated by Mosheim—the Adamites, Cainites, Abelites, Sethites, Florinians, Ophites—Tertullian mentions only the Cainites, who, according to him, were Nicolaitans under another name.[14] It has been already remarked that the female, against whom the tract *de Baptismo* was composed, was said to belong to this sect.[15]

1 *Century* ii. part ii. chap. v. sect. 16, note.
2 *Adv. Valentinianos*, c. 4. In c. 11 Tertullian says that the divisions among the followers of Valentinus arose chiefly out of their different notions respecting Christ. See *de Præscriptione Hæreticorum*, c. 42.
3 Cc. 4, 33. 4 C. 4. 5 C. 4.
6 C. 4 and c. 38, where the system of Secundus is stated.
7 C. 4. In the tract *de Resurrectione Carnis*, c. 5, Marcus is said to have maintained that the human body was the workmanship of angels.
8 C. 4. "Multum circa imagines Legis Theotimus operatus est."
9 *De Carne Christi*, c. 16. See chap. v. note 9, p. 133.
10 *De Carne Christi*, cc. 17, 20. 11 *De Præscriptione Hæreticorum*, c. 38.
12 Chap. i. p. 29; chap. ii. p. 75.
13 *Scorpiace*, cap. ult. Prodicus is mentioned again in the tract *against Praxeas*, c. 3, *sub fine*.
14 *De Præscriptione Hæreticorum*, c. 33. 15 Chap. i. note 2, p. 9.

From the Oriental heresies, Mosheim proceeds to those which he allows to be of Grecian origin, and which, according to him, principally owed their rise to the attempt to explain the Christian doctrines of the Trinity and Incarnation, upon the principles of the Grecian philosophy. To this class of heresies he refers the tenets of Praxeas, Artemon, and Theodotus. Of Artemon and Theodotus we find no notice in Tertullian's writings. Against Praxeas he wrote a treatise, from which we collect not only the opinions of that heretic, but also his own, upon the two fundamental articles of Christian faith just mentioned. The reader will remember that the consideration of them was deferred till we arrived at this division of our work; and their paramount importance must be our excuse for entering into a more detailed account of the treatise *against Praxeas* than has been given of the other tracts against the heretics.

Praxeas, according to our author, was a man of a restless temper, who had very recently come from Asia, and by false representations prevailed upon the Bishop of Rome to recall a letter, in which he had recognised the prophecies of Montanus, Prisca, and Maximilla, and had recommended the Asiatic Churches to continue in communion with them.[1] This circumstance doubtless contributed, as much as the heretical tenets of Praxeas, to excite our author's indignation against him. When, however, those tenets found their way to Carthage, they were successfully combated and to all appearance extirpated by Tertullian himself; the person who originally taught them having delivered to the Church a written recantation. But after a time the heresy again displayed itself, and called forth, from the pen of Tertullian, the treatise which we are now to consider.

The error of Praxeas appears to have originated in anxiety to maintain the unity of God,[2] which, he thought, could only be done by saying that the Father, Son, and Holy Ghost were one and the same.[3] He contended, therefore, according to Tertullian, that the Father Himself descended into the Virgin, was

[1] C. I. "Ipsa novellitas Praxeæ hesterni," c. 2.

[2] "Unicum dominum vindicat, omnipotentem, mundi conditorem, ut de unico Hæresim faciat," c. I.

[3] "Dum unicum Deum non alias putat credendum, quam si ipsum eundemque et Patrem et Filium et Spiritum Sanctum dicat," c. 2. "Quum eundem Patrem et Filium et Spiritum contendunt, adversus οἰκονομίαν Monarchiæ adulantes," c. 9.

born of her, suffered, and was in a word Jesus Christ.[1] Praxeas, however, does not appear to have admitted the correctness of this account of his doctrine, but to have declared his opinion to be—that the Father did not suffer in the Son, but sympathized (*compassus est*) with the Son.[2]

Tertullian enters upon the refutation of the doctrines of Praxeas by setting forth his own creed.[3] "We believe," he says, "in one God, but under the following dispensation or economy —that there is also a Son of God, His Word, who proceeded from Him;[4] by whom all things were made, and without whom nothing was made; who was sent by Him into the Virgin, and was born of her; being both man and God, the Son of man and the Son of God, and called Jesus Christ; who suffered, died, and was buried, according to the Scriptures; and was raised again by the Father;[5] and was taken up into heaven, there to sit at the right hand of the Father, and thence to come to judge the quick and the dead; who sent from heaven, from His Father, according to His promise, the Holy Ghost, the Comforter, the Sanctifier of the faith of all who believe in the Father, Son, and Holy Ghost."[6] Such, according to Tertullian, was the faith handed down in the Church, from the first preaching of the gospel—a faith which, far from destroying the unity, as Praxeas supposed, is perfectly consistent with it. "For though the Father, Son, and Holy Ghost are three, they are

[1] "Ipsum dicit Patrem descendisse in virginem, ipsum ex eâ natum, ipsum passum; denique ipsum esse Jesum Christum," c. 1.

[2] "Ergo nec compassus est Pater Filio; sic enim, directam blasphemiam in Patrem veriti, diminui eam hoc modo sperant, concedentes jam Patrem et Filium duos esse, si filius quidem patitur; Pater vero compatitur," c. 29. From this passage Lardner contends that Praxeas was not a Patripassian, and that Tertullian was mistaken in his view of that heretic's doctrines. According to Lardner, who follows Beausobre, Praxeas distinguished between the Word and the Son of God; deeming the former only an attribute or faculty of the divine nature, the communication of which to the man Jesus Christ, through His conception by the Holy Spirit, rendered Him the Son of God. *Credibility of Gospel History*, c. 41. *History of Heretics*, c. 20, sect. 7. But Wilson, in his *Illustration*, etc., pp. 312, 415, has satisfactorily shown that the earliest error on the subject of Christ's nature was that of those who denied, not His divinity, but His humanity; and that the error of Praxeas consisted in denying His distinct personality. Wilson compares Praxeas and his followers with the Swedenborgians.

[3] C. 2. This passage is quoted in chap. v. note 4, p. 159.

[4] "Qui ex ipso processerit." In c. 6 Tertullian, speaking of the generation of the Son, uses the word *protulit.* See also c. 7: "Hæc est nativitas perfecta Sermonis, dum ex Deo procedit." And c. 19: "In quo principio prolatus a Patre est."

[5] Here, as in the Epistle to the Galatians i. 1, the raising of Christ is attributed to the Father. See Pearson, article v. p. 256.

[6] In c. 4 the Holy Ghost is said to be from the Father, through the Son.

three, not in condition, but in degree;[1] not in substance, but in form; not in power, but in species; being of one substance, one condition, and one power, because there is one God, from whom those degrees, forms, and species, in the name of the Father, Son, and Holy Ghost are derived."

"The simple, indeed," Tertullian proceeds, "not to call them unwise and unlearned, who always constitute the majority of believers, are startled at the doctrine of the Trinity, thinking that it divides the Unity.[2] We, they say, maintain the monarchy, or sole government of God. But what is the meaning of the word monarchy? Sole empire;—and is it not perfectly consistent with singleness of rule that the ruler should have a son, or that he should administer the government through the agency

[1] "Tres autem, non statu, sed gradu; nec substantiâ, sed formâ; nec potestate, sed specie; unius autem substantiæ, et unius statûs, et unius potestatis; quia unus Deus, ex quo et gradus isti et formæ et species, in nomine Patris et Filii et Spiritûs Sancti, deputantur." C. 2. Compare c. 19. "Rationem reddidimus quâ Dii non duo dicantur, nec Domini, sed quâ Pater et Filius, duo: et hoc non ex separatione substantiæ, sed ex dispositione, quum individuum et inseparatum Filium a Patre pronuntiamus; nec statu, sed gradu alium; qui etsi Deus dicatur quando nominatur singularis, non ideo duos Deos faciat, sed unum; hoc ipso quod et Deus ex unitate Patris vocari habeat." See also cc. 9, 21.

[2] Tertullian's words are: "Simplices enim quique, ne dixerim imprudentes et idiotæ, quæ major semper credentium pars est," etc. In his controversy with Dr. Priestley, Bishop Horsley translated the word *idiotæ* by the English word *idiots*, for which translation he was severely reprehended by Dr. Priestley. The Bishop afterwards explained that by the word idiot he did not mean a person labouring under a constitutional defect of the faculty of reason; but a dull, stupid, ignorant person—a dunce or booby. Probably between the publication of his Letters and of his Supplemental Disquisitions, Bentley's animadversions upon Collins for translating "ab idiotis Evangelistis," *by idiot Evangelists*, had occurred to his recollection. *Remarks on Free-thinking*, c. 33.—Wilson, p. 444, thus translates the passage: "For *all the men of simplicity*" (alluding probably to their affectation of simplicity of doctrine, as well as to their ignorance), "not to call them unwise and unlearned, who always form the majority of Christians." We doubt whether the word *Simplices* was meant to convey the allusion which Wilson supposes. In the tract *against the Valentinians*, c. 2, Tertullian says that they called the orthodox *Simplices*, and themselves *Sapientes*. See also c. 3; *adv. Judæos*, c. 9, "Vel convertere simplices quosque gestitis." *Scorpiace*, c. 1, "Nam quod sciunt multos simplices ac rudes," where the word manifestly means, simple-minded, uninstructed. But that Wilson has rightly translated the word *idiotæ* will appear from the comparison of the following passages: "Male accepit idiotes quisque," c. 9. "Nec tantus ego sum ut vos alloquar; veruntamen et gladiatores perfectissimos non tantum magistri et præpositi sui, sed etiam idiotæ et supervacue quique abhortantur de longinquo, ut sæpe de ipso populo dictata suggesta profuerint." *Ad Martyres*, c. 1. "Sed est hoc solenne perversis et idiotis (et Rigault) hæreticis, jam et Psychicis universis." *De Pudicitiâ*, c. 16, *sub fine*. "Te simplicem et rudem et impolitam et idioticam compello." *De Testimonio Animæ*, c. 1. The word *imperitus* is used in nearly the same sense: "Secundum majorem vim imperitorum—apud gloriosissimam scilicet multitudinem Psychiorum." *De Jejuniis*, c. 11.

of whom he will?[1] When a father associates his son with himself in the empire, is the unity of the imperial power thereby destroyed? The Valentinians, it is true, destroy the monarchy of God, because they introduce other deities, who are wholly at variance with Him. The Son is of the substance of the Father;[2] He does nothing but by the will of the Father; He derives all His power from the Father, and will finally, as we learn from St. Paul, restore it to the Father.[3] How then can the doctrine of the Trinity, when thus explained, be deemed inconsistent with the sole government of God? The same reasoning is applicable in the case of the Holy Spirit." The very circumstance, that the Scriptures speak of one who delivers power, and of another to whom it is delivered, affords in Tertullian's estimation convincing evidence of a distinction of persons in the unity of the divine nature; yet expressions sometimes fall from him which seem at first sight to imply that the distinction only subsists for the purpose of carrying on the divine administration under the gospel.[4]

Having removed this popular objection to the doctrine of the Trinity, Tertullian turns to the immediate question between himself and Praxeas, and says that his object will be to inquire whether there *is* a Son, who He is, and how He exists.[5] In following Tertullian through his investigation of the first of these points, we must bear in mind the double sense of the word λόγος —which comprehends ratio and sermo, reason and speech. "Before all things God was alone, being His own world, and place, and universe; alone, because nothing existed without or beyond Him. Yet even then He was not alone, for He had with Him, within Himself, His Reason, called by the Greeks λόγος, by the Latins Sermo, though the word Ratio would be the more accurate translation, and it would be more proper to say, *In the beginning Reason* (*Ratio*) *was with God*, than *In the beginning the Word* (*Sermo*) *was with God;* since Reason is manifestly prior to the Word which it dictates.[6] Not that this distinction is of great

[1] "Facilius de Filio quam de Patre hæsitabatur." *De Præscriptione Hæreticorum*, c. 34. Semler insinuates that this part of Tertullian's reasoning verges towards Arianism.

[2] C. 4. [3] 1 Cor. xv. 28.

[4] "Videmus, igitur, non obesse monarchiæ Filium, etsi hodie apud Filium est; quia et in suo statu est apud Filium, et cum suo statu restituetur Patri a Filio; ita eam nemo hoc nomine destruet, si Filium admittat, cui et traditam eam a Patre, et a quo quandoque restituendam Patri constat," c. 4. Compare cc. 13, 16.

[5] C. 5.

[6] Tertullian's words are: "Cæterum ne tunc quidem solus; habebat enim

moment. For as God reasoned with Himself, and arranged the plan of creation, He may be accurately said, by so doing, to have made His Reason His Word. Thought, as we know from our own experience, is a species of internal conversation. This power and disposition of the divine intelligence (*Divini sensûs*) is called also in Scripture σοφία, or Wisdom; for what can be better entitled to the name of Wisdom than the Reason and Word of God?[1] When, therefore, God had determined to exhibit in their different substances and forms those things which He had planned within Himself in conjunction with the Reason and Word of His wisdom, He sent forth His Word[2]—who had also in Himself reason and wisdom inseparably united to Him—to the end that all things might be made by Him by whom they had been originally devised and planned—nay, had been actually made, as far as the divine intelligence was concerned (*quantum in Dei sensu*)—nothing more being wanting to them than that they should be known, and as it were fixed in their respective substances and forms. Such is the perfect nativity of the Word, as He proceeds from God: *formed* by Him first, to *devise*, under the name of wisdom; then *begotten*, for the purpose of carrying into effect what had been devised."[3] The reader will in this passage recognise a distinction, with which the early Fathers were familiar, between the λόγος ἐνδιαθέτος and the λόγος προφορικός. Tertullian's language would at first sight appear to imply that the generation of the Word took place when He was sent forth to create the world, and that His distinct personality commenced

secum, quam habebat in semetipso, Rationem suam scilicet. Rationalis enim Deus, et *Ratio* in ipso prius; et ita ab ipso omnia; quæ *Ratio* sensus ipsius est." Compare the conclusion of c. 15. *Sensus* in this passage, according to Bull, *Defensio Fidei Nicænæ*, sect. 3, c. 10, p. 238, corresponds to the Greek word ἔννοια. In the tract *de Præscriptione Hæreticorum*, c. 33, as was observed in note 2, p. 254, Tertullian uses it as synonymous with νοῦς. The difficulty is to reconcile this mode of explaining the generation of Word with the notion of distinct personality. The reader, however, may consult Horsley's fourth Supplemental Disquisition. There is towards the conclusion of c. 5 an expression on which Bull animadverts severely: "Possum itaque non temerè præstruxisse, et tunc Deum, ante universitatis constitutionem, solum non fuisse, habentem in semetipso proinde Rationem, et in ratione Sermonem, quem secundum a se faceret *agitando intra se*," p. 236.

[1] C. 6. Tertullian refers to Prov. viii. 22, introducing the quotation by the words, "Itaque Sophiam quoque exaudi, ut secundam personam *conditam*;" words which would at first sight seem to imply that the second Person in the Trinity was created; but he adds, "In *sensu suo* scilicet condens et generans (Deus)." Part of c. 7 is employed in proving the identity of the Word and Wisdom of God. Compare *adv. Hermogenem*, c. 20.

[2] Semler infers that, previously to this prolation, the Word had no distinct personality.

[3] C. 7. "Hæc est nativitas perfecta Sermonis, dum ex Deo procedit: *conditus* ab eo primum ad cogitatum in nomine Sophiæ—dehinc *generatus* ad effectum."

from that period. It is, however, certain that our author intended to assert the distinct personality of the λόγος ἐνδιαθέτος.

One of the objections urged by Praxeas was, that the Word of God meant nothing more than the Word of His mouth—not a distinct agent, but the emission of His voice, to which, in metaphorical language, agency was ascribed. "What," he asked, "do you make the Word a substance, when it is in truth a voice, a sound proceeding from the mouth; and, as the grammarians say, an impulse given to the air, and intelligible through the hearing?"[1] To this objection Tertullian answers, that the expressions in Scripture respecting the Word are of such a nature that they imply a Person, whom we call the Son, distinct from the Father; and that they cannot be accounted for on the supposition that they are metaphorical. Can the Word, of whom it is said that *without Him nothing was made that was made*, be supposed to be a mere empty sound? Can that which is without substance, create substances? "Whatever, then," concludes Tertullian, "may be the substance of the Word, I call that substance a Person, and give it the name of Son; and while I acknowledge a Son, I maintain that He is second to the Father."[2] Thus our author determines the first question which he proposed to discuss—whether there is a Son?

We have seen that Tertullian, in speaking of the generation of the Son, uses the words *protulit* and *procedit*.[3] He thinks it therefore necessary to refute by anticipation the charge of introducing the Valentinian προβολὴ, prolation of Æons.[4] "Their prolation," he says, "implies an entire separation of the substance emitted—mine does not prevent its most intimate union with that from which it proceeds." In order to explain his meaning, he borrows illustrations from natural objects. The three persons in the Trinity stand to each other in the relation of the root, the shrub, and the fruit; of the fountain, the river, and the cut from the river; of the sun, the ray, and the terminating

[1] C. 7. "Ergo, inquis, das aliquam substantiam esse Sermonem, Spiritu et Sophiæ traditione constructam? Plane." And again: "Quid est enim, dices, sermo nisi vox et sonus oris, et sicut Grammatici tradunt, aer offensus, intelligibilis auditu? cæterum vacuum nescio quid et inane et incorporale?"

[2] "Quæcunque ergo substantia Sermonis fuit, illam dico personam, et illi nomen Filii vindico; et dum Filium agnosco, secundum a Patre defendo." The expression, "Secundum a Patre," according to Semler, implies a complete separation of the Son from the Father—a separation of substance; but whoever reads the following chapter (viii.) will be convinced that such was not Tertullian's notion.

[3] Note 4, p. 261. [4] C. 8.

point of the ray.[1] For these illustrations he professes himself indebted to the revelations of the Paraclete. In later times, divines have occasionally resorted to similar illustrations, for the purpose of familiarising the doctrine of the Trinity to the mind; nor can any danger arise from the proceeding, so long as we recollect that they are illustrations, not arguments—that we must not draw conclusions from them, or think that whatever may be truly predicated of the illustration may be predicated with equal truth of that which it was designed to illustrate.

"Notwithstanding, however, the intimate union which subsists between the Father, Son, and Holy Ghost, we must be careful," Tertullian continues, "to distinguish between their Persons."[2] In his representations of this distinction, he sometimes uses expressions which in after times, when controversy had introduced greater precision of language, were studiously avoided by the orthodox. Thus he calls the Father the whole substance; the Son a derivation from or portion of the whole.[3] In proving the distinction of Persons he lays particular stress on John xiv. 16.[4] He contends also that Father and Son are correlative terms, one of which implies the existence of the other: there cannot be a Father without a Son, or a Son without a Father.[5] Consequently the doctrine of Praxeas, which confounds the Father and Son, must be erroneous. To this argument Praxeas replied, that nothing is impossible with God—that He, who could make a barren woman and even a virgin bear, could make Himself at once both Father and Son.[6] In support of this assertion he quoted the first verse of Genesis, in which he appears to have read, *In principio Deus fecit sibi filium.*[7] Tertullian rejoins, that

1 "Protulit enim Deus Sermonem, quemadmodum etiam Paracletus docet, sicut radix fruticem, et fons fluvium, et Sol radium;" quoted in note 1, p. 10 of chap. i. Again, "Tertius enim est Spiritus a Deo et Filio, sicut tertius a radice, fructus ex frutice; et tertius a fonte, rivus ex flumine; et tertius a Sole, apex ex radio." I know not whether I have rightly translated the words *rivus* and *apex*. Let me take this opportunity of observing that I undertake only to state, not always to explain or comprehend, Tertullian's notions.

2 C. 9.

3 "Pater enim tota substantia est, filius vero derivatio totius et portio, sicut ipse profitetur, *quia Pater major me est.*" Semler supposes *derivatio* to be a translation of ἀπόῤῥοια, a word which he states to have been rightly rejected by Irenæus and others. See c. 14, "Pro modulo derivationis," and c. 26. Bull, sect. 2, c. 7, p. 95.

4 "I will pray the Father, and He shall give you *another* Comforter—even the Spirit of Truth."

5 C. 10.

6 It appears from this passage that Praxeas admitted the miraculous conception.

7 C. 5. "Aiunt quidem et Genesin in Hebraico ita incipere, *In principio Deus fecit sibi filium.*" Semler doubts the truth of Tertullian's assertion. His note is, "*Mirum est sic quosdam finxisse.*"

our business is to inquire what God has done, not to conjecture what He can do; or to infer that, because He can produce a certain event, He has produced it. He could have given men wings, but He has not given them. In God, will and power are the same; what, therefore, He wills not to do, that in one sense He cannot do. Tertullian proceeds to say that Praxeas, in order to establish his point, ought to produce passages of Scripture in which the absolute identity of the Father and Son is as clearly expressed as is the distinction of Persons in the passages produced by the orthodox.[1] Our author then alleges various passages, many of them from the Old Testament,[2] and dwells particularly on Genesis i. 26—where God, when about to create man, speaks in the plural number, "Let *us* make man in our image, after our likeness."[3]

"But how," asked Praxeas, "do you clear yourself of the charge of polytheism — of teaching a plurality of gods?"[4] Having first shown by copious quotations from Scripture that the names Deus and Dominus are applied to Christ, and consequently that the sacred writers may with equal justice be accused of inculcating polytheism,[5] Tertullian answers, that "the orthodox never speak of two Gods or two Lords, though they affirm that each Person in the Trinity is God and Lord.[6] The design of those passages in the Old Testament, in which two Gods or two Lords are mentioned, was to prepare the minds of men to acknowledge Christ, when He should appear, as God and Lord. But now that Christ has appeared, the necessity for using this language has ceased, and we speak only of one God and one Lord. When, therefore, we have occasion to mention both the Father and Son, we imitate St. Paul, and call the Father, God; the Son, Lord.[7] When to mention the Son alone, we again imitate St. Paul, and call Him God."[8] "If," adds Tertullian, "you require additional proof

[1] C. 11. Tertullian here uses an expression which Semler conceives to savour of Arianism. "Probare autem tam aperte debebis ex Scripturis, quam nos probamus *illum sibi Filium fecisse Sermonem suum.*" But Tertullian had before said, in speaking of the Reason and Word of God, "Cum ratione enim suâ cogitans atque disponens Sermonem eam efficiebat, quam Sermone tractabat," c. 5. See also *adv. Marcionem*, l. ii. c. 27. "Sermonem ejus, quem ex semetipso proferendo filium fecit."

[2] Isa. xlii. 1, lxi. 1; Ps. cx. 1.

[3] C. 12. "Cum quibus enim faciebat hominem, et quibus faciebat similem? Cum Filio quidem, qui erat induturus hominem; Spiritu vero, qui erat sanctificaturus hominem; quasi cum ministris et arbitras, ex unitate Trinitatis, loquebatur." The Jews supposed the Almighty in this verse to speak to the angels.

[4] C. 15.

[5] For instance, Tertullian refers to Ps. xlv. 7, 8, cx. 1; Isa. xlv. 14, liii. 1; Gen. xix. 14; John i. 1.

[6] Compare c. 19.

[7] Rom. i. 4.

[8] Rom. ix. 5.

of our abhorrence of polytheism, you may find it in our refusal to acknowledge two Gods and two Lords, although by making the acknowledgment we might escape the pains of martyrdom."

Tertullian proceeds to argue that a distinction of Persons in the Godhead affords the only means of reconciling some apparent inconsistencies in the sacred writings.[1] At one time God says to Moses that no man can see His face and live;[2] at another we read that God appeared to Abraham, Jacob, and the prophets. These apparent contradictions can only be reconciled by supposing that it was the Son who appeared.[3] "But what," asked Praxeas, "do you gain by this supposition? Is not the Son, who is the Word and Spirit, equally invisible with the Father? And if it was the Son who conversed with Moses, it was the face of the Son which no man could see and live; you in fact establish the identity of the Father and Son. Father and Son are only names applied to the same God; the former, when He is invisible; the latter, when visible." "We grant," answers Tertullian, "that the Son, inasmuch as He is God, and Word, and Spirit, is invisible; but He was seen by the prophets in visions, and conversed with Moses face to face at the time of the transfiguration; for in that event was accomplished the promise made by God to speak with Moses face to face.[4] The New Testament confirms this distinction between the Father, who was never seen, and the Son, who appeared in early times in visions, but afterwards in the flesh.[5] The Son not only made all things, but has from the beginning conducted the government of this world.[6] To Him all power was given. He it was who executed judgment upon mankind, by causing the deluge, and by destroying Sodom and Gomorrah. He it was who descended to converse with man, appearing to Abraham, the patriarchs, and the prophets in visions, and thus as it were preparing Himself for His future residence on earth, when He was to assume the form and substance of man, and to become subject to human infirmities.[7] Praxeas, on the contrary, ignorantly imputes all these acts to the Father, and supposes the Omnipotent, Invisible God, who dwells

[1] C. 14.
[2] Ex. xxxiii. 13, 18, 20.
[3] Compare *adv. Judæos*, c. 9; *adv. Marcionem*, l. iii. cc. 6, 9; l. iv. cc. 10, 13; l. v. c. 19: *de Carne Christi*, c. 6.
[4] Num. xii. 2.
[5] C. 15. We have seen, chap. i. note 2, p. 12, that Tertullian applies to the Holy Spirit the names Christi Vicarius, Domini Vicarius. *De Virginibus velandis*, c. 1. In like manner he calls Christ, Vicarius Patris. *Adv. Marcionem*, l. iii. c. 6; *adv. Praxeam*, c. 24.
[6] C. 16.
[7] Compare c. 12.

in light inaccessible, to have been seen by man and to have suffered thirst and hunger. He makes this supposition, because the attributes and titles of God are ascribed in Scripture to Him who appeared to man, forgetting that those attributes and titles equally belong to the Son, though not precisely in the same manner as to the Father."[1]

Our author next enters upon the consideration of those passages of Scripture which were urged by Praxeas in proof of the identity of the Father and Son.[2] When it is said, for instance, that *there is one God the Father, and besides Him there is no other*, Tertullian affirms that the existence of the Son is not denied, who is indeed one God with the Father.[3] "These," he observes, "and similar expressions were directed against the idolatry and polytheism of the heathen; or designed to confute by anticipation the notions of those heretics who feigned another God by whom Christ was sent, distinct from the Creator. The error of Praxeas arises from confining his attention to those passages which favour his own opinion, and overlooking those which clearly bespeak a distinction of Persons, without however violating the unity of the Godhead." Praxeas appears to have insisted particularly on the following texts in St. John's Gospel:—*I and my Father are one. He who has seen me has seen the Father also. I in my Father, and my Father in me.*[4] "To these few texts," observes Tertullian, "he wishes to make the whole of the Old and New Testaments bend; whereas, had he been really desirous of discovering the truth, he would have sought for such an interpretation of them as would have reconciled them to the rest of Scripture." Our author then proceeds to show, by a minute analysis of St. John's Gospel, that the Father and Son are constantly spoken of as distinct Persons.[5] With respect to the first of the texts alleged by Praxeas—*I and my Father are one*, or as it stood in his Latin version, *Ego et Pater unum sumus*—he animadverts severely upon the folly of that heretic in urging it, who ought to have seen in the first place that two Persons are mentioned, *Ego et Pater;* in the next that the word *sumus* implies a plurality of persons.[6] "If," he continues, "the masculine noun *unus* had been used instead of the neuter *unum*, the passage might have afforded some countenance to the doctrine of Praxeas,—since *unus* might

[1] C. 17. [2] Cc. 18, 19. [3] C. 20. Isa. lxv. 5.
[4] C. 10, ver. 30, 38, and c. 14, ver. 10. [5] Cc. 21, 23, 24.
[6] C. 22. Tertullian's interpretation of the second text will be found in c. 24.

mean one with reference to number, whereas *unum* can only imply unity of substance." With respect to the third text, *I in my Father, and my Father in me*, Tertullian's remark is that Christ had just before referred to the miracles which He had wrought. He meant, therefore, to affirm that He possessed the same power as the Father; that they were *one* as to the power of working miracles. Our author urges incidentally, as an argument against the doctrine of Praxeas, that the Jews in his day did not look for the coming of the Father, but of a distinct Person—the anointed of the Father.

Tertullian comes at last to those passages relating to the mission of the Paraclete,[1] which, as has been already remarked, he conceived to afford decisive proof of the distinction of Persons in the Trinity. In his comment upon them, he has been supposed to allude to the celebrated verse in the First Epistle of St. John, which contains the three heavenly witnesses. It is not my intention to engage in the general controversy respecting the genuineness of the verse; but it may be expected that I should state my opinion upon that part of the question in which Tertullian is immediately concerned. We have seen that, according to him, Praxeas confounded the Persons in the Trinity; though, if we may judge from his mode of conducting the controversy, it turned principally upon the Persons of the Father and the Son. Praxeas quoted in support of his opinion, *Ego et Pater unum sumus*.[2] Tertullian replied, "That verse is directly against you; for though it declares a unity of substance in the Father and Son, it also declares a duality, if we may coin a word, of Persons." Having established his point with respect to the first and second Persons in the Trinity, Tertullian proceeds to the third. "We have seen," he says, "that the Son promised that, when He had ascended to the Father, He would ask the Father to send another Comforter; and we have seen in what sense He was called *another* Comforter.[3] Of this Comforter the Son says, *He shall take of mine*, as the Son Himself had taken of the Father's.[4] Thus the connexion of the Father in the Son, and of the Son in the Paraclete, makes three coherent Persons, one in the other;

[1] C. 25. See p. 266, note 4. [2] C. 22. [3] C. 9.

[4] "Cæterum *de meo sumet*, inquit, sicut ipse de patris. Ita connexus Patris in Filio, et Filii in Paracleto, tres efficit cohærentes, alterum ex altero; qui tres unum sunt, non unus; quomodo dictum est, *Ego et Pater unum sumus*, ad substantiæ unitatem, non ad numeri singularitatem."

which three are one in substance, *unum;* not one in number, *unus;* in the same manner in which it was said, *I and my Father are one.*" Now in case Tertullian had been acquainted with 1 John v. 7, a verse which as clearly proved, according to his own mode of reasoning, the unity of substance and distinction of Persons in the Father, Son, and Holy Ghost, as *Ego et Pater unum sumus* did in the Father and Son—I would ask whether it is not contrary to all reason to suppose that he would have neglected to quote it, and chosen rather to refer his readers to the latter text (John x. 30) and to John xvi. 14? An attempt has, I am aware, been made to evade the force of this argument, by saying that "Tertullian could not expressly quote 1 John v. 7, because it contains as just a description of the doctrine of Praxeas as that heretic could have given. The second Person in the Trinity is there designated as *the Word;* and Praxeas argued that the Word could not mean a distinct Person, but merely a voice—a sound proceeding from the mouth."[1] But if this reason was sufficient to prevent Tertullian from quoting the verse, it would also have prevented him from alluding to it. It is, however, quite incredible that any such reason should have occurred to him. A considerable portion of his tract is occupied in arguing that the Word (Sermo, not Filius) is a distinct Person from the Father;[2] and in proof of this position he quotes from Psalm xliv. (or xlv.), *Eructavit cor meum sermonem optimum.*[3] Would a writer, who alleged such a passage in support of the distinct personality of the Word, be deterred from quoting 1 John v. 7, because the name of Verbum is there given to the second Person in the Trinity? In my opinion, the passage in Tertullian, far from containing an allusion to 1 John v. 7, furnishes most decisive proof that he knew nothing of the verse. It is not unworthy of remark that throughout this tract, when speaking of the Word, he uses Sermo,[4] and not Verbum.

[1] C. 7.

[2] See cc. 5, 7.

[3] C. 11. "Aut exhibe probationem, quam expostulo, meæ similem; id est, sic Scripturas *eundem* Filium et Patrem ostendere, quemadmodum apud nos distincte Pater et Filius demonstrantur; distincte inquam, non divise. Sicut ego profero dictum a Deo, *Eructavit cor meum Sermonem optimum;* sic tu contra opponas alicubi dixisse Deum, Eructavit *me* cor meum Sermonem optimum; ut ipse sit et qui eructavit et quod eructavit; et ipse qui protulerit et qui prolatus sit, si ipse est et Sermo et Deus." This argument, in favour of the distinct personality of the Word, is lost in our version, *My heart is inditing of a good matter.* See Porson *to Travis,* p. 260.

[4] A great outcry was raised against Erasmus for translating λόγος, *Sermo,* in his version of the New Testament. See his Apology de *In principio erat Sermo,* Opera, tom. ix. p. 111, ed. Lugd. Bat. 1706, and his note on John i. 1.

To return to Tertullian's argument against Praxeas:—after briefly referring to different passages in the Gospels of St. Matthew and St. Luke, which prove the existence of the Son as a distinct Person from the Father,[1] he proceeds to the two remaining questions which he proposed to discuss—Who the Son is, and how He exists. In order to get rid of our author's conclusion respecting the distinction of Persons,[2] Praxeas contended that, in the passages on which it was founded, the Son meant the flesh, that is man, that is Jesus;[3] the Father meant the Spirit, that is God, that is Christ. "Thus," observes Tertullian, "he contradicts himself; for if Jesus and Christ are different Persons, the Son and Father are different—since the Son is Jesus and the Father Christ. Nor is this all; for he also divides the Person of Christ." Here our author undertakes to explain in what manner the Word was made flesh.[4] He was not transfigured into flesh, but put on flesh. Transfiguration implies the destruction of that which before existed. Neither must we suppose that the Word was so confounded with the flesh as to produce a third substance, in the same manner in which gold mixed with silver produces what is called electrum. Christ was both God and man:[5]—the Word and the flesh, that is, the divine and human natures were united in His Person, but were not confounded. Each displayed itself in its peculiar operations: in the former He worked miracles;[6] in the latter He hungered, thirsted, wept, was sorrowful even unto death, and died. "If," adds Tertullian, "we attend only to the meaning of the word Christus, we shall perceive the absurdity of supposing that the Father and Christ are one Person.[7] Christus means one who is anointed—anointed consequently by another; but by whom could the Father be anointed?" Tertullian concludes the treatise with observing that the doctrine of the Trinity constituted the great difference between the faith of a Jew and a Christian.[8] Praxeas, therefore, by confounding the Son and

[1] C. 26.

[2] C. 27.

[3] From this statement Lardner argues that Praxeas was not a Patripassian, since he believed that the Son alone suffered. *History of Heretics*, c. 20, sect. 7, 8.

[4] See the passage quoted in chap. vi. p. 225, note 2.

[5] "Sed hæc vox carnis et animæ, id est hominis, non Sermonis nec Spiritûs, id est non Dei, propterea emissa est ut impassibilem Deum ostenderet, qui sic filium dereliquit, dum hominem ejus tradidit in mortem," c. 30. The meaning seems to be that, as man, Christ had a body and soul; as God, He had also the Spirit, which left Him on the cross, and by the loss of which He became subject to death. Compare *de Carne Christi*, cc. 5, 17.

[6] Compare c. 16. *Apology*, c. 21. "Ostendens se esse λόγον Dei," etc.

[7] C. 28.

[8] C. 31.

the Holy Ghost with the Father, carried the believer back to Judaism.

After the detailed account which has been given of the tract *against Praxeas*, we need scarcely observe that Tertullian maintained a real Trinity; or, in the words of our first Article, that "in the unity of the Godhead there be three Persons of one substance, power, and eternity." Semler, in one of his notes, affirms that Tertullian was the earliest writer who used the words Trinitas and Persona, in speaking of the Persons in the Godhead.[1] He also asserts that Tertullian borrowed them from the Valentinians; but this assertion is unsupported by proof. There is undoubtedly a passage in the treatise *de Animâ*[2] in which he uses the word Trinitas to express the Valentinian distinction of men into three different species—spiritual, animal, and material; but it does not therefore follow that he borrowed the word from the Valentinians; for he has in the very same tract applied it to the Platonic division of the soul into λογικὸν, θυμικὸν, and ἐπιθυμητικόν.[3] We find also in the tract *de Resurrectione Carnis*, the expression "Trina Virtus Dei;"[4] but it is employed to denote the triple exercise of God's power, in rendering the devil subject to man, in raising the body of man from the grave, and in calling him to judgment hereafter.

Our analysis of the treatise *against Praxeas* further proves that the opinions of Tertullian respecting the Son and the Holy Ghost essentially coincided with the doctrines of our Church. According to him, "the Son, which is the Word of the Father,[5] begotten from everlasting of the Father, the very and eternal God, of one substance with the Father, took man's nature in the womb of the Blessed Virgin, of her substance;[6] so that two whole and

[1] C. 8. The word Trinitas occurs also in cc. 2, 11.

[2] C. 21. "Ut adhuc Trinitas Valentiniana cædatur." See also *de Præscriptione Hæreticorum*, c. 7. "Trinitas hominis apud Valentinum."

[3] C. 16. "Ecce enim tota hæc Trinitas et in Domino: rationale—indignativum—et concupiscentivum." See chap. iii. p. 99.

[4] C. 28. There is a singular representation of the Trinity in the tract *de Pudicitiâ*, c. 21, *sub fine*. "Nam et Ecclesia proprie et principaliter ipse est Spiritus, in quo est Trinitas unius divinitatis, Pater et Filius et Spiritus Sanctus. Illam Ecclesiam congregat quam Dominus in tribus posuit." We have already on more than one occasion referred to the notion, adopted by Tertullian after he became a Montanist, that three persons constitute a Church.

[5] *Adv. Praxeam*, c. 5.

[6] *Apology*, c. 21. "Necesse est igitur pauca de Christo, ut Deo.—Hunc (τὸν λόγον) ex Deo prolatum dicimus, et prolatione generatum, et idcirco Filium Dei et Deum dictum ex unitate substantiæ: nam et Deus Spiritus. Et quum radius ex

perfect natures, that is, the Godhead and manhood, were joined together in one Person,[1] never to be divided,[2] whereof is one Christ, very God and very man, who truly suffered, was dead and buried." According to him, "Christ did truly rise again from death, and took again His body, with flesh, bones, and all things appertaining to the perfection of man's nature, wherewith He ascended into heaven, and there sitteth until He return to judge all men at the last day."[3] Lastly, according to him, "The Holy Ghost, proceeding from the Father and the Son, is of one substance, majesty, and glory with the Father, very and eternal God."[4]

But though we think that Tertullian's opinions on these points coincided in the main with the doctrines of our Church, we are far from meaning to assert that expressions may not occasionally be found which are capable of a different interpretation; and which were carefully avoided by the orthodox writers of later times, when the controversies respecting the Trinity had introduced greater precision of language. Pamelius has thought it necessary to put the reader on his guard against certain of these expressions; and Semler has noticed with a sort of ill-natured industry every passage in the tract *against Praxeas* in which there is any appearance of contradiction, or which will bear a

sole porrigitur, portio ex summâ, sed sol exit in radio, quia solis est radius: nec separatur substantia, sed extenditur. Ita de Spiritu Spiritus, et de Deo Deus, ut lumen de lumine accensum—Iste igitur Dei radius, ut retro semper prædicabatur, delapsus in Virginem quandam, et in utero ejus caro figuratus, nascitur homo Deo mistus. Caro Spiritu instructa nutritur, adolescit, affatur, docet, operatur, et Christus est." Tertullian then proceeds to describe Christ's crucifixion, His resurrection on the third day, and ascension. Compare *adv. Marcionem*, l. iii. c. 12; *de Spectaculis*, c. 25. We learn incidentally from the passage in the *Apology* that the Jews expected a mere man in the Messiah.

[1] "Aliter non diceretur homo Christus sine carne; nec hominis filius sine aliquo parente homine; sicut nec Deus sine Spiritu Dei, nec Dei filius sine Deo patre. Ita utriusque substantiæ census hominem et Deum exhibuit: hinc natum, inde non natum; hinc carneum, inde spiritalem; hinc infirmum, inde præfortem; hinc morientem, inde viventem." *De Carne Christi*, c. 5.

[2] I have observed nothing in Tertullian's writings which corresponds to the expression *never to be divided*.

[3] *Adv. Praxeam*, c. 30; *de Carne Christi*, c. 24. "Sed bene quod idem veniet de cœlis, qui est passus: idem omnibus apparebit, qui est resuscitatus; et videbunt, et agnoscent, qui eum confixerunt; utique ipsam carnem in quam sævierunt; sine quâ nec ipse esse poterit, nec agnosci." See particularly *de Res. Carnis*, c. 51.

[4] "Tertius enim est Spiritus a Deo et Filio, sicut tertius a radice fructus ex frutice, et tertius a fonte rivus ex flumine, et tertius a sole apex ex radio; nihil tamen a matrice alienatur, a quâ proprietates suas ducit." *Adv. Praxeam*, c. 8. We have seen that in another place Tertullian speaks as if the Holy Ghost was from the Father through the Son. "Quia Spiritum non aliunde puto quam a Patre per Filium," c. 4.

construction favourable to the Arian tenets.[1] Bull, also, who conceives the language of Tertullian to be explicit and correct on the subject of the pre-existence and the consubstantiality, admits that he occasionally uses expressions at variance with the co-eternity of Christ. For instance, in the tract *against Hermogenes* we find the following passage:[2]—"Quia et Pater Deus est, et judex Deus est; non tamen ideo Pater et judex semper, quia Deus semper. Nam nec Pater potuit esse ante Filium, nec judex ante delictum. Fuit autem tempus quum et delictum et Filius non fuit, quod Judicem et qui Patrem Deum faceret." Here it is expressly asserted that there was a time when the Son was not. Perhaps, however, a reference to the peculiar tenets of Hermogenes will enable us to account for this assertion. That heretic affirmed, as we shall shortly have occasion to show more in detail, that matter was eternal, and argued thus: "God was always God and always Lord; but the word Lord implies the existence of something over which He was Lord; unless, therefore, we suppose the eternity of something distinct from God, it is not true that He was always Lord." Tertullian boldly answered that God was not always Lord; and that in Scripture we do not find Him called Lord until the work of creation was completed. In like manner he contended that the titles of Judge and Father imply the existence of sin and of a Son. As, therefore, there was a time when neither sin nor the Son existed, the titles of Judge and Father were not at that time applicable to God. Tertullian could scarcely mean to affirm, in direct opposition to his own statements in the tract *against Praxeas*, that there was ever a time when the λόγος, or Ratio, or Sermo internus, did not exist.[3] But with respect to Wisdom and the Son, Sophia and Filius, the case is different. Tertullian assigns to both a begin-

[1] We call it an ill-natured industry, because the true mode of ascertaining a writer's opinions is, not to fix upon particular expressions, but to take the general tenor of his language. If anything is expressly affirmed in the tract *against Praxeas*, it is that the Son is of the substance of the Father; yet Semler, finding in c. 27 this passage, "Quis Deus in eâ natus? Sermo, et Spiritus qui cum Sermone de Patris voluntate natus est," makes the following remark: "Sic, *i.e.* de Patris *voluntate*, Ariani, non ἐξ οὐσίας."

[2] C. 3. Compare c. 18. "Agnoscat, ergo, Hermogenes idcirco etiam Sophiam Dei natam et conditam prædicari, ne quid innatum et inconditum præter solum Deum crederemus. Si enim intra Dominum, quod ex ipso et in ipso fuit, sine initio non fuit—Sophia scilicet ipsius, exinde nata et condita, ex quo in sensu Dei ad opera mundi disponenda cœpit agitari; multo magis non capit sine initio quicquam fuisse, quod extra Dominum fuerit."

[3] With respect to the Sermo externus, Tertullian speaks of a time antecedent to his emission. "Nam etsi Deus *nondum* Sermonem suum miserat." *Adv. Praxeam*, c. 5.

ning of existence. Sophia was created or formed in order to devise the plan of the universe; and the Son was begotten in order to carry that plan into effect.[1] Bull appears to have given an accurate representation of the matter when he says that, according to our author, the Reason and Spirit of God, being the substance of the Word and Son, were co-eternal with God; but that the titles of Word and Son were not strictly applicable until the former had been emitted to arrange, the latter begotten to execute, the work of creation.[2] Without, therefore, attempting to explain, much less to defend, all Tertullian's expressions and reasonings, we are disposed to acquiesce in the statement given by Bull of his opinions: "Ex quibus omnibus liquet, quam temerè ut solet, pronuntiaverit Petavius, *Quod ad æternitatem attinet Verbi, palam esse, Tertullianum minime illam agnovisse.*[3] Mihi sane, atque, ut arbitror, post tot apertissima testimonia a me adducta, lectori etiam meo prorsus contrarium constat; nisi verò, quod non credo, luserit Petavius in vocabulo *verbi.* Nam Filium Dei, docet quidem Tertullianus Verbum sive Sermonem factum ac denominatum fuisse ab aliquo initio: nempe tum, quando ex Deo Patre exivit cum voce, *Fiat Lux*, ad exornandum universa.[4] Atqui ipsam illam hypostasin, quæ sermo sive verbum et Filius Dei dicitur, æternam credidisse Tertullianum, puto me abunde demonstrâsse."

In speaking also of the Holy Ghost, Tertullian occasionally uses terms of a very ambiguous and equivocal character. He says, for instance, that in Genesis i. 26 God addressed the Son,

[1] C. 7. "Hæc est nativitas perfecta Sermonis, dum ex Deo procedit: *conditus* ab eo primum ad *cogitatum* in nomine Sophiæ—dehinc *generatus* ad effectum."

[2] *Defensio Fidei Nicænæ*, sect. iii. c. 10, p. 242. Bull refers to the following passages in support of his interpretation:—"Sermo autem Spiritu structus est, et, ut ita dixerim, Sermonis corpus est Spiritus. Sermo ergo et in Patre semper, sicut dicit, *Ego in Patre;* et apud Deum semper, sicut scriptum est, *Et Sermo erat apud Deum.*" *Adv. Praxeam*, c. 8. "Nos etiam Sermoni atque rationi, itemque virtuti, per quæ omnia molitum Deum ediximus, propriam *substantiam* Spiritum inscribimus." *Apology*, c. 21. "Quæcunque ergo substantia Sermonis fuit, illam dico Personam, et illi nomen Filii vindico." *Adv. Praxeam*, c. 7. To these may be added, "Quia ipse quoque Sermo, ratione consistens, priorem eam ut substantiam suam ostendat." *Adv. Praxeam*, c. 5. "Virtute et ratione comitatum, et Spiritu fultum." *Apology*, c. 21. "Hic Spiritus Dei idem erit Sermo; sicut enim, Ioanne dicente, *Sermo caro factus est*, Spiritum quoque intelligimus in nomine Sermonis; ita et hic Sermonem quoque agnoscimus in nomine Spiritûs. Nam et Spiritus substantia est Sermonis, et Sermo operatio Spiritûs: et duo unum sunt." *Adv. Praxeam*, c. 26. See, however, *adv. Hermogenem*, c. 45. "Non apparentis solummodo, nec adpropinquantis, sed adhibentis tantos animi sui nisus, Sophiam, valentiam, sensum, sermonem, Spiritum, virtutem."

[3] Sect. 3, c. 10, p. 246.

[4] *Adv. Praxeam*, c. 7, *sub in.*

His Word, the second Person in the Trinity, and the third Person, the Spirit in the Word.[1] Here the distinct personality of the Spirit is expressly asserted, though it is difficult to reconcile the words *Spiritus in sermone* with the assertion. It is, however, certain, both from the general tenor of the tract *against Praxeas*, and from many passages in his other writings, that the distinct personality of the Holy Ghost formed an article of Tertullian's creed.[2] The occasional ambiguity of his language respecting the Holy Ghost is perhaps in part to be traced to the variety of senses in which the word Spiritus is used. It is applied generally to God, for God is a Spirit;[3] and for the same reason to the Son, who is frequently called the Spirit of God,[4] the Spirit of the Creator.[5] Bull also, following Grotius, has shown that the word Spiritus is employed by the Fathers to express the divine nature in Christ.[6]

In our remarks upon the eighth Article of our Church, we stated that, in treating of the tract *against Praxeas*, an opportunity would present itself of ascertaining how far the opinions of Tertullian coincided with the language employed in the Nicene and Athanasian Creeds.[7] That the general doctrine of those creeds is contained in Tertullian's writings cannot, we think, be doubted by any one who has carefully perused them. With respect to particular expresssions, we find that he calls the Son—God of God and Light of Light.[8] In referring to that verse in the fifteenth chapter of St. Paul's First Epistle to the Corinthians in which it is said that Christ died for our sins according to the Scriptures, Tertullian observes that the apostle inserted the words *according to the Scriptures*, for the purpose of reconciling men, by the authority of Scripture, to the startling

[1] *Adv. Praxeam*, c. 12. "Imo, quia jam adhærebat illi filius, secunda Persona, Sermo ipsius; et tertia, Spiritus in Sermone."

[2] See for instance *ad Martyres*, c. 3. "Bonum agonem subituri estis, in quo agonothetes Deus vivus est; xystarches Spiritus Sanctus; corona æternitas; brabium Angelicæ substantiæ politia in cœlis, gloria in secula seculorum. Itaque epistates vester Christus Iesus."

[3] *Adv. Marcionem*, l. ii. c. 9, *sub in.*

[4] *De Oratione*, c. 1, *sub in.* "Dicimus enim et Filium suo nomine eatenus invisibilem, qua Sermo et Spiritus Dei." *Adv. Praxeam*, c. 14. See also c. 26; *adv. Marcionem*, l. v. c. 8.

[5] *Adv. Marcionem*, l. iii. c. 6. "Nam quoniam in Esaiâ jam tunc Christus, Sermo scilicet et Spiritus Creatoris, Ioannem prædicârat," l. iv. c. 33, *sub fine.*

[6] *Defensio Fidei Nicænæ*, sect. 1, c. 2, p. 18.

[7] Chap. v. p. 160.

[8] See the passage from the *Apology* quoted in note 6, p. 273 of this chapter, and *adv. Praxeam*, c. 15, "Nam etsi Deus Sermo, sed apud Deum, quia ex Deo Deus."

declaration that the Son of God had been made subject to death.[1] With respect to the expressions in the Athanasian Creed, we find Tertullian, while he asserts the distinction of the Persons in the Trinity, careful to maintain the unity of the substance; or, in the language of the creed, neither to confound the persons nor divide the substance.[2] We find also, in the tract *against Hermogenes*,[3] an expression which, although there used without any reference to the Trinity, bears a strong resemblance to that clause in the Athanasian Creed which declares that "in the Trinity none is afore or after other; none is greater or less than another." The creed speaks of the Christian verity as compelling us to acknowledge that every Person in the Trinity by Himself is God and Lord, and of the Catholic religion as enforcing the unity of God. Tertullian speaks of the Christian verity as proclaiming the unity.[4] On the subject of the Incarnation, the reader who compares the passages in the note with the corresponding clauses in the creed will be almost disposed to conclude that the framer of the creed had Tertullian's expressions immediately in his view.[5]

There is, however, a passage in the tract *de Carne Christi*, which appears at first sight to be at variance with the following clause of the creed, *One, not by conversion of the Godhead into flesh*.[6] The heretics against whom Tertullian was contending argued that "God could not possibly be converted into man, so as to be born and to be embodied in the flesh; because that which is

[1] "Nam et Apostolus, non sine onere pronuntians *Christum mortuum*, adjicit *secundum Scripturas*, ut duritiam pronuntiationis Scripturarum auctoritate molliret, et scandalum auditori everteret." *Adv. Praxeam*, c. 29.

[2] "Alium autem quomodo accipere debeas, jam professus sum; personæ, non substantiæ nomine; ad distinctionem, non ad divisionem." *Adv. Praxeam*, c. 12.

[3] Tertullian is arguing upon the consequences which he conceived to flow from the doctrines of Hermogenes respecting the eternity of matter. "That doctrine," he says, "places matter on a perfect equality with God." "Neutrum dicimus altero esse minorem, sive majorem; neutrum altero humiliorem, sive superiorem," c. 7.

[4] "Sed veritas Christiana districtè pronuntiavit, Deus si non unus est, non est." *Adv. Marcionem*, l. i. c. 3.

[5] "Sed enim invenimus illum directò, et Deum et hominem expositum—certe usquequaque Filium Dei et Filium hominis, quum Deum et hominem, sine dubio secundum utramque substantiam, in suâ proprietate distantem; quia neque Sermo aliud quam Deus, neque caro aliud quam homo—Videmus duplicem statum; non confusum, sed conjunctum in unâ Personâ, Deum et hominem Iesum." *Adv. Praxeam*, c. 27. See also the passage from c. 30, quoted in note 5, p. 272, where it is said that Christ, as man, had a soul and flesh. For the inferiority of the Son in His human nature, see c. 16, referred to in note 6, p. 272.

[6] C. 3. "'Sed ideo,' inquis, 'nego Deum in hominem verè conversum, ita ut nasceretur et carne corporaretur' (Rigault has operaretur); 'quia qui sine fine est,

eternal must necessarily be inconvertible. Conversion into a different state is the termination of the former state. If the Godhead was converted into manhood, it was entirely lost." To this argument Tertullian replied, that "although it might be right with respect to all other natures, it was not so with reference to the divine nature. We read in Scripture that at different times angels were converted into the human shape, and yet did not cease to be angels. Much more then might God assume the nature of man, and yet continue to be God." Here Tertullian appears to admit that in the mystery of the Incarnation there was a conversion of the Godhead into flesh, though he disallows the inference drawn by the heretics from it. If, however, we compare this passage with another in the tract *against Praxeas*, we shall find our author's opinion, when accurately stated, to have been, that God took upon Himself manhood.[1]

The present appears to be the proper opportunity for observing that, among other appellations given by Tertullian to Christ, we find those of Persona Dei and Spiritus Personæ Dei; the former derived from Psalm iv. 6,[2] which stands thus in the Septuagint version, ἐσημειώθη ἐφ' ἡμᾶς τὸ φῶς τοῦ προσώπου σου, Κύριε; the latter from an erroneous reading of Lamentations iv. 20, πνεῦμα προσώπου ἡμῶν, Χριστὸς Κύριος, where αὐτοῦ appears to have been substituted for ἡμῶν.[3]

One of the questions on which theological ingenuity has

etiam inconvertibilis sit necesse est. Converti enim in aliud finis est pristini. Non competit ergo conversio cui non competit finis.' Plane natura convertibilium eâ lege est, ne permaneant in eo quod convertitur in iis; et (ut) ita non permanendo pereant; dum perdunt convertendo quod fuerunt. Sed nihil Deo par est; natura ejus ab omnium rerum conditione distat. Si ergo quæ a Deo distant, aut a quibus Deus distat, quum convertuntur, amittunt quod fuerunt; ubi erit diversitas divinitatis a cæteris rebus, nisi ut contrarium obtineat; id est, ut Deus et in omnia converti possit, et qualis est perseverare?"

[1] "Quod ergo Angelis inferioribus licuit, uti conversi in corpulentiam humanam Angeli nihilominus permanerent; hoc tu potentiori Deo auferas? quasi non valuerit Christus, *vere hominem indutus*, Deus perseverare?" Compare *adv. Praxeam*, c. 27, quoted also in chap. vi. note 2, p. 225. "Igitur Sermo in carne; dum et de hoc quærendum quomodo Sermo caro sit factus? utrumne quasi transfiguratus in carne, *an indutus carnem?* imo, indutus."

[2] "Cui respondet Spiritus in Psalmo ex providentiâ futuri: *Significatum est*, inquit, *super nos lumen personæ tuæ, Domine.* Persona autem Dei, Christus Dominus." *Adv. Marcionem*, l. v. c. 11.

[3] "Nam et Scriptura quid dicit? *Spiritus personæ ejus, Christus Dominus.* Ergo Christus personæ paternæ Spiritus est," etc. *Adv. Praxeam*, c. 14, *sub fine.* But in the third book *against Marcion*, c. 6, we find "*Personam Spiritûs nostri, Christum Dominum.*" Rigault, however, in this passage, reads "Spiritus personæ ejus, Christus Dominus." See Jerome's comment on the verse.

exercised itself is, whether the flesh of Christ was corruptible or incorruptible. We have seen that Valentinus asserted a difference between Christ's flesh and human flesh. In replying to this assertion, Tertullian observes, that Christ would not have been perfect man had not His flesh been human, and consequently corruptible.[1] Tertullian ascribes ubiquity to Christ as God, but not as the conductor of the gospel economy.[2] We find also in his writings a notion, derived from Isaiah liii. 3, which was very common among the early Fathers, that the personal appearance of Christ was mean and ignoble.[3]

The next heretic in Mosheim's catalogue is Hermogenes. He was a painter by profession, and contemporary with our author, from whose language it might be inferred that he actually apostatised from Christianity to paganism;[4] but I believe Tertullian's meaning to be, that he adopted the notions of the pagan philosophers, the Stoics especially, respecting matter, which he conceived to be self-existent, and consequently eternal. From this matter, according to him, God made all things. His mode of arguing was, "Either God made all things from Himself, or from something, or from nothing.[5] He could not make them from Himself, because they would then be parts of Himself; but this, the divine nature, which is indivisible and always the same, does not allow.[6] He could not make them from nothing, because, being infinitely good, He would not in that case have allowed evil to exist: but evil does exist; it must consequently have existed independently of God, that is, in matter." Hermogenes urged another argument of a very subtle character, to which we have already had occasion to allude.[7] "There never was a time when the title of Dominus or Lord was not applicable to God; but that title is relative—it implies the existence of something over which God was Lord: that something was

[1] *De Carne Christi*, c. 15.

[2] *Adv. Praxeam*, c. 23. "Habes Filium in terris, habes Patrem in cœlis. Non est separatio ista, sed dispositio divina. Cæterum scimus, Deum etiam intra abyssos esse, et ubique consistere, sed vi et potestate, Filium quoque, ut individuum cum ipso, ubique. Tamen in ipsâ οἰκονομίᾳ, Pater voluit Filium in terris haberi, se vero in cœlis." See Bull, *Defensio Fidei*, sect. 4, c. 3, p. 271.

[3] *De Idololatriâ*, c. 18; *de Carne Christi*, cc. 9, 15; *adv. Marcionem*, l. iii. c. 7, *sub in.*, c. 17, *sub in.*; *adv. Judæos*, c. 14.

[4] *Adv. Hermogenem*, c. 1. "Hermogenis autem doctrina tam novella est; denique ad hodiernum homo in seculo." Compare *de Præscriptione Hæreticorum*, c. 30. "Cæterum et Nigidius nescio quis et Hermogenes, et multi alii qui adhuc ambulant, pervertentes vias Dei." See also *adv. Valentinianos*, c. 16; *de Monogamiâ*, c. 16.

[5] C. 2. [6] Compare c. 39. [7] C. 3. See p. 275.

matter." To this argument Tertullian answers without hesitation that there was a time when the title was not applicable, that is, before the creation—as there was a time when God was neither Father nor Judge; which are also relative terms, implying the existence of a Son, and of sinners to be judged. "If we turn," he adds, "to Scripture, we shall find that, while the work of creation was carrying on, the language is always *God said*, *God saw*, not *the Lord said*, *the Lord saw*; but when it was completed, the title of Lord is introduced, *the Lord God took man whom He had made.*"

Tertullian objects, in the first place, to the opinion of Hermogenes respecting the eternity of matter, that its effect is to introduce two Gods.[1] "You ascribe," he says, "eternity to matter; and thereby invest it with the attributes of the Deity. You join matter with God in the work of creation; for though you may pretend that eternity is the only attribute ascribed to matter, and that the supremacy is still reserved to God,—inasmuch as He is active and matter passive, and He it is who gives a form to matter—yet this is a mere evasion, since the very foundation of your doctrine is, that matter existed independently of God, and consequently out of the range of His power. Nay more, you make matter superior to God.[2] He who grants assistance is surely superior, in that respect at least, to him to whom it is granted. But God, according to your doctrine, could not have made the universe without the assistance of matter. Had God possessed any dominion over matter, He would, before He employed it in the work of creation, have purged it of the evil which He knew to exist in it. You are at least in this dilemma: you must either deny the Omnipotence of God, or admit that God was the Author of evil by voluntarily using matter in the creation of the world. Yet you adopted this notion respecting the eternity of matter, under the idea that you thereby removed from God the imputation of being the Author of evil. Like the other heretics, you were blind to the defects of your own reasoning, and did not perceive that it really furnished no solution of the difficulty."

Tertullian proceeds to inquire whether the reasons for which

[1] Cc. 4, 5, 6, 7, 11, 42. Compare *de Præscriptione Hæreticorum*, c. 33. It is evident that Tertullian here draws consequences from the opinions of Hermogenes, which that heretic himself disavowed. Compare c. 5 with *adv. Marcionem*, l. i, c. 3.

[2] Cc. 8, 9, 10.

Hermogenes imputed evil to matter, might not afford as good ground for imputing it to God Himself.[1] Among other arguments he urges the following:—"If matter is eternal, it is unchangeable in its nature; and that nature, according to Hermogenes, is evil.[2] How then could God create that which is good out of evil matter?[3] Hermogenes ought rather to have said that matter was of a mixed character, both good and evil." "At least," Tertullian continues, "it is more honourable to God to make Him the free and voluntary Author of evil than to make Him as it were the slave of matter, and compelled to use it, although He knew it to be evil, in the work of creation."[4] We find incidental mention of an opinion entertained by some, that the existence of evil was necessary in order to illustrate good by contrast; but Tertullian states that it was not entertained by Hermogenes.[5] Tertullian further argued that by making matter self-existent and eternal, Hermogenes placed it above the Word or Wisdom, who, as begotten of God, had both an Author and beginning of His being.[6] We have already seen in what sense Tertullian ascribed a commencement of existence to the Word or Wisdom.[7]

Hermogenes endeavoured to support his opinions by appealing to Scripture. He began with the very first words of the Book of Genesis, asserting that, by the expression, *In the beginning*, or as it is in the Latin, *In principio*, was meant some principle or substance out of which the heaven and earth were created: as it might be said that the clay is the principle of the vessel which is made from it.[8] Tertullian replies that the words were only designed to mark the commencement of this visible frame of things. But not content with this sound explanation, he has recourse to others of a very different character: he supposes, for instance, that the word *principium* may refer to the Wisdom of God,[9] of whom it is said in the Book of Proverbs, "Dominus condidit me *initium* viarum suarum in opera sua."[10] If, however, this argument is weak, the praise of subtlety at least must be allowed to that which I am about to subjoin. "In every work, for example, in making a table, there must be a combination of

[1] C. 11.
[2] Cc. 12, 13. Hermogenes appears sometimes to have contended that matter was neither good nor evil, c. 37.
[3] The reference is to Gen. i. 21.
[4] C. 14.
[5] C. 15.
[6] Cc. 17, 18.
[7] P. 275.
[8] C. 19.
[9] Cc. 20, 21, 22.
[10] C. 8, ver. 22. The words of the English version are, *The Lord possessed me in the beginning of His way.*

three things—of him who makes—of that which is made—and of that out of which it is made.[1] But in the account of the creation only two of these are mentioned—God the Creator, and the heavens and earth the thing created; we are not told out of what they were created; therefore they were created out of nothing." Is there not here some confusion between what Johnson has called the positive and negative meanings of nothing?

The next passage on which Hermogenes relied was also taken from the first chapter of Genesis: *the earth was without form and void.*[2] The earth here spoken of was, according to him, the matter out of which the present earth and all other things were made. But we will not weary the reader's patience by detailing Tertullian's observations upon this and upon other portions of Scripture alleged by his opponent. Both are justly liable to the charge of drawing inferences which were never intended by the sacred writer.

Having proved to his satisfaction that the universe was not created out of pre-existent matter, Tertullian proceeds to notice the inconsistencies of which Hermogenes was guilty with respect to his supposed matter;[3] saying at one time that it was neither corporeal nor incorporeal—"as if," observes Tertullian, "everything in the universe must not fall under one or other of the two descriptions;"[4] saying at another that it was partly corporeal and partly incorporeal[5]—corporeal, because bodies are formed out of it; incorporeal, because it moves, and motion is incor-

[1] Tertullian urges an argument of a similar nature in c. 34. "It appears," he says, "from the Scriptures, that in the final consummation of all things the universe will be reduced to nothing; we may therefore presume that it was created out of nothing." Hermogenes appears to have interpreted the dissolution of the universe spiritually.

[2] C. 23. Tertullian's Latin is, "Terra autem erat invisibilis et incomposita."

[3] C. 35.

[4] "Nisi fallor enim, omnis res aut corporalis aut incorporalis sit necesse est, ut concedam interim esse aliquid incorporale de substantiis duntaxat, quum ipsa substantia corpus sit rei cujusque." This passage was quoted in note 3, p. 96 of chap. iii. Bull, *Defensio Fidei Nicænæ*, sect. 3, c. 10, p. 236, observes, "Sed Tertulliano solenne est Deo corporales affectiones intrepide adscribere. Unde viri quidam docti existimârunt, revera sensisse Tertullianum, corporeæ esse naturæ Deum; a quibus tamen ego quidem dissentio."

[5] C. 36. The motion ascribed by Hermogenes to matter was of an irregular, turbulent kind, like the bubbling of boiling water in a pot. "Sic enim et ollæ undique ebullientis similitudinem opponis," c. 41. "Materiam vero materiarum, non sibi subditam, non statu diversam, non motu inquietam, non habitu informem," c. 18. See also cc. 28, 42.

poreal. "But in what sense," asks Tertullian, "can motion be made a part of matter? Man moves; but we do not say he is partly corporeal and partly incorporeal, because he has both body and motion. His actions, passions, duties, appetites are incorporeal; but we do not call them parts or portions of his substance. Motion is not a substance, but a particular state of a substance. With equal inconsistency and absurdity Hermogenes sometimes says that matter is neither good nor evil.[1] Moreover, he assigns it a place below God;[2] forgetting that, by assigning it a place, he assigns it limits, and thus admits that it is not infinite—an admission at variance with all his previous reasoning."

Tertullian next alludes to a notion of Hermogenes, that God did not use the whole, but only a portion of this pre-existent matter in the creation of the universe; and notices various absurd consequences which, in his opinion, proceed from the doctrine of Hermogenes: such as that good and evil are substances.[3] He ridicules also the notion that God, in the work of creation, performed no other act than that of merely appearing and drawing near to matter; "as if," he observes, "there ever was a time when God did *not* appear or draw near to matter.[4] On this supposition not only matter, but the universe also, is eternal." "Noli," continues Tertullian, "ita Deo adulari, ut velis illum solo visu et solo accessu tot ac tantas protulisse substantias et non propriis viribus instituisse"—a sentiment for which he is severely reprehended by Bull, who says that he seems to have cared little what he said, if he did but contradict his adversary.[5]

Such were the speculations of Hermogenes on the eternity of

[1] C. 37.

[2] Cc. 38, 39, 40. Hermogenes seems to have contended that matter was infinite only in duration; that is, eternal, not infinite in extent.

[3] C. 41.

[4] C. 44. Hermogenes illustrated his meaning by saying that God brought order out of confused and indigested matter by merely appearing or drawing near to it; as beauty affects the mind of the spectator by its mere appearance, and the magnet attracts iron by mere approximation. "At tu non inquis, pertransiens illam (materiam) facit (Deus) mundum, sed solummodo appropinquans ei, sicut facit quis decor solummodo apparens, et magnes lapis solummodo appropinquans. Quid simile Deus fabricans mundum, et decor vulnerans animum, aut magnes adtrahens ferrum?"

[5] *Defensio Fidei Nicænæ*, sect. 3, c. 10, p. 236. Tertullian afterwards says on the same subject, "Non apparentis (Dei) solummodo, nec adpropinquantis; sed adhibentis tantos animi sui nisus, Sophiam; valentiam, sensum, sermonem, Spiritum, virtutem," c. 45. Compare Warburton, Sermon 2, vol. ix. p. 39. *But what shall we say*, etc. He appears rather to lean to Tertullian's opinion.

matter, and such the arguments by which our author answered him. In one part of his reasoning he must be allowed to have been successful—in showing that the theory of his opponent removed none of the difficulties in which the question respecting the origin of evil is involved. He has also given no slight proof of discretion—a quality for which he is not generally remarkable—in not attempting himself to advance any counter-theory upon that inexplicable subject.

In conformity with the opinions already detailed, Hermogenes maintained that the human soul was made out of matter. This notion Tertullian confuted in an express treatise, entitled *de Censu Animâ, Concerning the Origin of the Soul*, which is not now extant.[1] In our account of Marcion we stated that Tertullian charged that heretic with denying the freedom of the will. We founded this statement on the following passage, in the tract *de Animâ*, in which the name of Hermogenes is coupled with that of Marcion.[2] "Inesse autem nobis τὸ αὐτεξούσιον naturaliter jam et Marcioni ostendimus et Hermogeni." On this passage Lardner observes, "Tertullian asserted human liberty; and I think he does not deny it to have been held by Marcion and Hermogenes."[3] He appears to have forgotten that he had before referred to this very passage as furnishing proof that the Marcionites did not allow the freedom of human actions, but were believers in a kind of necessity.[4] The zeal of Tertullian against Hermogenes was doubtless quickened by the boldness with which that heretic asserted the lawfulness of second marriages.[5] In one place Hermogenes is connected with Nigidius, of whom nothing more is known.[6]

Besides the heretics enumerated by Mosheim in his history of the second century, Tertullian mentions some who belonged to the first. He speaks of Simon Magus;[7] and repeats the story, which had been handed down by Justin Martyr and Irenæus, that a statue had been erected to Simon at Rome, bearing an inscription in which his divinity was recognised.[8] In the tracts

1 "De solo censu animæ congressus Hermogeni, quatenus et istum ex materiæ potius suggestu, quam ex Dei flatu constitisse præsumpsit." *De Animâ*, c. 1. See also cc. 3, 11, and *de Monogamiâ*, c. 16.

2 C. 21.

3 *History of Heretics*, c. 18, sect. 9.

4 *History of Heretics*, c. 10, sect. 15.

5 *Adv. Hermogenem*, c. 1; *de Monogamiâ*, c. 16.

6 *De Præscriptione Hæreticorum*, c. 30.

7 *De Præscriptione Hæreticorum*, cc. 10, 33.

8 *Apology*, c. 13.

*de Idololatriâ*[1] and *de Præscriptione Hæreticorum*,[2] allusions are found to his practice of magic. His disciples pretended that by their magical arts they could call up the souls of the deceased prophets.[3] In the treatise *de Animâ*,[4] it is said that Simon, indignant at the reproof which he received from St. Peter, determined in revenge to oppose the progress of the gospel, and associated with himself in the undertaking a Tyrian prostitute named Helena. He called himself the Supreme Father; Helena his first conception, through whom he formed the design of creating the angels and archangels. She, however, becoming acquainted with the design, went out from the Father into the lower parts of the universe; and there, anticipating his intention, created the angelic powers, who were ignorant of the Father, and were the artificers of this world.[5] They detained her with them through envy; lest, if she went away, they should be deemed the offspring of another—that is, as I interpret the words, not self-existent. Not content with detaining her, they subjected her to every species of indignity, in order that the consciousness of her humiliation might extinguish even the wish to quit them. Thus she was compelled to take the human form; to be confined, as it were, in the bonds of the flesh, and to pass through different female bodies; among the rest through that of the Spartan Helen, until at length she appeared as the Helena of Simon. She was the lost sheep mentioned in the parable, whom Simon descended to recover and restore to heaven. Having effected his purpose, he determined in revenge to deliver mankind from the dominion of the angelic powers; and in order to elude their vigilance, he pretended to assume the human form, appearing as the Son in Judæa, as the Father in Samaria. On this strange account it will be sufficient to remark that it is taken almost *verbatim* from Irenæus.

Tertullian mentions Menander, the Samaritan, as the disciple of Simon Magus and the master of Saturninus.[6] One of his assertions was that he was sent by the Supreme and Secret Power to make all who received his baptism, immortal and incorruptible; in other words, his baptism was itself the resurrection, and delivered all who partook of it from liability to death.[7] Another of his

[1] C. 9. [2] C. 33. [3] *De Animâ*, c. 57. [4] C. 34.

[5] Instead of artificis, we must read artifices, as is evident from the corresponding passage in Irenæus, l. i. c. 20.

[6] *De Animâ*, c. 23.

[7] *De Animâ*, c. 50, from which passage we also learn that Menander dissuaded his followers from encountering martyrdom.

opinions was that the human body was created by angels.[1] Tertullian mentions the Nicolaitans;[2] but says nothing respecting them which may not be immediately inferred from the Book of Revelation.[3]

There is a passage in the tract *de Resurrectione Carnis*, in which, if the reading is correct, Tertullian speaks of heretics who asserted the mortality of the soul.[4]

In the tract *de Jejuniis* our author mentions another heretic of his own day ("apud Jovem, hodiernum de Pythagorâ hæreticum"), who borrowed his tenets from the Pythagorean philosophy.[5]

To this account of the particular heresies mentioned by Tertullian, we will subjoin a few observations collected from his works, which apply generally to them all. We have seen that he traces their origin to the Grecian philosophy,[6] and conceives that their existence was ordained or permitted by God in order to prove the faith of Christians.[7] In the tract *de Præscriptione Hæreticorum* he draws a very unfavourable picture of the heretics in general, and of their modes of proceeding.[8] He says that their practice, like their faith, was without gravity, authority, or discipline—that all was confusion amongst them—that they received indiscriminately every person who came to them, however different his opinions from their own; the mere fact that he joined in opposing the truth being a sufficient recommendation to their favour—that they were puffed up with the conceit of their own knowledge, all being in their own estimation competent to instruct others, and even their women exercising the ministerial functions—that they conferred orders without previous inquiry into the qualifications of the candidates. Passing from their practice to their doctrine, he says that their object was to destroy, not to build up; to unsettle, not to instruct; to pervert the

1 *De Res. Carnis*, c. 5.

2 *De Præscriptione Hæreticorum*, c. 33; *adv. Marcionem*, l. i. c. 29; *de Pudicitiâ*, c. 19.

3 C. 2, vv. 15, 20.

4 "Quanquam in hâc materiâ admittamus interdum mortalitatem animæ assignari ab Hæreticis," c. 18.

5 C. 15.

6 P. 235. Tertullian supposed that the founders of the different heresies were led astray by the suggestion of the devil and his evil spirits. *De Præscriptione Hæreticorum*, c. 40; *Apology*, c. 47.

7 Chap. v. p. 171; *de Præscriptione Hæreticorum*, cc. 2, 3, 5, 39.

8 Cc. 41, 42.

orthodox, not to convert the Gentiles:—that there was no agreement among them, each following his own fancies and despising his superiors—that many of them were even without assemblies for public worship. Another charge which he brings against them on the subject of doctrine is that, from consciousness of the weakness of their cause, they purposely argued in an inverted and perplexed manner.[1] With respect to their morals, he accuses them of holding intercourse with fortune-tellers and astrologers, and of acting as if they were released from all moral obligation.[2] He charges those heretics in particular, who denied the resurrection of the body, with leading sensual and vicious lives.[3] That many of the accusations brought by him against the heretics were true, cannot, we think, be reasonably doubted; but there seems to be as little doubt that some rested on no solid foundation, and that others were grossly exaggerated. "We should not," to borrow Jortin's words,[4] "trust too much to the representations which Christians after the apostolic age have given of the heretics of their times. Proper abatements must be made for credulity, zeal, resentment, mistake, and exaggeration." It appears that the heretics were in the habit of appealing, in confirmation of the truth of their tenets, to the miraculous powers exerted by the founders of their respective sects.[5]

We shall conclude the present chapter by a remark which the subject naturally suggests. The Roman Catholics are in the habit of urging the division among Protestants as an argument against Protestantism; and their own pretended freedom from dissensions as a proof that they compose the true Church. If this is a valid argument against Protestantism, the long catalogue of heresies which have been just enumerated must furnish an equally valid argument against Christianity itself. But the divisions which arose, both among the early proselytes to the gospel and the early Reformers, were the natural consequences

[1] *De Res. Carnis*, c. 2; *adv. Praxeam*, c. 20; *de Pudicitiâ*, cc. 8, 16, *sub fine*. In the tract *against Hermogenes*, cc. 19, 27, Tertullian accuses the heretics of torturing the words of Scripture, and obscuring the plainest passages by their subtleties and refinements.

[2] *De Præscriptione Hæreticorum*, c. 43.

[3] *De Res. Carnis*, c. 11. In the tract *de Pœnitentiâ*, c. 5, Tertullian mentions certain persons (he does not call them heretics) who held that God was to be worshipped with the heart and mind, not by outward acts; and under this persuasion thought that they might sin with impunity.

[4] *Discourses concerning the Truth of the Christian Religion*, p. 72, 3rd ed.

[5] *De Præscriptione Hæreticorum*, c. 44.

of the change effected in the condition of mankind by the new light which had burst upon their minds. Their former trains of thinking were interrupted—their former principles to a certain extent unsettled—they were to enter upon a new and enlarged field of speculation and of action. When, therefore, we consider how many sources of disagreement existed in their passions and prejudices—in the variety of their tempers and the opposition of their interests—it cannot be matter of surprise that all did not consent to walk in the same path, or that truth was occasionally sacrificed to the ambition of founding a sect.

---

It was originally the author's intention to add some observations upon the quotations and interpretations of Scripture in Tertullian's works; but the present volume has already exceeded the limits within which he purposed to confine it, and he must consequently defer those observations to a future opportunity.

# ADDENDA, Etc.

PAGE

32, note 2. Dr. Neander observes that the tract *de Spe Fidelium* is mentioned by Jerome in *Ezechielem*, c. 36.

65, note 2, *add*, compare *de Cultu Fœminarum*, l. ii. c. 11: "Ac si necessitas amicitiarum officiorumque *gentilium* vos vocat," etc.; from which it appears that the Christians did not think themselves called upon to interrupt their former friendships, much less to break off all intercourse with the heathen.

66, third line, *for* charity *read* chastity.

117, line 13, *add*, in the tract *de Jejuniis*, c. 17, we find an allusion to the practice of allotting a double portion to the presidents in the feasts of charity, founded on a misapplication of 1 Tim. v. 17. "Ad elogium gulæ tuæ pertinet, quod duplex apud te Præsidentibus honor *binis partibus* deputatur; quum Apostolus duplicem honorem dederit, ut et fratribus et præpositis."

126, note 4, *add*, "Et tamen ejusmodi neque congregant neque participant nobiscum, facti per delicta denuo vestri: quando ne illis quidem misceamur, quos vestra vis atque sævitia ad negandum subegit." *Ad Nationes*, l. i. c. 5.

133, note 9. With respect to the reading of Rom. viii. 3, Dr. Neander has pointed out two passages, *de Res. Carnis*, c. 46, and *de Pudicitiâ*, c. 17, in which Tertullian has "*damnavit* or *damnaverit* delinquentiam in carne."

137, note 5, *add*, compare *de Monogamiâ*, c. 10, where Tertullian's reasoning proceeds on the supposition that we shall recognise our relations and friends in a future state.

160, Lord King, in his *Critical History of the Apostles' Creed*, infers from a passage in the tract *de Baptismo*, c. 6, that a recognition of the Holy Catholic Church formed a part of the profession of faith made by the candidates for baptism. "Quum autem sub tribus et testatio fidei et sponsio salutis pignerentur, necessario *adjicitur Ecclesiæ mentio*: quoniam ubi tres, id est Pater et Filius et Spiritus Sanctus, ibi Ecclesia quæ trium corpus est." The same noble writer considers *the Communion of Saints* as merely an appendix to the preceding clause, the *Holy Catholic Church*, and understands by the expression, the mutual

PAGE

society and fellowship which subsisted between particular Churches and between their members. To this fellowship, Tertullian's writings contain frequent allusions; and the external marks of this fellowship are expressed in the following passage from the tract *de Præscriptione Hæreticorum*, c. 20:—"Communicatio pacis, et appellatio fraternitatis, et contesseratio hospitalitatis; quæ jura non alia ratio regit, quam ejusdem sacramenti una traditio;" where, in the expression *contesseratio hospitalitatis*, Tertullian refers to the commendatory letters, on the production of which members of one Christian community, when travelling abroad, were hospitably received, and allowed to communicate by the members of other communities.

167, note 4, *add*, "Ethnici, quos penes nulla est veritatis plenitudo, quia nec doctor veritatis Deus," etc. *De Spectaculis*, c. 21.

181, note 4. The reference to *de Res. Carnis*, c. 26 (not c. 62), is misplaced; it should have followed the word *copiâ* in the first line, p. 182.

204, note 2, *add*, In further proof that in Tertullian's time the Lord's Day was deemed a day of rejoicing, see the tract *de Coronâ*, c. 11. "Jam stationes aut ulli magis faciet quam Christo? aut et dominico die, quando nec Christo?"

205. I have said that Tertullian makes no allusion to the Paschal controversy. The passage in the work entitled *Prædestinatus* (c. 26) escaped me, in which the author quotes Tertullian as affirming, in his reply to Soter, Bishop of Rome, and to Apollonius, that the Montanists kept Easter according to the Roman custom. Dr. Neander refers, in confirmation of this statement, to the tract *adversus Judæos*, c. 8, *sub fine*, where Tertullian says that Christ was sacrificed on the first day of unleavened bread, on the evening of which the Jews killed the Paschal Lamb. Tertullian must therefore have supposed that the last meal which Christ ate with His disciples was not the Paschal Feast—a supposition at variance with the Asiatic mode of celebrating Easter.

223, note 8, *add*, *Apology*, c. 30; *ad Scapulam*, c. 2.

268, note 7, *add*, *Adv. Marcionem*, l. ii. c. 27.

www.ingramcontent.com/pod-product-compliance
Lightning Source LLC
LaVergne TN
LVHW020534100826
845148LV00010B/1453

* 9 7 8 1 5 9 7 5 2 6 7 2 2 *